Penguin Education

Sociology of Mass Communications

Edited by Denis McQuail

Penguin Modern Sociology Readings

D0723270

Sociology of Mass Communications

Selected Readings

Edited by Denis McQuail

Penguin Books

Penguin Books Ltd, Harmondsworth,
Middlesex, England
Penguin Books Inc, 7110 Ambassador Road,
Baltimore, Md 21207, USA
Penguin Books Australia Ltd,
Ringwood, Victoria, Australia

First published 1972
This selection copyright © Denis McQuail, 1972
Introduction and notes copyright © Denis McQuail, 1972

Copyright acknowledgement of items in this volume
will be found on page 461

Made and printed in Great Britain by
Richard Clay (The Chaucer Press) Ltd
Bungay, Suffolk
Set in Monotype Times

Contents

For my students at the
Annenberg School of Communications
with gratitude

Introduction

Any collection of articles on a broad subject is inevitably open to the charge of arbitrariness, and in seeking to demonstrate a rationale for this particular selection, it is as well to acknowledge that the charge is likely to have some justice. In the first place, pieces tend to be included because of their attractiveness to the editor, and while he may regard the result as forming a consistent whole, the pattern of consistency is not always so clear to the reader. Secondly, there are constraints on his choice which may reduce the overall consistency of the finished work: he will be inclined, as I have been, to omit pieces, however excellent in themselves and relevant to the theme, which have already been anthologized and are relatively accessible – and this happens to be a field which is already well served by such collections. Or again, limitations of space will prevent the inclusion of more than two or three pieces on a theme or sub-theme. Or things that he might like to include may be denied him. Thirdly, there are those accidents of experience and awareness during the period of selecting articles which lead some items to come to the attention of the editor rather than others. Finally, there are blind spots and areas of ignorance which any collator suffers from and which lead to the omission of important contributions.

Despite these admissions, some claim to a coherent rationale can be made. First, one can make a general claim in justification of this anthology. The field of study of mass communications does not reside securely in any one discipline, unless the study of communications as such can be regarded in this light. For the student of sociology, the literature is widely scattered and often low in accessibility, and it is useful to have a selection made with the interests of such a person in mind. That is a primary, though hardly novel, aim of this book. Another similarly general purpose, which might be expected of any such collection, is to try and represent some recent trends in thinking and research, and the Readings which follow are certainly weighted in that direction, since a high proportion of contributions are published or translated here for the first time.

The precise policy adopted in selecting must be explained in terms of exclusions as well as inclusions. Certain broad subject areas have been deliberately, and for a variety of reasons, omitted. There is little or nothing about the direct, empirically measured effects of mass communications on individuals or society, although a good deal of the contents does bear indirectly on such questions. Reasons of policy as well as shortage of space have dictated this decision. Much valuable evidence is now available about the effects of mass communication and there is a strong case for a continued updating of the excellent summaries of research evidence that have already been published (for example by Klapper, 1960; Halloran, 1965; Weiss, 1969). But from the perspective of sociology as such it can be argued that knowledge of the empirically measured 'effects' of the media, as they are usually conceived, does not contribute a great deal to the understanding of the part played by mass media in modern society. The view of the media adopted by the propagandist, the advertiser, the editor or proprietor, or by those concerned with what the media may be doing directly to their audiences is inevitably a partial one and has already received its share of attention in writing on this subject. Reasons of space largely account for other areas of omission, many of which are equally deserving of attention. They include the part played by the media in education and in economic and social development; the history and development of mass communications; mass media content analysis; the study of news flow and news values; cross-cultural comparisons of mass communications. In each of these fields there is a growing body of published material and a strong case for inclusion without inconsistency with the general policy adopted.

What then are the positive aspects of the rationale adopted? Certain guiding principles can be mentioned, present in aspiration even if not realized fully. I have wished to devote particular attention to contributions of a conceptual kind, to articles which have important theoretical implications or which are generally reflective in character, in the belief that empirical research can be valuably complemented and stimulated by contributions of this kind. Secondly, I have wished to draw attention to the organizational and societal settings in which the media operate and to emphasize the link between audience behaviour and the social context of audience members. Thirdly, I have concentrated particularly on what might be termed issues of public policy or social concern, although with the rather obvious omission of contributions dealing with violence and sex on the media, with censorship, and with children or young people as special groups. A final intention guiding selection has been to include, as a matter of policy, contributions from sources other than Britain or America. The problems dealt with are not peculiar to the Anglo-Saxon world and the inclusion of works from several different countries may in itself contribute to the cross-cultural study of mass communications.

As measured by the amount and quality of research, by volume of publications, by the attainment of high academic standards and of a firm institutional base, the study of social aspects of mass communication has achieved in recent years a degree of maturity. Even so, it has been more troubled by uncertainty and self-doubt than is usual even for sociology (for example, see Berelson, 1959; Nordenstreng, 1968). Research findings have too often seemed negative or slight in importance, there has been little development of theory, and the accumulation of general findings has seemed slow and inadequate. The initial excitement of trying to discover the 'effects' of the new communications media gave way to a growing realization of the conceptual and methodological complexity of such an enterprise. The process was educative, but to some, depressing. The degree of uncertainty engendered by this particular cause can easily be exaggerated, and certainly there is no longer any widespread pessimism or shortage of ideas. Nevertheless, the remainder of this Introduction is taken up with some brief and partial remarks about future directions which the sociology of mass communications may follow, and the contents of the collection taken as a whole are designed to back up these ideas.

As an object of sociological study, the institution of mass communications has often proved rather elusive. When one sets out to examine the media directly, one frequently ends up talking about something else – the social background of audience members, the group or societal context associated with particular uses of mass communications, the organizational settings in which mass communications are produced, the opinions and attitudes of the producers and receivers of mass communications, the pressures which shape content, and so on. Many of the best and most successful studies of mass communications have turned out to be more illuminating about general social processes and relationships than about the media themselves. In part this stems from the fact that the mass media as a social institution have no monopoly over the exchange and flow of information and ideas in a society, in part because of the diversity of forms and haziness of boundaries which characterize the institution. The common core, cutting across cultures and societies, is a particular technology and a set of comparable activities based on this technology. No doubt a sociology of the motor car or of farm implements would raise similar problems, but compared to the major institutions of social life, such as the family, law, politics and work, it is less easy to locate stable value patterns, or to identify the personal and collective needs, which govern the institution. Nor is it certain how long the mass media will survive in a currently recognizable institutional form. As instituted at present, they take their predominant character from other features of modern society – from its level of technology and economic development, its particular class and status structure, its centralized and bureaucratic forms of organization, its ways of handling work and leisure, its predominantly democratic political forms. Changes in technology and social structure have had, and probably will have, more sharp and immediate repercussions on the media than on other social institutions. In short, media institutions are highly dependent on other social forces and on external circumstances, and it has taken a minor revolution in thinking to alter predominant ways of thinking about the mass media so as to acknowledge this dependent status. If the media are more acted upon than acting it has profound implications for the kinds of questions one asks. However, once accepted, a view of the media as being variable and in some degree unstable in respect of content, production and audience behaviour opens up more options than it closes. Most obviously, it raises a large number of questions about the nature of the interdependence, the forms it takes, the strength and direction of links with other aspects of society and the conditions governing these links. The questions in this area are too numerous and particular to list here, but instead I will suggest three or four directions of inquiry which the sociological study of mass communications might well take and which merit particular attention.

The question of what it is essentially, in terms of human needs and purposes, which sustains mass media institutions has already been raised in passing. We cannot assume these human elements to be insubstantial, ephemeral or beyond the reach of investigation. The fact that attitudes, interests and needs of people constitute key variables in determining the attention paid to different mass communication sources has long been recognized, just as an appeal to what the audience wants, as if this were something known and fixed, has been a standard defence of the *status quo* of organized mass communications, at least in market systems. But we know relatively little about these phenomena, and in particular, very little about the independent contribution made by stable patterns of need and expectation to sustaining particular kinds of media provision and institutional forms. Are such patterns stable over time, and how stable are they? How are they composed? What variables of culture and social structure help to shape these patterns? There is plenty of rather imprecise opinion on such questions, but so far little attempt to draw together the evidence we have and look for more. It is a matter of more than academic importance to attempt to draw some outline of the social and psychological attachment between audience and mass communications, since the key to any projected or hoped-for change must lie in the realities of the present.

A second focus of attention which merits emphasis has to do with the part played by the mass media in shaping the individual and collective consciousness. This they do by organizing and circulating the knowledge which people have of their own everyday life and of the more remote context of their lives. The media are used both by agencies of institutional authority to achieve social control, and also by individuals as a source of reference in their interaction with others. The mass media, in consequence, both make it easier for people to conform to the view of society which others hold and also offer people the materials for shaping and maintaining their own view of the social world and their place in it. In no known modern society is there either total freedom of choice in this process or total determination, but normally we find a series of possible options which vary in their availability and occurrence between different societies. These remarks raise questions about broad social effects, about the supply and content of mass communications and about audience behaviour and perceptions.

A related perspective on the media, which until recently has not attracted sustained attention, is one which treats media content as an object of cultural analysis. Despite the many pitfalls of interpretation and difficulties of methodology, there is potentially much to be learned about the culture, values and living ideology of a society from the totality of mass communication content. The basic consensual elements, the unspoken and unacknowledged assumptions, the models of conduct to be followed, the knowledge selected as important for a culture or sub-culture are open to view and even to systematic observation in what is disseminated, or attended to, in mass communications. It would be possible and desirable to conduct those kinds of analysis of mass media content which could help to answer fundamental questions about the society and culture in which mass communications are located. The intellectual history of sociology must share some blame for the neglect of cultural analysis of the kind suggested. Its espousal of action theory, structural functionalism and social system analysis as the recommended paradigms for scientific inquiry into society has tended to exclude the study of culture expressed in symbolic (rather than behavioural) forms from the sociological fold.

The sociology (and social psychology) of mass communications has in the past owed much to the need to solve practical communication problems and to contribute to issues of believed social importance. A good part of the accumulated findings of research, the kinds of techniques used, the direction of past orientations, some elements of theory, have all been strongly influenced by the need to count and classify audiences, measure and predict effects, design effective persuasive or informational mass communications, placate anxious parents, educators and other guardians of morality. The whole idea of an applied social science of mass communications may be deservedly suspect and unpopular on the grounds that it is likely to involve serious bias and deliver yet another tool into the hands of manipulators of consciousness and behaviour.

Even so, there is a strong case to be made against rejecting the idea of policy-related or purposive inquiry in principle. A considered focus on practical issues or issues of social concern, as these may be defined in different societies, can even be recommended. The case does not rest on a general argument that the scientist or scholar should be a responsible member of society or human being, since there are many alternative ways in which such responsibilities can be met. Rather, if one looks at what seem to be the key issues of social concern, one could argue that they bear very directly on areas of great theoretical importance for understanding the mass communication process. Three such questions may be instanced, each frequently posed and yet still without agreed answers:

1. Why is it that when public demand is allowed to express itself freely and is then met by mass media provision, the content seems to be so low in aesthetic and moral quality?

2. Why have the mass media, which in many countries do purvey in absolute terms large quantities of knowledge and information, and even truth and beauty, failed to have had marked liberating effects on people's outlook, beliefs and behaviour, and why are such a limited range of content options taken up by the publics concerned?

3. Why have the media not been more successful in increasing sympathy and understanding between nations, races and cultures?

These questions are formulated in ways which make very broad assumptions, but they will probably be recognizable and comprehensible. If these and other questions could be clarified and tenable answers obtained they would do more than point the way to improved mass communications, since some notable advances in theory would be a prerequisite of any such answers.

The argument for taking problems of policy as a guide to academic inquiry is inextricably linked with an argument for clarifying our ideas about the 'freedom' and purpose of mass communications. Fundamental to the proposal is the idea that the media have not in any society been neutral in respect of furthering the interests of different groups and the attainment of some values rather than others. The mass media are potentially an instrument of social power, and no policy-related inquiry is going to be possible without taking up some position about how this power should be used and by whom. The starting point for the kind of sociology recommended here is thus, inevitably, some fundamental thinking about the purpose and objectives of mass media institutions in society. To neglect such thinking is not particularly conducive to scientific integrity since it cuts off inquiry at critical points and promotes muddled thinking; to engage in it can be productive of extremely interesting and coherent sets of hypotheses.

References

BERELSON, B. (1959), 'The state of communication research', *Public Opinion Q.*, vol. 23, pp. 1–6.

HALLORAN, J. D. (1965), *The Effects of Mass Communication*, Leicester University Press.

KLAPPER, J. T. (1960), *The Effects of Mass Communication*, Free Press.

NORDENSTRENG, K. (1968), 'Communication research in the United States: a critical perspective', *Gazette*, vol. 14, no. 3, pp. 207–16.

WEISS, W. (1969), 'Effects of the mass media of communication', in G. Lindzey and E. Aronson (eds.), *The Handbook of Social Psychology*, vol. 5, ch. 38.

Part One
General Perspectives

Both contributions to this section present and document two
points of view which would find wide acceptance in this as in
other fields of sociology. Smythe's case (Reading 1) is not
against the scientific method as such, since this is uniquely
capable of answering certain kinds of questions, but against a
'scientistic' approach which has no place for historical, qualitative
and interpretive approaches to the phenomena of mass
communications. An imaginative use of very diverse evidence is
required in order to understand how mass media institutions
actually work in modern societies, and to assess their importance.
Gerbner's much more recently expressed views are
complementary and provide a measure of the progress which
has been attained in formulating questions about the link
between mass media and society and in directing attention to the
most critical points of this linkage (Reading 2). It should be very
useful to those looking for a carefully ordered commentary on
the most relevant literature.

1 Dallas W. Smythe

Some Observations on Communications Theory[1]

Dallas W. Smythe, 'Some observations on communications theory',
Audio-Visual Communication Review, vol. 2, 1954, pp. 24–37.

What do we think we know about the effects of mass communications (motion pictures, radio, television, newspapers,
magazines and books)? Research in a number of academic disciplines and in the business organizations of the United States has
been increasingly directed towards this question in the past
twenty years. Without attempting an over-all synthesis, this essay
is addressed to the logic of research in the communications field,
and to its value systems.

I

Our common sense tells us that these agencies of mass communication have had enormous effects. It has been observed for
several decades how the Hollywood motion pictures have affected
the peoples of the world. It could never be forgotten how a Hitler
and a Roosevelt obtained effects through the use of radio. The
social revolutionary history of the past hundred years would
testify to the effects of the pamphlet, the book and the newspaper
in facilitating the creation of certain kinds of public opinion.
And in its short history to date, television has demonstrated
in the United States its undoubted power to effect changes in
people's behavior if only through changes in their use of time in
looking at it.

Yet, withal, can social scientists parallel this common-sense
observation with the corresponding 'laws' of communications?
The answer must be: They can not. What, then, is the reason for
this? What are the prospects for their doing so?

My thesis is a compound of a series of interrelated propositions:
1. that we are a long way from being able to codify the laws of

1. This paper was written for publication in Italian in the Spring 1953
issue of *Lo Spettacolo*.

communications; 2. that one of the reasons for this state of affairs is an immaturity in research methodology manifested in 'scientism'; 3. that a mature situation in communications research would balance empiricism with a methodological 'open-door' policy, welcoming, with the stature of 'science', observation and logical rigor outside the controlled-experiment situation; 4. that in this field possibly more than most others the ethical value issues implicit in the normative aspects of communications research demand searching self-examination by scholars. If, in the course of a short paper, the proof offered for all of these related propositions seems scanty, then I must console myself that it may be worthwhile even to have stated and briefly elaborated the issues.

Our distance from being able to measure adequately the effects of communications may be illustrated in relation to the most substantial single empirical research work yet done in communications: *Experiments on Mass Communication* (Hovland, Lumsdaine and Sheffied, 1949). This report on experiments in the training and indoctrination by film of the American soldiers in the second World War shows that films were quite effective in imparting skills of the 'nuts and bolts variety' but that for changing attitudes toward the war, films produced very little change in the intended direction. For altering motivation the films showed practically no effect. While we have many suggestive clues which may shortly lead us to more sweeping generalizations than these, the Hovland report typifies the present state of affairs. Obviously our experimental approach has thus far yielded results which are by no means commensurate with the common-sense judgements as to the effects of communications, illustrations of which were given in the second paragraph.

Among the several contributing factors to this state of affairs, 'scientism' is not least. The bulk of the research in the inter-disciplinary field coming to be known as 'communications research' has been in the hands of persons who more or less consciously adopt the stance of 'scientism'. By this I mean that they will accept as 'knowledge' only what has been demonstrated through 'controlled experiments'; and that their assumptions and preconceptions are often inexplicit and seriously biasing.[2]

2. A salutary experience in this connection is to re-read Thorstein Veblen's essays on methodology (1919).

One of the more serious of these preconceptions has been that there is a simple cause-and-effect relation between the content of the mass media and the behavior and attitudes of the audience.

While doubtless unintended by Hovland and his colleagues, their virtuosity in the use of controlled experimental methods has to some extent provided a model for a 'scientistic' approach to later communications research. Thus an otherwise admirable survey of the literature of social science on communications effects performed by Klapper is marred by scientism (1949). This survey was conducted to provide answers to certain policy-oriented questions posed by the director of the Public Library Inquiry, a Social Science Research Council project devoted to analysing the position of the public library movement in the United States. One question posed for Klapper was whether a plethora of escapist entertainment is conducive to social apathy. Klapper finds some 'evidence' to support the view that escapist material provides 'relaxation', 'compensation', and that it some-times has a 'boomerang' effect which is personally and socially harmful. But when he comes to the 'safety valve for social tensions' hypothesis, he summarily denies that a social apathy effect of escapist entertainment has yet

. . . been demonstrated by any direct evidence. Nor could any evidence be adduced except by the most prolonged and elaborate experiment or survey. In the absence of such evidence, then, the thesis remains a thesis – a conjecture held in common by acute observers, but by no means an established fact (1949, ch. 3, p. 12).

He admits the 'probability that mass media tend to sanctify the *status quo*', but argues that this tendency is 'the result of various forces rather than the product of escapist communication alone'.

Perhaps the semantic stance in which the question was posed is responsible in part for the nature of the response. But this passage illustrates the crippling effect of an assumption that the only evidence worthy of credence must come from the laboratory blessed with statistical measures of variance. Neither in the social nor the physical sciences can the validity of information be tested by whether it is 'an established fact' in the sense used by Klapper. This fallacy is the essence of scientism, and its exposure as a

Dallas W. Smythe 21

fallacy hardly needs documentation.[3] For Klapper, moreover, multiple correlations of forces produce 'evidence' in a 'laboratory', but not outside. The evidence from the fields of history, sociology, political science and economics is ignored as being unfit for acceptance as 'science'. Here we have scientism serving to obscure.

Lest this illustration be thought too slender a basis for my conclusion, let us look to Klapper's answer to the question: How is persuasion with regard to important civic attitudes carried on with the greatest likelihood of success? Here, to be sure, Klapper does use evidence derived from observation of social institutions to support the view that the monopoly propagandist operates under conditions of maximum likelihood of effect (Lazarsfeld and Merton, 1948). But his naiveté in methodology is evident in his apology for the fact that 'the "research" on this topic has included no controlled experiments. . . .' (Klapper, 1949, ch. 4, p. 21). To accept institutional observations as *exceptions* to the scientific 'rules' of evidence is methodologically on a par with rejecting them for the same reason; in both events their validity is unrecognized.

Klapper's study also provides us with an example of the unconscious or at least unacknowledged normative bias which often accompanies 'scientism'. In considering how the public libraries might use the monopoly propaganda characteristics of the mass media to promote the libraries' cultural objectives, he *himself* uncritically accepts the *status quo* as unchangeable:

3. A recent affirmative statement on this fallacy by two psychologists might well put a quietus on it: 'Philosophers, educators and scientists have perhaps written more truth and nonsense about 'The Scientific Method' than about any other single subject of common concern. . . . The scientific method . . . is at some time or other all things to all scientists. There is no such thing as *the* scientific method. It is more accurate to speak of science as a kind of adaptive behavior resulting from the special assignment which a certain class of people set for themselves. The assignment for the scientist is to apply himself to a domain of events in order to achieve so much understanding of it that his control of it and the predictions he makes about it will occur with a minimum of surprise (i.e. 'error'). . . . There can be no rules or presumptions that will be invariant from scientist to scientist: effective solution of this problem as of any other problem may be tried via manifold routes' (Klein and Krech, 1951, pp. 14–15).

Because American mass media are controlled by commercial interests who are concerned with maintaining the *status quo*, monopoly propaganda in America *is and can be* directed only upon the reinforcement or activation of attitudes already almost universally sanctioned (Klapper, 1949, ch. 4, p. 38 – emphasis added).

Had his theoretical stance been otherwise, obviously the question might have been answered in terms which regarded the mass media as communicating units the policies and organization of which change through time. Conceivably the public library movement might have found policy use for such an analysis which recognizes the nature of institutional change.

There is hopeful evidence that this constrictive view is being broken through. Thus Lazarsfeld in his foreword to the Klapper report verbalizes the common feeling of frustration with the limited knowledge now available on communications effects. He says:

In some quarters, there is a feeling that if we only had more and better studies, the answers would be quickly forthcoming. But this isn't likely to be the case. The main difficulty probably lies in formulating the problem correctly. For the trouble started exactly when empirical research stepped in where once the social philosopher had reigned supreme. To the latter there was never any doubt that first the orator and then the newspaper and now television are social forces of great power. But when specific studies were made about the effect of educational radio programs or the influence of the library on the community, these facts could only rarely be demonstrated. It is possible, of course, that our measuring instruments are not yet fine enough. But most likely the difficulty is due to the nature of the effects themselves (Klapper, 1949, pp. 1–2).

Moreover, recent studies have, as Fearing remarks, pointed the way out from the limitations set by the simple causal relationship preconception. Two studies in particular (Cooper and Dinerman, 1951; Wiese and Cole, 1946) show that:

The viewer and listener are dynamic participants in the situation. They react *on* the content presented rather than reacting to it. How they react is determined by many factors *only one of which is the content of the film itself*. This is not equivalent to saying that film and radio have no effects. Rather, it raises the much more complicated question of what effects under what conditions (Fearing, 1951, pp. 139–40).

To follow the implications of this conclusion is to widen the methodological outlook. For now it becomes relevant to hypothesize concerning the needs of members of the audience, concerning the character structure of the members of the audience, towards the institutional setting in which the audience exists – indeed towards all that can be meant by the concept of the dynamics of the personalities of audience members.

The theoretically self-conscious researcher is now invited to frame studies both in and outside of the controlled-experiment situation. For example, one might take account of the evidence about personality dynamics as given to us in *The Authoritarian Personality* (Adorno et al., 1950). These social scientists were studying the general population – not avowed fascists – and were concerned with the analysis of the deep-lying as well as the surface aspects of prejudice. Quite aside from providing the communications researcher with techniques of identifying various syndromes of prejudice they offer some suggestive conclusions. Rational arguments, they say, cannot be expected to have deep or lasting effects upon a phenomenon such as social discrimination which is essentially irrational. Appeals to sympathy for the plight of minority groups may do as much harm as good when directed to people one of whose deepest fears is that they might be identified with weakness or suffering. Urging closer association with members of minority groups will be futile in influencing people who are so built that they cannot experience relations with others. And establishing liking for minority groups is next to impossible for people who are really unable to like anyone, including themselves. Of some importance for us is their final conclusion that no lasting increase in people's capacity to see and be themselves can be expected from manipulative devices. In other words, they say, the devices of salesmanship won't work to make people less authoritarian.

Other examples could be provided but they would unduly extend the present paper. I cannot refrain from mentioning, however, the possibility that empirical studies might be framed which would test the hypotheses advanced by Innis, that cultures exist in space and time (1951); that media of communication confer monopolies or oligopolies on the knowledge which gives being to cultures.[4]

4. See especially Innis (1951, pp. 61–91).

The main point to be made here is that the way may now be open for integration of the content of the social sciences as it bears on the process of communication. If this hope is justified then we may expect to find the 'quantifiers' endeavoring to measure variables constructed on hypotheses previously not admitted to the laboratory situation. Also one might hope that the results of rigorous logic and observation pursued *outside* the laboratory might in this area acquire status as intellectually valid 'evidence'.

II

At this point I should like to sketch one 'non-scientistic' approach to the social science of communications. The following remarks are intended to make a methodological point and a substantive one. The methodological point is that new and stimulating insights may be revealed by admitting institutional observations as evidence. The substantive thesis is that such an historical view as follows suggests that as our culture has developed it has built into itself increasing concentrations of authority and nowhere is this more evident than in our communications activities. The reader will observe that the substantive fruit of this methodological approach has normative implications which raises a final topic for consideration.

I would begin by reformulating the issue of the 'effects of the mass media' in terms of the 'effects of the kind of communications used before the mass media came into existence.'[5] The kinds of services which we must look for in the pre-mass media era will be entertainment (principally), and information and orientation (interpretation of experience).

How did mankind get its entertainment, its information and its orientation before the electronic age? Before the age of the film? Before the age of the printing press? What functions were performed by these services as thus rendered?

We might begin with the Middle Ages. In that period, most of the entertainment in the form of fiction (stories, folk tales, etc.)

5. In this portion of the present article I am profoundly indebted to David Riesman, author of *The Lonely Crowd* (1950). Standing back of him in this respect are Max Weber and the historians, sociologists and economists who developed some of Weber's ideas.

which was available to children was what they heard from senior members of their own families. The children's unsophisticated reactions of alarm or pleasure at the tales they heard might encourage the story teller to soften or expand the story as it developed. As far as specialized entertainment services were concerned, adults depended on ballad singers, minstrels, jesters and groups of actors. From them they heard the folk tales, fairy tales, morality stories, and so forth which constituted the non-clerical forms of entertainment. The pageantry of church and community ceremonies also had its entertaining aspects. As Pellizzi has pointed out the entertainment was primarily ritualistic in character (1951).

News and other information was similarly transmitted through face-to-face communications in feudal Europe. The market place, the inn, provided the location. Travelers, merchants, seamen, soldiers, etc., transmitted news to the general public in this way, while for the nobility and clergy special couriers brought information in person.

For the bulk of the population which had no formal schooling available to it, the main source of orientation was conversation – conversation between parents and children, between children, between men at the bench or at the pump or tavern, between women at their washing. For the church-goer, for the member of a medieval guild, for the merchant and for the noble, appropriate institutional orientation was provided by religious, occupational or political organizations.

In looking back, we are struck with the extent to which the medieval man's communications intake was *traditionally* directed. Custom, superstitious and irrational though it might be, ruled his individual life and conditioned the content of his communications. You might say that the medieval man internalized at his parents' side the traditions which he then used to direct his life.

Apart from its tradition-directed content, communications in the middle ages had one other very significant characteristic: they were face-to-face. There was ample opportunity for what today is called 'feedback'. (What the communicator receives back from his audience is feedback.) The listener registered pleasure, bore-dom, skepticism, excitement, blunt disbelief, or some other reaction to what he heard. The communicator – whether story-telling grandpa, the court jester, the newly-returned veteran of the Crusades, or the traveling troupe of actors – could *see* and *feel* and *hear* the emotional response of his audience. On the basis of this feedback, he could and usually would modify his content if necessary in order to achieve the desired effect on later renditions. From the listeners' viewpoint, this interplay permitted direct – even initimate – 'controls' on the communicator. His performance was subject to immediate review. His responsibility was personal, direct and unshiftable.

The personal nature of medieval communications had still another implication. The success of the communicator depended in large measure on his skill and his personality. He was an individual, not a corporation. His policy was made under his own hat, not in an air-conditioned Board room by Board members mostly unskilled in the art of communication. Under these conditions the style of delineation of the characters, the story-line, the news report and the interpretation was free and fluid.

Our second snapshot view of communications history begins with the age of the Reformation, the rise of national states in Western Europe, and of the commercial revolution in economic life. It ends during the nineteenth century. This one covers about five hundred years. It was the era of the growth of modern capitalism. It includes the period of the Industrial Revolution, and the pioneering growth of American life down to the disappearance of the frontier. Progress was in the air. The Church and the nobility remained powerful forces in the new national states for most of this period. And tradition and status still were influential, especially among rural and working folk.

A new character type – the inner-directed character – came into being with the rise of Protestantism. Protestantism supplied the religious justification for the rising business class. It held with Calvin and Luther that business was not necessarily a sinful affair. For the individual, Protestantism meant that his conscience was more important than it had been under the traditional Roman Catholic system of the Middle Ages. It was as if, as Riesman says, he had swallowed a gyroscope. His conscience, like a gyroscope, kept him on course. The course was one which avoided the pitfalls of sin and waste in pursuit of material success here on earth and salvation in the hereafter. This inner-directed character system was diffused through the business community and from it to the population at large with the aid of the printing press.

The entertainment function of communications in early modern times was carried on by the successors of the medieval entertainers on the stage and in community ceremonies of one kind or another. The medieval function of the parents as story-tellers to the children was continued, but the content of the stories shifted somewhat to introduce inner-directed themes. With the printing press came books, newspapers and the predecessors of our magazines. Increasingly these media assumed the function of providing information and orientation. *Communications began to be mechanized, began to be a business.* To this extent communications lost their personal, face-to-face nature. Now if the story-teller's readers threw his book into the fireplace in disgust, he didn't know it. There was no direct feedback. The readers had lost their direct control over those who spoke to them through the medium of the printing press. The market came between communicator and reader. Moreover, with the market for publications came the alienation of the creative writers from the policy-making of the press. Editors began to make policy on the selection of books and information for their newspapers – in line with the business appraisal of the market. Writers became specialists in writing in contrast to the full-functioned creative story-tellers of medieval times. The style of entertainment in the inner-directed era was unique and appropriate to its *Weltanschauung*. One can almost take it as axiomatic that with a decrease in possible feedback there goes a proportionate decrease in the humanity of communications. I mean by humanity all of the kaleidoscopic diversity of human elements of strength and weakness, humor, pathos, spontaneity, candor, imagination and originality.

Though *direct* feedback was lost with the advent of commercial publishing, the market did provide one partly compensatory indirect control to the readers. New talents could enter the market easily. If a new writer didn't like the best deal he could get from an established publisher, he could find his own printer and publish his own work. Or, he could even start his own printshop and do the whole thing himself. It was relatively easy and inexpensive.

Up to the latter fourth of the past century in the western world there was predominantly face-to-face communication. An enlarged school system, the Chatauqua circuit, the orators so popular one hundred years ago, the family fireside where stories were told and retold, the legitimate stage for big and small cities, the early chambers of commerce, the early labor unions – all of these were the principal means of communication as recently as seventy-five years ago.

Our third historical snapshot covers less time than either of the first two. It is the era beginning in the last quarter of the nineteenth century. In it the scope of the business operation of our entertainment rituals has widened to include virtually all attention given to drama and music through the agency of the mass media.

This era was ushered in when as a result of the developments in our technology, productive capacity 'caught up' with the capacity of the bulk of the population to buy the fruits of their labor. From that time on our system was capable of producing more goods and services than could easily be sold at the producers' desired prices. This led to the rapid growth of advertising and other methods of manipulating the customer into buying things. The disappearance of the old-style small businessman and the predominance of large-scale business organization has shifted the center of gravity of our population into white-collar jobs. Along with this shift has, of course, gone the increase in urbanization. This concentration of population in cities necessarily has increased the dependence people feel toward others.

Deference to the presumed value standards of others is at the root of the character structure which is growing to be typical of the marketing era. Such standards tend to displace the conscience and tradition as the guide. 'Other-direction' is the essence of the appeals of advertising and salesmanship. The method of character operation here may be likened to the radar. It is as if the other-directed person had swallowed a radar in his childhood, by which he guides himself according to the real or fancied standards of his peer-groups, the latter usually scaled somewhat ethnocentrically. The agencies of mass communications both facilitate and themselves create these standards.

As the army of white-collar employees has grown, business and government have mechanized their duties and rationalized their operations. As Mills puts it, the 'managerial demiurge' sets up an impersonal 'system' which manipulates the population to the presumed advantage of the organizations, but without personalization of responsibility (1951). For those who head the organizations, as for the remainder of the 'other-directeds', virtue comes no longer to be its own reward; rather policies are justified in terms of their results in meeting group-determined objectives. Group loyalties are exalted above conscience and tradition.

The procedures involved in training for the new outlook on life and business become pervasive. Personality tends to replace skill as a requirement for hiring and promotion. What began as an attempt to prepare employees for successful business has been diffused as a way of life. As Mills says rather bitterly, there is a public-relations aspect to private relations of all sorts, including even relations with oneself.

Without common values and mutual trust, the cash nexus that links one man to another in transient contact has been made subtle in a dozen ways and made to bite deeper into all areas of life and relations. People are required by the salesman ethic and convention to pretend interest in others in order to manipulate them. In the course of time, and as this ethic spreads, it is got onto. Still it is conformed to as part of one's job and one's style of life, but now with a winking eye, for one knows that manipulation is inherent in every human contact. Men are estranged from one another as each secretly tries to make an instrument of the other, and in time a full circle is made: one makes an instrument of himself, and is estranged from it also (1951).

The mass media now supply entertainment which more than fills the quantitative void left by the displacement of the older rituals for entertainment. As far as information is concerned, radio and TV have completed the attenuation of face-to-face communication begun by newspapers, magazines and books. The role of the family in interpreting information has also shrunken. Children, no less than their parents, now depend on radio, TV and publications for direct orientation on public affairs. More subtly, the comic books, the pulps, the movies, plus radio and TV provide in fictional form the behavior patterns which imply orientation towards public – and private affairs.

What becomes of feedback from the audience to the communicator under these conditions? Direct feedback is shrunken to the small volume of fan mail. Indirectly a sort of feedback is supplied by pressures exerted for 'codes' of ethics in the operation of the mass media. Being administered by the same groups to which they apply, these codes are inherently weak and unenforceable except through the operation of conscience.

The economic open-endedness of the publishing industry which was a partial corrective for the loss of feedback until late in the nineteenth century has now virtually disappeared as a characteristic of the mass media. The huge capital sums required to start a successful newspaper, TV station, or motion picture production effectively exclude fresh and experimental ventures to the point where their occasional appearance is regarded as a 'curiosity'. The banker's approval, necessary to the loans required for investment in the complex technical equipment of our day depends on offering something *safe* – that is *like* what the existing mass media already sell. Patent restrictions also bar easy entry. And in the radio and television fields, the shortage of spectrum space limits the numbers of stations. On the whole the possibility of effective feedback to the men who run our mass media is negligible today. They are in effect autonomous – irresponsible, except through their own consciences, to the viewer, reader, or listener.

The style of writing and production used in our mass media is in keeping with the ethical and aesthetic values of other-direction. Riesman, in *The Lonely Crowd*, finds stereotyping characteristic of our mass media. Invulnerable authority symbols appear as stereotypes in most entertainment offered the young. In our current entertainment the hero wins so quickly that it cannot help but seem effortless. In the process neither the hero nor the listener has time to experience internal moral conflict (as in the inner-directed story), nor the desirability on occasion of asserting his individual goals in the face of hostile authority (as in the tradition-directed story).

There is a stereotyped tightness of fit in portraying the physical externals of the characters on our mass media. Details of speech and costume are carefully filled in. Typecasting with faithful repetition of familiar mannerisms is essential in order that the picture, article or program may be distinguishable from their competitors. Exceptions to this style are most often to be found in book publishing, occasionally in magazines, rarely in the other media.

Still another aspect of stereotyping in the mass media comes from the assumption on the part of the advertisers that the fictitious mass audience wants more of the same sort of programs currently available. Thus we find slavish imitativeness in the multiplication of a few types of entertainment programs. This fallacy parades under the label of 'giving the public what it wants (as determined by Hooper-ratings, and the like)', and has even been glorified by the president of Columbia Broadcasting System as 'cultural democracy'. Obviously the public cannot vote for what it has never experienced.

If the forgoing analysis has any validity, the hypothetical conclusion might be drawn that as our social organization has become more tightly integrated on the basis of modern technology, authority has increasingly been built into it. To be tested is the further hypothesis that our mass media, through cutting off feedback, through dealing in stereotypes, through specializing in a manipulative view of humanity (both directly through advertising and indirectly through the plot structures and motivations portrayed in entertainment and other program material) are capable of molding us more and more into authoritarianism. Such a conclusion is translatable into terms of a general theory of communication – provided all parts of it are not required to be demonstrated in controlled experiments simultaneously and immediately. An adequate general theory has yet to be fully developed. Perhaps a beginning lies in a theoretical model currently being developed by my colleague, Professor Charles E. Osgood. This model, as yet unpublished, conceives of the communications field as consisting of communicating units (individuals and social institutions) simultaneously functioning in all stages of the communications process. These stages are regarded as the *receiving* of information, the *interpreting* of received information and the *transmitting* of information to other units. Account has also to be taken of 'noise' (in the sense employed by Shannon and Weaver (1949)), and 'feedback'.

Having identified the normative aspects of both the 'scientistic' approach and an alternative one, a final word is necessary concerning the ethical value issues involved in the *application* of communications research techniques. In the United States there have been numerous expressions of concern on this score. For example, one of the leading scholars in this field, Dr Robert K. Merton says,

The technicians of mass opinion . . . cannot escape the moral issues which permeate propaganda as a means of social control . . . the pressure of immediate objective tends . . . to exact a price of the prevailing morality for it expresses a manipulative attitude toward men and society (quoted in Whyte, 1952, ch. 14, p. 233).

A foremost economist in North America, Innis, is heard to say:

The political realization of democracy invariably encourages the hypnotist. The behavioristic and psychological testers have their way. In the words of one of them: 'Great will be our good fortune if the lesson in human engineering which the war has taught us is carried over, directly and effectively, into our civil institutions and activities' (C. S. Yoakum). Such tactlessness and offense to our good sense is becoming a professional hazard to psychologists (Innis, 1951, p. 90).

The quotations could be multiplied. Quite recently, William H. Whyte, Associate Editor of *Fortune* magazine, in his *Is Anybody Listening?* delivered a biting attack on the social scientists who apply the techniques and theories of 'social engineering' under many labels. It may be argued whether such a sweeping indictment is justified. Perhaps on balance, Whyte's view may be well taken, if the results of social science in the field of communications are to be judged solely on the basis of the use made of this material in the current scene. However, an excellent case may be made for separating the ethically self-conscious social scientists from those who practice pseudo-social science. My point here is no more and no less than to establish the proposition that a greater degree of concern with communications theory, its premises and its preconceptions, is the best safeguard communications social scientists can use to ensure the integrity of their scientific work. In the interest of the values of our cultural heritage this, it seems to me, is our ultimate obligation.

References

ADORNO, T. W., FRENKEL-BRUNSWICK, E., LEVINSON, D. J., and SANFORD, R. N. (1950), *The Authoritarian Personality*, Harper & Row.

COOPER, E., and DINERMAN, H. (1951), 'Analysis of the film *Don't be a Sucker*: a study in communication', *Pub. Opinion Q.*, vol. 15, pp. 243–64.

FEARING, F. (1951), 'A word of caution for the intelligent consumer of motion pictures', *Q. Film, Radio, Television*, vol. 6, pp. 139–40.

HOVLAND, C. L., LUMSDAINE, A. A., and SHEFFIED, F. D. (1949), *Experiments on Mass Communication*, volume 3 of *Studies in Social Psychology in World War II*, Princeton University Press.

INNIS, H. A. (1951), *The Bias of Communication*, University of Toronto Press.

KLAPPER, J. T. (1949), *The Effects of Mass Media*, Columbia University Bureau of Applied Social Research.

KLEIN, G. S., and KRECH, D. (1951), 'The problem of personality and its theory', *J. Person.*, vol. 20, pp. 2–23.

LAZARSFELD, P. F., and MERTON, R. K. (1948), 'Mass communication, popular taste and organized social action', in L. Bryson (ed.), *Communication of Ideas*, Harper & Row.

MILLS, C. W. (1951), *White Collar*, Oxford University Press.

PELLIZZI, C. (1951), 'The show as a form of social activity', *Lo Spettacolo 1*, (summary in English).

RIESMAN, D. (1950), *The Lonely Crowd*, Yale University Press.

SHANNON, C. E., and WEAVER, W. (1949), *The Mathematical Theory of Communications*, University of Illinois Press.

VEBLEN, T. (1919), *The Place of Science in Modern Civilization*, B. W. Huebach.

WHYTE, W. H. (1952), *Is Anybody Listening?*, Simon & Schuster.

WIESE, M., and COLE, S. (1946), 'A study of children's attitudes and the influence of a commercial motion picture', *J. Psychol.*, vol. 21, pp. 151–71.

2 George Gerbner

Mass Media and Human Communication Theory

George Gerbner, 'Mass media and human communication theory'
in F. E. X. Dance (ed.), *Human Communication Theory*,
Holt, Rinehart & Winston, 1967, pp. 40–57.

I

The fundamental questions raised by media of communications
are usually those of new or different ways of looking at life.

When printing became a practical possibility, it disturbed
existing assumptions about the capacity – and right – of ordinary
people to acquire knowledge beyond their own experience, and
about the point of view from which public knowledge was to be
produced.

The questions raised by mass media today are similarly profound. These questions reflect the cultural transformation of our
time. To take the full measure of this transformation, we have to
start at least one hundred million years ago – give or take a few
million.

Lush forests covered the land from the Arctic Circle across the
Sahara Desert to the Antarctic. Arboreal existence in damp
tropical forests freed the forearms of one group of mammals
from having to carry the burden of the body, and shaped these
forearms into strong, sure, delicate instruments. Deft manipulation required a hand that could grasp, a brain that could do the
same, and an exceptionally large and complex control system.
This came about with the development of erect posture and the
ability to focus the eyes on small objects at arm's length. The
ability to grasp with the hand and the mind literally developed
'hand in hand'.

The last million years robbed hominoids of their 'paradise'.
The featherless and furless creatures were hard-pressed to develop
all their resources of collaboration, community and communication – and thus to transform themselves into *Homo sapiens*.

Communication is the most uniquely 'humanizing' element of

the pattern. It is unique especially in its symbolic representation and re-creation of aspects of the human condition, in forms that can be learned and shared. Only the hominoid brain could regulate the body, respond to the immediate environment, and still retain the reserve capacity and mechanical calm necessary to hold an image long enough to reflect on it, record it, store it, and retrieve it in the form of messages. This ability was the prerequisite for human communication – social interaction through messages. Communication in the broadest 'humanizing' sense is the production, perception and grasp of messages bearing man's notions of what is, what is important and what is right.

For a long time the messages and images that compose the fabric of popular culture were woven by the tribe and village out of the same homespun yarn of everyday experience, which also gave rise to the folkways of rearing, teaching and preaching. The process was mostly interpersonal. It was slow-moving and fixed as long as the local and limited circumstances that governed it were fixed. Studies of Japanese folklore, for example, suggest that in the closed traditional rural village people knew each other so well that one could understand what his neighbor was intending to communicate even from his facial expression or his slightest move.

As more and more people became aware of cultural influences beyond their own tribe or village, social interaction became primarily oral and increasingly regional rather than purely tribal. It was still adjustable to time, place, circumstance, function, and yet was long-enduring. A tale heard from one's grandfather and told to one's grandchild would span a century. Until recently, then, the common culture in which man learned to think and act 'human' seemed part of a relatively fixed universe, like the air in which a young bird must learn to act like a bird.

After a long, slow build-up, the Industrial Revolution burst into the cultural sphere. Instead of the age-old process of filtering-down and person-to-person transmission of most information that ever comes to a human, we have the mass production and almost simultaneous introduction of information, ideas, images and products at all levels of society and – at least potentially – in all inhabited parts of the globe.

A change in man's relationship to the common culture marks

the transition from one epoch to another in the way members of our species are 'humanized'. The rate of this change has increased (and the life-span lengthened) to such an extent that different generations living side by side may now be 'humanized' in different ways and live in essentially different (but overlapping) cultural epochs.

The shared communicative context of messages and images through which a culture reveals the varieties, limitations and potentials of the human condition is no longer woven out of a homespun yarn of private everyday experience. Even the meaning of 'everyday experience' has changed. Much of our experience is in a new type of cultural environment. We listen to the morning newscast or music program while we sip our breakfast coffee and drive to work. The commuter reads his newspaper oblivious of the 'real' world around him. Much of our behavior is in response to things we do not directly 'experience'. What happens in Paris, Moscow, Tokyo, Havana, Washington, Berlin, New Delhi, or London; what happens in art, science, technology, medicine, education, public administration – all these and many other constantly changing relationships affect us quickly and profoundly. Faraway storytellers mass produce new tales every hour and tell them to millions of children, fathers and grand-fathers *at the same time*. Never have so many people in so many places shared so much of a common system of messages and images and have the assumptions about life, society, and the world imbedded in them while having so little to do with their making. The fabric of popular culture that relates elements of existence to each other and structures the common consciousness of what is, what is important, and what is right, is now largely a manufactured product.

The new situation is a radical transformation in the ways members of our species become human. Social structure and industrial organization have a more central and direct bearing upon the common consciousness than ever before. With the ability of industrial societies to produce the material requirements of subsistence and welfare, the strains and stresses of a social system come to be transferred to the mass-cultural sphere. The struggles for power and privilege, participation in the conduct of human affairs, more equitable distribution of resources, all other forms of social justice, and, indeed, for survival in a nuclear age, are increasingly shifting from older arenas and methods of struggle to the newer spheres of control, contest and attention in mass-produced communications.

To sum up: The ways we reflect on things, act on things and interact with one another are rooted in our ability to compose images, produce messages, and use complex symbol systems. A change in that ability transforms the nature of human affairs. We are in the midst of such a transformation. It stems from the mass production of symbols and messages – a new industrial revolution in the field of culture. New media of communication provide new ways of selecting, composing and sharing perspectives. New institutions of communication create new publics across boundaries of time, space and status. New patterns of information animate societies and machines. Along with other dramatic changes, we have altered the symbolic environment that gives meaning and direction to man's activity.

These developments present new problems and demand fresh insights. But the new also sheds light on the old. An assessment of basic communicative processes and cultural traditions is part of the response to the transformations of our time. The search for a new grasp on the affairs of man crosses established disciplines, strains the organization of knowledge and leads to the emergence of new fields and new schools.

A part of this search is the quest for a theory that might help us to study, understand, judge and control the conduct of events in which mass media and mass communications play an increasingly significant role. There is no such theory now. Most attempts to construct theories have taken parochial or tangential approaches of established disciplines or the partial view of journalistic scholarship.[1]

After exploring definitions of terms and concepts, I shall note some of these contributions. The work of political scientists and others concerned with the public policy functions of mass media

1. Since this essay was written De Fleur (1970) has given further impetus to theoretical analysis, viewing the study of mass communication 'emerging as a new academic discipline in its own right' (p. xiii). Other significant new publications whose thrust is consistent with the present effort but whose relevant contributions could not be noted in this essay are Edelstein (1966) and Fagen (1966), see pp. 456 and 459.

will receive a greater share of attention than will those of sociologists, social psychologists, psychologists and others. Finally, I shall attempt to summarize some of my own notions and questions (derived, of course, from the work of many others, and spelled out in greater detail in other publications) pointing, hopefully, toward a theory of mass media and mass communications.

II

Communication can be defined as 'social interaction through messages'. Messages are formally coded, symbolic, or representational events of some shared significance in a culture, produced for the purpose of evoking significance (Gerbner, 1958a). The distinction between the 'communication approach' and other approaches to the study of behavior and culture rests on the extent to which; 1. messages are germane to the process studied; 2. concern with the production, content, transmission, perception and use of messages is central to the approach. A 'communication approach' (or theory) can be distinguished from others in that it makes the nature and role of messages in life and society its central organizing concern.

   Media of communication are the means or vehicles capable of assuming forms that have characteristics of messages or that transmit messages. *A Dictionary of the Social Sciences* defines *mass media* as

all the impersonal means of communication by which visual and/or auditory messages are transmitted directly to audiences. Included among the mass media are television, radio, motion pictures, newspapers, magazines, books and billboards (Gould and Kolb, 1964, p. 413).

Two features of the definition receive further elaboration. One is the technical means of transmission, and the other is the nature of the audience. Klapper considers the technical means sufficient. He writes:

The term connotes all mass media of communication in which a mechanism of impersonal reproduction intervenes between speaker and audience. By this criterion radio, screen, books and other media of impersonal communication would be classified as mass media (1949, p. 3).

This definition appears to exclude only such communications as drama, personal conversation and public address.

The nature of the audience is emphasized in a definition offered by Wiebe, who writes:

The two essential characteristics of mass media are: (i) their product is easily available – in a physical sense – to most of the public, including a sizable number of people in all major subgroups; and (ii) their cost is so small to the individual that they are generally available to these same people in a financial sense (1952, pp. 164–5).

This criterion emphasizes the size of the audience and appears to exclude not only personal communications but also the more expensive or less readily available communication products such as hard-cover book and educational film. A further qualification is introduced by Sherif and Sherif, who assert not only that a large audience is necessary for the proper usage of the term but that mass media must 'reach millions of people simultaneously or within very brief periods of time' (1956, p. 562). Another conception of *mass* is emphasized by Wirth, who writes that the mass media of communication transcend 'the peculiar interests and preoccupations of the special and segmental organized groups and direct their appeal to the mass' (1948, p. 10). This conception stresses not only the size and heterogeneity of the audience but also the contention that members of the audience respond to the communication as separate individuals.

Perhaps the most comprehensive attempt to delineate essential characteristics of mass communication comes from Wright (1959, pp. 12–15). In addition to modern technology, he writes, mass communication involves distinctive operating conditions, primary among which are the nature of the audience, of the communication experience and of the communicator. First, 'mass communication is directed toward a relatively large, heterogeneous and anonymous audience'. Second, 'mass communications may be characterized as public, rapid and transient'. And third, the communicator in mass media usually works through a complex corporate organization embodying an extensive division of labor and an accompanying degree of expense.

Common to most definitions is the conception that mass media are technological agencies and corporate organizations engaged in the creation, selection, processing and distribution of communications that are (or can be) produced at speeds and in quantities possible only by mass-production methods. Mass media, therefore, provide the broadest common currencies of public interaction in a society.

This broad 'public-making' significance of mass media of communications – the ability to create publics, define issues, provide common terms of reference and thus to allocate attention and power – has evoked a large number of theoretical contributions. Other theories of mass media have their origins in political thought, social-economic analysis and historical-artistic-literary scholarship.

Until recently the motivation for theorizing about the mass media came mostly from a desire for, or resistance to, cultural change. It came from philosophers and revolutionists, defenders of 'classical' or of 'folk' cultures, critics of 'elite' and aristocratic traditions, propagandists and propaganda-analysts, historians and sociologists embroiled in a 'popular culture debate', economists and lawyers defending or fighting the trend toward cultural oligopolies, and crusaders alarmed by the drift of events or dismayed at the tenacity of the *status quo*. It is only in the last few decades that, whatever the motivation, theorizing has come to reflect a growing body of systematic information and scientific methodology becoming available for the serious student.

III

The allocation, distribution and exercise of attention and power are always related to communication (whether over roads, or by water, wire or air). In recent times the possibility of nearly simultaneous large-scale social interaction through mass communications changed the nature of politics. 'As we look back upon previous social aggregations,' wrote Wirth

such as those of the ancient kingdoms, or at their greatest extent the Roman Empire, we wonder how, given the primitive communications that obtained, such impressive numbers and territories could be held together under a common regime over any considerable span of time. If we discover, however, that these aggregations were not truly societies but were little more than administrative areas, creatures of military domination along the main arteries of communication from some center of power, and that the economic base of their cohesion rested on exploitation of the outlying territories and peoples by the power-holders at a center through their representatives who were scattered thinly over the territory, the magnitude of these aggregations does not seem too impressive. Mass societies as we find them today, however, show greater marks of integration. They are aggregations of people who participate to a much greater degree in the common life and, at least in democratic parts of the world, comprise people whose attitudes, sentiments and opinions have some bearing upon the policies pursued by their governments. In this sense mass societies are a creature of the modern age and are the product of the division of labor, of mass communication and a more or less democratically achieved consensus (1948, p. 2).

The possibilities inherent in a 'more or less democratically achieved consensus' motivated many political scientists and social critics to theorize about propaganda and mass communications. In an early statement on 'the theory of political propaganda', Lasswell (1927, p. 627) defined propaganda as 'the management of collective attitudes by the manipulation of significant symbols', and wrote:

Propaganda rose to transitory importance in the past whenever a social system based upon the sanctions of antiquity was broken up by a tyrant. The ever-present function of propaganda in modern life is in large measure attributable to the social disorganization which has been precipitated by the rapid advent of technological changes. . . . Literacy and the physical channels of communication have quickened the connection between those who rule and the ruled. Conventions have arisen which favor the ventilation of opinions and the taking of votes. Most of that which formerly could be done by violence and intimidation must now be done by argument and persuasion. . . .

'Propaganda analysis' made a contribution to mass media theory in developing methods for the systematic and comparative examination of large-scale, mass-produced message systems. Such examination need not be restricted to messages of persuasive intent. Students of propaganda such as Jacques Ellul (1965) have come to feel that a total cultural perspective – such as can stem from political, commercial or any other single basis of mass media ownership and control – constitutes the most pervasive form of 'propaganda'. A study of political perspectives inherent in non-political news reporting (Gerbner, 1964b) seems to bear out this contention.

Ithiel de Sola Pool sketched the rise of political theory and research in mass communications (1965):

Studies of politics of a kind that could be included in a bibliography on communication start with the ancient Greeks. Among the classic studies are Plato's *Gorgias*, which considers morality in propaganda; Aristotle's *Rhetoric* and John Stuart Mill's *System of Logic* (1846) which analyse the structure of persuasive argumentation; Lenin's *What is to be Done* (1902), a large part of which is devoted to a discussion of the role that an all-Russian newspaper might play in the revolutionary politics of the Bolsheviks; Milton's *Areopagitica* and Mill's *On Liberty* (1885) which consider the systematic effects of permitting freedom of expression in communication; Dicey's *The Development of Law and Opinion in England in the Nineteenth Century* (1905) which considers the effects of the ideological context on public actions; Marx's *German Ideology* (1832), and Sorel's *Reflections on Violence* and Pareto's *The Mind and Society* which distinguish the social function from the truth value of beliefs.

While all of these are books on communication, only some of the most recent ones (e.g. Lenin's *What is to be Done*) focus on mass communication as such. The growth of mass media to the point where they dominate the communication system of society is a phenomenon of recent times. Every society has some communication system for man is a communication animal, but only in the last century have we had the emergence of an extraordinary phenomenon – societies organized around mass media systems.

The growth of mass media has had many profound effects on the quality of life. With the growth of the mass media there have also arisen exaggerated beliefs in the efficacy of the propaganda. A number of factors are responsible for the myth of the all-powerful propagandist. In the period after the First World War the extreme right in Germany, unwilling to admit that their nation had been defeated in battle, proposed the myth that German victory had been snatched away from the soldiers by civilian acceptance of allied propaganda. This belief in a 'Schwindel' led to much writing about the supposed magical powers of propaganda.

In the United States advertising and public relations men were disseminating the same illusions since overestimation of propaganda was often useful in selling their own services. Popular writers who have believed their claims have written books about the vast powers of 'The Hidden Persuaders'. . . .

One cannot doubt that if the mass media were non-existent or differently structured our politics would be different. The point we are trying to make is that the effects of the mass media must be conceived much more broadly than simply as persuasion of people to accept the views presented in the media. The mass media have many more subtle and complex effects both through what they say and through their existence as institutions. . . .

Political scientists have paid more attention to the non-persuasive effects of communication than have some other social scientists. Perhaps this has been because they were interested in the ideologies being communicated and their use in power politics, even where persuasion was minimal. For example, Harold Lasswell has long argued the importance of securing exact quantitative data on the distribution in the world of ideological symbols. In the 1930s he initiated the use of content analysis as a device to compare political propaganda in different times and places. This research was continued at the Library of Congress during the Second World War and at the Hoover Institute during the post-war years. The RADIR studies at the latter Institution canvassed the political symbols used in editorials in major newspapers in five countries over a sixty-year period. They demonstrated such trends as a decline in attention to ideas of property and a rise in concern for welfare (Pool, 1951; 1952; Lasswell, Lerner and Pool, 1952).

In his recent book on *The Future of Political Science*, Lasswell described some of the reasons for and circumstances of pioneering political studies in mass communications (1964, pp. 161–2):

It is generally recognized that the scientific study of communication has made giant strides in recent decades. An important date in the growth of the field was the early 1930s, when the Humanities Division of the Rockefeller Foundation and the Social Science Research Council interested themselves in the state of knowledge regarding propaganda and communication.

An observer of the academic world of the time might have taken it for granted that the initiative for accelerated research would originate with specialists in linguistics. After all, students of language were primarily responsible for investigating the most distinctive social patterns devised by man in aid of mutual comprehension. But the observer would have been mistaken. The most successful step was taken by political scientists. They provided a unified map of the field that brought specialists of many kinds to sudden awareness of a common frame of reference. The step was taken because political scientists were increasingly aware of the strategic significance for arenas of power of the control of communication. Looking at the many practitioners and technicians of the arts of communication at local, national and international levels, political scientists were startled by the lack of communication among them.

The committee appointed by the Social Science Research Council to report on the situation was composed, for the most part, of political scientists who had previously concerned themselves with the use of guided communication by political parties, pressure groups or by official agencies in war and peace. The integrative, community-wide perspective of political scientists had already begun to make an impression on schools of journalism by seeking to transform the curriculum from over-absorption in ephemeral technicalities.

The conferences and bibliographic aids prepared by the council's committee were helpful in bringing together the fragments of knowledge and the diversities of technique among political scientists, historians, journalists, advertising men, public-relations experts, social psychologists, sociologists and many other specialists (Lasswell, Casey and Smith, 1935; Lasswell, 1958).

Acting as team members or as independent research workers, political scientists conducted descriptive or analytic studies and devised or adapted many data-gathering and data-processing procedures. Among technical innovations can be mentioned various modes of analysing content and of interviewing message-senders and receivers.

A summary of 'Recent trends in political theory and political philosophy' by Deutsch and Rieselbach (1965, pp. 150–3) stressed the contributions of cybernetics as well as of content analysis. The authors posed the 'great issue that concerned theorists from Aristotle to Montesquieu – to what extent is human nature uniform in politics, and to what extent is it shaped by the spirit of times and of countries or peoples . . . ?'

A major approach toward finding answers to these questions is through the study of communication [they suggested]. The theory of communications and control – sometimes also called cybernetics, that is, the theory of steering or of government – arose in the late 1940s and the 1950s in science and technology, but some of its intellectual implications were spelled out in the work of Claude Shannon, Norbert Wiener, John Von Neumann, W. Ross Ashby, George A. Miller, Colin Cherry, Herbert Simon, Allen Newell, and others. Some inferences have been drawn from this body of thought to the theory of government and politics. This general theoretic configuration of communication channels in a society; of language and culture as habits of complementary communication; of the media of mass communication, their content and their control; the memories held by individuals and groups; the visible and invisible filtering mechanisms influencing the selective perception, transmission and recall of information in large populations or small social groups or within the minds of individuals. Communication theory further permits us to conceive of such elusive notions as consciousness and the political will as observable processes. It defines the latter as the process by which postdecision information is so selected and censored as to subordinate it to the outcome of the predecision messages which 'hardened' into the decision. Independent evidence for this process of subordinating postdecision or postcommitment messages has been presented recently within another theoretical framework by Leon Festinger and his associates.

From the viewpoint of communication theory, the content of message flows and of memories is crucial. It is the content of the memories recalled for purposes of recognition of items in current messages from the outside world – it is this content which often determines which messages will be recognized and transmitted with special speed and attention, and which other messages will be neglected or rejected. The consonance or dissonance of messages, of memories and of several projected courses of action is thus decisive for behavior. The dissociation of items from old memories and then recombination to new patterns is seen from this viewpoint as an essential step in the processes of initiative, of innovation, and of essential human freedom. Communication channels do have an influence upon the composition of message flows and memories, and hence on the content of their ensembles, but the content of messages in turn may change the operating preferences and priorities – that is, the values – of the system. . . .

The study of the content of messages has been getting a strong impetus from the development of electronic computing methods of content analysis, lending powerful technological support to the long-standing interest in content analysis pioneered earlier in the Stanford studies by Harold Lasswell and his associates and now being reissued in revised editions (Lasswell, Lerner and Pool, 1952; Pool, 1951; Pool, 1952). A new series of Stanford studies, this time called 'Studies in International Conflict and Integration', under the leadership of Robert C. North, Richard Brody, Ole Holsti and others, is making extensive use of content analysis by computer, within a communications-oriented framework of concepts (North *et al.*, 1963; North, Holsti and Brody, 1965).

Several major recent studies have stressed channel configurations and political communication systems. They have done so, however, usually in combination with an effective concern for the content of the messages transmitted and remembered, and of the value changes produced in the course of time. Outstanding studies of this kind are the volume edited by Lucian Pye on *Communications and Political Development* (Pye, 1963); Daniel Lerner's *The Passing of Traditional Society*

(1958); and the prize-winning volume by Raymond Bauer, Ithiel Pool and Lewis Dexter on *American Business* and *Public Policy* (1963).

Deutsch also made a contribution in the application of theories of communication and control to problems of nationalism and political integration. He described how a study of the flow of everyday communication transactions can help determine the extent to which people belong to a particular community (1964). Deutsch again stressed the importance of message and memory systems, and suggested methods for using communication transaction flow analysis as an indicator of political cohesion.

Edelman, working in the tradition of Lasswell, Mead, Burke and Dewey, contributed an incisive analysis of the significance of symbolic acts and content to the political process itself (1964). Summarizing relevant research and theory, Edelman suggested that the myths, rites and other satisfactions of the electoral and legislative process may confer a sense of public participation, which is only indirectly, if at all, related to what administrators and courts actually do. There is an intricate interplay between the actual allocation of power and benefits on one hand, and the cultivation of beliefs in the reality and rationality of the allocating institutions, on the other.

These contributions stress different aspects of the relationship between the processes of mass communication and the dynamics of social policy. They spell out how the patterned flow of messages, both hierarchical and lateral, defines consensus and community, delineates functional cohesion and effective policy-making, and cultivates public-belief systems. Mass media are dominant shapers of this flow because they are the only agencies of public acculturation capable of mass-producing and distributing common systems of messages beyond previous limitations of face-to-face and any other personally mediated interaction.

IV

Combining the political and sociological approaches are the contributions of Wright Mills (especially 1953, pp. 332–40, and 1956, pp. 306–24). Seminal works in the political economy of mass communications are those of Innis (1950, 1951) and Smythe (1960, 1962). Levin has contributed one of the few systematic economic studies of media ownership and operation (1960). Organizational and decision-making studies have been reported by Breed (1960) and Gieber (1964).

Probably the best review of the sociologically and social-psychologically oriented contributions to mass-media theory and research has been given by Wright (1959). His *Mass Communication: A Sociological Perspective* summarizes contributions to a theory of mass media functions developed elsewhere by Lasswell (1960), Merton (1957), Lazarsfeld and Merton (1960) and Wright himself (1964), as well as theories of mass media advanced by Inkeles (1951), Siepmann (1950) and Siebert, Peterson and Schramm (1963).

Wright's discussion of 'The Sociology of the Audience' (1959, ch. 3) presents the conclusions of pioneering studies on patterns of influence and information diffusion, and such theoretical implications as 'selective exposure', the 'reinforcement effect' and the 'two-step flow' theory. The latter theory, developed by Merton (1949) and Katz and Lazarsfeld (1955) suggests that some mass media content reaches audiences indirectly through the mediating efforts of opinion leaders. The theory affected much subsequent research and led to a call for a more sophisticated treatment of social structures. Wilensky tried to resolve the paradox of simultaneous growth of structural differentiation and cultural uniformity by reexamining media exposure and response patterns (1964, p. 196). He suggested that, on the whole,

men who have confidence in the major institutions of American society tend to distrust 'TV and radio networks'; men who trust media distrust other institutions. Finally, men whose social relations are stable tend to have fluid party loyalties. *To be socially integrated in America is to accept propaganda, advertising and speedy obsolescence in consumption.* (Italics in the original.)

Pioneering works in the historical-artistic-literary tradition are those of Gilbert Seldes, Leo Lowenthal, Raymond Williams and Marshall McLuhan. Seldes (1950, 1956, 1962) has called for, and contributed to, the development of a 'physics, or perhaps the physical geography, of the popular arts'. Lowenthal (1950, 1961; Lowenthal and Fiske, 1957) traced the origins of the debate about popular culture in the eighteenth century and sketched some historical perspectives for contemporary analysis. Williams (1958, 1961, 1962) discussed culture and society in the light of the 'long revolution' in mass communications and education. McLuhan (1951, 1962, 1964) started from Innis's contention that monopoly over the raw materials and media of communications confers control over knowledge, and developed a theory that argues that any technology ('extension of man') creates a new environment whose content is the old technology in altered form. Furthermore, contends McLuhan, the shift from print to other media produces a basic change in the 'ratio of the senses' dealing with the external world, and thus a new 'rationality'; hence 'the medium is the message'.

Contributions of Altick (1957), Watt (1957) and Hoggart (1957) sketched parts of the social and literary background against which the massive cultural transformation of our time may be examined.

The role of mass media in national development, social change and international communications has received increasing attention in the work of Lerner (1958), Pye (1963), Doob (1961), Schramm (1964), Davison (1965) and their collaborators.

The most prolific writer, researcher, summarizer and popularizer in the field, Schramm, left his mark on nearly every aspect of mass media theory and research (1954, 1960, 1963). Anthologies edited by Rosenberg and White (1957), Larrabee and Meyersohn (1958), Dexter and White (1964), Jacobs (1959), Berelson and Janowitz (1966) and Steinberg (1966) contain selections (and bibliographies) reflecting much of the significant theoretical and research contributions of recent decades. More specialized summaries of research on content analysis have been written by Berelson (1952), Budd and Thorp (1963), Pool (1959) and North *et al.* (1963). Klapper summarized research on the effects of mass communication (1960). Berelson's critique of 'The State of Communication Research' (1964) evoked dissent in the same publication by Schramm, Riesman and Bauer, comment by Katz (1959), and new surveys of the field by White (1964, 1965). A 'Quantitative Group' presented a symposium on the research of a decade published in the *Journalism Quarterly* (1965).

The growing body of research and the almost inexhaustible fund of theorizing have not yet produced historically inspired, empirically based, institutionally oriented, comparative and critical theories adequate to the study of the cultural role and public policy significance of the mass media. The following notes attempt to raise some issues and advance questions pertinent to such a theory.

V

A central concern of the study of communications is the production, organization, composition, structure, distribution and functions of message systems in society.

Concern with these patterns and processes involves basic questions of popular culture and public policy, especially in societies where mass-produced message systems provide widely distributed common currencies of social interaction. The questions are necessarily those of social science. Practitioners in the arts and industries of communications; policy-makers in business or government; critics, participants and observers of popular culture – no matter how perceptive and well-informed in their own spheres of interest – do not have systematic, objective and reliable information about the overall operation of the cultural processes in which they – and all of us – live and work.

The cultivation of dominant image patterns is the major function of the dominant communication agencies of any society. There is significant change in that process when there is a change in the clientele, position or outlook of the dominant agencies of communications in culture. Such change, when it occurs, changes the *relative meaning* of existing images and behavior patterns even before it changes the patterns themselves. The history and dynamics of continuities as well as of change in the reciprocal relationships between social structures, media-message systems and image structures are the 'effects' of communications in culture.

Mass communication is the extension of institutionalized public acculturation beyond the limits of face-to-face and any other personally mediated interaction. This becomes possible only when technological means are available and social organizations emerge for the mass production and distribution of messages.

The key to the historic significance of *mass* communication does not rest on the usual concept of 'masses'. There were 'masses' (large groups of people) reached by other forms of public communication long before the advent of modern mass communication. But new means and institutions of production and distribution, the mass media, provided new ways of reaching people. These new ways were not only technologically, but eventually also conceptually and ideologically different from the old. They were associated with and coming at a time of general transformation in the productive base of society. Their cumulative impact burst upon the western world in the age of revolutions which was to shake the old foundations of world order and to introduce into the language most common words dealing with society, communications and industry. The continuing transformation brought about not only concentrations of people but also a conception of 'masses' related more to the movement of messages than of people. This is a conception of 'mass' publics as groups so large, heterogeneous, and dispersed that only mass production and mass distribution systems are capable of reaching them with the same messages within a short span of time, and thus of creating and maintaining some community of meaning and perspective among them.

The key to the historic significance of mass media is, therefore, the association of 'mass' with a process of production and distribution. Mass communication is the technologically and institutionally based mass production and distribution of the most broadly shared continuous flow of public messages in industrial societies. The rise of mass media to popular cultural dominance in the twentieth century represents a major continuing transformation in human affairs, extending the impact of the industrial revolution into the cultural field.

The media of mass communications – print, film, radio, television – present institutional perspectives, i.e. their own ways of selecting, composing, recording and sharing symbols and images. They are products of technology, corporate (or other collective) organization, mass production, and mass markets. They are the cultural arms of the industrial order from which they spring.

Mass media perspectives reflect a structure of social relations and a stage of industrial development. American mass media, for example, established as adjuncts of an already high degree of productive development, became generally consumer and market oriented. In countries where mass media were established at less advanced stages, as agents of planned industrialization, these media are more oriented toward production and development.

Mass media policies reflect not only stages of industrial development and the general structure of social relations but also particular types of institutional and industrial organization and control (Gerbner, 1958b, 1958c, 1959). Corporate or collective organization, private or public control, and the priorities given to artistic, political and economic policy considerations govern their overall operations, affect their relationships to other institutions, and shape their public functions (Gerbner, 1961a, 1961b, 1964a, 1964b).

Popular self-government is possible when people, acting as citizens, collectively create policy alternatives rather than only respond to them. This can come about when knowledge of events and ways of looking at events are public, that is, shared with full knowledge of their being shared. Private systems of 'knowings and viewings' have to be transformed into public systems of 'knowings and viewings' in order to form publics whose perspectives will bear upon social policy in ways that can create policy alternatives. The process by which private knowledge is transformed into public knowledge is literally the process of *publication*.

Publication as a general social process is the creation of shared ways of selecting and viewing events and aspects of life. In its most advanced form, it is mass production and distribution of message systems transforming private perspectives into broad public perspectives. This transformation brings publics into existence. Once created, these publics are maintained through continued publication. They are supplied with selections of information and entertainment, fact and fiction, news and fantasy or 'escape' materials, which are considered important or interesting or entertaining and profitable (or all of these) in terms of the perspectives to be cultivated.

Publication is thus the basis of self-government among large groups of people too numerous and too dispersed to interact face-to-face or in any other personally mediated fashion. That is why 'the press' has a special place in the constitutions and laws of all modern states. Publication is the formation and information (and 'entertainment') of publics; the creation and cultivation of public perspectives; the ordering and weighting of shared knowledge; the maintenance through mass-produced message systems of vast and otherwise heterogeneous communities of perspective and meaning among people who could interact no other way. The truly revolutionary significance of modern mass communications is its 'public-making' ability. That is the ability to form historically new bases for collective thought and action quickly, continuously and pervasively across previous boundaries of time, space and status.

These notions of what I called elsewhere the institutionalized approach to mass communications (Gerbner, 1967) present mass media as creators of technologically produced and mediated message systems, as new forms of institutionalized public acculturation, and as the major common carriers of social interaction and public-policy formation in modern societies. Thus conceived, studies of mass media revolve around problems of message system theory and analysis, institutional process theory and analysis, and the investigation of relationships between message systems, social and organizational structure, image formation and public policy. A theory of mass media would, therefore, deal with these questions: How do media compose and structure their message systems at different times and in different societies? How are message-production systems and mass-distribution systems organized, managed, controlled? What perspectives and what patterns of choices do these systems make available to what publics? In what proportions, and with what kinds and degrees of attention, emphasis and appeal do they weight these choices? What general systems of public images, and what common perspectives on existence, priorities, values and relationships does each structure of choices tend to cultivate?

When we ask about the composition and structure of mass-produced message systems, we ask about mass media content. When we ask what types of mass-produced message systems tend to be produced under different cultural, institutional, technological, conditions, we ask about mass media content in a comparative setting (Gerbner, 1961b, 1964b). In the analysis of content, we want to know about the dynamics of representation of what is, what is important, what is right, and what is related to what else. That is, we want to know the distribution of attention (selection and frequency of topics); the ordering of items in some order of priority (by emphasis); how items are evaluated or judged in context and in relation to some norm; and what groups of items tend to cluster together in certain contexts.

When we ask about influences, relationships, decision-making procedures governing the mass-production of message systems we ask about the institutional process in mass communications (Gerbner, 1964a). And when we ask about information flow, cultivation of images and belief systems, formation and maintenance of publics, delineation of issues and weighting of choices in given frameworks of knowledge, we are asking about communication consequences of mass media content and process.

It may be premature, only thirty years or so after the pioneers have begun to ask such questions, to speak of the emergence of a discipline devoted to the search for answers. But the questioning has become more systematic and persistent, methods of research have become more sophisticated and rigorous, theorizing has become better informed and disciplined, and academic organizations have been established to lead the search for answers and the quest for a theory.

References

ALTICK, R. D. (1957), *The English Common Reader*, University of Chicago Press.

BAUER, R. A., DE SOLA POOL, I., and DEXTER, L. A. (1963), *American Business and Public Policy: The Politics of Foreign Trade*, Atherton Press.

BERELSON. B. (1952), *Content Analysis in Communication Research*, Free Press.

BERELSON, B. (1964), 'The state of communication research', *Pub. Opinion Q.*, vol. 23, Spring, pp. 1–15. Also reprinted in L. A. Dexter and D. M. White (eds.), *People, Society and Mass Communication*, Free Press.

BERELSON, B., and JANOWITZ, M. (1960), 'Social control in the news room', in W. Schramm (ed.), *Mass Communications*, University of Illinois Press.

BREED, W. (1960), 'Social control in the news room', *Social Forces*, vol. 33, pp. 326–35. Reprinted in W. Schramm (ed.) *Mass Communications*, University of Illinois Press.

BUDD, R. W., and THORP, R. K. (1963), *An Introduction to Content Analysis*, School of Journalism, University of Iowa.

DAVISON, W. P. (1965), *International Political Communication*, Praeger.

DE SOLA POOL, I. (1951), *Symbols of Internationalism*, Stanford University Press.

DE SOLA POOL, I. (1952), *The Prestige Papers*, Stanford University Press.

DE SOLA POOL, I. (ed.) (1959), *Trends in Content Analysis*, University of Illinois Press.

DE SOLA POOL, I. (1965), 'Mass communication and political science', in L. W. Kindred (ed.), *Communication Research and School-Community Relations*, Temple University College of Education, pp. 133–50.

DEUTSCH, K. W. (1964), 'Communication theory and political integration', and 'Transaction flows and indicators of political cohesion', in P. E. Jacob and J. V. Toscano (eds.), *The Integration of Political Communities*, Lippincott, pp. 46–9.

DEUTSCH, K. W., and RIESELBACH, L. N. (1965), 'Recent trends in political theory and political philosophy', *Ann. Amer. Acad. polit. soc. Science*, vol. 360, July, pp. 139–62.

DEXTER, L. A., and WHITE, D. M. (eds.) (1964), *People, Society and Mass Communications*, Free Press.

DOOB, L. (1961), *Communication in Africa*, Yale University Press.

EDELMAN, M. (1964), *The Symbolic Uses of Politics*, University of Illinois Press.

ELLUL, J. (1965), *Propaganda: The Formation of Men's Attitudes*, translated from the French by K. Kellen and J. Lerner, with an introduction by K. Kellen, Knopf.

GERBNER, G. (1958a), 'Content analysis and critical research in mass communication', *AV Communication Review*, vol. 6, pp. 85–108. Reprinted in L. A. Dexter and D. M. White (eds.), *People, Society and Mass Communication*, Free Press.

GERBNER, G. (1958b), 'The social anatomy of the romance-confession cover girl', *Journalism Q.*, vol. 35, Summer, pp. 299–306.

GERBNER, G. (1958c), 'The social role of the confession magazine', *Soc. Problems*, vol. 6, Summer, pp. 29–40.

GERBNER, G. (1959), 'Mental illness on television: a study of censorship', *J. Broadcasting*, vol. 3, Autumn, pp. 292–303.

GERBNER, G. (1961a), 'Psychology, psychiatry and mental illness in the mass media: a study of trends 1900–1959', *Mental Hygiene*, vol. 45, January, pp. 89–93.

GERBNER, G. (1961b), 'Press perspectives in world communications: a pilot study', *Journalism Q.*, vol. 38, Summer, pp. 313–22.

GERBNER, G. (1964a), 'Mass communication and popular conceptions of education: a cross-cultural study', cooperative research project no. 876, US Office of Education, pp. 562.

GERBNER, G. (1964b), 'Ideological perspectives and political tendencies in news reporting', *Journalism Q.*, vol. 41, Autumn, pp. 495–509.

GERBNER, G. (1967), 'An institutional approach to mass communications research', in L. Thayer (ed.), *Communication: Theory and Research*, Charles C Thomas.

GERBNER, G. (1966), 'Images across cultures: teachers and mass media fiction and drama', *School Rev.*, vol. 74, Summer, pp. 212–30.

GERBNER, G. (1966), 'Mass media and the crisis in education', *A Symposium on Technology and Education*, Syracuse University, School of Education.

GIEBER, W. (1964), 'News is what newspaper men make it', in L. A. Dexter and D. M. White (eds.), *People, Society and Mass Communications*, Free Press.

GOULD, J., and KOLB, W. L. (eds.) (1964), *A Dictionary of the Social Sciences*, Free Press.

HOGGART, R. (1957), *The Uses of Literacy*, Essential Books; Penguin, 1958.

INKELES, A. (1951), *Public Opinion in Soviet Russia: A Study in Mass Persuasion*, Harvard University Press.

INNIS, H. A. (1950), *Empire and Communication*, Clarendon Press.

INNIS, H. A. (1951), *The Bias of Communication*, University of Toronto Press.

JACOBS, N. (ed.) (1959), *Culture for the Millions? Mass Media in Modern Society*, Van Nostrand.

KATZ, E., and LAZARSFELD, P. F. (1955), *Personal Influence: The Part Played by People in the Flow of Mass Communications*, Free Press.

KATZ, E. (1959), 'Mass communications research and the study of popular culture', *Studies in Public Communication*, vol. 2, pp. 1–6.

KLAPPER, J. T. (1949), *The Effects of Mass Media*, Columbia University Bureau of Applied Social Research.

KLAPPER, J. T. (1960), *The Effects of Mass Communication*, Free Press.

LARRABEE, E., and MEYERSOHN, R. (1958), *Mass Leisure*, Free Press.

LASSWELL, H. D. (1927), 'The theory of political propaganda', *The American Political Science Review*, vol. 21, pp. 627–30. Reprinted in B. Berelson and M. Janowitz *Reader in Public Opinion and Communication*, Free Press, 1966.

LASSWELL, H. D., CASEY, R. D., and SMITH, B. L. (1935), *Pressure Groups and Propaganda: An Annotated Bibliography*, University of Minnesota Press.

LASSWELL, H. D., LERNER, D., and DE SOLA POOL, I. (1952), *The Comparative Study of Symbols*, Stanford University Press.

LASSWELL, H. D. (1958), 'Communication as an emerging discipline', *Audio-Visual Communication Rev.*, vol. 6, pp. 245–54.

LASSWELL, H. D. (1960), 'The structure and function of communication in society', in W. Schramm (ed.), *Mass Communications*, University of Illinois Press.

LASSWELL, H. D. (1964), *The Future of Political Science*, Atherton Press.

LAZARSFELD, P. F., and MERTON, R. K. (1960), 'Mass communication, popular taste and organized social action', in W. Schramm (ed.), *Mass Communications*, University of Illinois Press, pp. 492–512. Also in B. Rosenberg and D. M. White (eds.), 1957, *Mass Culture. The Popular Arts in America*, Free Press, pp. 457–73.

LERNER, D. (1958), *The Passing of Traditional Society*, Free Press.

LEVIN, H. J. (1960), *Broadcast Regulation and Joint Ownership of Media*, New York University Press.

LOWENTHAL, L. (1950), 'Historical perspectives of popular culture', *Amer. J. Sociol.*, vol. 55, pp. 324–5. Also in B. Rosenberg and D. M. White (eds.), *Mass Culture: The Popular Arts in America*, Free Press.

LOWENTHAL, L., and FISKE, M. (1957), 'The debate over art and popular culture in eighteenth century England', in M. Komarovsky (ed.), *Common Frontiers in the Social Sciences*, Free Press. Condensed as 'Reaction to mass media growth in eighteenth century England', *Journalism Q.*, vol. 33, Autumn, 1956, pp. 442–55. Also in Lowenthal, L., *Literature, Popular Culture, and Society*, Prentice-Hall, 1961.

LOWENTHAL, L. (1961), 'An historical preface to the popular culture debate', in Jacobs (ed.), *Culture for the Millions: Mass Media in Modern Society*, Van Nostrand.

MCLUHAN, M. (1951), *The Mechanical Bride*, Vanguard Press.

MCLUHAN, M. (1962), *The Gutenberg Galaxy: The Making of Typographic Man*, Toronto University Press.

MCLUHAN, M. (1964), *Understanding Media*, McGraw-Hill.

MERTON, R. K. (1949), 'Patterns of influence', *Communications Research 1948–1949*, Harper & Row, pp. 180–219.

MERTON, R. K. (1957), 'Manifest and latent functions', *Social Theory and Social Structure* (rev. edn), Free Press, ch. 10.

MILLS, C. W. (1953), *White Collar: The American Middle Classes*, Oxford University Press.

MILLS, C. W. (1956), *The Power Elite*, Oxford University Press.

NORTH, R. C., HOLSTI, O. R., ZANINOVICH, M. G., and ZINNES, D. A. (1963), *Content Analysis: A Handbook With Applications for the Study of International Crisis*, Northwestern University Press.

NORTH, R. C., HOLSTI, O. R., and BRODY, R. A. (1965), 'Perception and action in the study of international relations: the 1914 crisis', in J. D. Sanger (ed.), *The International Yearbook of Political Behavior Research: Empirical Studies in International Relations*, Free Press.

PYE, L. W. (ed.) (1963), *Communications and Political Development*, Princeton University Press.

'Quantitative group looks back over decade of research', (1965), in *Journalism Q.*, vol. 42, Autumn, pp. 591–622.

ROSENBERG, B., and WHITE, D. M. (eds.) (1957), *Mass Culture: The Popular Arts in America*, Free Press.

SCHRAMM, W. (ed.) (1954), *The Process and Effects of Mass Communication*, University of Illinois Press.

SCHRAMM, W. (ed.) (1960), *Mass Communications*, 2nd edn., University of Illinois Press.

SCHRAMM, W. (ed.) (1963), *The Science of Human Communication*, Basic Books.

SCHRAMM, W. (1964), *Mass Media and National Development*, Stanford University Press.

SELDES, G. (1950), *The Great Audience*, The Viking Press.

SELDES, G. (1956), *The Public Arts*, Simon & Schuster.

SELDES, G. (1962), *The Seven Lively Arts*, Barnes.

SHERIF, M., and SHERIF, C. W. (1956), *An Outline of Social Psychology*, rev. edn., Harper & Row.

SIEBERT, F. S., PETERSON, T., and SCHRAMM, W. (1963), *Four Theories of the Press*, University of Illinois Press.

SIEPMANN, C. (1950), *Radio, Television and Society*, Oxford University Press.

SMITH, B. L., LASSWELL, H. D., and CASEY, R. D. (1946), *Propaganda Communication and Public Opinion*, Princeton University Press.

SMYTHE, D. W. (1960), 'On the political economy of communications', *Journalism Q.*, vol. 37, pp. 563–72.

SMYTHE, D. W. (1962), 'Time, market and space factors in communication economics', *Journalism Q.*, vol. 39, pp. 3–14.

STEINBERG, C. S. (ed.) (1966), *Mass Media and Communication*, Hastings House Publishers Inc.

WATT, I. (1957), *The Rise of the Novel: Studies in Defoe, Richardson and Fielding*, University of California Press.

WIEBE, G. D. (1952), 'Mass communication', in E. L. Hartley and R. E. Hartley, (eds.), *Fundamentals of Social Psychology*, Knopf.

WHITE, D. M. (1964), 'Mass communications research: a view in perspective', in L. A. Dexter and D. M. White (eds.), *People, Society and Mass Communications*, Free Press.

WHITE, D. M. (1965), 'The role of journalism education in mass communications research', in L. W. Kindred (ed.), *Communications Research and School-Community Relations*, University College of Education, Temple, pp. 29–57.

WILENSKY, H. L. (1964), 'Mass society and mass culture: interdependence or independence', *Amer. sociol. Rev.*, vol. 29, April, pp. 173–97.

WILLIAMS, R. (1958), *Culture and Society, 1780–1950*, Chatto & Windus; Penguin, 1961.

WILLIAMS, R. (1961), *The Long Revolution*, Columbia University Press; Penguin, 1965.

WILLIAMS, R. (1962), *Britain in the Sixties: Communications*, Penguin.

WIRTH, L. (1948), 'Consensus and mass communication', *Amer. sociol. Rev.*, vol. 13, pp. 1–14.

WRIGHT, C. R. (1959), *Mass Communication: A Sociological Perspective*, Random House.

WRIGHT, C. R. (1964), 'Functional analysis in mass communication', in A. L. Dexter and David M. White (eds.) *People, Society and Mass Communication*, Free Press, pp. 91–109.

Part Two
Mass Media and Mass Society

No concept has been more potent in shaping views of the social
significance of mass communications than that of mass society
(see Bramson, 1961), but it has, in its turn, suffered a decline in
currency. The critique of the media offered, for example, by
Wright Mills (1956) as part of a wider attack on the
prevailing social order, while still compelling, has itself been
subjected to a re-evaluation. Of the three pieces which follow,
only Enzenberger's seeks directly to advance the line of left-
wing criticism from the point where it was left by mass society
theorists (Reading 5). In doing so he raises a number of
interesting questions, about how the technology of mass
communications might, under certain conditions, be a cause of
or means to the reshaping of modern society. Baumann
(Reading 3) takes a lucid look at the concept of mass culture,
and by linking it to other aspects of social change and defining
it as a more universal culture, opens it to a more objective
analysis than it has often received. Alberoni is also concerned
with the transition from traditional social forms to those which
are more open and complex, and chooses an area of
discussion which has been surprisingly neglected in the sociology
of mass communications – the phenomenon of the stars
(Reading 4). Amongst public personages few are more widely
known or more significant to more people than the stars of the
world of entertainment, yet the fact has been largely ignored by
serious social inquiry. The interpretive framework developed
by Alberoni should be of considerable interest both to
students of social change and of the mass media.

References

BRAMSON, L. (1961), *The Political Context of Sociology*, Princeton University Press.
MILLS, C. W. (1956), *The Power Elite*, Oxford University Press.

3 Zygmunt Baumann

A Note on Mass Culture: On Infrastructure

Excerpt from Zygmunt Baumann, 'Two notes on mass culture', *The Polish Sociological Bulletin*, no. 2, 1966, pp. 58–74.

It was probably the historical circumstances of the birth of the term 'mass culture' that have determined the particular cognitive context in which problems pertaining to it have usually been treated in American and other sociological writings. First came the 'discovery' by sociologists of what came to be known as the media of mass communication and their satanic role in the revolutionary change in the mechanisms of perceiving the world, and in the extent to which these mechanisms can be manipulated; the term 'mass culture' was an offspring of the term 'mass communication' coined to denote all that derived from the fact of communication having acquired a mass character. In this manner, due to the causal structure of thinking, the concept of mass culture became linked with that of mass communication. More than that: the two were bound up in a relationship of cause and effect. The modern technical means of mass communication were the cause. Mass culture was the effect. Occasionally, the dependence has been formulated openly; more often, it has been taken for granted, sometimes with no thought given to it. The term 'mass culture' provokes mental associations with television, the radio and the mass-circulation newspaper. And that is all. In most arguments, the circle is perfectly complete: the media of mass communication are the parent of mass culture; mass culture is the child of the mass communication media. Even Stefan Żółkiewski, the leading Polish Marxist theoretician of mass culture, while having broken the circle, has not wholly succeeded in escaping from it: in his excellent study *O kulturze Polski Ludowej* (*On the Culture of People's Poland*), he links with the peculiarities of social structure no more that the 'style' of mass culture, attributing the 'mass' character ('type') of culture itself to the mass range of the means of cultural communication and their public.

The present note has been written to question the cognitive sense of closing the mentioned circle and substantiate the supposition that the media of mass communication are not so much cause of mass culture as a tool to shape it: they serve as channels to convey cultural contents, which have filled already, and independently of those media, the cells of a social structure which has assumed a 'mass' character. The technical and social peculiarities of the media of mass communication provide the explanation for their being able to perform that function. But, only peculiarities of the social structure can explain why they perform their function effectively. For culture to become 'mass', it is not enough to set up a television station. Something must first happen to social structure. Mass culture is in a way a superstructure resting upon what we shall tentatively call 'mass social structure'.

The dispute about the definition of mass culture is a long one, involving many participants. I do not want to join it as protagonist number one thousand and one. And I am now interested not in a definition, but merely in what is usually meant when the term 'mass culture' is applied. And this is the following: within cultures embracing entire societies (national cultures) there traditionally existed relatively disparate variants – regional, ecological (village, small town, big city), class. With all its general features, the culture of a nation was a collection of 'subcultures'. Its acquisition of a 'mass' character in fact amounted to a disappearance of these subcultures and their replacement by a universal culture, common to all the members of the society. To put it more cautiously, it amounted to a weakening of the 'subcultural' features with a concurrent increase in the importance of the common features.

I would not like, either, to be drawn into the dispute about the definition of culture. In this case, too, it will be enough to record the cognitive localization of the problems most commonly put into the 'culture' pigeon-hole: the norms, institutions and patterns of individual behaviour, which combine into 'culture' in fact constitute both the product and the prerequisite of the active mutual adjustment of man and his environment. Culture is the product of the accumulated life experience of many generations, while at the same time it 'serves' these life processes. In this service consists the social function of culture, whereas in this function resides the principal mechanism of selection of cultural elements; even though not every element of culture that functions socially is 'functional', a human community with an ecological equilibrium close to norm displays an inclination to absorb functional elements and a resistance to elements alien to the cultural system.

If we agree with what has just been said about the content of the term 'culture' in general, and the term 'mass culture' in particular, we can draw the following conclusion: the existence within the framework of a 'national' culture of various subcultures – distinguished by regional, ecological or class differences – is probably evidence of none other than these differences being responsible for human social situations becoming so strongly diversified as to lead to these situations having to be served by diverse cultural norms, institutions and patterns. Human communities, differentiated on account of the diversity of regional, ecological or social-class factors, create what might be called – to paraphrase a term used in genetics, intra-breeding populations – that is to say, populations distinguished by the fact that cultural exchanges and the accumulation of cultural elements on the internal plane are much more intensive than those on the external plane. It is for this reason – and even if account is taken of the continuous inter-population exchange, which 'straightens the front' – that in every such intra-breeding population the mutations of cultural elements and the institutionalization of the products of these mutations, which occur with relative independence and in relative mutual isolation, produce a relatively independent evolutionary tendency of culture. From the point of view of the society taken as a whole, this leads to a progressive diversification of the subcultures. The significance of this diversification is the greater the more diversified are the features of the environment – being, in an abstract way, common – that each population selects for its 'own environment'. And since the social situation of the community, as reflected above all in its manner of production, distribution and acquisition of the goods that serve its needs, is the principal criterion of such selection, we are entitled to say that the diversification of the general culture of the society and the dissimilarity of the subcultures are the greater the more disparate are the respective social situations of the members of the respective intra-breeding populations. And vice versa: the more pronounced the 'mass' character, in the sense as defined above, of the culture of the entire society, the greater is the share in that culture of cultural universals, while the smaller the part played by elements which are specific for the formerly intra-breeding groups, the less 'endo-cultural' these populations become – that is, the more convergent become their environments, in the social meaning of the word – the more uniform become the ways of acquiring goods by various individuals and groups constituting the total society. In other words, for a culture to acquire a 'mass' character (it would perhaps be more correct to say, for it to become 'universal') the social situations of the members of the society – and, consequently, also the criteria determining the functional utility of elements of culture – must become standardized.

I think the above statement to be important in its methodological rather than ontological sense. I am not interested at the moment in re-telling the story of how culture acquired a mass character: what I am interested in is the phenomenological reference system, in which the problems of mass culture ought to be placed in order that they might be made as understandable as possible and in order that the interdependence of the two variables resulting from the intervention of a third variable, remaining in the shadow, should not be regarded as a relationship of cause and effect.

Television, the radio and the mass-circulation newspaper are all recent discoveries; which is not to say that media of mass communication were unknown to earlier ages. It is believed – correctly – that the peculiarities of these media consist in the following: 1. the communication of the same unit of information to very many people at one and the same time, with no differentiation introduced into it according to the status of the addressees; 2. the communication of this unit of information in one irreversible direction and the virtual exclusion of the possibility of an addressee to reply, leaving aside any discussion on an equal footing; a sharp polarization of the system of communication into those sending the information and those receiving it; 3. the remarkable persuasiveness of the information being passed on, based on the exalted social authority of the sources, their semi-monopolistic position, and the conviction, of much psychological significance, that 'everybody' is listening – and listening with respect – to the same message. It will readily be noted that all those things were enjoyed by, for example, the Catholic Church – that great broadcasting centre of medieval Europe, with the pulpits of its parish churches playing the part of television sets. The landowner, the serf and the craftsman would all attend the same mass; the same words of the sermon would be spoken to them all, and the same appeal addressed to all. The flow of information was decidedly one-directional and no more reversible than that in present-day television. And as for authority and the universality of reception, even the most clever of television experts would find it hard to compete. Nonetheless, the Church failed to produce a mass culture. Not only the ways of dress and ways of life, but also the ideals and moral standards, and even beliefs which are the least dependent on one's position in life – all remained diversified among the public the Church had. The words spoken from the pulpit were the same for all the faithful, but apparently the ears of the listeners were covered with different kinds of adhesive, designed to absorb different kinds of substances, with the result that to every pair of ears different contents adhered. The chemical composition of the adhesive had first to be standardized for the messages that were uniform when broadcast to become uniform also when received. Culture began to acquire a mass character not when the branches of the same broadcastng system began to reach a mass audience, but when certain conditions of life and social situations became the lot of the masses – when these conditions and these situations, no longer diversified, ceased to diversify the selectivity of reception.

If the media of mass communication today augment the content resources of a culture that is of an increasingly mass character (one would again like to say: increasingly universal), the causes of this fact must be sought in the universalization – supra-regional, supra-ecological and supra-class – of the essential components of the social situation. To be more exact: the effectiveness of the media of mass communication in making culture a mass culture is the greater the farther has the process of universalization of these components progressed. Let us consider, then, what possible components can be involved.

Component number one is *dependence on the market*. Even a hundred or two hundred years ago most people satisfied most of their needs without the intermediary of a market; with the help of unsold manpower – or the unsold part of it – they produced commodities which they then themselves consumed. The process of satisfaction of the needs of that majority was, as a consequence, excluded from the macro-social circulation of commodities and relatively independent of inter-regional, inter-ecological or inter-class exchanges. It constituted a specific infrastructure of the endoculture of the individual and his immediate environment – the environment within which there was a closed circle of undeveloped exchange.

Today – in countries with a developed industry and, consequently, a developed market – a relatively insignificant proportion of people satisfy a relatively insignificant part of their needs by goods excluded from macro-social circulation – goods which they themselves produce and which personify the identity of producer and consumer. The great majority sell that commonest of commodities – manpower – in order subsequently to purchase consumer goods. They enter the market twice – as sellers and as buyers. Everybody, or virtually everybody, is a merchant. And, just as merchants, they are dependent on the market for their successes and failures, their hopes and disappointments. They are dependent on the labour market and the wages market, on the price of manpower and the price of bread. Fascination with one's personal needs cannot in these conditions be expressed otherwise than by fascination with the market. 'Market orientation' is, in these conditions, a social norm and a symptom of mental health. For what are almost psycho-physical reasons, a man placed in the macro-social situation of the circulation of commodities is exposed to the culture-forming influences of the market. He finds the actual products of culture indispensable for the satisfaction of culturally modelled needs, and he cannot acquire these products otherwise than through the intermediary of the market. Nobody can – rich or poor, boss or subordinate, townsman or farmer. This is the common element of their social situation, an infrastructural universal of culture.

And the market standardizes things, as all markets do. Especially this market, based as it is on mass and serial production. From the very outset of the Industrial Revolution the development of industry has consisted – from the point of view of the market – in a serialization and universalization of the production of commodities which had previously, on account of their rarity, been accessible only to the privileged, and which for this reason had enjoyed a special prestige and had been particularly coveted. As consumers, the upper classes performed the function of tasters; the industry for the privileged became the scout that paved the way for the massed columns of serial goods. (A note on the margin: hence, probably, the extraordinary jump in the price of the 'rare' combined with the 'unique', characteristic of our own times: possession of no industrial product gives any longer the sweet sense of security and of the stability of the material symbols of superior social status; exclusive and 'unique' today, every industrial product will become tomorrow – as soon as it wins an appropriate amount of prestige, due precisely to its exclusiveness – a common commodity, and will at once lose its prestige-generating quality. Hence the fantastic prices of the originals of paintings, sculptures, works of antique craftsmanship, and all collector's items; they alone provide a guarantee that rarity will not turn into ordinariness tomorrow. Thus what one pays for is uniqueness, and the price is out of proportion to any aesthetic or useful value. One buys a symbol of superior status, and such symbols are harder and harder to come by in the market.) So, it is not only that everybody satisfies his needs through the intermediary of the market. As serial production develops, more and more often one satisfies these needs with things that are the same for everybody. This is another of the infrastructural universals of culture.

Component number two is *dependence on organization*. When a society was composed of masters and their servants, or of entrepreneurs and their hirelings, two different cultures were needed to service the two disparate social situations – those of rule and subordination, of potency and helplessness. When a society is largely composed of functionaries of organizations, one culture suffices. The behaviour of a director affects that of many more people than does the behaviour of a clerk or labourer working under him; but the director, the clerk and the labourer are all functionaries to an equal extent. The feudal lord was bound to be a master, just as a serf was bound to be a serf; the capitalist tycoon of the Industrial Revolution was bound to model his fate on his own; the director, clerk or labourer of the era of great organizations are bound to have their lives shaped not so much by third persons as by third 'unpersons', whom they do not master and on whom they have no influence – in fact, of whose nature they are hardly aware. The tangled web of organizational links and dependences (a web that is disentangled only in sociological abstraction distant from realities), coupled with the far-reaching autonomy of decision-making in specialized formal organisms, account for the fact that there is hardly any social development that would exert no influence on the fate of the individual, and that there are extremely few such influence-exerting elements on which the individual himself can have an influence, or even such as he can as much as enumerate. Sociologists time and again find to their horror that a worker does not usually know what is produced in the factory where he himself bores tiny holes in steel tubes. Still, only occasionally do these sociologists hit upon the idea that in that factory there is not a single person who would be mentally aware of the entire set of partial functions, of the process of production in its entirety. It is said that a foreman knows more than an ordinary worker, a department head more than a foreman, and a manager more than a department head. But this is a view from the window of the manager's office. The opposite saying is no less true: there are things known to the worker but unknown to the foreman, known to the department head but not to the manager. Nobody knows all. Everyone of us is in a situation in which the number of unknowns exceeds that of equations. This is the case in a factory, in an office, in a multi-organizational society – to a degree incomparably greater than in an abstract factory 'taken separately'. Organization is supra-personal rather than non-personal – absolutely and without exception. And this is yet another infrastructural universal of culture.

To satisfy his needs, to acquire the goods indispensable for it, man must win a position in an organization. This becomes for everybody, whatever his or her profession, the supreme instrumental value. Organizations differ one from the other, and so do the positions in the organizations, but the need for some position in some organization is common to everyone. Also the ways of winning a position are, on the whole, similar: an education appropriate for the position, a behaviour appropriate for the organization's requirements and crowned by an appointment decided upon by appropriate organizational bodies. The fascination with needs turns in a socially natural manner into a fascination with the organization and with the position within it – and it cannot turn into anything else. The position in the organization is the fundamental determinant of all social situations and a social certificate of identity. The question: 'Who is he?' is unhesitatingly answered by modern man: 'He is director X at office Y' rather than 'He's a very nice chap' or 'He's a noble dreamer.' And this, again, is an infrastructural universal of culture.

But, in a pluralist society, the power of every organization extends to only a fraction of the goods of social importance and only a fractional human community. No individual can restrict the process of satisfying his needs to the range of the goods and people that are within the domain of one organization. On the contrary: in the course of this process he inevitably enters into the spheres of influence of a great number of different and mutually autonomous organizations, in a few of which only he himself is an influential person. Thus, everyone is alternately the order-giver and the applicant, alternately the subject and the object of the influence. Individual bilateral acts of cooperation become polarized into subjects and objects – but society does not. The closer that society is to the perfectly pluralist model, the closer to zero is the number of exceptions to the rule. The proportion in which the elements of subjection and command are mixed vary from one individual situation to another, but both elements occur in each. The differences are quantitative rather than qualitative. Thus, this aspect of the situation, which is traditionally one of the principal sources of cultural diversification, gradually becomes also a premise for infrastructural universals.

Component number three is *dependence on technology*. The peasant who wove linen on a hand-loom at his own home depended on himself for the satisfaction of his needs. The farmer who buys his shirt in a shop in town depends on technology. A man who uses a razor is less dependent on technology than one who employs an electric razor. If a stone gets into the gears of a turbine at some power station hundreds of miles away, he will have to go unshaved. Technical equipment makes all our actions considerably easier, but at the same time renders us helpless when faced by the adversities of fate, however trivial. It is easier to sweep a room using a vacuum cleaner rather than a brush, but we are unable to repair the vacuum cleaner when it breaks down. There is the macabre American joke about the American family going to bed without dinner after the TV set has broken down: the mother of the family, not having watched the latest advertisements, did not know what to buy for a meal. Technology has displaced the elemental disasters of old: if just one tram runs off the rails, we are unable to return home from work. The fear of motorcars in the road has taken over in family lore the part once played by the fear of vipers and wolves. However, let us return to what is for us the most important matter: more and more people to an increasing extent satisfy their needs with the help of technology – a technology which they do not create themselves, the principles of whose functioning they do not understand, and which they are unable to master without the assistance of other people. Technology is a blessing, but it is also a materialized and ever-present nightmare. The ambivalence is notorious, and so is the ambiguity of the sentiments it generates – admiration intertwined with apprehension. The man-in-the-street accepts the news that a computer thinks on the same principle as Nootka the Indian accepted the shaman's explanation that the catch was bad because the fish had been insulted by the failure to dance the prescribed ritual dance before the canoe was set afloat. The man-in-the-street demands an explanation about the computer for the same reason for which Nootka the Indian needed information about the touchy fish – because there is some connection between the computer and the satisfaction of his needs. The fascination with one's personal needs is expressed in a fascination with technology. This is one more infrastructural universal of culture.

But in the case of Nootka the Indian the connection between the irritability of the fish and his next dinner was direct and obvious. For our own man-in-the-street the connection between the technology he reads about in his paper and his dinner today, or even tomorrow, is a far cry from this mentally delectable obviousness. The connection between some new tool and the craftsman's or farmer's personal position was once clear, and the criteria of its assessment simple: there was progress if one found one's work easier, or if one got more out of one's work, or if both these things happened together. When following in his newspaper reports about the introduction of some new bulldozer or crushing-machine, the man-in-the-street is by no means sure whether there is in fact a link between these events and his personal situation, and, if there is one, what it is. For the two variables to be mutually linked, abstract thinking is now needed – theory, macro-social syntheses. Not everybody is capable of that, all the less since their verification is beyond the possibilities of the individual. A new technical device certainly implies an increment in human power. But, will it increase also the power of the individual? We are far from sharing the individualistic optimism of an Adam Smith or the collectivist optimism of Charles Wilson of General Motors. The progress of mankind and the progress in the situation of the individual are not now identical in either practice or human consciousness. Dependence on technology thus generates disorientation and anxiety, if only of the kind which always goes together with uncertainty and incomplete knowledge. Everybody feels threatened. Nobody is master of this jinn released from the bottle. And this fact, too, we must include among the infra-structural universals.

The importance of all the three components, listed here, of the social situation of people living in an industrial civilization – supra-regional, supra-ecological, and supra-class, and, quite simply, common – consists in that they are components of the most important process of life – that of satisfaction of human needs. Man becomes dependent on the market, on organization and on technology because he cannot by-pass them on the road from the expenditure of his creative energy to the acquisition of the goods indispensable for its regeneration. Thus, it is in the growing similarity of these roads that I perceive the fundamental reason for the increasing preponderance of these features in the life situations of people which are common and general over those which are still diverse – and, consequently, also for the increasing preponderance of those elements in the culture of the entire society which have become macro-social universals over those which are still subject to subcultural (regional, ecological, class) diversification. Culture services the life situations of individuals: mass (universal) culture services mass (universal) situations. This, of course, is a dependence of pattern. Because, on the one hand, the universalization of culture has to overcome the resistance of tradition, custom and group homeostasis, and that is why it usually lags behind the universalization of infrastructural elements; while, on the other hand, the impact of the current cultural peak may introduce to the cultural system of one society or another elements adapted to servicing an infrastructure that has not yet emerged; these elements will then run ahead and speed up (if considered within the context of a single national society, and not mankind in general) corresponding changes in the infrastructure.

In what I have said so far I was able to employ the term 'need' by invoking the interpretation it is commonly given, without caring for deciphering it. But, if the list of infrastructural universals is to be completed, the collection of the elements covered by the term 'needs' must be put in rough order. The differentiation proposed by Abraham H. Maslow – into 'deficiency needs' and 'Being needs' – seems to be the most useful for this purpose. The former category includes, for example, the need to satisfy hunger and to secure personal safety; the latter, the need for the enjoyment flowing from aesthetic experiences and a sense of one's own creative potentialities. The mutual relationship between the two categories can, in general terms, be characterized as follows: when the deficiency needs are not satisfied, they suppress or even annihilate the Being needs; when the deficiency needs are satisfied, it is the Being needs that vex the strongest and are the most obtrusive in making themselves felt. Let us add to this that, in Maslow's view, the deficiency needs and the Being needs differ in that the former disappear as soon as they are satisfied, while the latter, on the contrary, are further stimulated by their satisfaction; and that the reward that the former can bring may result merely from the elimination of the tension that was caused by the failure to satisfy them (it is thus a 'negative reward!'), whereas the latter, on the contrary, create such tensions as are of themselves a source of enjoyment. Satisfaction of the deficiency needs, Maslow says, is merely the prerequisite for an absence of sickness: health further requires the Being needs to appear.

Borrowing Maslow's terminology, we can now say that a successive component of the life situation of people living in an industrial civilization – a component which, if not universal, is certainly becoming more and more common – is the shrinking of that portion of time and energy which is socially indispensable for the satisfaction of the deficiency needs of such people – and – as a result – the universalization of the Being needs. Over the past several thousand years, in many parts of the globe and most certainly within the orbit of our *oikoumene*, the needs of existence, potentially accessible to every human individual, were revealed only in those individuals who happened to belong to the idle and rich classes. The lives of all people centred on the satisfaction of their needs, but these needs differed not only in quantity but also in kind. The minority searched for ways of satisfying the needs of growth, while the majority grappled with the deficiency needs. Consequently, the minority and the majority were each in the need of a different culture. As the abundance of the goods that serve the satisfaction of the deficiency needs increased, and as the contribution of direct human effort to their production simultaneously decreased, while at the same time the lower limit of participation in these goods was raised, a different situation arose: fewer and fewer people centre their life activity on the satisfaction of the deficiency needs, whereas the Being needs come to the fore more and more commonly. They slowly become a psychological universal which, similarly to the infrastructural universals, becomes an element in the universalization of culture -- or, in other words, the birth and triumph of mass culture.

Note One might as well end here. The idea I have tried to express is relatively simple. On the model plane it can be presented as follows: for the culture of society X to become a mass culture, i.e. one universally accepted and diversified only insignificantly according to criteria of region, ecology or class, it is necessary for the social situations of the individuals in this society X and for the structure of their needs to become uniform to such an extent that they must and can be serviced by one and the same cultural system. The model character of this dependence rests upon, among other things, the assumption – silently accepted, though not fulfilled in practice – about the cultural isolation of society X – that is to say, about the absence of external cultural diffusion, and just because this assumption does not hold good in practice, the connection between culture on the one hand, and the infra-structure and structure of needs on the other, may in some society be more complex than would result from the model state-ment. Nonetheless, I am inclined to persist in affirming the cogni-tive value of the methodological directive to the effect that the processes occurring in social infrastructure and the structure of personality should serve as the reference system for an analysis of the origin and content of mass culture.

4 Francesco Alberoni

The Powerless 'Elite': Theory and Sociological Research
on the Phenomenon of the Stars[1]

Francesco Alberoni, 'L'Élite irresponsable; théorie et recherche
sociologique sur *le divismo*', *Ikon*, vol. 12 – 40/1, 1962, pp. 45–62.

This Reading is presented in this volume in a new translation by
Denis McQuail.

General conditions for the existence of the phenomenon

In every society are to be found persons who, in the eyes of other
members of the collectivity, are especially remarkable and who
attract universal attention. This applies most often to the king
and nobles, to priests, prophets and men of power, although often
in very diverse ways and in varying degrees. In general it is a
question of persons who hold power (political, economic or
religious) – that is to say, of persons whose decisions have an
influence on the present and future fortunes of the society which
they direct. This rule holds true even in modern western society.
However, besides these persons, one finds others, *whose institutional power is very limited or non-existent, but whose doings and
way of life arouse a considerable and sometimes even a maximum
degree of interest*. This interest is not related to the consequences
which the activities and decisions of these particular individuals
(stars, idols, '*divi*') can have on the lives and future expectations
of members of the society. They belong to another sphere of
evaluation.

The existence, at the heart of a society, of two categories of
persons whose behaviour is an object of great attention, is
accompanied effectively by a difference *in orientations and in
criteria of evaluation*. Because the holders of power are 'evaluated' almost exclusively according to the direct or indirect consequences of their activities for the attainment of societal goals
and for the organization of the community, with them it is a
question of a specific criterion of evaluation. With the second

1. Extract from research conducted for the Institute of Sociology of the
Catholic University of Milan, with financial help from UNESCO.

group, a more complex system, which we are going to analyse in the course of the present research, is involved.

Such a separation stems from the fact that decision-making activities which concern the collectivity (power) are made up of autonomous and specific social roles: these activities, engaged in by persons who hold institutionally established positions have their effects in a real sphere of decision and are subject to forms and criteria of evaluation which are fixed in advance. At a given stage of social development, it follows that an impersonal evaluation of activities of collective interest is possible. The preliminary conditions for a situation of this type comprise the establishment of a state of law and of an efficient bureaucracy.

A phenomenon like 'stardom' does not exist unless certain systems of action are institutionally considered as *unimportant from a political point of view*. In other words 'stars' exist in that measure to which their activities are not mainly evaluated according to the consequences which they involve for the collectivity. There is a social mechanism of separation which, put schematically, holds that the 'stars' do not occupy *institutional positions of power*. One may note that this situation could not, in theory, hold in a marxist social system where every member of a social group has a function for the collectivity and is responsible for the consequences of his action. It could, however, hold in these circumstances in respect of persons who, living outside the system and belonging to the capitalist world, have no power over the system itself. In this sense, 'stardom' does not so much presuppose a pluralism of evaluation or culture, as the existence of autonomous centres of power, whether private or not, which are institutionally guaranteed against the intervention of the State.

These conditions hold today in the western world, just as they did in Greece and above all in imperial Rome (it does not seem that 'stardom' in the true sense of the term existed in the Egypt of the Pharaohs – a fact which can be explained without inconsistency with earlier remarks: in this particular case the governing bureaucracy did not permit the existence of autonomous centres of private power, governed and guaranteed by public power).

Besides these two conditions which we have indicated, we can mention several others: the degree of structuring of the social system; the growth in size of societies; the increase in economics wealth; social mobility.

As far as the *structuring* of the social system is concerned, what we have already said has implied this. The separation out of specific principles of evaluation, important for the growing institutional cadres of decision-making power, cannot help but produce a complex structure in a society.

As to the size of the social system, we observe that in public–star relationships, each individual member of the public knows the star, but the star does not know any individuals. The star views the public as a collectivity. This does not mean that personal relationships between the star and other actors cannot exist, but that it is not these personal relationships which characterize the phenomenon. For a relationship of this kind to be set up, one must presuppose a large number of spectators and the existence of certain specific social mechanisms. Even if the star is perceived in his or her individuality, the spectators cannot be perceived in theirs. This situation is best exemplified in a large-scale society, with a high level of interdependence, at the core of which and by virtue of its very large size, only a small number of persons can provide a point of reference for all. In a more restricted community, the same process would be possible, bearing in mind the existence of those institutional barriers of the type which separate the king, or certain priests or nobles. In this case, the phenomenon would be something other than 'stardom', since for the latter there is no institutional barrier. On the contrary, the obstacle arises in most cases either because observation of the person concerned cannot be direct or because of the sheer number of aspirants to such a type of relationship. We can see that the relationship between star and public lacks an element which we would label 'mutuality'.

An increase of economic wealth is a third basic condition. In effect, only an income above subsistence level allows the mobilization of interests and attention which gives rise to the phenomenon of stardom. Nevertheless, one must be cautious in establishing a correlation between these two orders of phenomena. On the one hand, the rise in income above subsistence level is always the fruit of an economic and structural transformation of society – a point which connects with the two earlier conditions – on the other hand, we can find the phenomenon of 'stars' at very low levels of income and economic development (football-players in South America; cinema actors in India). One might even wonder whether the phenomenon in its most accentuated form is not peculiar to societies which are socially and economically under-developed.

Social mobility, which is dependent on the transformation of the system, is also a fundamental condition for enabling one to have admiration, rather than envy, for the star.

Stardom and charisma

We will use the word 'stars' and 'stardom' with a rather wider meaning than common usage allows, especially in Italy.[2] Following Panzini's definition (1963, p. 202), one would understand by this word the phenomenon by which a certain individual attracts, in the eyes of many others, an unconditional admiration and interest. The cry of the crowd to the victorious champion 'you are a god' provides a typical example. The champion is credited with capacities superior to those of all other men, and thus with super-human qualities. Weber defined this situation as *charismatic* (1968, vol. 1, p. 241). He writes

By charisma we mean a quality regarded as extraordinary and attributed to a person. . . . The latter is believed to be endowed with powers and properties which are supernatural and superhuman, or at least exceptional even where accessible to others; or again as sent by God, or as if adorned with exemplary value and thus worthy to be a leader.

We can, first of all, ask ourselves what the relevance of this example is in assessing the phenomenon of stardom as we have presented it. Are the stars truly gods in the literal meaning of the word, or rather charismatic figures?

2. In French, the word '*divismō*' has been retained as a concept, and 'divi', in the plural as a related term; but the word 'vedette' has usually been used instead of the singular 'divo'.

Translator's note: In this English translation, 'divi' has been rendered as 'stars'; similarly, the key term 'divismo', for which there is no English synonym, has been translated usually as 'stardom', and occasionally as 'star system' or 'phenomenon of the stars' (as in the title). It is hoped that the context fully conveys the intended meaning of these related concepts.

According to Max Weber, charisma leads to a power relationship by virtue of the fact that the possessor of charisma is perceived as a leader or chief (thus producing an internalized feeling of obligation); under his leadership, those who submit derive benefits which constitute proof of charisma. In the definition of 'stardom' we have made it clear that the star is not endowed with authoritative power and that his decisions are not collectively felt to have any influence on the life and the future of members of the collectivity. How is it that the charismatic element of 'stardom' does not get transformed into a power relationship? The explanation must be sought in the mechanisms which, in a highly structured society, give rise to the specificity of social roles. Whoever occupies a social position is appraised according to the specific content of the function which characterizes this position (see Parsons, 1949). In the case of a multiple classification, the specificity of the function and of the evaluation does not disappear (see Alberoni, 1960, pp. 37–42).

In other words, a bank employee is judged in the light of specific criteria which relate to the kind of work he does. If at the same time he is a member of some association, the kind of normative qualities required of him in the second system and the evaluative criteria used in relation to it, are not only specific, but often will not relate to the former. It is exactly this independence of social roles which, in modern societies, leads to conflicts between the roles themselves. Thus the bank employee or the unattached person who rejoices at the victory of his sporting hero and who calls out 'you are a god' does not cease to be a bank employee or a private citizen in order to follow his idol and share in his idol's charisma. The behaviour in which charisma is expressed is in reality behaviour in a particular role, while the behaviour of the spectator is defined by exclusion from this role and by the retention of his ordinary roles. The spectator is present at, shares in, but does not act. The manifestation of charisma which concerns us presupposes, therefore, a stable social structure – that is, a system of pre-established and internalized roles, of such a kind that the sharing in charisma does not result in the restructuring of habitual systems of action. In this way, the charisma is highly specific.

The racing cyclist who is a demi-god in the eyes of his

enthusiastic admirer does not necessarily show competence in other fields. The specificity of charisma should be understood as a specificity relating to one class of actions, all requiring the same kind of skill. This is why a great racing cyclist can also be a great athlete. Specialization lies at the heart of any particular field. Besides, a champion's superiority in fields different from his speciality, but within the same category, can furnish confirmation of his true charismatic nature. It would be very interesting to make an empirical study of the size of this area of generalization, in terms of conscious and unconscious expectations. Nevertheless, there exist institutional limits to such generalizations: political activity is one example.

By contrast, in a society where there is no complexity of social structures, nor mechanisms for separating out social roles, charisma tends to become generalized. This is one of the reasons why stardom does not exist in small-scale societies. The exceptional man raises himself to a charismatic level and becomes a hero. He thus acquires over the community a power which, at the same time, exposes him to aggressively violent reactions on the part of his opponents and to the envy of those who are less adept than he. Change occurs within two limiting points: either the hero is overthrown by envy and aggression, or he succeeds over his enemies and his power is institutionalized. Neither case would be expected in large-scale societies with a high level of structuring. In such cases, charisma is not generalized, the star does not acquire power and as a result is not exposed to envy or aggression. The sharp separation between roles which prevents the stars from acquiring an institutionalized position of power in a highly structured society is the social system's protection mechanism against the menace of generalized charisma. The separation of roles in this respect offers much stronger guarantees than does simply specificity of roles. In the case of multiple allocation, the specification of roles is only efficacious up to the point where the corresponding modes of evaluation are deeply internalized. If the specificity of evaluation were strongly internalized, the star would be able to occupy a power position because he or she would be evaluated quite differently as a holder of power than as artist, football champion, etc. But if the internalization is shallow, there is always the danger in this situation that charisma will become generalized. The great actor, the great athlete, the personage known to all, sympathetic, attractive – all these could be raised to power, not independently of the fact of their being actors, cyclists or well-known figures, but precisely because they are such. This would occur especially in countries where the structuring is still weak and where specific and rational modes of evaluation are little internalized.

(We have recently seen a case of a country choosing as parliamentary deputies football players who were victorious in a world championship. In Italy we have had the candidature of Bartali in parliamentary elections. Elia Kazan, in his film 'Face in the Crowd' shows a situation in which a very gifted singer becomes a charismatic leader and, supported by unscrupulous politicians, finds himself on the point of attaining power.)

The mechanism by which social roles are sharply separated seems therefore to have the function of a defence against the generalization of charisma. In the light of these considerations one may assume that the condition of sharp separation of roles will lose its importance along with a greater internalization of specific modes of evaluation.

The 'stars' as an elite

In any society which is socially stratified, normal methods for the study of stratification always enable us to identify a more exalted social stratum which has sharply different characteristics from other social strata. A primary feature of this difference is the existence, amongst members of this particular stratum, of a higher degree of interaction than is found between members of other strata.

A second feature derives from the fact that in this group, competition, and often very active competition, always takes place with a high regard for the rules and mores of the group, thus ensuring that the decisions of members of the 'elite' do not have too sudden and sharp repercussions on the non-privileged.

The third feature is a certain degree of isolation, compared with other strata and groups. In general this is a question of ensuring a degree of secrecy for the activities of competition and cooperation, since these might not accord with the those of the non-privileged. The reduction in what we will call observability has the effect of enabling those who hold power to follow strategies for conserving it, and sometimes constitutes a means for preserving privilege. In contrast, an increase in observability is often an expression of the diminution of power. All of which comes back to the point that a power elite can never be exposed to a high degree of observability. In any case, the forms and the nature of observability, as far as the holders of institutional power are concerned, are institutionally established (in democracy in very liberal measure); this characteristic, which is most important, is respected even when there is a high degree of observability. In the case of the stars, on the contrary, observability is practically unlimited.

The highest degree of observability in a power elite is to be found in aristocratic or monarchic states whose legitimacy is securely founded on popular consent, and in popular democracies. The king, court and nobles are objects of valuation in varied ways, including, amongst other things, that type of valuation reserved for 'stars'. In this case the situation is very close to that of very small communities. This is facilitated by the lack of influence which observability has on power, attributable in turn to the particular criteria which affect selection for, and participation in, the elite (for example the requirement of membership of certain noble families).

Charismatic totalitarianism accords with this situation only superficially. In fact the chief or leader parades a total observability, even of his private life, which is presented as exemplary. But the behaviours truly deserving attention (as far as power is concerned) are kept carefully hidden and removed from all control. The observability of the charismatic leader is carefully foreseen and manipulated. Its purpose is to guarantee that only those evaluative orientations conducive to the exercise of power itself and favourable to it, will be set working.

On the other hand, in the democracy typical of industrial societies, there develop specific traditional evaluative orientations towards the power elite. It is, in general, a question of highly specific evaluations, from which are eliminated all elements which are not functionally important. Other evaluative orientations are no longer directed towards elites, but towards 'significant others' whose observability is not institutionally limited, that is to say the 'stars'. By comparison the observability of the latter is thus very heightened, and the evaluative orientations very complex.

One must, nevertheless, admit that the specificity of evaluations concerning persons who occupy institutionalized positions of power in a democracy can vary in degree. In long-established and well-consolidated democracies, where the internalization of the values of the social system is deepest, observability is greater and more diffused. This probably stems from the fact that the danger represented by the generalization of charisma is least; the institutionalized rules coincide in greater measure with the mores of the community. The limitation of evaluations within highly specific limits here loses its importance. In England, or in the United States, politicians are evaluated (in a greater measure than in Italy, for example) with regard to activities which are not strictly or specifically political. The President of the United States, in order to be elected, must present a total image of his private life, of his relations with the community, etc., something which is inconceivable in a democracy of recent origin, menaced by the generalization of charisma. The mode of behaviour in the community becomes the object of evaluation in order to demonstrate the adherence of the candidate to the mores of the society, mores which constitute the fundamental basis of evaluation internalized from the political system. The President will become a symbol for the nation, an ideal model for universal reference; he crystallizes in himself many of the characteristics belonging to stardom. Hence a necessity for an *a priori* evaluation of his manner of life and of his capacities in office. The latter is possible when the values inspired by the political system are widely shared and deeply internalized. A very slight deviation can then rapidly provoke the condemnation of the person, whatever may be his institutional power position. The case is very different if this internalization does not exist. Satisfaction can easily transform itself into admiration, qualities into superhuman properties, superiority into charisma, and admiration into devotion.

In democracies of recent date, where the process of consolidation of democratic institutions is under way, where the progressive change of the system is leading towards industrial rationalization, a specific evaluation should be interpreted either as a latent function or as an anticipatory manifestation of socialization, ensuring that the evolution of the system remains in accord with the model of rationalization. One would predict that when a deeper internalization of democratic values occurs and of specific and rational modes of evaluation, there will appear, in this type of social system, forms of values which are more general, while still retaining a specific character.

We can say that the stars are, like the power elite, an object of reference for the community, but of a different kind. It seems to us useful to stress that a good many of these stars appear in the eyes of the public as being in close interaction and making up a true elite which occupies a central place (although without power) in a community of an industrialized kind. They constitute a genuine core of the community, and although deprived of any fixed or stable location, they do at least partially congregate as a group in certain privileged places.[3]

If we were to choose any list whatsoever of people of this kind, based on a sampling of weekly magazines, we would soon find that the majority has been or is effectively in interaction. We are here concerned with a world of entertainment, related to everyday society by reason of business or profession, or because they frequent the same fashionable places, the same receptions, etc.

In the eyes of the public, this commonality probably seems higher than it really is, either by reason of the false impression of proximity suggested by television shows, or through the juxtaposition of photographic evidence with press articles, or because of the care which is taken to present to the public friendly and cooperative forms of interaction and to soften hostile and competitive forms. The members of this elite thus appear, contrary to fact, as being potentially in interaction. (It would be interesting to study how this type of relationship is perceived by the public and what sort of constellations, especially of a spatial kind, they imagine to exist).

One can say that the stars form a social group with very fluid and uncertain limits. The group is not structured, but it shows

3. These are the star 'communities', as in Hollywood, or the Via Veneto, Rome, and all other places where the fashionable set meet. The most frequent occasions are for film premières, festivals, exhibitions, cruises, receptions and presentations of literary and artistic prizes, etc.

certain centres of interaction which sometimes take on the character of sub-group or sub-community: for example, the community group of the Via Veneto in Rome, the Frank Sinatra clan, etc. Those who make up a lower group (the fringe constituted by those who, in the eyes of the public, interact only occasionally with the group, like certain writers, painters or fashionable thinkers) do not, however, exhaust the totality of these personages who are 'significant', *although lacking in power or authority*. The protagonists in national scandals (as Brusadelli or Giuffre in Italy), those accused of famous crimes like Giuliano, are not part of this elite: participants in televised competitions or television plays enter it in a rather fleeting manner. One knows of people who have become famous as a result of an exceptional exploit like Lindberg or Gagarin who can enter into interaction with the core we have spoken of, but who often remain completely separate from it, or, in contrast, can even belong marginally to the elite of power as did Gagarin. Even when they lack interactive relationships with the community core, or when they are institutionally excluded from it, these people (even the criminals) are nevertheless potential members of it in the eyes of the public.

Evaluation of modes of conduct in the community

We have said that the stars are those members of the community whom *all* can evaluate, love or criticize. They are the chosen objects of collective gossip, the channels of which are the mass media of communication.

To fulfil such a social function, they must be observable to people of all degrees. In a small-scale community, observability is very much heightened, and the tension which accompanies observability is very great, but there also exist specific mechanisms for reducing observability and for preserving an area of privacy. All members of the social groups are subject to continual observation and other members of the group evaluate their behaviour (often by means of gossip) in order to:

1. Decide whether, according to group values and rules, their morality or character is deviant.

2. Compare performance with expectation.

3. Verify culturally established predictions and expectations, based on earlier behaviour and the pressures exerted by the milieu.

4. Assess the influence of their behaviour on the community (for instance, the effect of their example on morals).

The result is to encompass behaviour in a system of value-norms and procedure-results, which is predetermined but also in a continual, if rather slow, state of revision. Each behaviour is, therefore, a matter to be experienced by the collectivity and the result serves to test the systems of expectation (normative or not) of the group under consideration.

5. One other source of tension associated with observability lies in its direct correspondence with conscious or unconscious desires or impulses (voyeurism, release of aggression, love, etc.);

6. There is, finally, one class of evaluations from which several advantages might be expected in connection with interactive relations. In this case observation is useful to an individual to the extent that the behaviour is particularly instrumental for him.

This is notably the case when the behaviour concerned has an economic bearing, more generally it is true of the behaviour of persons who have some power in relation to the observer. We should bear in mind that in a small village each inhabitant has a certain power in relation to every other and, as a result, that this last mentioned component is always present and linked inextricably to others. The greater the power possessed by one person, the greater is the interest of the others in increasing his observability. An increase in observability signifies, in effect, an increase in the possibilities of predicting the actions of the other, and therefore means for the observer an increase in his own possibilities for action.

As the community increases in size, direct interactions lose their importance and observability diminishes. The large city guarantees to its members a weak degree of observability or a high degree of anomie. On this account it is impossible to examine collectively the behaviour of all the members of a populous community, in the light of the principles of evaluation which we have noted. This evaluation is reserved by each member for those with whom he is in direct interaction and for those particularly 'significant' personages.

In particular, as far as the evaluative orientation of the sixth type is concerned, it can apply to persons with whom the subject is in interaction (members of his family, friends, acquaintances, rivals, etc.) and persons who hold power in the community (the power elite). Orientations of types 1, 2, 3, and 5 are, in a large-scale community, directed towards the stars, while orientations of types 4 and 6 are specifically directed towards the power elite. We can note that, even when limited to evaluations of types 1, 2, 3, and 5, there is a profound difference between the gossip which goes on in small villages and that which applies to the stars. The former is more critical, aggressive, scandalous than the latter. The majority of the stars chooses freely, or at least accepts its collective role, and the group to which they belong retains a sufficient degree of stability. These two conditions would not be realizable if the aggressive and competitive components which develop in community life were free to attach to them.

One other interesting fact is that the stars are not objects of envy. Further, the elite of the stars is not in general perceived as a privileged class; their very existence is not regarded as a clear and brutal witness to social injustice.

The lack of slander, of envy and of class demands – these are the phenomena between which one can see a correlation, but which, from a sociological point of view, are not necessarily linked.

In general, scandal occurs without those who are its object being considered as a privileged group. It consists essentially in sharing with someone else the knowledge and reprobation of some moral act of another known to both, and in deriving a satisfaction from the condemnation which compensates for a personal aggressiveness in relation to the person who is the object of scandal. Such a satisfaction exists when, in a small community, the shared condemnation effectively harms the intended person; from this condemnation issue collective punitive acts (sanctions). The fact that such a condemnation is made according to shared standards of evaluation avoids, on the other hand,

any feelings of guilt which might be provoked by the consciousness of personal aggression. The unconscious aggression which is
the driving force of the action is transformed in this manner into
'moral disdain'. From the point of view of the community, this
process functions as a mechanism for assessing all behaviour
according to the values and rules of the group. This mechanism
presupposes the existence of rigorous principles of evaluation and
the possibility of an effective prejudice against the deviant person
(sanction), and moreover the existence of prior motives of
aggressiveness. In relation to the stars these three conditions
exist only in very small measure.

The shared principles of evaluation which are present in a
modern industrial society are less integrated and less rigorous
than those of a small community, by reason especially of the
continuous transformation which an industrial society under-
goes. The possibilities of effective prejudice against a deviant
person are very few. Only by collective acquiescence could it be
achieved, and the latter, in the absence of a direct interaction
between the members of a social group, is limited to the means of
mass communication, and as a result finds itself in large measure
controlled by the elite with which it is concerned. As for the
existence of an aggressiveness which can be transformed into
'moral disdain' this is equally very weak, as we will have occasion
to see in speaking of envy.

Actions are not only evaluated in the light of the values and
rules of the group, but also according to the results which are
expected; their efficacy is also evaluated. A large part of scandal
fulfils the important social function of assessing the correspondence between normal behaviour and the success achieved in the
realization of certain ends. As a result of this, one can anticipate
the results of all behaviour in terms of its efficiency. In scandal
such a process of prediction has a sharply pessimistic character,
because negative and inefficient consequences are foreseen and
desired for nearly all actions which are capable of modifying the
status of an actor in the community. This is to be understood
according to the degree to which any modification of status is
reprehensible in a stable society.

This negative prediction has, by its collective character,
according to Thomas's theorem, the effect of increasing the

probability that things will turn out as expected. Moreover, the verification of results contrary to expectations (or desires) sets into motion an interpretive mechanism of the following kind: since the actor could not, by conforming to common models of behaviour arrive at this result, this must signify: (a) that the actor has behaved randomly, and it does not follow that next time the same result would be produced; (b) or that he has acted dishonestly, that is to say that he has not conformed to the 'rules of the game', to the established modes of behaviour (even if we do not know exactly how).

His behaviour is then examined afresh from a critical point of view, in order to discover the proof of the deviation from the values and norms. It is in the implicit and basic acceptance that behaviour according to rule cannot modify the status of the member of a group and, correlatively, that an alteration of status must mean that he has not behaved morally that we find one of the most basic signs of the lack of evolution in a system.

The testing of efficiency in such a system has for its main function the guaranteeing of its static character. In contrast, the verification of efficiency in an industrial society has a totally different function, because in this system it is acknowledged that the individual status or the social structure can be modified.

Those behaviours which can result in modification can be classified as either conformist with, or different from, or neutral in respect of social norms. In other words, men can be considered as virtuous, neutral or dishonest. Hence the possibility of conflict when these are behaviours which differ from the norm yet are not the most likely to assure success. While in a traditional society successes which are attained by deviant means are rejected, in an industrial society, on the other hand, a selection is effected to assure maximum success consistent with respect for the norms. The criterion of efficiency in this type of society becomes a principle of evaluation and acts as a principle of rationalization of behaviour. In a community of this kind, predictions about the outcomes of any behaviour are no longer required to be pessimistic, and the attained success is not considered to imply a social fault.

The fact that in a static society any aspiration towards a modification of status is resented as a failing signifies that such a modification is regarded as socially dangerous. The acquisition by someone of any new advantage takes on the implication of harm done to others.

We thus arrive at a discussion of envy. In envy an acquisition of some kind, or an advantage obtained by a person, is considered by some other person as an injustice. The roots of envy, as psychologists have demonstrated, lie in infancy. In most cases it is the *transfer* from competitive infantile situations concerning a frustrated love object, which is internalized to allow its exclusive possession. An analogous mechanism can be found in static societies. Competition for some good in limited supply (like land) develops on the supposition that acquisition of one part of the good by an individual automatically implies the potential deprivation of all other individuals.[4] This mechanism tends to disappear in an economic system in which goods are capable of accumulation without limit by means of rationally controlled individual and collective action (following the principle of efficiency). In such a reference system, any action which is revealed as efficient for attaining an end is judged as likely not to diminish but to increase the probability that other individuals can attain the same result. In place of the mechanism of envy there is released the mechanism of admiration.

A powerful component of stardom is the admiration for the success achieved by the stars. Gina Lollobrigida, Sophia Loren, Marilyn Monroe bear witness, by their existence, to the large possibilities for social mobility. From the point of view of communal orientations of evaluation, the problem is to demonstrate that such a great improvement of status has been obtained not by illicit means but thanks to meritorious conduct and to excepttional or charismatic qualities. A major part of 'gossip' about stars performs this function. It is evident that this interpretation depends on the existence of a certain degree of social distance between the star and the public, so as to permit only an indirect or partial confrontation between the one and the other. This can be verified without difficulty when information is provided by the more remote means of communication, and in particular by mass communication. This absence of direct interaction is often

4. Alberoni (1961, pp. 69–80). This phenomenon is well described in Banfield (1961).

felt by the public as a limitation, a hindrance to full and entire knowledge of the stars. But this last aspiration, if it were satisfied, would lead to a complete development of a moral critique and the freeing of components of aggression and envy which exist all the time, but under control. These components would threaten the existence even of the stars.

Let us conclude this point with a last observation. We have noted in passing, and it has been verified in our experimental research, that the moral evaluation of the stars is more 'indulgent' than that reserved by the public for those who are socially nearer to them. This shows itself particularly in the case of small communities where social control is rigorous and where the contrast is very obvious between this control and the tolerance shown towards the stars. This phenomenon can be explained in part by the absence of those aggressive components which underlie slander and envy, and in equal part by social distance. On the basis of previously stated considerations, we can understand the reasons for this fact in sociological terms. Amongst the modes of evaluation already discussed, the fourth type has, in small communities, a very great importance where the evaluation aims to test the consequences of a way of acting for the community (the influence of example on morals). Moral vigilance and negative evaluation equally function to protect the community against the threat represented by the example of deviant behaviour which goes unpunished. In the case of stars, this category of evaluation loses its importance because they are not judged institutionally responsible for the results of their actions on the community. In small communities, there is an awareness of the potentially scandalous and corrupting character of their behaviour, but there is no possibility of applying sanctions. In the more generalized community, the separation of roles has such an important function that it makes this danger pass to a second level. As a result, a strong component of moral evaluation disappears or is attenuated. At the psychological level, this reduction is achieved by a relative evaluation: in effect each person judges, not in relation to the standards of his own community, but in relation to those of the stars (elite) who serve as a reference group. A big gap between the rules of the community of membership and those of the reference group requires continual recourse to a mechanism of separation between 'us' and our community and 'them' and their community. This can lead to an opposition between the reference group and the community of membership. We will see how strong are the critico-aggressive components which are then released.

Action within the community and action on the part of the community

Taken together, these factors which we have illustrated strongly reduce the aggressive and competitive components which develop in action in a community. However, they do not suffice to explain why the elite of stars is not considered as a privileged class, witness to the injustice of the social system. Their wealth, the manner of life they lead, constitute evident affronts to egalitarian ideals. The most commonly given explanations of this phenomenon appeal on the one hand to the mechanisms of the 'star system' and on the other to the 'narcotizing illusion'.

In the former case, one observes that stardom is the product of an important publicity organization which is useful to the entertainment industry. Thanks to the media of communication, the public are presented with the image of the person who has most chance of attracting attention and sympathy, of exciting human warmth or curiosity. The whole life of the stars is thus astutely orchestrated and arranged, so that nothing is left to chance. This type of explanation suffers from a certain naiveté. It is simplistic and naive to think that a phenomenon like stardom can be the intentional result of artful manoeuvres. Publicity agents, by their actions, do no more than facilitate and direct into a chosen path, a phenomenon which is an expression of the society as a whole. They are no more than part of the social mechanism which they are supposed to create.

Moreover, this thesis is contradicted by the history of stardom. In the early days film producers were opposed to the development of the system which nevertheless became established; and it was only after the event that they came to favour it, realizing that they could exploit it to their own ends, rather than find themselves crushed by opposing it. Furthermore, one cannot say that the star system has tended to cover up the wealth of the stars, their luxury, or their extraordinary earnings, in order to stress their social merits and their social function, etc. The star system has never, indeed, sought to legitimate the position of the stars on any other basis than their personality, their private life, their friends, their intimate tragedies and their eccentricities. Without any doubt it has attenuated the competitive elements of their ways of acting in the community, and has proclaimed the existence of amicable relations between such and such amongst them, and between them and the public. That could have contributed, marginally, to the avoidance of any growth of class resentment, but it certainly would not have been possible so to act if resentment of this kind was clearly manifested.

The theory of the 'narcotizing illusion' sees in the star system a cultural product of the economic power elite, having as its object to supply the masses with an escape into fantasy and an illusion of mobility, in such a way as to prevent their taking stock of their real condition as exploited masses. Against this theory, which has achieved considerable success, there is the fact that the star system has prospered, and prospered in nearly all countries and at all social levels—even amongst groups which adopt a marxist perspective. Interest in stars can be found through the whole range of the political keyboard, without any distinction. It would be interesting to make a closer study of the changing attitude of the press, and especially of the communist press, towards the stars. Immediately after the war (until about 1950) the stars were criticized or condemned. Subsequently they, and their way of life, were given a warm welcome. Many amongst them were men of the left who had never in their lives sought to become stars and who, on the contrary, had even denounced the phenomenon. The stars are proclaimed as such by the collectivity. It is not they themselves who impose themselves on the latter by a power acquired independently of the collectivity. This does not stem only from the fact that the stars are an open elite. Things would not be different if the stars were self-perpetuating, and if what is the case for some individuals like, for example, Greta Garbo and Clark Gable, were a universal rule. What counts is the fact that their *status* is always potentially revocable: by the public. The star system thus never creates the star, but it proposes the candidate for 'election', and helps to retain the favour of the 'electors'. Certainly those who activate the star system have an ascendancy of power which they hold over the public, but that is precisely why it is towards them and not towards the stars, that there can and does form some class resentment. In the eyes of the public, the producer is someone of quite a different order from the star whom he launches. Even when he enters into the elite of the stars he always remains an ambivalent figure, and the public forgets his power only when his personal affairs, as also his way of acting in the community, assume an autonomous interest.[5]

We can now appreciate a last and interesting phenomenon peculiar to stardom. Although most stars are not dispersed, but grouped together, the evaluative orientation is not directed towards the group. It is almost always the individual and not the group, that is, the ways of acting within the community and not the community itself, which become the object of evaluation. It can turn out that the community itself becomes an object of evaluation, but in this case the framework changes completely and the critical-aggressive components of which we have spoken are released.

In this case, the elite of the stars, instead of becoming the centre of the community as a whole, is detached from it and is differentiated as a distinct and privileged community, an expression of organized social forces and, as a result a holder of power. In such a case the star no longer belongs to the wider community, that is to say to ours, but to an opposed community.

The innumerable denunciations of the moral poverty and the corruption of Hollywood, together with marxist critiques, or again films like *La Dolce Vita*, tend towards the production of a frame of meaning of this kind. But this restructuring does not persist and tends quickly to dissolve. It gives way, on the whole, to an evaluation of each individual and his influence on the community. That is why men can scorn and condemn the morals of Hollywood, the way of life of the Via Veneto and of criminal circles, and continue meanwhile to be touched by the vicissitudes

5. What we have just said is of great sociological interest, since we can establish in the same way that class resentment and the experience of injustice do not depend on the fact of contrasting inequalities with egalitarian ideals, but that they depend essentially on the fact that one perceives the existence of an autonomous illegitimate power underpinning the inequality. If the autonomous power goes by default (as in stardom) class resentment and the experience of injustice are consequently lacking.

which affect Carla Gravina and Sacha Distel, to admire Lana Turner, to express sympathy for Frank Sinatra and to respect the memory of Clark Gable.

Meaning and perspectives of stardom

In the light of the foregoing considerations, stardom appears as a phenomenon appropriate to a certain moment in the development of industrial societies, in which it fulfils certain variable functions which depend on the socio-political configuration of the society. Stardom carries a time dimension, which enables us to make a dynamic study of it.

The development of industry, the rise in population, urbanization, the increasing interdependence of the economic system and the appearance of the means of mass communication all tend to break down traditional social relationships. Society becomes differentiated and develops associations and organizations which are impersonal, rational and variable, controlled by a limited number of men who possess particular qualities and who monopolize the instruments of control. The information which, transmitted by the traditional channels of communication, sufficed in more limited communities to provide the coordinates of orientation in the heart of the general system, rapidly became insufficient because of the increasing complexity of the latter, because of its novelty and variability. The political organization of the whole society and of the state is largely controlled by new strata and by classes under formation; in addition the society and the state become rationalized according to the model of economic arrangements. The system presents a new structure formed from an articulated assemblage of positions defined in universalist ways, to which correspond specific roles, which are themselves universal, neutral and subject to the criteria of efficiency. The culture ceases to be a collection of pre-ordained solutions to recurring problems; it is differentiated in two directions. On the one hand it becomes a science capable of obtaining results wished for by means of procedures open to theoretical deduction; on the other hand the culture depends on a large area of consensus concerning the implicit meaning of given situations or about the possibility of attaining certain ends and realizing certain values. In this process the horizon of the community widens. The symbols of power of the community constitute the emotional centre of the social system as a whole. Sometimes one might see the emergence of national fascism, sometimes, when conflict between classes occurs in the absence of a dominant class, the community is identified with the class.

In such a case the community sees itself in those individuals who have symbolic value, and who at the same time occupy positions of symbolic power. They are the charismatic leaders who interpret new and former values of the whole community; on this basis they give unity to the experiences and expectations of members of the community, while creating the consensus which permits the whole process to go forward. In other countries with a democratic tradition, representative institutions are modified so as to welcome and meet the new demands which continually arise.

In those countries (an example is provided by Italy before the rise of fascism) the daily demands for orientation of community life (met in the small community by relations of neighbourhood, by gossip, by the exercise of applied morals, etc.) begin to be met at the level of a more general community life. The media of mass communication begin to present to the public persons who belong to the extended community and who become an object of interest, identification and collective evaluation. With the progress of visual information persons of the entertainment world begin, to an increasing degree, to make their mark. Their lives, their social relationships, become an object of identification or a projection of the needs of the mass of the population, a benchmark for positive or negative evaluation, the chance to have experience in the domain of the morally possible, and a living testimony to the possibility of achieving a rise in personal status. Thanks to a collective consensus, their capacity and their skill readily acquire a charismatic dimension. However, the generalization of charisma is impeded by the simultaneous articulation of the structuring in the form of specific roles. Correspondingly, a preponderance is established of modes of evaluation which are impersonal, neutral and specific. On the other hand, since the danger of charisma exists in a much higher degree where the internalization of new evaluative orientations is shallowest (that is to say that it exists especially when the process of nation-forming is at its beginning) one also sees appearing mechanisms for the rigorous separation of roles. For this reason one must posit a more or less sharp distinction between the elite of power and the elite of stars. This mechanism of separation acquires a particular importance in countries which, after an experience of charismatic power, becomes democratic again (like Italy) at the moment when the process of economic development and rationalization is unleashed.

We are witnessing a rigorous separation of roles. Alongside a political class considered as responsible for the results of its decisions on the collectivity, there develops an elite of politically irresponsible stars, whose whole way of life and personal relationships excite interest, and whose influence on morals is profound. Members of small isolated communities which make up the large general community meet and discover the stars before they come across political men for whom they retain feelings of distrust and incomprehension. It is television in particular, which by its violation of the intimacy of family life introduces figures representative of the community into each isolated group and contributes to the development of consciousness of common belonging. The fact of taking part in this experience makes the psychic domain more isomorphic and constitutes, as a result, a condition which facilitates reciprocal comprehension (mutuality) and hence social interaction.

Our account has been concerned with progress towards a particularly interesting stage of transition, where a society is both rationalized and democratic, where the manifestations of charisma are henceforth under control, where the mythic forms of stardom tend to disappear and where regard for the wider society is strong and has already lost the implication of a euphoric participation in its 'power', although it has not yet become a responsible participation. How should this phenomenon be projected into the future? It is difficult to predict future developments, but it is at least very probable that the stars will continue to exist, both as privileged members of the wider community and as an object of reference for members of the latter. This might follow from the great extension of the wider community which only allows a few members to be a collective object of reference; or it could be so because, in a society under transition, there is always some insufficiency in the culture and consequently a need for a collective consensus about the new implications of reality and new solutions to be found to the problems of family, neighbourhood, of production and consumption, etc.

The progressive increase in interdependence in industrial society ought to lead us to take account of the responsibilities of all public personages, with rather more rigour than one finds in practice. We have seen that the stars are not held institutionally responsible for the consequences of their own actions on the community, since this responsibility rests uniquely on those men who occupy positions of institutional power. A decrease in the sharp separation of social roles and in their specificity can create the necessary conditions for opening to evaluation the 'private' life of the stars as well as of men engaged in politics, according to the consequences which their actions have for the collectivity.

Other likely changes can be foreseen if the tension of aspirations is reduced: this might create, or add to, the chances for individuals to satisfy personal ambition while at the same time supporting the institutional mechanisms provided by the society.

References

ALBERONI, F. (1960), *Contributo all' Integrazione sociale dell' Immigrato*, Milano, Vita e Pensiero.

ALBERONI, F. (1961), 'Saggio critico delle differenze socioculturali tra due region meridionali', *Internat. soc. Science Rev.*, vols. 1 and 2.

BANFIELD, E. (1961), *Una Communita del Mezzogiorno*, Bologna, Il Mulino.

PANZINI, A. (1963), *Modern Dictionary of Words which are not Found in Ordinary Dictionaries*, Milano, Hoepli.

PARSONS, T. (1949), *The Social System*, Free Press.

WEBER, M. (1968), *Economy and Society*, Bedminster Press.

5 Hans Magnus Enzensberger

Constituents of a Theory of the Media

Excerpt from Hans Magnus Enzensberger, 'Constituents of a theory of the media', *New Left Review*, vol. 64, November–December 1970, pp. 13–36.
Translated from the German by Stuart Hood

With the development of the electronic media, the industry that shapes consciousness has become the pacemaker for the social and economic development of societies in the late industrial age. It infiltrates into all other sectors of production, takes over more and more directional and control functions, and determines the standard of the prevailing technology.

(In lieu of normative definitions here is an incomplete list of new developments which have emerged in the last twenty years: news satellites, colour television, cable relay television, cassettes, videotape, videotape recorders, video-phones, stereophony, laser techniques, electrostatic reproduction processes, electronic high-speed printing, composing and learning machines, microfiches with electronic access, printing by radio, time-sharing computers, data banks. All these new forms of media are constantly forming new connections both with each other and with older media like printing, radio, film, television, telephone, teletype, radar and so on. They are clearly coming together to form a universal system.)

The general contradiction between productive forces and productive relationships emerges most sharply, however, when they are most advanced. (By contrast, protracted structural crises as in coalmining can be solved merely by getting rid of a backlog, that is to say, essentially they can be solved within the terms of their own system and revolutionary strategy that relied on them would be short-sighted.)

Monopoly capitalism develops the consciousness-shaping industry more quickly and more extensively than other sectors of production; it must at the same time fetter it. A socialist media theory has to work at this contradiction. Demonstrate that it cannot be solved within the given productive relationships – rapidly increasing discrepancies – potential destructive forces. 'Certain demands of a prognostic nature must be made' of any such theory (Walter Benjamin).

(A 'critical' inventory of the *status quo* is not enough. Danger of underestimating the growing conflicts in the media field, of neutralizing them, of interpreting them merely in terms of trade unionism or liberalism, on the lines of traditional labour struggles or as the clash of special interests (programme heads—executive producers, publishers—authors, monopolies – medium sized businesses, public corporations – private companies, etc.). An appreciation of this kind does not go far enough and remains bogged down in tactical arguments.)

So far there is no Marxist theory of the media. There is therefore no strategy one can apply in this area. Uncertainty, alternations between fear and surrender, mark the attitude of the socialist Left to the new productive forces of the media industry. The ambivalence of this attitude merely mirrors the ambivalence of the media themselves without mastering it. It could only be overcome by releasing the emancipatory potential which is inherent in the new productive forces – a potential which capitalism must sabotage just as surely as Soviet revisionism, because it would endanger the rule of both systems.

The mobilizing power of the media

The open secret of the electronic media, the decisive political factor, which has been waiting, suppressed or crippled, for its moment to come, is their mobilizing power.

(When I say *mobilize* I mean *mobilize*. In a country which has had direct experience of fascism (and Stalinism) it is perhaps still necessary to explain, or to explain again, what that means – namely, to make men more mobile than they are. As free as dancers, as aware as football players, as surprising as guerillas. Anyone who thinks of the masses only as the object of politics cannot mobilize them. He wants to push them around. A parcel is not mobile; it can only be pushed to and fro. Marches, columns, parades, immobilize people. Propaganda, which does not release self-reliance but limits it, fits into the same pattern. It leads to depoliticization.)

For the first time in history, the media are making possible mass participation in a social and socialized productive process, the practical means of which are in the hands of the masses themselves. Such a use of them would bring the communications media, which up to now have not deserved the name, into their own. In its present form, equipment like television or film does not serve communication but prevents it. It allows no reciprocal action between transmitter and receiver; technically speaking it reduces feedback to the lowest point compatible with the system.

This state of affairs, however, cannot be justified technically. On the contrary. Electronic techniques recognize no contradiction in principle between transmitter and receiver. Every transistor radio is, by the nature of its construction, at the same time a potential transmitter; it can interact with other receivers by circuit reversal. The development from a mere distribution medium to a communications medium is technically not a problem. It is consciously prevented for understandable political reasons. The technical distinction between receivers and transmitters reflects the social division of labour into producers and consumers, which is why the consciousness industry becomes of particular political importance. It is based, in the last analysis, on the basic contradiction between the ruling class and the ruled class – that is to say between monopoly capital or monopolistic bureaucracy on the one hand and the dependent masses on the other.

(This structural analogy can be worked out in detail. To the programmes offered by the broadcasting cartels there correspond the politics offered by a power cartel consisting of parties constituted along authoritarian lines. In both cases marginal differences in their platforms reflect a competitive relationship which on essential questions is nonexistent. Minimal independent activity of the part of the voter/viewer. As is the case with parliamentary elections under the two-party system the feedback is reduced to indices. 'Training in decision making' is reduced to the response to a single, three-point switching process: Programme 1; Programme 2; Switch off (abstention).)

Radio must be changed from a means of distribution to a means of communication. Radio would be the most wonderful means of communication imaginable in public life, a huge linked system – that is to say, it would be such if it were capable not only of transmitting but of receiving, of allowing the listener not only to hear but to speak, and did not isolate him but brought him into contact. Unrealizable in this social system, realizable in another, these proposals, which are, after all, only the natural consequences of technical development, help towards the propagation and shaping of that *other* system (Brecht, 1932).

The Orwellian fantasy

George Orwell's bogey of a monolithic consciousness industry derives from a view of the media which is undialectical and obsolete. The possibility of total control of such a system at a central point belongs not to the future but to the past. With the aid of systems theory, a discipline which is part of bourgeois science – using, that is to say, categories which are immanent in the system – it can be demonstrated that a linked series of communications or, to use the technical term, switchable network, to the degree that it exceeds a certain critical size, can no longer be centrally controlled but only dealt with statistically. This basic 'leakiness' of stochastic systems admittedly allows the calculation of probabilities based on sampling and extrapolations; but blanket supervision would demand a monitor that was bigger than the system itself. The monitoring of all telephone conversations, for instance, postulates an apparatus which would need to be n times more extensive and more complicated than that of the present telephone system. A censor's office, which carried out its work extensively, would of necessity become the largest branch of industry in its society.

But supervision on the basis of approximation can only offer inadequate instruments for the self-regulation of the whole system in accordance with the concepts of those who govern it. It postulates a high degree of internal stability. If this precarious balance is upset, then crisis measures based on statistical methods of control are useless. Interference can penetrate the leaky nexus of the media, spreading and multiplying there with the utmost speed by resonance. The regime so threatened will in such cases, in so far as it is still capable of action, use force and adopt police or military methods.

A state of emergency is therefore the only alternative to leakage in the consciousness industry; but it cannot be maintained in the long run. Societies in the late industrial age rely on the free exchange of information; the 'objective pressures' to which their controllers constantly appeal are thus turned against them. Every attempt to suppress the random factors, each diminution of the average flow and each distortion of the information structure must, in the long run, lead to an embolism.

The electronic media have not only built up the information network intensively, they have also spread it extensively. The radio wars of the 1950s demonstrated that in the realm of communications, national sovereignty is condemned to wither away. The further development of satellites will deal it the *coup de grâce*. Quarantine regulations for information, such as were promulgated by fascism and Stalinism, are only possible today at the cost of deliberate industrial regression.

(Example. The Soviet bureaucracy, that is to say the most widespread and complicated bureaucracy in the world, has to deny itself almost entirely an elementary piece of organizational equipment, the duplicating machine, because this instrument potentially makes everyone a printer. The political risk involved, the possibility of a leakage in the information network, is accepted only at the highest levels, at exposed switchpoints in political, military and scientific areas. It is clear that Soviet society has to pay an immense price for the suppression of its own productive resources – clumsy procedures, misinformation, *faux frais*. The phenomenon incidentally has its analogue in the capitalist west, if in a diluted form. The technically most advanced electrostatic copying machine, which operates with ordinary paper – which cannot, that is to say, be supervised and is independent of suppliers – is the property of a monopoly (Xerox); on principle it is not sold but rented. The rates themselves ensure that it does not get into the wrong hands. The equipment crops up as if by magic where economic and political power are concentrated. Political control of the equipment goes hand in hand with maximization of profits for the manufacturer. Admittedly this control, as opposed to Soviet methods, is by no means 'watertight' for the reasons indicated.)

The problem of censorship thus enters a new historical stage. The struggle for the freedom of the press and freedom of ideas has, up till now, been mainly an argument within the bourgeoisie itself; for the masses, freedom to express opinions was a fiction since they were, from the beginning, barred from the means of production – above all from the press – and thus were unable to join in freedom of expression from the start. Today censorship is threatened by the productive forces of the consciousness industry which is already, to some extent, gaining the upper hand over the prevailing relations of production. Long before the latter are overthrown, the contradiction between what is possible and what actually exists will become acute.

Cultural archaism in the Left critique

The New Left of the 1960s has reduced the development of the media to a single concept – that of manipulation. This concept was originally extremely useful for heuristic purposes and has made possible a great many individual analytical investigations, but it now threatens to degenerate into a mere slogan which conceals more than it is able to illuminate, and therefore itself requires analysis.

The current theory of manipulation on the Left is essentially defensive; its effects can lead the movement into defeatism. Subjectively speaking, behind the tendency to go on the defensive lies a sense of impotence. Objectively, it corresponds to the absolutely correct view that the decisive means of production are in enemy hands. But to react to this state of affairs with moral indignation is naive. This is in general an undertone of lamentation when people speak of manipulation which points to idealistic expectations – as if the class enemy had ever stuck to the promises of fair play it occasionally utters. The liberal superstition that in political and social questions there is such a thing as pure, unmanipulated truth, seems to enjoy remarkable currency among the socialist Left. It is the unspoken basic premise of the manipulation thesis.

This thesis provides no incentive to push ahead. A socialist perspective which does not go beyond attacking existing property relationships is limited. The expropriation of Springer is a desirable goal but it would be good to know to whom the media should be handed over. The Party? To judge by all experience of that solution, it is not a possible alternative. It is perhaps no accident that the Left has not yet produced an analysis of the pattern of manipulation in countries with socialist regimes.

The manipulation thesis also serves to exculpate oneself. To cast the enemy in the role of the devil is to conceal the weakness and lack of perspective in one's own agitation. If the latter leads to self-isolation instead of mobilizing the masses, then its failure is attributed holus-bolus to the overwhelming power of the media.

The theory of repressive tolerance has also permeated discussion of the media by the Left. This concept, which was formulated by its author with the utmost care, has also, when whittled away in an undialectical manner, become a vehicle for resignation. Admittedly, when an office-equipment firm can attempt to recruit sales staff with the picture of Che Guevara and the text *We would have hired him*, the temptation to withdraw is great. But fear of handling shit is a luxury a sewer-man cannot necessarily afford.

The electronic media do away with cleanliness; they are by their nature 'dirty'. That is part of their productive power. In terms of structure, they are anti-sectarian – a further reason why the Left, in so far as it is not prepared to re-examine its traditions, has little idea what to do with them. The desire for a cleanly defined 'line' and for the suppression of 'deviations' is anachronistic and now serves only one's own need for security. It weakens one's own position by irrational purges, exclusions and fragmentation, instead of strengthening it by rational discussion.

These resistances and fears are strengthened by a series of cultural factors which, for the most part, operate unconsciously, and which are to be explained by the social history of the participants in today's Left movement – namely their bourgeois class background. It often seems as if it were precisely because of their progressive potential that the media are felt to be an immense threatening power; because for the first time they present a basic challenge to bourgeois culture and thereby to the privileges of the bourgeois intelligentsia – a challenge far more radical than any self-doubt this social group can display. In the New Left's opposition to the media, old bourgeois fears such as the fear of 'the masses' seem to be reappearing along with equally old bourgeois longings for pre-industrial times dressed up in progressive clothing.

(At the very beginning of the student revolt, during the Free Speech Movement at Berkeley, the computer was a favourite target for aggression. Interest in the Third World is not always free from motives based on antagonism towards civilization which has its source in conservative culture critique. During the May events in Paris the reversion to archaic forms of production was particularly characteristic. Instead of carrying out agitation among the workers in a modern offset press, the students printed their posters on the hand presses of the École des Beaux Arts. The political slogans were hand-painted; stencils would certainly have made it possible to produce them *en masse*, but it would have offended the creative imagination of the authors. The ability to make proper strategic use of the most advanced media was lacking. It was not the radio headquarters that were seized by the rebels, but the Odéon Theatre, steeped in tradition.)

The obverse of this fear of contact with the media is the fascination they exert on left-wing movements in the great cities. On the one hand, the comrades take refuge in outdated forms of communication and esoteric arts and crafts instead of occupying themselves with the contradiction between the present constitution of the media and their revolutionary potential; on the other hand, they cannot escape from the consciousness industry's programme or from its aesthetic. This leads, subjectively, to a split between a puritanical view of political action and the area of private 'leisure'; objectively, it leads to a split between politically active groups and sub-cultural groups.

In western Europe the socialist movement mainly addresses itself to a public of converts through newspapers and journals which are exclusive in terms of language, content and form. These news-sheets presuppose a structure of party members and sympathizers and a situation, where the media are concerned, that roughly corresponds to the historical situation in 1900; they are obviously fixated on the *Iskra* model. Presumably the people who produce them listen to the Rolling Stones, follow occupations and strikes on television, and go to the cinema to see a Western or a Godard; only in their capacity as producers do they make an exception, and, in their analyses, the whole media sector is reduced to the slogan of 'manipulation'. Every foray into this territory is regarded from the start with suspicion as a step towards integration. This suspicion is not unjustified; it can however also mask one's own ambivalence and insecurity. Fear of being swallowed up by the system is a sign of weakness; it presupposes that capitalism could overcome any contradiction – a conviction which can easily be refuted historically and is theoretically untenable.

If the socialist movement writes off the new productive forces of the consciousness industry and relegates work on the media to a subculture, then we have a vicious circle. For the Underground may be increasingly aware of the technical and aesthetic possibilities of the disc, of videotape, of the electronic camera, and so on, and is systematically exploring the terrain, but it has no political viewpoint of its own and therefore mostly falls a helpless victim to commercialism. The politically active groups then point to such cases with smug *Schadenfreude*. A process of un-learning is the result and both sides are the losers. Capitalism alone benefits from the Left's antagonism to the media, as it does from the de-politicization of the counter-culture.

Democratic manipulation

Manipulation – etymologically, handling – means technical treatment of a given material with a particular goal in mind. When the technical intervention is of immediate social relevance, then manipulation is a political act. In the case of the media industry that is by definition the case.

Thus every use of the media presupposes manipulation. The most elementary processes in media production, from the choice of the medium itself to shooting, cutting, synchronization, dubbing, right up to distribution, are all operations carried out on the raw material. There is no such thing as unmanipulated writing, filming, or broadcasting. The question is therefore not whether the media are manipulated, but who manipulates them. A revolutionary plan should not require the manipulators to disappear; on the contrary, it must make everyone a manipulator.

All technical manipulations are potentially dangerous; the manipulation of the media cannot be countered, however, by old or new forms of censorship, but only by direct social control, that is to say, by the mass of the people, who will have become productive. To this end, the elimination of capitalistic property relationships is a necessary, but by no means sufficient condition. There have been no historical examples up until now of the mass self-regulating learning process which is made possible by the electronic media. The communists' fear of releasing this potential, of the mobilizing capabilities of the media, of the interaction of free producers, is one of the main reasons why even in the socialist countries, the old bourgeois culture, greatly disguised and distorted but structurally intact, continues to hold sway.

(As a historical explanation it may be pointed out that the consciousness industry in Russia at the time of the October Revolution was extraordinarily backward; their productive capacity has grown enormously since then, but the productive relationships have been artificially preserved, often by force. Then, as now, a primitively edited press, books and theatre, were the key media in the Soviet Union. The development of radio, film and television, is politically arrested. Foreign stations like the BBC, the Voice of America, and the *Deutschland Welle*, therefore, not only find listeners, but are received with almost boundless faith. Archaic media like the handwritten pamphlet and poems orally transmitted play an important role.)

The new media are egalitarian in structure. Anyone can take part in them by a simple switching process. The programmes themselves are not material things and can be reproduced at will. In this sense the electronic media are entirely different from the older media like the book or the easel-painting, the exclusive class character of which is obvious. Television programmes for privileged groups are certainly technically conceivable – closed-circuit television – but run counter to the structure. Potentially the new media do away with all educational privileges and thereby with the cultural monopoly of the bourgeois intelligentsia. This is one of the reasons for the intelligentsia's resentment against the new industry. As for the 'spirit' which they are endeavouring to defend against 'depersonalization' and 'mass culture', the sooner they abandon it the better.

Properties of the new media

The new media are orientated towards action, not contemplation; towards the present, not tradition. Their attitude to time is completely opposed to that of bourgeois culture which aspires to possession, that is to extension in time, best of all, to eternity. The media produce no objects that can be hoarded and auctioned.

They do away completely with 'intellectual property' and liquidate the 'heritage', that is to say, the class specific handing-on of non-material capital.

That does not mean to say that they have no history or that they contribute to the loss of historical consciousness. On the contrary, they make it possible for the first time to record historical material so that it can be reproduced at will. By making this material available for present-day purposes, they make it obvious to anyone using it that the writing of history is always manipulation. But the memory they hold in readiness is not the preserve of a scholarly caste. It is social. The banked information is accessible to anyone and this accessibility is as instantaneous as its recording. It suffices to compare the model of a private library with that of a socialized data bank to recognize the structural difference between the two systems.

It is wrong to regard media equipment as mere means of consumption. It is always, in principle, also means of production and, indeed, since it is in the hands of the masses, socialized means of production. The contradiction between producers and consumers is not inherent in the electronic media; on the contrary, it has to be artificially reinforced by economic and administrative measures.

(An early example of this is provided by the difference between telegraph and telephone. Whereas the former, to this day, has remained in the hands of a bureaucratic institution which can scan and file every text transmitted, the telephone is directly accessible to all users. With the aid of conference circuits, it can even make possible collective intervention in a discussion by physically remote groups.

On the other hand those auditory and visual means of communication which rely on 'wireless' are still subject to state control (legislation on wireless installations). In the face of technical developments, which long ago made local and international radio-telephony possible, and which constantly opened up new wavebands for television – in the UHF band alone, the dissemination of numerous programmes in one locality is possible without interference, not to mention the possibilities offered by wired and satellite television – the prevailing laws for control of the air are anachronistic. They recall the time when the operation of a printing press was dependent on an imperial licence. The socialist movements will take up the struggle for their own wavelengths and must, within the foreseeable future, build their own transmitters and relay stations.)

One immediate consequence of the structural nature of the new media is that none of the regimes at present in power can release their potential. Only a free socialist society will be able to make them fully productive. A further characteristic of the most advanced media – probably the decisive one – confirms this thesis: their collective structure.

For the prospect that in future, with the aid of the media, anyone can become a producer, would remain apolitical and limited were this productive effort to find an outlet in individual tinkering. Work on the media is possible for an individual only in so far as it remains socially and therefore aesthetically irrelevant. The collection of transparencies from the last holiday trip provides a model.

That is naturally what the prevailing market mechanisms have aimed at. It has long been clear from apparatus like miniature and 8 mm cine cameras, as well as the tape recorder, which are in actual fact already in the hands of the masses, that the individual, so long as he remains isolated, can become with their help at best an amateur but not a producer. Even so potent a means of production as the shortwave transmitter has been tamed in this way and reduced to a harmless and inconsequential hobby in the hands of scattered radio hams. The programmes which the isolated amateur mounts are always only bad, outdated copies of what he in any case receives.

(Private production for the media is no more than licensed cottage industry. Even when it is made public it remains pure compromise. To this end, the men who own the media have developed special programmes which are usually called 'Democratic Forum' or something of the kind. There, tucked away in the corner, 'the reader (listener, viewer) has his say', which can naturally be cut short at any time. As in the case of public opinion polling, he is only asked questions so that he may have a chance to confirm his own dependence. It is a control circuit where what is fed in has already made complete allowance for the feedback.

The concept of a licence can also be used in another sense – in an economic one; the system attempts to make each participant into a concessionaire of the monopoly that develops his films or plays back his cassettes. The aim is to nip in the bud in this way that independence which video-equipment, for instance, makes possible. Naturally, such tendencies go against the grain of the structure and the new productive forces not only permit but indeed demand their reversal.)

The poor, feeble and frequently humiliating results of this licensed activity are often referred to with contempt by the professional media producers. On top of the damage suffered by the masses comes triumphant mockery because they clearly do not know how to use the media properly. The sort of thing that goes on in certain popular television shows is taken as proof that they are completely incapable of articulating on their own.

Not only does this run counter to the results of the latest psychological and pedagogical research, but it can easily be seen to be a reactionary protective formulation; the 'gifted' people are quite simply defending their territories. Here we have a cultural analogue to the familiar political judgements concerning a working class which is presumed to be 'stultified' and incapable of any kind of self-determination. Curiously, one may hear the view that masses could never govern themselves out of the mouths of people who consider themselves socialists. In the best of cases, these are economists who cannot conceive of socialism as anything other than nationalization.

A socialist strategy

Any socialist strategy for the media must, on the contrary, strive to end the isolation of the individual participants from the social learning and production process. This is impossible unless those concerned organize themselves. This is the political core of the question of the media. It is over this point that socialist concepts part company with the neo-liberal and technocratic ones. Anyone who expects to be emancipated by technological hardware, or by a system of hardware however structured, is the victim of an obscure belief in progress. Anyone who imagines that freedom for the media will be established if only everyone is busy transmitting and receiving is the dupe of a liberalism which, decked out in contemporary colours, merely peddles the faded concept of a pre-ordained harmony of social interests.

In the face of such illusions, what must be firmly held on to is that the proper use of the media demands organization and makes it possible. Every production that deals with the interests of the producers postulates a collective method of production, It is itself already a form of self-organization of social needs. Tape recorders, ordinary cameras and cine cameras, are already extensively owned by wage-earners. The question is why these means of production do not turn up at workplaces, in schools, in the offices of the bureaucracy, in short, everywhere where there is social conflict. By producing aggressive forms of publicity which were their own, the masses could secure evidence of their daily experiences and draw effective lessons from them.

Naturally bourgeois society defends itself against such prospects with a battery of legal measures. It bases itself on the law of trespass, on commercial and official secrecy. While its secret services penetrate everywhere and plug in to the most intimate conversations, it pleads a touching concern for confidentiality, and makes a sensitive display of worrying about the question of a privacy in which all that is private is the interest of the exploiters. Only a collective, organized effort can tear down these paper walls.

Communication networks which are constructed for such purposes can, over and above their primary function, provide politically interesting organizational models. In the socialist movements the dialectic of discipline and spontaneity, centralism and decentralization, authoritarian leadership and anti-authoritarian distintegration has long ago reached deadlock. Network-like communications models built on the principal of reversability of circuits might give indications of how to overcome this situation: a mass newspaper, written and distributed by its readers, a video network of politically active groups.

More radically than any good intention, more lastingly than existential flight from one's own class, the media, once they have come into their own, destroy the private production methods of bourgeois intellectuals. Only in productive work and learning processes can their individualism be broken down in such a way that it is transformed from morally based (that is to say as individual as ever) self-sacrifice to a new kind of political self understanding and behaviour.

An all too widely disseminated thesis maintains that present-day capitalism lives by the exploitation of unreal needs. That is at best a half-truth. The results obtained by popular American sociologists like Vance Packard are not unuseful but limited. What they have to say about the stimulation of needs through advertising and artificial obsolescence can in any case not be adequately explained by the hypnotic pull exerted on the wage-earners by mass consumption. The hypothesis of 'consumer terror' corresponds to the prejudices of a middle class, which considers itself politically enlightened, against the allegedly integrated proletariat, which has become petty-bourgeois and corrupt. The attractive power of mass consumption is based not on the dictates of false needs, but on the falsification and exploitation of quite real and legitimate ones without which the parasitic process of advertising would be redundant. A socialist movement ought not to denouce these needs, but take them seriously, investigate them and make them politically productive.

That is also valid for the consciousness industry. The electronic media do not owe their irresistible power to any sleight-of-hand but to the elemental power of deep social needs which come through even in the present depraved form of these media.

Precisely because no one bothers about them, the interests of the masses have remained a relatively unknown field, at least in so far as they are historically new. They certainly extend far beyond those goals which the traditional working class movement represented. Just as in the field of production, the industry which produces goods and the consciousness industry merge more and more, so too, subjectively, where needs are concerned, material and non-material factors are closely interwoven. In the process old psycho-social themes are firmly embedded – social prestige, identification patterns – but powerful new themes emerge which are utopian in nature. From a materialistic point of view neither the one nor the other must be suppressed.

Henri Lefèbvre has proposed the concept of the *spectacle*, the exhibition, or show, to fit the present form of mass consumption.

Goods and shop windows, traffic and advertisements, stores and the world of communications, news and packaging, architecture and media production come together to form a totality, a permanent theatre, which dominates not only the public city centres but also private interiors. The expression 'beautiful living' makes the most commonplace objects of general use into props for this universal festival, in which the fetishistic nature of the commodities triumphs completely over their use value. The swindle these festivals perpetrate is, and remains, a swindle within the present social structure. But it is the harbinger of something else. Consumption as spectacle contains the promise that want will disappear. The deceptive, brutal and obscene features of this festival derive from the fact that there can be no question of a real fulfilment of its promise. But so long as scarcity holds sway, use-value remains a decisive category which can only be abolished by trickery. Yet trickery on such a scale is only conceivable if it is based on mass need. This need – it is a utopian one – is there. It is the desire for a new ecology, for a breaking-down of environmental barriers, for an aesthetic which is not limited to the sphere of 'the artistic'. These desires are not – or are not primarily – internalized rules of the games as played by the capitalist system. They have physiological roots and can no longer be suppressed. Consumption as spectacle is – in parody form – the anticipation of a utopian situation.

The promises of the media demonstrate the same ambivalence. They are an answer to the mass need for non-material variety and mobility – which at present finds its material realization in private car-ownership and tourism – and they exploit it. Other collective wishes, which capital often recognizes more quickly and evaluates more correctly than its opponents but naturally only so as to trap them and rob them of their explosive force, are just as powerful, just as unequivocally emancipatory: the need to take part in the social process on a local, national and international scale; the need for new forms of interaction, for release from ignorance and tutelage; the need for self-determination. 'Be everywhere!' is one of the most successful slogans of the media industry. The readers' parliament of *Bild-Zeitung*:[1] direct democracy used against the interests of the *demos*. 'Open spaces' and

1. The Springer press mass publication.

'free time' – concepts which corral and neutralize the urgent wishes of the masses.

(The corresponding acceptance by the media of utopian stories. For example, the story of the young Italo-American who hijacked a passenger plane to get home from California to Rome was taken up without protest even by the reactionary mass press and undoubtedly correctly understood by its readers. The identification is based on what has become a general need. Nobody can understand why such journeys should be reserved for politicians, functionaries and business men. The role of the pop star could be analysed from a similar angle; in it the authoritarian and emancipatory factors are mingled in an extraordinary way. It is perhaps not unimportant that beat music offers groups, not individuals, as identification models. In the productions of the Rolling Stones (and in the manner of their production) the Utopian content is apparent. Events like the Woodstock Festival, the concerts in Hyde Park, on the Isle of Wight and at Altamont, California, develop a mobilizing power which the political Left can only envy.)

It is absolutely clear that, within the present social forms, the consciousness industry can satisfy none of the needs on which it lives and which it must fan, except in the illusory form of games. The point, however, is not to demolish its promises but to take them literally and to show that they can be met only through a cultural revolution. Socialists and socialist regimes which multiply the frustration of the masses by declaring their needs to be false, become the accomplices of the system they have undertaken to fight.

Summary

Repressive use of media	Emancipatory use of media
Centrally controlled programme	Decentralized programme
One transmitter, many receivers	Each receiver a potential transmitter
Immobilization of isolated individuals	Mobilization of the masses
Passive consumer behaviour	Interaction of those involved, feedback

Repressive use of media	Emancipatory use of media
Depoliticization	A political learning process
Production by specialists	Collective production
Control by property owners or bureaucracy	Social control by self-organization

Reference

BRECHT, B. (1932), *Theory of Radio*, Gesammelte Werke, Band 8, pp. 129 ff., 134.

Part Three
The Audience of Mass Communications

Why do people attend to mass communications? What functions do the media fulfil in the lives of audience members? These, broadly, are the two questions to which most of this section is addressed. There has been a long-standing interest in this aspect of media use, as Fearing's article (Reading 6), written nearly twenty-five years ago, testifies. And the fact that it still reads so freshly is also a measure of how little cumulative knowledge we have yet. The contributions by McQuail, Blumler and Brown (Reading 7) and by Rosengren and Windahl (Reading 8) offer both evidence and ideas to help solve the puzzle of much mass media use. Piramidin's article (Reading 10) is only one which might have been chosen from what is now a quite extensive body of Russian research on mass communications, an outcome of the notable revival of sociology in the Soviet Union during the last decade. It is typical of the particular interest taken in media research in that country in the relationship between audience member and mass communication source. The inclusion of one piece (Reading 9 by Emmett) relating some findings of regular audience research should provide up-to-date factual information about the use of broadcasting in one country, and serve as a useful background to the discussion of audience motives.

6 Franklin Fearing

Influence of the Movies on Attitudes and Behaviour

Franklin Fearing, 'Influence of the movies on attitudes and behavior', *Annals of the American Academy of Political and Social Science*, no. 254, 1947, pp. 70–79.

With a few special exceptions, everybody – social scientists, movie makers and laymen – seems to agree that there are profoundly important relationships between motion pictures and human behavior. The initially important question is concerned with the way in which these relationships are to be conceived. Any investigations in this field will be predicated on certain assumptions about human collective behavior, about how human beings give and receive communications, and about how the individual apprehends his social role and identifies the social roles of others. Bartlett, in his classic study entitled *Remembering*, states:

. . . it is fitting to speak of every human cognitive reaction – perceiving, imaging, remembering, thinking and reasoning – as an *effort after meaning*. Certain of the tendencies which the subject brings with him into the situation with which he is called upon to deal are utilized so as to make his reaction the 'easiest', or the least disagreeable, or the quickest and least obstructed that is at the time possible. When we try to discover how this is done we find that always it is by an effort *to connect what is given with something else*.[1] Thus, the immediately present 'stands for' something not immediately present, and 'meaning', in a psychological sense, has its origin (1932, pp. 44–5).

For Bartlett, the processes by which the individual comes to terms with his environment, which in the language of traditional psychology have been called by such terms as remembering, thinking, perceiving and imaging, are dynamic and creative rather than passive and static. The individual does not passively respond *to* the situation. Rather he responds *in* the situation selectively and creatively. This is cognition. Motion pictures achieve their effects because they help the individual to cognize his world.

1. These italics supplied.

Significance to the individual

Like the folk tale, classic drama, primitive story-telling, or the medieval morality play, the film may be regarded as a means through which the individual understands himself, his social role and the values of his group. It is also a means by which the individual orients himself in a universe of events which appear to occur haphazardly and chaotically. His need for meaningful experience is a need for order. This need has emotional components, since the lack of coherence in experience creates anxiety within the individual, from which he seeks relief.

The motion picture is not a fixed pattern of meanings or ideas which are received by a passive mind. Rather, what the individual 'gets' is determined by his background *and his needs*. He takes from the picture what is usable for him or what will function in his life. The stuff of films is action, movement, characterization, conflict, expressed in swiftly changing images. Whatever sense they have for the individual observer, however they are 'cognized', to use Bartlett's term, will depend on the particular configuration of needs which the individual brings with him. He utilizes the pictured situation in the process of coming to terms with the larger environment. This is the conceptual framework within which the significant analyses of the effects of motion pictures and other mass media of communication on behavior and attitudes must occur.

Psychologically, an important aspect of this process is that of participation. It is the special characteristic of these media that the individual has an opportunity to project himself into situations and in some degree share in experiences otherwise denied him. He may move into a world other than his own and acquire social identities and play social roles in many groups otherwise inaccessible to him. He may vicariously experience how other people react in a variety of situations.

'Effects' and 'impact'

The phrasing of the question in terms of simple 'effects' which a motion picture 'has' is inadequate, because it implies that films, as stimuli, have specific effects on an audience that is more or less inert or in some manner especially impressionable, and hence may be affected or swayed in a given direction.

This one-directional conception of effects is widely held. The supposed passivity of the motion picture audience has impressed many people and forms the basis of many attitudes and beliefs about the supposed good and bad effects of films. A more adequate statement of our problem would be: What is the nature of the impact of the content of motion pictures on the audience? More simply it might be put: What do people get out of the films they see – and why?

When phrased in these terms, the question is raised regarding the stimulus *value* of the motion picture. This is a question of the cultural values in our society which films express and the extent to which films communicate these values. In order to understand this extraordinarily complex process which involves both expression and communication, it is necessary to know something about the content of the film, the psychological needs of the persons who are exposed to it, the immediate setting, and the social and cultural forces operating on the persons who make films and the audiences for whom they are intended.

It must be confessed that we have very little in the way of tested answers to any of these questions. It is remarkable that an industry which has accepted status as the fifth largest in the United States has done so little systematic research on its product or the factors influencing the acceptance of the product. It is true that there have been a number of cliches which in the main seem to express the wishful attitudes toward films held by persons within and without the industry. Such a point of view, for example, is the frequently expressed statement that films are 'pure entertainment', providing a means of escape from the world of reality. An opposing view held by many outside the industry would have it that far from being 'just' entertainment, films have definite and presumptively bad effects on the population. For these, Hollywood is the synonym for sin, and its product so likely to be morally debauching, or so filled with subversive propaganda, that constant policing is thought to be necessary.

The lay and professional attitudes toward the problem of the effects or, as we have rephrased the question, the impact of films on human behavior are curiously diverse and frequently contradictory. They are based on a variety of assumptions about human nature and how the human animal reacts in social situations.

Since these attitudes in effect constitute the frames of reference within which the thinking of both the layman and the professional regarding the role of the motion picture in our society has occurred, it may be useful to summarize them.

'Mere entertainment'

There is the view that the effects of motion pictures on behavior and attitudes are negligible and transitory. This seems to be the underlying attitude of those who characterize the motion pictures as 'mere entertainment' or as 'escapist entertainment'. The much publicized statement that Hollywood's chief function is to provide 'dreams' for millions falls in this category. These formulations assume that the essential role of motion pictures in our society is to entertain and amuse or to afford an opportunity for a harassed and anxiety-ridden population to 'get away from it all' by escaping into a land of phantasy.

The term 'entertainment' is psychologically ambiguous. Applied to films, the term 'pure entertainment' would appear to mean that motion pictures may be made without meaningful content and without effects on those exposed to them. This is a formulation which affords a ready rationalization for not making 'serious' films, that is, films which are concerned with current problems, particularly if those problems are controversial. Many of those who support this view are fearful that films may be made which have meaningful content and hence have effects on behavior and attitudes. They rationalize this position by insisting that such films are without entertainment value.

The use of the term 'entertainment' as if it were some unique and special quality which may or may not be added seems obscure if not actually mystical. Any dramatic presentation which is coherent enough to hold attention and interest of a group is in some degree entertaining. Regardless of content, films may be dull and uninteresting or exciting and possibly disturbing with correspondingly low or high entertainment values.

Measuring effects

A diametrically opposed position states that the effects of motion pictures on behavior and attitudes are marked, particularly on certain groups. This type of answer is very popular with those who find in motion pictures the causes of a variety of social ills. These ills range from juvenile delinquency and crime to the alleged effects of films on the styles of women's hair-dos. It is doubtless this point of view which lies behind the current debate on whether there is something called 'propaganda' in films. This debate reaches an acute stage when there are legislative investigations to determine whether or not foreign, presumably subversive, ideas have infiltrated the commercial Hollywood product.

At the more sophisticated levels there is the accumulated experience from the use of a vast variety of educational films. These films have been made with the express purpose of affecting behavior or modifying attitudes in a specific manner. Their use and the studies which have been made regarding their effects present unequivocal evidence that motion pictures *do* affect human attitudes.

Perhaps the most extensive body of data validating the view that films have specific effects on attitudes and behavior was that obtained in a series of studies conducted by a number of sociologists and psychologists under the aegis of the Motion Picture Research Council and financed by the Payne Fund. The results of these studies, usually known as the Payne Fund Studies, were published in a series of monographs in 1933.[2] These investigations were especially concerned with the effects of motion pictures on children, on the production of juvenile and adult delinquency, on children's emotions, and on certain specific social attitudes. They were the subject of a prolonged and severe critical appraisal by Adler, published in a book entitled *Art and Prudence: A Study in Practical Philosophy* (1937). Professor Adler's book was summarized and his criticisms defended by Moley in a brochure entitled *Are We Movie-Made?* (1938).

It is impossible here to review the controversies which the Payne Fund Studies precipitated, nor is it useful at this late date to examine the strictures regarding their methodology and theoretical suppositions made by Adler and Moley. It may be

2. Following is a list of these monographs: Blumer (1933), Blumer and Hauser (1933), Charters (1933), Dale (1935a), Dale (1935b), Dale (1933), Dysinger and Ruckmick (1933), Holaday and Stoddard (1933), May and Shuttleworth (1933), Peters (1933), Renshaw, Miller and Marquis (1933), and Thurstone and Peterson (1933).

said, however, that the Payne studies were the first systematic attempt, with the use of experimental and other presumably rigorous techniques, to find out the effects of commercial motion pictures on specific human attitudes and behavior. It may be granted that some of the studies were imperfect as judged by rigorous methodological standards and that some of the results were publicized beyond their scientific merit. However, many of the criticisms brought forward by Adler and Moley were on grounds that many contemporary social scientists find difficult to understand and to share. The general conclusion of the Payne studies was that motion pictures have definite and measurable effects on attitudes and behavior, particularly in the case of children and adolescents, and that these effects are on the whole bad.

Methods of testing

Among these studies, the investigation of Thurstone and Peterson is notable because it follows a design which has become more or less standard in investigations of this type. It consists in testing a group of subjects as regards certain attitudes before the presentation of a film, and repeating the test immediately afterwards or after a lapse of time. In the case of the Thurstone and Peterson study the test consisted of the administration of scales designed to measure attitudes relevant to the content of the picture. Attitudes toward war, toward Negroes, and toward Orientals were measured in this study before and after a series of 'entertainment' or commercial feature films dealing with these subjects. The results indicated that in the case of the children tested there were measurable changes in their attitudes in the direction indicated by the film as a result of exposure to it. In the case of at least one group, these effects persisted in a significant amount for a period of five months. Among the motion pictures used as stimuli were *The Birth of a Nation* (anti-Negro), *Sons of the Gods* (pro-Chinese), and *Welcome Danger* (anti-Chinese).

Although not one of the Payne Fund Studies, the investigation of Rosenthal demonstrated that pictures with certain types of content has measurable effects on socio-economic attitudes (1934). A more recent study of the effects on children of a single motion picture, in which a somewhat different method is utilized, is that of Wiese and Cole (1946). Instead of attitude scales, this study made use of a free association technique in which the subjects wrote answers to questions regarding the ideological points in the film before and after being exposed to it. The film was a commercial motion picture, '*Tomorrow the World*', and dealt with the problem of the adjustment of an expatriated Nazi youth in the United States. Approximately three thousand children of different socio-economic backgrounds served as subjects.

These investigations all yield evidence that films have measurable effects on attitudes and that the effect is in the direction indicated by the film. The Wiese and Cole study is particularly interesting since it indicates that the effects of the film were in large degree determined by the social, economic and cultural origins of the individuals. This study documents an important generalization, namely, that the socio-economic backgrounds of the audience determine in large measure what a film 'means'. The underprivileged children saw meanings in Emil's behavior in '*Tomorrow the World*' which did not exist for middle- and upper-class children.

The small number of such studies is perhaps an index of the difficulties involved. It is worth noting that the uniform result that films do affect specific attitudes as measured still leaves unanswered the larger question of the impact of the motion picture on culture.

Film content and audience need

A third category of attitudes regarding the nature of the impact of motion pictures assumes that films have effects but that they are reciprocal to the socially determined needs of the audience. This view regards the motion picture as a cultural product in that in the film the individuals find affirmations or negations which are related to their tensions and needs.

This view assumes that there is a broad functional relationship between the thematic content of films (or other mass media of communication) and the needs of the mass audience. The term 'need' as used here refers to the fact that the individual seeks experience beyond that furnished by his immediate environment, which will assist him in understanding that environment. This, in Bartlett's terminology, is the act of cognizing. The experience which the individual obtains through the medium of dramatic presentation in its various forms provides him with interpretive frames of reference. These either reaffirm the norms of his culture or group or reveal previously unsuspected and possibly contrasting alternatives to these norms. He sees how other people behave in a wide variety of situations, and is thus provided with patterns of behavior which he may accept or reject. But whether he accepts or rejects them, his area of significant meanings has been enlarged and his awareness of the range of possibilities or his degrees of freedom for action is increased. The 'need' is not necessarily consciously experienced by the individual, but is assumed to underlie his behavior in seeking the entertainment or amusement provided by the motion picture. It finds expression in the pattern of his acceptances or rejections, approvals or disapprovals, of specific films.

Such a view, of course, does not regard the individual in the audience as neutral and unbiased, or as one who merely seeks to be amused or distracted. Rather, the audience is assumed to be made up of individuals with interests, fears and anxieties which gain expression through opportunities for identification in the dramatic situations presented in the film.

Research more or less identified with this point of view has concerned itself especially with content analysis of films or other mass media of communication. A few studies have been published mostly in the field of radio. In motion pictures, the study of Jones illustrates the method (1942). One hundred commercial Hollywood films released between April 1941 and February 1942 are analysed as regards types of characters, themes, goals sought and so forth.

Types of reaction

To be truly significant, studies of this type should attempt to correlate the themes with existing patterns of interest and stress in the individuals who compose the mass audience. Box-office attendance figures are ambiguous as an index of the significance of the film with regard to the needs of the audience. Special research techniques are required. Studies in the mass reaction to radio have yielded important data which indicate the character of the factors underlying the effects of the mass media of communication.

Herzog's investigations of the nature of the impact of daytime radio serials revealed one type of reaction to the stories which is particularly significant to the present discussion. The stories were not accepted as substitutes for reality by her listeners. Rather,

they identify themselves with them only in so far as they provide adjustment to the kind of life they are living. [The stories] *give meaning to a world which seems nothing but a humdrum existence by offering a continuous sequence of events.*[3] ... They give the listener a sense that the world is not as threatening as it might seem by supplying formulas of behavior for various troublesome situations ... and they explain things by providing labels for them (1941, p. 65).

Merton, in his penetrating analysis of the reactions of the mass audience to Kate Smith's famous eighteen-hour radio war-bond campaign, arrives at similar conclusions (1946). People bought thirty-one million dollars' worth of bonds in response to the appeal of a single person. Merton finds that the basic factor was Kate Smith's value as a symbol of sincerity. He notes that in a highly competitive urban society most people live in 'a climate of reciprocal distrust'; Smith signifies something that is stable and honest. It is this image with which the audience makes identification and to which they respond.

Films as reflectors

The conception of the film as a reflector of the stress patterns and the emotional needs of its audience is discussed by Houseman, producer and playwright, in a recent article.

Every generation has its myth – its own particular dream in which are mirrored the preoccupations of its waking hours. ... I have argued elsewhere against the notion that Hollywood enjoys any real free-will in the choice of its subjects. The best it can do, in the general run of its product, is to reflect as honestly and competently as it can the interests and anxieties of its hundred million customers (1947, p. 14).

When this analysis is applied to the current cycle of 'tough' films (for example, 'Blue Dahlia', 'The Big Sleep', 'Double Indemnity'), Houseman finds that they reflect some of the basic aspects of contemporary American life. Houseman's stress on

3. Italics supplied.

the films as reflectors is extremely important. It fails, however, to present an adequate picture of forces which make the audience expose themselves to the picture. In this connection psychological cliches should be avoided. It is dangerous, for example, to interpret the popularity of the current cycle of 'tough' films on the basis that they 'satisfy' an alleged sadistic or other fixed component in human nature. Aggression, hostility and conflict are prime characteristics of the contemporary scene. It may be that the motion picture audience is seeking interpretive frames of reference within which such phenomena become intelligible. Whether the films they see (and find entertaining) furnish adequate interpretation is, of course, another question.

'Collective unconscious'

Finally, there is an approach to the problem which is very similar to the one just described. It might, in fact, be bracketed under it. It also supports the thesis that films have content which is related to the underlying needs of mass audiences. It differs, however, from the foregoing view in that it has made use of a specific type of psychological theory as its theoretic framework.

From this point of view the material in the film is conceived to present two levels of meaning in so far as its impact on the audience is concerned. On the top level are its obvious and explicit meanings. At a deeper level are to be found the meanings which reflect or express the unconscious desires and compulsion of a whole people. This view of the relationship of motion pictures to the mass audience in effect states that a society, nation or population possesses a collective unconscious, and that motion pictures reflect and satisfy these needs.

A somewhat modified form of this approach is found in the recent book by Kracauer (1947). Kracauer's book is a study of the German films produced between 1922 and the beginning of the Hitler regime. It is its thesis that in these films are found reflected the needs, strivings and tensions of the German people. Further, Kracauer assumes that the analysis of these films not only reveals the characteristics of the German mass mind, but enables the historian to understand and predict the appearance of Nazism. Embedded within the manifest content of the films of this period, Kracauer finds motifs which had a special significance both for those who made the films and for those who saw them. He states: 'What films reflect are not so much explicit credos as psychological dispositions – those deep layers of collective mentality which extend more or less below the dimension of consciousness'.

Similar views are presented in a recent book by Mayer (1946). Mayer makes the point that there is an element of myth in what he calls the 'contemporary longing for the cinema'. He adds: 'Just because traditional structures of life are uprooted and are on the verge of disappearing forever the modern cinema-goer is seeking a *participation mystique* in the events on the screen.' Mayer derives the phrase *participation mystique* from the anthropologist Lévy-Bruhl's conceptions regarding the alleged prelogical character of the primitive mind. The reaction of the modern cinema audience to film content, like the primitives' reaction to and use of myth, is explained as non-rational and childlike.

In this sense we are all savages. Anyone who is familiar with recent developments in child-psychology knows that the non-rational character of the child's reaction towards the world persists even when the rationalization of the child's mind is already fully developed. The same applies to the adult. . . . Play, *participation mystique*, behavior patterns and conduct are certainly interlocked. This interlocked structure I have in mind, when I speak of the mythical element in our passion for the cinema (p. 19).

It is interesting to note that Mayer finds the same meaning in certain German films that Kracauer found.

The psychoanalytic tinge

The resemblance between these conceptions and the psychological assumptions underlying psychoanalysis is obvious. The film is understood psychologically in much the same way that the psychoanalyst understands the dream. In both there is a manifest and a latent content, and in both there are assumptions regarding the role and the significance of symbols. Thus, Kracauer notes the preoccupation of certain German films with the manifestations of tyrannical power. For example, the character Caligari, in *The Cabinet of Dr Caligari*, embodies these tendencies. In the story as originally written, Caligari, the insane psychiatrist, according to Kracauer, symbolizes remorseless power which is symbolically abolished. When the film was produced by Wiene, however, the story was placed within a framing plot which reversed its meaning although retaining its general form. Kracauer's analytical method is illustrated in his interpretation:

If it holds true that during the postwar years most Germans eagerly tended to withdraw from a harsh outer world into the intangible realm of the soul, Wiene's version was certainly more consistent with their attitude than the original story. . . . By putting the original into a box. this version faithfully mirrored the general retreat into a shell. . . . The film reflects the double aspect of German life by coupling a reality in which Caligari's authority triumphs with a hallucination in which the same authority is overthrown. There could be no better configuration of symbols for that uprising against the authoritarian dispositions which apparently occurred under cover of a behavior rejecting uprising (p. 67).

This psychoanalytic view is made explicit in its most extreme form in the recent book by Tyler when he says:

Briefly, movies, similar to much else in life, are seldom what they seem. In this sense . . . movies are dreamlike and fantastic, their fantasy and dreamfulness having actually come to the fore at the moment of writing as consciously embodying certain assumptions of my previous book. These assumptions are simple: the existence of the unconscious mind as a dynamic factor in human action, and the tendency of screen stories to emphasize – unintentionally – neuroses and psychopathic traits discovered and formulated by psychoanalysis. Hollywood movie-makers are used to combining their own automatism of mental and physical behavior with that of the characters of their products (1947, p. xiii).

Inadequate interpretation

In spite of the plausibility of these interpretations and the useful insights which they occasionally reveal, methodologically they are unsatisfactory to many social scientists. They suggest that there is something approaching a mystical communion between the minds which write, direct and produce a film and the minds of the mass audience. We have no indication as to the manner in which the makers of films gain access to the collective unconscious of the population for whom they are intended. Nor do we know whether the film as made actually carries the symbolic meanings to the mass audience. The 'collective unconscious' and 'participation mystique' are scarcely adequate conceptualizations.

Questions are unanswered

Although incomplete, the foregoing categories probably represent the principal ways in which laymen and professionals conceptualize the relationships between film content and human behavior.

Some of these approaches are more cogent, more testable, than others. However, many of these formulations are little more than plausible cliches about human nature or what the public 'wants', in place of scientific hypotheses. Such questions as: Why do people go to the picture houses? – What do they get out of the picture? are unanswered. Research has not been systematic. The Payne studies were ground-breaking, but in a sense were premature. They were conducted in a let's-see-what's-wrong-with-the-movies atmosphere. This nervousness still persists and constitutes a barrier for a completely free inquiry.

It is the trite but expected thing for the social scientist to recommend 'further research'. But the field offers exciting possibilities, and the questions are pressing. The movies reflect life and also may alter it, but we do not know precisely *how*. The investigation of the effects of such a film as *The Birth of a Nation* indicates that race prejudice may be increased. As an eminent psychologist once asked the author, if you could make any kind of a film you wished, with complete control of content and an unlimited budget, and you wished to affect anti-Negro or anti-Semitic attitudes, *what kind of a film would you make*? Where would you begin to alter the stereotypes?

This is an embarrassing question, because we do not know with even approximate precision what it is in the complex Gestalt which is the film, that would have the sought-for effect. It is psychologically naive to think of these questions in terms of 'propaganda' or 'entertainment', as if these were qualities which could be added or subtracted at will. Rather, we are confronted with the basic problem of how meaning is communicated. It is possible that recently developed research techniques in social psychology would yield significant results if applied to these problems.

Two generalizations

Two generalizations regarding the relations between film content and human behavior and attitudes seem justified.

Inevitable response

In the first place, on the basis of evidence from several lines of research it is possible to demonstrate that any film, regardless of its character – documentary, musical, western or realistic – has some measurable effects on specific attitudes of those exposed to it, provided a measuring instrument (e.g. attitude scale) is devised for it, and provided the audience is sufficiently interested to give it sustained attention. This is equivalent to saying that it is probably impossible to construct a coherent sequence of audio-visual images involving human action and interaction without at the same time presenting an attitude or ideological position toward that action. This constitutes its meaning or significance, and this may be communicated. These are the effects of the film *as measured by some test instrument*. Whether they express themselves in other patterns of behavior, that is, independently of the response to the test itself, is another question. The measured effects may or may not be those intended by the makers of the film.

This last point has more than academic interest. The question of intent involves the whole matter of propaganda in films. The intent of the makers of the film to produce a particular effect does not guarantee that the effect will be produced. A current controversy regarding the film classic *The Birth of a Nation* is a case in point. Griffith has recently stated:

I am not now and never have been 'anti-Negro' or 'anti' any other race. My attitude towards the Negroes has always been one of affection and brotherly feeling. . . . In filming *The Birth of a Nation*, I gave to my best knowledge the proven facts, and presented the known truth, about the Reconstruction period in the American South. These facts are based on an overwhelming compilation of authentic evidence and testimony (1947, p. 32).

For Griffith this film was a historically accurate presentation, produced without intent to affect attitudes towards the Negro. The study of Thurstone and Peterson (1933) demonstrated that this film made those exposed to it much less favorable toward Negroes.

It is within the framework of this first generalization that much of the research on specific effects of films has been done.

Films and the personal world

In the second place, motion pictures afford an opportunity for the expression of the basic meanings inherent in the relationships of human beings to each other, to their environment, and to the society of which they are a part. This is not limited to a passive reflection of those meanings, but may be a dynamic and creative interpretation. Nichols, the distinguished screen writer, expresses this when he states:

A storyteller is passionately interested in human beings and their endless conflicts with their fates, and he is filled with desire to make *some intelligible arrangement out of the chaos of life*,[4] just as the chairmaker desires to make some useful and beautiful arrangement out of wood (1943, p. xxxvii).

It is this intelligible arrangement that the movie-goer seeks, whatever his level of sophistication and regardless of whether he is able to be articulate about it. He finds affirmations for his doubts, alternative solutions for his problems, and the opportunity to experience vicariously ways of behaving beyond the horizons of his personal world. A useful bit of psychological jargon expresses this in the statement that films (and many other agencies) assist the individual in structuring his world. And, rightly or wrongly, effectively or ineffectively, all individuals must structure their worlds. This is a psychological principle, not alone an aesthetic principle, without which it is impossible to understand the nature and the results of the impact of films on human culture. It expresses the basic organic relationship between motion pictures and human life.

4. Italics supplied.

References

ADLER, M. J. (1937), *Art and Prudence: A Study in Practical Philosophy*, Longman.
BARTLETT, F. C. (1932), *Remembering: A Study in Experimental and Social Psychology*, Cambridge University Press.
BLUMER, H. (1933), *Movies and Conduct*, Macmillan Co.
BLUMER, H., and HAUSER, P. M. (1933), *Movies, Delinquency and Crime*, Macmillan Co.
CHARTERS, W. W. (1933), *Motion Pictures and Youth*, Macmillan Co.
DALE, E. (1933), *How to Appreciate Motion Pictures*, Macmillan Co.

DALE, E. (1935a), *Children's Attendance at Motion Pictures*, Macmillan Co.

DALE, E. (1935b), *The Content of Motion Pictures*, Macmillan Co.

DYSINGER, W., and RUCKMICK, C. A. (1933), *The Emotional Responses of Children to the Motion Picture Situation*, Macmillan Co.

GRIFFITH, D. W. (1947), in *Sight and Sound*, vol. 16, no. 61.

HERZOG, H. (1941), 'On borrowed experience', *Stud. Philos. Soc. Science*, vol. 9, no. 65.

HOLADAY, P., and STODDARD, G. D. (1933), *Getting Ideas from the Movies*, Macmillan Co.

HOUSEMAN, J. (1947), 'Today's hero; a review', *Hollywood Q.* vol. 2, January.

JONES, D. B. (1942), 'Quantitative analysis of motion picture content', *Pub. Opinion Q.*, vol. 6, pp. 411–28.

KRACAUER, S. (1947), *From Caligari to Hitler: A Psychological History of the German Film*, Princeton University Press.

MAY, M. A., and SHUTTLEWORTH, F. K. (1933), *The Social Conduct and Attitudes of Movie Fans*, Macmillan Co.

MAYER, J. P. (1946), *Sociology of the Film*, Faber & Faber.

MERTON, R. K. (1946), *Mass Persuasion: The Social Psychology of a War-Bond Drive*, Harper & Row.

MOLEY, R. (1938), *Are we Movie-Made?*, Macy-Masius.

NICHOLS, D. (1943), 'The writer and the film', in *Twenty Best Film Plays*, Crown Publishers.

PETERS, C. J. (1933), *Motion Pictures and Standards of Morality*, Macmillan Co.

RENSHAW, S., MILLER, V. L., and MARQUIS, D. (1933), *Children's Sleep*, Macmillan Co.

ROSENTHAL, S. P. (1934), 'Change of socio-economic attitude under radical motion picture propaganda', *Arch. Psychol.*, no. 166.

THURSTONE, L. L., and PETERSON, R. C. (1933), *Motion Pictures and the Social Attitudes of Children*, Macmillan Co.

TYLER, P. (1947), *Magic and Myth of the Movies*, Holt, Rinehart & Winston.

WIESE, M., and COLE, S. (1946), 'A study of children's attitudes and the influence of a commercial motion picture', *J. Psychol.*, vol. 21, pp. 151–71.

7 Denis McQuail, Jay G. Blumler and J. R. Brown

The Television Audience: A Revised Perspective

Published for the first time in this volume

The single concept which seems to have assumed most prominence in discussions of mass media experience has been that of 'escape'[1] – whether applied to the dominant character of mass media content or to the motives of the typical audience member. The phenomenal rise in popularity of the cinema may have particularly encouraged this way of thinking about mass communications in general and its subsequent transfer to television – despite the very different characteristics of that medium in content and organization. There developed a frame of reference for handling the film experience, common to critics, students of film and often the filmgoer himself, which accentuated the elements of dream, hallucination, fantasy and withdrawal from real-life problems. Kracauer's study of film theory contains a number of passages which suggest that escapism can be taken for granted as a universal component in film experience. He notes that:

from the twenties to the present day, the devotees of film and its opponents alike have compared the medium to a sort of drug and have drawn attention to its stupefying effects (1960, p. 159).

And later he maintains that 'to the extent that films are mass entertainment they are bound to cater for the alleged desires and daydreams of the public at large' (1960, p. 163). Another writer has described Hollywood as a 'Dream Factory' and the aptness of the label has never been challenged (Powdermaker, 1950).

As it happened, the growth of the cinema audience coincided,

1. For an authoritative discussion of the notion of 'escape', see Katz and Foulkes (1962). As they point out 'The favourite answer of the popular-culture writers to [the] question "What do people do with the media?" is that they use it for escape.'

in industrialized countries, with the incidence of widespread unemployment and hardship, high rates of population mobility, the decline or extinction of traditional cultures and the experience of war or threats of war. In these circumstances, the images, associations and modes of thinking offered by many films seemed to provide a series of contrasts to predominant life experiences: reassurance instead of insecurity; reward instead of deprivation; the grandeur of the picture house instead of the generally mean and cramped home; freedom instead of constraint; an expanded horizon in the mind as against sharply restricted real-life chances; an idealized world instead of an anxious and imperfect one; and a temporary remission from the rationality and calculativeness of daily life in modern society. It is hardly surprising that the cinema gave rise to an image of the medium-audience nexus which has played a formative part in interpretations of modern cultural phenomena. Nor is it surprising that orientations to television, in many respects heir to that mass audience which the film had helped to create, should have been powerfully affected in turn by those expectations and associations which the cinema had attracted.

The interpretation of a communication medium as escapist is not in itself a novel development. Lowenthal has traced essentially the same notion back to the writings of Pascal and Montaigne (1950) and has elsewhere described a strand of criticism and social comment in nineteenth-century Britain that was concerned with the escapist nature of the culture and entertainments of the working-class people, linking the phenomenon with urban social conditions. We may suggest, however, that even if the idea is not new, it is now so widely held and applied to the main contemporary medium of mass communication, that it has acquired a new significance.

The degree to which the concept of escape figures in studies of television can readily be illustrated. In a judicious review of escapist communication, Klapper notes that the content concerned might include anything which 'presents a picture of life and the world which is not in accord with reality'. He would include in this genre:

family comedy . . .; musical variety shows on radio, television and screen; the daytime serials of radio and television; much light fiction . . .; adventure stories; and a good deal of what the mass media consider serious drama (1960, p. 168).

Clearly such a list covers a major part of the full spectrum of television programming. An outstanding American study of the place of television in children's lives gives escapism as the first and, significantly the 'obvious' reason for watching television. This is elaborated as :

the passive pleasure of being entertained, living in a fantasy, taking part vicariously in thrill play, identifying with exciting and attractive people, getting away from real-life problems and escaping real-life boredom (Schramm, Lyle and Parker, 1961, p. 57).

The authors go on to say of television that it:

leads not toward human interaction, but rather toward withdrawal into private communion with the picture tube and the private life of fantasy. It is aimed less often at solving the problems of life than escaping from them (p. 58).

The study then discovers that:

when children talk about the gratifications they get from television, the fantasy gratifications come out first and in greater number. When they list favorite programs, fantasy types of program are likely to outnumber reality programs by a ratio of twenty to one (p. 69).

The centrality of the concept of escape in discussions of the television audience may stem from the concurrence or convergence of several factors, apart from the suggested 'halo' effect of the cinema. Firstly, there is some evidence to support the view that heavy use of mass media, and especially of television, is associated with various forms of personal or social deprivation.[2] Although direct evidence about the motivations which underlie such heavy media use has in the main been lacking, the common-sense view that it tokens a seeking of relief from persistent problems has been widely accepted. Second, the findings of media content analysis have testified to the presence of strong and systematic patterns of reality distortion – a distortion which, *inter alia*, appears to favour the assumed aspirations, wishes and dreams of the audience member by over-representing higher status occupations and life-styles and more exciting and

2. The most relevant studies are summarized in Katz and Foulkes (1962). But for some contrary evidence see Sargent and Stempel (1968).

glamorous surroundings, than are normally found (Jones, 1942; Smythe, 1954). Again, it has usually been assumed that these content characteristics owe their origin to the contribution they make to escape-seeking by the audience. A third factor tending in the same direction is the persistent popularity of cultural material which is apparently without intrinsic merit or communicative purpose – the light entertainment and drama which is produced according to formula, entirely unmemorable, undemanding and unstimulating. The phenomenon again seems to lend itself most readily to the view that what the media are offering, and what the audience is primarily looking for, is something to fill time and to absorb without disturbance, requiring no expertise or relearning and having cheerful and diverting associations. A fourth observation, obvious enough but easily lost sight of, is that media use is confined typically not only to leisure time, but to 'out of role time' in general. There is an implication, in the words of one commentary, of 'checking one's social roles at the movie-house door' (Katz and Foulkes, 1962). Watching television is something to do when not at work, a facility bought by work. But in addition, it is an activity that is typically disengaged from other social roles – of parent, spouse, member of group or association. Attending to the media, and watching television in particular, is typically a matter of free personal choice, carrying few or no obligations to the communicator or to fellow members of an audience or social group. This lends further weight to the escapist thesis, since it establishes media use as a type of behaviour which is remarkably unconstrained, free from feelings of duty and obligation, a collectively sanctioned withdrawal from social life.[3] Finally, one can note the disillusion of those who have had high aspirations for television as a potentially educative force, who have wished to see it used to widen horizons, increase knowledge and broaden the base of participation in civic life. While in some measure television may have helped to further such developments, there seem to be strict limits to the willingness and capacity of many people to respond actively to the fund of social and political information presented in the press and on

3. See Steiner (1963). This view is supported by Steiner's evidence, but he also calls attention to the accompanying feelings of guilt, especially amongst the better-educated.

television. Even where news and current affairs materials are provided and followed in large amounts, there is a strong suspicion that they do not succeed in forging any enduring links between the ordinary citizen and decision-taking processes of the society. In fact, the term, 'narcotizing dysfunction', was coined by Merton and Lazarsfeld to refer to an apparent tendency of audiences to accept the vicarious media experience as a substitute for actually doing anything about social or political problems (1948). So even many of those who had hoped that a medium like television could contribute to the building of a more participatory democracy are on the whole inclined to fear that the mass audience has little taste for reality as presented over the most popular mass medium.

Taken together, these several factors have all strongly underlined what we have identified as a key explanatory tendency in relation to television. It would be misleading, however, to suggest that such views have been put forward without qualification. Serious commentators have recognized that not all television content is escapist nor are heavy users of television exclusively motivated by a desire to escape from reality. Equally, the complexity of the notion of 'escape' has been acknowledged. In the discussion previously cited, Klapper notes that the term 'escapist' is itself unfortunate since, in its accepted meaning, it does not adequately describe the kind of media material normally thought of in this connection nor does it accurately describe all of its supposed effects (1960, p. 167). In their analysis of the 'escape' concept, Katz and Foulkes draw attention to the need to distinguish between escape via the media as withdrawal and uses of 'escapist' media which have a positive feedback on the performance of the individual's other social roles – by providing a needed respite and relaxation (1962). Hence we need to allow for the existence of different kinds of feedback from the same content at different times and for different people. In an empirical study of children's uses of pictorial media, Bailyn identified escape as the main function of the mass media for children, but distinguished between (a) those escapist uses which might 'preclude more realistic and lasting solutions' to problems, and (b) those which at one level were 'escapist' but which should more properly be categorized as 'supplementation' (1959). For her the latter term had positive associations and implied a widening of horizons and the provision of relaxation. Schramm, Lyle and Parker also contrast media use which is 'reality-seeking' or socializing with the fantasy uses which they find prevalent. But they confine their list of television materials in the domain of reality to 'news, documentaries, interviews, public affairs programs and educational television' (1961, p. 64). The effect is to exclude from consideration under this heading a wide range of television content which could have an important bearing on the individual's perception and understanding of the real world without appearing in an explicitly cognitive form. When all due allowance is made for distinctions and reservations, it must be admitted that the escapist hypothesis still occupies much of the central ground in discussion and study of the television audience.

Like several other notions that are deeply entrenched in the vocabulary of discourse about culture and society, the concept of escape is exceptionally potent because it inextricably intermingles what might otherwise by a merely descriptive assertion in the scientific spirit (hypothesizing that most viewers predominantly use television in order to forget stressful and disliked features of their environment) with a strongly held normative standpoint. Deployed in the latter sense, the escapist thesis has helped to precipitate and perpetuate certain derogatory assumptions about the typical relationship between television and the viewer, from which even the qualifications and reservations mentioned above are usually excluded.

Firstly there is the view that popularity is inconsistent with high quality, since the latter is assumed to connote educational attainment, critical standards, sensitivity of judgement, effort and creativity, all of which stand in contrast to the dominant meanings of the escape concept. Second, there is an assumption of homogeneity; the content of a mass medium like television is regarded virtually as a single commodity, in which one programme could stand in quite readily for any other. The audience is unselective because all or most programmes offer essentially the same satisfaction and are watched for broadly the same motive. A third and related point is that the experience of television is uninvolving and, by implication, unimportant according to a widely held scale of values. It is regarded as shallow, undemanding and trivial. Fourth, television is regarded as a residual category of leisure activity; it is a time-filler, a substitute for doing nothing or something more worthwhile, shaped more by variations in other demands on one's time than by any positive attractions or considered motivations. This view finds some support in the phenomenal *quantity* of time devoted to it. The general bearing of this set of views is to see the experience of watching television as largely lacking in meaning, hardly deserving of serious interest or respect, a chance outcome of a set of market circumstances. The explanatory formula is thus closed and virtually self-validating. So the evidence showing long hours of time spent watching television is not interpreted as pointing to the influence of powerful attraction or strong need, but as indicative instead of a vacancy of outlook, an emptiness of life and a uniformity of response. And when evidence shows that people do actually depend a good deal on television and are upset when it is not available, this is taken more as a sign of their stupidity than of the constructive role which the medium plays in their lives.

The main purpose of this essay is neither radically to revise the concept of escape itself, nor to dispute the validity of its reference to one important dimension of audience involvement in mass communications. We would strongly question, however, the appropriateness of its virtually all-embracing application to a possibly quite diverse range of content appeals, motives, satisfactions and experiences. After all, the greater part of the plausibility of the escapist hypothesis derives from indirect evidence. Direct tests of the predominance of escapist concerns in the audience have not yet been devised or administered. Moreover, although a link between social deprivation and heavy mass media use is often postulated, the associations actually detected so far by research have tended to be rather limited in direction and type and open to more than one interpretation. The danger is that an uncritical acceptance of the escapist thesis will go hand-in-hand with a simplistic view of the relations between audience and media content and an underestimation of the diversity and complexity of motives that may sustain the mass audience. It could also have undesirable consequences for the organization of television and the evolution of policies that determine its place in society – undesirable, that is, if television is not in fact so constrained as the escapist theory makes out from performing a wider range of social functions than is generally assigned to it in western societies today.

In this essay we aim, then, to advance, on the basis of empirical research evidence, a typology of viewer gratifications which can both enlarge our understanding of what escape implies and help to place it in a context of a number of other equally important orientations, motives and links between people and television. We strive to substantiate the claim that escape does not represent the only, or even the invariably most appropriate, formulation of the needs served by the mass communication process and to direct attention towards several other formulations of what this process may fundamentally involve and signify.

The evidence presented for illustration and support derives from a programme of investigation initiated in 1969 at the Centre for Television Research in the University of Leeds.[4] It was designed to further in a systematic way the tradition of inquiry which has been concerned with audience 'uses and gratifications', and which seeks to explain, usually on the basis of the audience member's own subjective account of the media experience, just what functions a particular kind of content serves in particular circumstances. Our research programme had the following objectives:

1. To investigate the main types of motive and satisfaction relevant to diverse kinds of television content.

2. To establish a set of categories covering the main types of audience gratification.

3. To find ways of classifying members of the television audience according the these main categories.

4. To investigate the links between the social circumstances, background and experience of viewers and the incidence of different types of gratifications sought from television.

5. To develop empirical methods for measuring and interrelating data about social background and motives and gratifications, suitable for deployment in large-scale surveys and amenable to statistical analysis.

4. The research was supported by a grant from the Social Science Research Council.

6. Eventually to make general statements about the range of satisfactions provided by television and the salience of each of them for different groups, defined in demographic or personality terms.

While these aims are far short of being fully accomplished, a number of studies have been completed which bear closely on the problem we have raised – the need for a conceptual framework within which findings about the audience experience and interpretations of it can be more adequately accommodated. On the basis of evidence already accumulated we can present, in simplified form, a typology of the main kinds of satisfaction which are sought or gained by the television audience. This typology is essentially hypothetical in character and requires revision and extension, but even in its present form it has a number of implications for some of those prevalent assumptions about the mass audience which have been outlined above.

Our work was guided by certain presuppositions, which should be briefly outlined. Most fundamentally, we adopted the view than an important part of television viewing is goal-directed. While this premise may seem question-begging, we could not proceed far with our investigation without it, and it does not imply in advance any single kind of motive. Second, we assumed that the goals of television viewing can only be discovered from viewers themselves and that people will be sufficiently self-aware to be able to report their interests and motives in particular cases or at least to recognize them when confronted with them in an intelligible and familiar verbal formulation. Third, we were prepared to find diverse and overlapping patterns of motive and satisfaction; if a viewer was moved by several different concerns to follow the same content, we want our instruments of investigation to disclose, not to ignore, this fact. Fourth, we were prepared to treat as a conceptually independent unit of analysis something which might variously be described as a satisfaction, a motive, a gratification, an interest or a function. These units could be distributed in varying ways amongst a given population of television viewers and also be associated with different programmes and programme types in varying degrees.

Because it stands on the same plane of generality as the assumptions specified above, a final orientation deserves to be mentioned here, even though it only emerged explicitly as evidence was collected and analysed. This is that media use is most suitably characterized as an interactive process, relating media content, individual needs, perceptions, roles and values and the social context in which a person is situated. Our model of this process is that of an open system in which social experience gives rise to certain needs, some of which are directed to the mass media of communication for satisfaction. It is also possible that media content may occasionally help to generate in the audience member an awareness of certain needs in relation to his social situation. The linkage is necessarily a complex one and may take diverse forms; it may involve a process of deprivation-compensation in which the media offer substitute satisfactions for something desired or valued, but relatively unavailable; or it may involve a process of value reinforcement in which salient values, beliefs or attitudes are sustained by attention to certain content forms; or materials taken from the media may contribute to certain processes of social interchange which go with the occupancy of certain roles. The essential point to be stressed is our belief that media use is interactive. That is, it does not conform to the typical lineaments of a subject–object relationship, and should not be treated merely as a one-way tension-reducing mechanism. Such a model would leave out of account the many ways in which, according to our evidence, audience members seem to bring back into their lives, their patterns of activity and their circles of familiar acquaintances some of the broadcast programmes to which they have become attached.

In collecting empirical evidence about viewer gratifications, a major concern was to move from a qualitative and descriptive approach to a quantitative one, to develop instruments designed to operationalize the notion of the media-related gratification and to open it to statistical treatment. As a result a good deal of experimentation with research techniques was undertaken, which could have the effect of complicating any account of our methodology and substantive results. Nevertheless, our several investigations followed a broadly similar course which can be briefly described.

An initial task was to select particular types of content as foci of research (having decided to begin at this point rather than with types of viewer or types of satisfaction). The choice was guided by several criteria – links with earlier work in the field, the popularity and familiarity of the content itself, or its relevance to hypotheses about the social origin of audience motives. So far six main programmes or programme types have been investigated: a domestic radio serial, *The Dales*; a domestic television serial, *Coronation Street*; certain television quiz programmes; news on television; and two television adventure serials, *Callan* and *The Saint*. Some other kinds of material have incidentally been studied, but each of the programme areas mentioned have been subjected to an intensive investigation following a similar pattern. The first move was to undertake unstructured small-group discussions with regular members of the audience. These discussions were tape-recorded and the material was analysed for its references to the programme under study. On this basis, a list was compiled of statements which people had made expressive of their attitude to the programme or their motives for following it, or of any satisfactions derived from it. These lists, together with a battery of questions concerning social-background particulars and other variables, were incorporated into a structured interview conducted with a small sample of respondents (ranging from seventy to one-hundred-and-eighty persons), who frequently saw the programme concerned or regarded it as one of their favourites. Quota controls ensured that each sample included 'fans' drawn from different age groupings and social backgrounds.

The basic form of questioning about programme gratifications was the submission to the respondent of the list of statements relating to the programme (up to forty-five in number) with a request to say whether each applied to his own viewing of it and to what degree. These results were then subjected to an item-by-item intercorrelation, and the whole matrix of correlations was further examined (by a procedure described below) to reveal the underlying structure of response. For each programme or type, a set of clusters emerged, grouping together those kinds of audience gratification that were empirically associated. It is these data which constitute the basis of the typology set out below. A final stage of the research process involved the allocation to respondents of scores reflecting their position in relation to each cluster and facilitating a statistical analysis of the background variables that are associated with each main kind of satisfaction.

In order to illustrate these procedures and the nature of the evidence from which the typology was derived, a brief account follows of one programme study, that which was concerned with television quiz programmes. This was the second study carried out and the first in which a group of programmes as a type, rather than a single programme, was examined. The choice was influenced by the fact that quiz programmes form a distinctive and popular category of television content with a seeming diversity of associations. In addition, there existed a link with early research in the form of an interesting study of a small sample of listeners to an American radio quiz programme, providing material for comparison and a source of some hypotheses (Herzog, 1940).

A series of tape-recorded discussions was first held with followers of television quiz programmes, and a questionnaire compiled in the light of the analysis of material thus obtained. This questionnaire was then administered to a quota sample of seventy-three Leeds residents (with controls for sex, age, housing type and social grade), all of whom had designated as among their favourite television programmes one of several quiz programmes from a wider list. The three quiz programmes were *University Challenge*, *TV Brain of Britain*, and *Ask the Family*, each of them involving genuine tests of knowledge rather than being merely parlour games with big prizes, gimmicks and a prominent element of chance.

The most relevant part of the questionnaire consisted of an inventory of forty-two statements about quiz programmes, divided into three sections, which were presented to respondents for endorsement on a four-point scale. The first section contained statements indicating expected satisfactions and accompanied by the wording: 'When I think of watching a quiz [the statement] applies very much, quite a lot, a little, not at all.' The second referred to experienced satisfactions in the following way: 'When watching quizzes [the experience] has happened very often, quite often, only now and then, never.' In the third section respondents were asked whether certain descriptive phrases applied 'very well', 'slightly', or 'not at all' to quiz programmes.

The purpose of splitting up the items was to introduce distinctions of meaning into the concept of a gratification or function and to guard against dangers of response set, although in the event the distinctions were ignored in the analysis, and the intercorrelations of item endorsements ranged meaningfully across boundaries. The inventory as a whole was given to each respondent by an interviewer for self-completion. The rest of the questionnaire consisted mainly of items about general media use habits, as well as a series of 'social indicator' measures – which were intended to aid clarification in terms of social position and social attitudes.[5]

The pattern of the gratifications viewers seek from quiz programmes emerged from an analysis involving two stages. First, associations between endorsements of the scales were set out in a 42×42 matrix of intercorrelations. Second, the statements were re-arranged into sub-sets by means of a cluster analysis (McQuitty's elementary linkage analysis, 1957). This technique is designed to arrange intercorrelated items into clusters which maximize the average internal correlation of the clustered items and minimize the correlation between sub-sets. It is an approximate method, easy to apply, which provides an entirely empirical solution to the problem of ordering inter-related data. Every item is assigned to one and only one cluster, although it may be the case that a particular statement could equally well fit in more than one cluster.

The results of the quiz programme cluster analysis are presented in Table I. We find four main clusters of items emerging, with several small groups in pairs also separated out. Following recommendations made and methods described by McKennel (1970), we calculated measures of homogeneity (indicating the degree of intercorrelation) and of reliability, which appeared in the case of the four main clusters to reach the specified levels of acceptability.

These findings confirm the point made thirty years earlier by Herta Herzog that quiz programmes have a multiple appeal: 'different aspects of them appeal to different people' (1940). In

5. The measures employed covered customary demographic variables plus an array of background particulars including subjective social status, reactions to work, experience of social mobility, attachment to locality, sociability, family experience and attitudes to education.

Table I Results of cluster analysis of statements relating to television quiz programmes

	Coefficients of homogeneity	reliability
Cluster 1 Self-rating appeal	0·24	0·69
I can compare myself with the experts		
I like to imagine that I am on the programme and doing well		
I feel pleased that the side I favour has actually won		
I imagine that I was on the programme and doing well		
I am reminded of when I was in school		
I laugh at the contestant's mistakes		
Hard to follow		
Cluster 2 Basis for social interaction	0·31	0·79
I look forward to talking about it with others		
I like competing with other people watching with me		
I like working together with the family on the answers		
I hope the children will get a lot out of it		
The children get a lot out of it		
It brings the family together sharing the same interest		
It is a topic of conversation afterwards		
Not really for people like myself		
Cluster 3 Excitement appeal	0·34	0·78
I like the excitement of a close finish		
I like to forget my worries for a while		
I like trying to guess the winner		
Having got the answer right I feel really good		
I completely forget my worries		
I get involved in the competition		
Exciting		

	Coefficients of	
	homogeneity	reliability

Cluster 4 Educational appeal	0·30	0·68

Cluster 4 Educational appeal

I find I know more than I thought

I feel I have improved myself

I feel respect for the people on the
programme

I think over some of the questions
afterwards

Educational

Cluster 5

It is nice to see the experts taken down a peg

It is amusing to see the mistakes some of the
contestants make

Cluster 6

I like to learn something as well as to be
entertained

I like finding out new things

Cluster 7

I like trying to guess the answers

I hope to find that I know some of the
answers

Cluster 8

I find out the gaps in what I know

I learn something new

A waste of time

Cluster 9

Entertaining

Something for all the family

Cluster 10

I like the sound of voices in the house

I like seeing really intelligent contestants
showing how much they know

addition they form a strikingly clear and interpretable pattern, or so we can conclude about the four relatively large clusters. The six later clusters add little to the results, partly because most of their meanings have already been covered and partly because two- or three-item groups are inevitably low in reliability.

According to this analysis, then, four main kinds of gratifications are involved in the viewing of quiz programmes. One stems from a *self-rating appeal*, whereby watching a quiz enables the viewer to find out something about himself. Inspection of the individual items in Cluster 1 suggests that it embraces several related elements. There is the possibility of assessing one's ability by comparing one's own responses to the questions with the performance of other contestants. There is the possibility of testing one's judgement by guessing which group of competitors will turn out to be the winners. There is the theme of projection, whereby the viewer can imagine how he would fare if he were on the programme himself. And there is the possibility of being reminded of what one was like as a schoolchild. In the last context it is interesting to note that Herzog also detected a self-rating appeal of quiz programmes and speculated that one of its ingredients was the attraction of 'being taken back to one's own school days' (1940).

The meaning of Cluster 2 seems equally definite. A second major appeal of quiz programmes is their provision of a *basis for social interaction* with other people. Each item in the cluster (with only one exception) bears this interpretation. A quiz programme offers shared family interest; there is the possibility of observing 'what the children get out of it'; the whole family can work together on the answers; alternatively, viewers can compete with each other in trying to answer the questions; and the occasion can form a topic of conversation afterwards. Clearly quiz programmes are well adapted to serving a 'coin of exchange' function.

A third main appeal of TV quizzes arises from the *excitement* they can engender. Many of the items in Cluster 3 convey this emphasis. Quiz programmes apparently offer the excitement of competition itself, guessing who might win and seeing how one's forecast turns out, and the prospect of a close finish. Herzog seemed to have this gratification in mind when referring to the so-called 'sporting appeal' of *Professor Quiz* (1940). Perhaps what is distinctive about the composition of Cluster 3 in this study is its injection of an 'escapist' note into the associated group of items ('I like to forget my worries for a while', and 'I completely forget my worries'). It is as if the various tensions of a quiz programme facilitate its 'escapist' function and help the viewer to shed his everyday cares for a while.

Finally, Cluster 4 picks out an *educational appeal* of quiz programmes. Here, too, several ingredients are involved. It is not just that quizzes can help to stimulate thought ('I think over some of the questions afterwards'). In addition, two of the items sound a note of 'self-improvement' ('I feel I have improved myself', and 'I find I know more than I thought'), in terms which suggest that people who feel insecure in their educational status may use quizzes to reassure themselves about their own knowledgeability. And this suggests yet another way of interpreting Cluster 4 – as expressive of the function of quiz programmes in projecting and reinforcing educational values.

Subsequent analysis involved the testing of relationships between the appeals represented by these main clusters and variables representative of social experience and attitudes. In effect we wished to know what kinds of people were most attracted to quiz programmes for reasons implied in these different clusters. It lies outside the scope of this paper to elaborate on the findings, but the procedure can be briefly described and a few results mentioned, partly because they bear on the issue of validating our gratification measures.

The first step was the relatively simple one of converting the cluster-analysis results into scores for each respondent according to the degree to which he had endorsed the items included in a particular cluster. The analysis was then carried out by applying a computer programme known as Automatic Interaction Detector (AID – improved and adapted for work of this kind by Dr A. C. McKennel), the main purpose of which is to locate the best predictor, amongst a set of independent variables, of a given criterion variable.[6] In our case the independent variables

6. We are grateful to Dr McKennel for much help and advice in applying this AID programme to our data and to Mr J. Reeves of the Computing Laboratory of Southampton University.

are those relating to a respondent's social background and the criterion variable was his score on each of the clusters. The application of the AID programme results in the location of respondent sub-groups, defined according to those independent variables which show maximum average scores for each of the clusters. What we wish primarily to know is what kinds of social circumstances are associated with, and hence possibly causative of, liking the programme in question for a given type of reason. The results are of interest both as tests of certain hypotheses and as means of validating the distinctiveness of the separate clusters. The findings are complex, but for each of four quiz clusters we can report the sub-group or groups which are maximally involved.

Cluster 1 Self-rating appeal

The analysis separates out as relatively high scorers those members of the sample (thirty-six out of seventy-three) living in council housing. This suggests that the working-class fans of a programme type which in fact had a generally stronger appeal for middle-class people were more concerned to use it to 'learn things about themselves' than were other viewers.

Cluster 2 Basis for social interaction

Here the strongest associations were with social contact variables. The first high-scoring group to emerge from the analysis consisted of those respondents who reported having a very large number of acquaintances in their neighbourhoods. Among the other sample members, those with a large extended family were then distinguished as particularly high-scoring on this cluster. The use of quiz material as a 'coin of exchange' seemed, then, to be directly related to the number of opportunities for interaction available in the individual's immediate social environment.

Cluster 3 Excitement

The highest scoring group consisted of working-class viewers who had measured low on an index of acts of sociability and who were late-born children of large families. While the significance of the role of family background here is not clear, the predominant meaning of the link to low sociability seems to favour an escapist or compensatory explanation of this motive for watching quiz programmes.

Cluster 4 Educational appeal

The strongest and most clearcut association here was with educational background, since the analysis, after first distinguishing Leeds-born respondents from the 'immigrants' to the city, then split the former into a high-scoring group whose education had finished at the minimum school-leaving age. Thus the educational appeal of quiz programmes was strongest for those individuals with the most limited school experience.

These and other results which related to quiz programmes were not without ambiguity and left many questions unanswered, but they appeared to lend support to some of our basic working assumptions. They also foreshadowed some of the categories that figure in the typology of viewer gratifications which stemmed from our attempt to organize the results of several different studies, of which the quiz investigation was but one example.

The four most successful studies yielded a total of nineteen clusters to which substantive labels could be attached, and when these were regarded as a whole a relatively small number of recurrent categories were found to emerge. It was this striking, and only partly anticipated, degree of overlapping in the gratification clusters which makes it possible, without further detailed research, to prepare the outlines of the overall framework of appeals by which television may meet the needs of its audience. A major implication of this phenomenon of overlapping dispositions is that people can look to quite different kinds of material for essentially the same gratification and, correlatively, find alternative satisfactions in the same televised material. Thus an 'escape' motive seemed to feature in the structure of orientations to broadcast materials as diverse as *The Dales* radio serial, *The Saint*, television news and quiz programmes. It should be noted that these types of content are hardly comparable in terms of the degree to which they provide a faithful representation of reality; yet they still offer a recognizably similar kind of satisfaction to audience members. Other gratification types ranged with equal facility across a similarly diverse set of programme areas.

In fact, this repetition of a small number of themes was the starting point for the development of an overall framework of

Denis McQuail, Jay G. Blumler and J. R. Brown 153

gratification types. Several ordering principles were then employed to help in arranging the separate categories of audience response in relation to each. The first of these involved the acceptance of a distinction akin to that made by Schramm between the immediate and delayed rewards of media content (1949). It was noticeable that some of our clusters reflected a disposition to use television to get away from or forget certain restricting or unpleasant features of the viewer's environment, while others represented a concern to acquire some information about the respondent's wider environment. A second set of considerations affected the way in which certain of the more immediate satisfactions should be treated. It was decided to refer to these, as far as possible, by the term 'diversion' rather than that of 'escape'. This was partly to avoid some of the accumulated associations, often perjorative or ambiguous, which attach to the latter term and partly to allow for a further division of this category into sub-types according to empirically occurring differences of meaning. A third general observation affecting our classification scheme relates to an apparent dichotomy between a reference to self and a reference to others; hence the need to separate out media uses which involve relations with others – even where the 'others' are imaginary characters or media performers – and those which are primarily inward-looking.

The conceptual status of the typology calls for a brief comment. What, exactly, it may be asked, *are* the sorts of things that we are classifying? However appropriate otherwise, the language of functionalism is so overworked, ambiguous and imprecise that we prefer to avoid it, and to attempt a new start. In keeping with our view of mass media use as being potentially highly involving and also two-way, we propose to use the expression, 'media–person interaction', to refer to the orientations distinguished in the typology. Our clusters of items seem to reveal certain types of relationship between the user and the communicated content that depend on the perceptions of the audience member. A good deal of imprecision remains in the concept, but this stems from the variability inherent in the situation. What we wish to avoid is any specific inference about the presence of a discrete motive or the occurrence of a precise 'effect'. The audience member temporarily occupies a particular position in relation to what he is viewing, a position affected by a large number of factors, including those deriving from his personality, social background, experience, immediate social context, and, of course, from the content itself. He brings certain expectations and responds in line with these, and he derives certain affective, cognitive and instrumental satisfactions.

The typology of media–person interactions is intended to differentiate certain common constellations of disposition and response. It does so only very approximately and at present hypothetically. Its main strength as a heuristic device or source of hypotheses derives from its empirical base and its main weakness from the possibly limited character of this base.

The categories of our typology can first be presented in a summary form and then elaborated and illustrated more fully:

1. Diversion
   (a) Escape from the constraints of routine
   (b) Escape from the burdens of problems
   (c) Emotional release
2. Personal Relationships
   (a) Companionship
   (b) Social utility
3. Personal Identity
   (a) Personal reference
   (b) Reality exploration
   (c) Value reinforcement
4. Surveillance

Diversion

The meaning of the three sub-types listed under this heading can be illustrated from the results of the programme studies mentioned above. The first sub-type of the category labelled 'diversion' is instanced by the first main clustering of responses to *The Saint*. This cluster included the following set of empirically linked items:[7]

'It helps you escape from the boredom of everyday life'
'It takes you out of yourself'

7. The items reproduced on this and subsequent pages are not generally complete clusters of items, but are confined to those most unambiguously reflective of the inferred meaning.

'The stories often have interesting backgrounds'
'It does you good to see somebody doing things you can't do yourself'
'*The Saint* keeps me in suspense'

What a programme of this kind offers is a fantasy world which is attractive in itself, and which the viewer can temporarily occupy.

A somewhat different relationship, justifying a second sub-type, is indicated by one of the clusters concerning quiz programmes where the item 'I completely forgot my worries' is closely linked with two others that refer to the mechanism involved: 'I like the excitement of a close finish', and 'I like trying to guess the winner'. Another expression of this kind of diversion seems implicit in one of the news-viewing clusters which linked the following items:

'It helps me to get away from my problems'
'It's like having a good gossip'
'I like the sound of voices in my house'

Third, the category of media function, which we have labelled 'emotional release' (familiar from Herzog's pioneering study (1944) of radio soap operas of thirty years ago) appeared in connection with *The Dales* radio serial. Only two linked items of response can bear this meaning – 'Sometimes I think "I wish that were me"', and 'Sometimes it makes me want to cry' – and probably it applies to only a minority of the audience for certain limited kinds of media material. Even so, the appropriate content may have been under-represented in the small sample of programmes studied, and additional evidence obtained in a follow-up study of the original sample of *The Dales* listeners seemed to confirm the presence of this kind of response. Thus, when fifty-five members of the sample were reinterviewed and asked directly if *The Dales* did provide an opportunity 'to relieve their feelings', sixteen answered affirmatively. The existence of this kind of reaction to books, films and plays is so familiar that it perhaps needs no further proof. More important is our wish to treat it as a form of 'diversion' and to distinguish it from an escape into a more desirable imaginary world or out of an oppressive reality.

Personal relationships

Two gratification types have been placed under this heading because they both refer to the viewer's relationships with other people – either real-life persons or media personalities. The 'companionship' category stands for a process whereby the audience member enters into a vicarious relationship with media personalities (fictional characters, entertainers, or presenters) as if he was on friendly terms with them, and as if they could stand in for real persons. Two perceptive observers have termed this tendency a 'para-social relationship' (Horton and Wohl, 1956). The clearest expression of the wish to use media in this way is represented in one of *The Dales* clusters, the most frequently endorsed item of which was 'It is good company when you're alone'. Some of the other related items were:

'The characters have become like close friends to me'
'It gives me something in common with other *Dales* listeners'
'I like the sound of the characters' voices in my house'

A familiar assumption about the mass media, and a phenomenon which will be within the experience of most people is attested to by the occurrence of this set of attitudes in relation to a programme which attracted a large number of solitary listeners, *The Dales*. What our evidence about this programme suggested, however, was that the companionship element was even stronger than is often supposed: the characters may become virtually real, knowable and cherished individuals, and their voices are more than just a comforting background which breaks the silence of an empty house. This point can be illustrated by some further data, relating this time to the TV serial, *Coronation Street*. In the course of interviewing the sample of viewers, an opportunity arose of asking respondents how they felt about a road crash which had occurred in the programme. Amongst the many replies demonstrating the ease with which fictional events are integrated into real life were a number relevant to the idea of substitute companionship: 'I'm sorry. I like all of them. Minnie's just like Auntie; you feel you know them. You know you feel as if they had been in a real accident and you'd like to do something for them'; or 'Shattered. I'm very upset. I hope they'll be all right'; and 'My wife was very upset. So was I. I hope they'll be all right.'

The category we have called 'social utility' is a disparate one, but would cover those uses of the media which are instrumental for social interaction with real people in familiar surroundings. Social utility here may refer to media use as a source of conversational material, as a subject of conversation in itself, as a common activity for a family or other group engaging, say, in viewing together, or as something that helps an individual to discharge a definite social role or to meet the membership requirements of one or more of his peer groups. The research literature includes a number of examples describing a 'coin of exchange' function served by the media in conversational and other social situations (Riley and Riley, 1951). One of the clearest illustrations from our own work is provided by many of the items included in the second cluster of responses to television quiz programmes:

'I look forward to talking about it with others'
'I like competing with other people watching with me'
'I like working together with the family on the answers'
'It brings the family together sharing the same interest'
'It is a topic of conversation afterwards'

And a prominent cluster in the analysis of television news-viewing located a somewhat more specific information-relaying use of television, grouping the following items:

'I like to be the first with the news so that I can pass it on to other people'
'It satisfies my sense of curiosity'
'Keeping up with the news gives you plenty to talk about'
'Somehow I feel more secure when I know what is going on'

Perhaps this category of media use provides the best support for our contention that the relationship between medium and audience is not one-sided and that the role and social situation of the viewer may help to govern his selection and response. It also serves to make plausible the view that the specific content of the media can be relatively unhelpful in predicting the grounds of audience response; consequently, categorization of content based on overt meaning may have a limited value in mass communications research. The 'meaning' of an example of viewing behaviour is not self-evident from knowledge of content alone, or of the social-demographic parameters of the audience.

Personal identity

The set of gratification types classified under this heading brings together ways of using programme materials to reflect upon or to give added salience to something important in the viewer's own life or situation. One such disposition – a use of television for what has been termed 'personal reference' – provided perhaps that most novel outcome of the exploratory research, for few previous uses and gratification studies have reported anything like it. This reflected a use of programme content to characterize or highlight for the viewer some feature of his own situation, character or life, past or present. For example, the dominant item of the first *Dales* cluster was worded 'The programme reminds me that I could be worse off than I am', while other items with which this was associated included:

'I can compare the people in the programme with other people I know'
'It reminds me of things that have happened in my own life'
'It sometimes brings back memories of certain people I used to know'

In addition, the first quiz cluster brought together a group of items which reflected the viewer's interest in rating his abilities by responding to the questions asked on the programmes and comparing his achievement with that of the performers. This orientation is reminiscent of the perspective of symbolic inter-actionism, according to which a central element in the world of every person is some notion of himself, and such a notion is formed in great part by looking at oneself through the eyes of others. Apparently, not only interpersonal exchanges but also mass communications can help some people to form or reassess impressions of their own 'selves'.

A second version of this concern of people to explore their own personal identity was distinguished from the first mainly by the kind of reflection that was evoked. In contrast to the more descriptive activities of classification and labelling subsumed under 'personal reference', the process of 'reality exploration' involved a use of programme content to stimulate ideas about certain problems which the viewer was experiencing, or might at some time experience, in his more immediate social environment. The *Dales* cluster which seemed to express this tendency included such items as : 'The people in *The Dales* sometimes have prob-lems that are like my own', and 'It sometimes helps me to understand my own life'. The emergence of a similar cluster from the *Saint* analysis – centering on the dominant item 'It provides food for thought' – was more surprising, since this series would seem to many observers to provide no more than a succession of wish-fulfilling fantasies. The result suggests that keen 'fans' of almost any kind of fictional content may regard it as a stimulus relevant to their own real-life problems.

Less surprisingly, amongst the appeals of television news, we located a small group of items which together indicated an empathic response to news viewing. This cluster separated out the following: 'It helps me realize my life is not so bad after all'; 'It helps me to understand some of the problems other people have'; 'It sometimes makes me feel sad'. While the allocation of this type of response between the categories of 'personal reference' and 'reality exploration' is uncertain, there is little doubt that news enters into the process of establishing and maintaining identity and of relating the self to the wider society.

The third gratification category under 'personal identity' in the typology, termed 'value reinforcement', is more or less self-explanatory. It locates the appeal to a viewer of a programme which upholds certain values that he also believes in. This particular mode of media–person interaction is most clearly illustrated by one of the *Dales* clusters, the dominant item of which, worded, 'It's nice to know there are families like the Dales around today', was linked with two others: 'It reminds me of the importance of family ties', and 'It puts over a picture of what family life should be like'. Two other instances of a value-reinforcing relationship involving broadcast material may be noted. One of these emerged from the quiz study where a set of items expressive of a positive attitude to self-improvement and educational values generally was picked out by the analysis. The second was also found in *Dales* study and involved a valuation of the serial as a programme for women, including in this assessment an appreciation of its gentility and moral respectability in contrast to other media content deemed to emphasize sex and violence.

Surveillance

We have no empirical basis for subdividing this category which has been labelled in accordance with Lasswell's original classification of media functions (1948), although further research might make this necessary. As one would expect, our own work shows it to have an important place in news viewing dispositions. One large cluster included the following items:

'Television news provides food for thought'
'It tells me about the main events of the day'
'I like to see how big issues are finally sorted out'
'I follow the news so I won't be caught unawares by price increases and that sort of thing'
'Watching the news helps me to keep an eye on the mistakes people in authority make'
'Television news helps me to make my mind up about things'

Although the meaning of this cluster seems similar to that of the 'reality exploration' category, its main thrust is directed elsewhere – more towards having some information and opinions about events in the wider world of public affairs than towards stimuli for reflecting upon a set of more immediately experienced personal problems. In fact this very distinction was preserved in the analysis itself, since another cluster of attitudes to the news conveyed just such a more personal emphasis.

Conclusions

Our intention has been to outline a framework for the systematic ordering of gratification data and (at this stage) to provide a basis for classifying viewer concerns according to their meanings, rather than their relative frequency of occurrence or salience to audience members. The interest of this typology, its provisional character notwithstanding, stems in our view from its basis in empirical evidence collected by similar methods from comparable samples of television viewers. The numerous earlier studies of audience 'gratifications' which have been reported in the literature could not so readily be treated as source material for a typology because of the diversity in time, place, culture, communication media, methods of study and characteristics of the populations studied. Nevertheless, many, if not all, the earlier findings seem amenable to incorporation into this or an enlarged schema.

As it stands, the typology has a number of evident weaknesses. It is probably incomplete, since it is based on the study of only a limited number of programme types, using rather small samples of respondents. Further evidence would presumably require an extension of its range and the addition of further sub-classifications. It also requires a good deal more validation, in respect both of the meaning attributed to discrete categories and of the distinctions drawn between category boundaries. In any case it is unlikely that any universally valid structure of media–person interactions could ever be erected on an empirical basis, since the phenomena in question are to some extent variable according to changes in audience experience and perception and also to changes in communication content and differences of social context. But there is no reason why, with further research along the reported lines, a good deal more precision could not be attained. Moreover, we would be surprised if more extensive inquiry, using the same methods, were to necessitate a fundamental revision of the pattern we have located and described.

The main implications for the problems discussed at the outset of this essay are also fairly self-evident. If the typology is accepted as approximating to the true state of affairs, then the escapist formula, as it has often been applied to the television viewing experience, is clearly inadequate. For one thing the motives and satisfactions to which the term 'escape' has customarily been applied are far from exhaustive of audience orientations. Although we have grouped an important set of interactions under the heading of 'diversion' in our typology, it is clear that in many people these coexist with several other very important kinds of expectation and outlook. (Whether there is, nevertheless, a type of person who more single-mindedly seeks 'diversion' from broadcasting, how numerous is the group of like-minded viewers to which he belongs, and by what psychological and social forces he is driven, remain, of course, as topics for investigation by means of research mounted on a larger scale than the studies that have so far been undertaken at Leeds).

Second, the relationship between content categories and audience needs is far less tidy and more complex than most commentators have appreciated. It is not just that most popular programmes are multi-dimensional in appeal. It is also the case that we have no single scale by which we can reliably attach a value to any given content category. Given the heterogeneity of materials transmitted over the broadcast media, not only is one man's meat another man's poison, but one man's source of escape from the real world is a point of anchorage for another man's place in it, defining or underlining certain features of his personality, of the problems he has encountered in daily living, and of the values he adheres to. There is neither a one-to-one correspondence between communication content and audience motivation, nor any such correspondence between the place on a presumed scale of cultural worth to which programme material may be assigned (according to prevailing standards of aesthetic judgement) and the depth of meanings that may be drawn from them by many of their most keen attenders.

And third, the supports of any sweepingly dismissive attitude to the popular viewing experience tend to crumble in so far as the predominently escapist interpretation of its meaning is successfully challenged. Of course mass communications research is still unable to shed much light on the lasting contributions made by time spent viewing television, but at least much of what they look for no longer seems quite so ignoble as depicted in the light of the escapist perspective.

But why should so many of the common assumptions about the television audience which were outlined on earlier pages have proven to be at odds with the evidence? Several explanations suggest themselves. An obvious one is the paucity in the past of the kind of data that might have better informed the views of critics and commentators. In addition, many vocal commentators are culturally disposed to adopt a superior attitude towards a popular medium like television, perhaps supposing that people deprived of the richness and diversity of the communication materials made available by literature, the arts, the specialist press and personal association with educated people, must simply go without altogether. In reality, people who, for whatever reason, lack access to multiple communication sources are much less functionally specific in their use of television; for them it is much more of an all-purpose medium than for the kinds of special population groups from which many critics and students of the mass media tend to be drawn. Finally, one must point to the dominance in television content of material which, on the face of it, is oriented to escape and diversion and which is often represented as such by its presenters because they believe that this will help to attract larger audiences. If one assumes a one-to-one relationship between the overt category of content and the kind of response it elicits, and if one also assumes a determining power in the media to shape audience response beyond what evidence and theory warrants, then the escapist interpretation becomes virtually inevitable. In effect, we have returned to the earlier point at which we noted a strong element of self-validation in prevalent images of the mass audience. The research we have described should pose a challenge to closed ways of thinking about mass communications. The typology which has emerged from it should provide a stimulus to further studies of the place of television in the lives of members of its audience.

References

BAILYN, L. (1959), 'Mass media and children', *Psychol. Monogr.* vol. 71, pp. 1–48.

HERZOG, H. (1940), 'Professor Quiz: A gratification study', in P. F. Lazarsfeld (ed.), *Radio and the Printed Page*, Duell, Sloan and Pearce.

HERZOG, H. (1944), 'What do we really know about daytime serial listeners', in P. F. Lazarsfeld and F. N. Stanton (eds.), *Radio Research, 1942–1943*, Duell, Sloan and Pearce.

HORTON, D., and WOHL, R. (1956), 'Mass communication and para-social interaction', *Psychiat.*, vol. 19, pp. 215–219.

JONES, D. B. (1942), 'Quantitative analysis of motion picture content', *Pub. Opinion Q.*, vol. 6, pp. 411–28.

KATZ, E., and FOULKES, D. (1962), 'On the uses of the mass media as "escape": clarification of a concept', *Pub. Opinion Q.*, vol. 26, pp. 372–88.

KLAPPER, J. T. (1960), *The Effects of Mass Communication*, Free Press.

KRACAUER, S. (1960), *Theory of Film*, Oxford University Press.

LASSWELL, H. D. (1948), 'The structure and function of communication in society', in L. Bryson (ed.), 1964, *The Communication of Ideas*, Institute for Religious and Social Studies, New York.

LOWENTHAL, L. (1950), 'Historical perspectives of popular culture', *Amer. J. Sociol.* vol. 55, pp. 323–32.

McKENNEL, A. C. (1970), 'Attitude measurement: use of coefficient alpha with cluster or factor analysis', *Sociol.* vol. 4, pp. 227–45.

McQUITTY, L. L. (1957), 'Elementary linkage analysis', *Educ. Psychol. Measurement*, vol. 17, pp. 207–29.

MERTON, R. K., and LAZARSFELD, P. F. (1948), 'Mass communication, popular taste and organized social action', in L. Bryson (ed.), *The Communication of Ideas*, Institute for Religious and Social Studies, New York.

POWDERMAKER, H. (1950), *Hollywood: The Dream Factory*, Little, Brown & Co.

RILEY, J., and RILEY, M. W. (1951), 'A sociological approach to communications research', *Pub. Opinion Q.* vol. 15, pp. 445–60.

SARGENT, L., and STEMPEL, G. H. III (1968), 'Poverty, alienation and mass media use', *Journalism Q.*, vol. 45, pp. 324–6.

SCHRAMM, W. (1949), 'The nature of news', *Journalism Q.*, vol. 26, pp. 359–69.

SCHRAMM, W., LYLE, J., and PARKER, E. B. (1961), *Television and the Lives of our Children*, Oxford University Press.

SMYTHE, D. W. (1954), 'Reality as presented by television', *Pub. Opinion Q.*, vol. 18, pp. 143–56.

STEINER, G. (1963), *The People Look at Television*, Knopf.

8 Karl Erik Rosengren and Swen Windahl

Mass Media Consumption as a Functional Alternative

Published for the first time in this volume

In the first, theoretical, part of this paper, a series of typologies of individuals' mass media behaviour, mass media content and functions are established and related to each other. Earlier concepts such as escape and fantasy are expressed in terms of these typologies. In the second and empirical part of the paper the focus is narrowed down to a special type of relations between the mass media and their public, sometimes called para-social interaction (PSI). Results from an exploratory empirical study are presented, in which PSI is related to indices of interaction potential, actual interaction and amount of mass media consumption. Finally, some suggestions for further research are made.

I

Studies of the relationship between the mass media and their audiences or society at large are often divided into two different kinds: effect studies and so-called uses and gratifications studies. Uses and gratifications studies are usually said to imply a functional approach. The functions of the media and their usage may be looked upon from the point of view of the individual or from that of society. Many functions, broad and narrow, have been suggested, discussed and sometimes even measured: socialization, recreation, escape, information, etc. (see Wright, 1959, pp. 16–23; Müller, 1970, pp. 60–70; Rosengren, 1971, pp. 67–9). Often a close relationship between media content and media function has been argued or taken for granted, but it seems as if there is now a growing consensus that almost any type of content may serve practically any type of function.

Our aim in this paper is to investigate a special family of media functions for the individual. We are trying to relate a certain type of gratification to a certain type of audience characteristic. Underlying this attempt is the conviction that sooner or later mass media research must cease using raw demographic variables for its independent variables, and simply amount of consumption for its dependent variable. Instead, various sociological and social psychological variables should be introduced as independent or intervening variables, while the dependent variable, the mass media consumption, should be qualitatively differentiated into various types of consumption. Before presenting our version of this programme, we must first discuss some relations between the individual, his needs and his possibilities to satisfy these needs in various ways.

We all have the most various types of needs. Suppose that we are interested in the study of one special, fairly well defined need.[1] Suppose there is more than one way of satisfying this need, ways numbering 1, 2, 3,... n. These are functional alternatives, one of which may, but not necessarily must, stand out as the natural one – for biological, psychological or cultural reasons.[2] Let us call this alternative 'way 1'. The possibilities to use way 1 of need satisfaction are supposed to vary on the individual and environmental levels. (Environment is here taken to include all extra-individual variables: social-psychological, social and societal.) When his individual and/or environmental possibilities to use this way of need satisfaction are small or even non-existent, the individual tends to satisfy the same need by means of one or more of the functional alternatives offered by society and its culture, ways 2, 3,... n.

Given these assumptions, a typology of possibilities for need satisfaction may be established. Individual and environmental possibilities for need satisfaction in way 1 may each be divided into satisfactory and non-satisfactory, which gives us a typology of four cases.

1. We loosely equate need with drive. In many or most cases we are probably thinking of acquired drive: 'a motive, need, or source of motivation (rarely defined) that is a product of learning' (Brown, 1968, p. 280).
2. Merton (1963, p. 34 *passim*). The arguments of the rest of this paper hold true even if the functional alternatives are equivalent, so there is no more or less self-evident 'way 1' among them.

Once the possibilities are organized in this way the four cells of the typology may be seen as the values of a new variable, *degree of dependence on the functional alternatives*. When an individual has satisfactory individual and environmental possibilities to satisfy the need in way 1, he is only to a small degree dependent on the functional alternatives. When he has non-satisfactory possibilities to satisfy the need in this way, he is very dependent on the alternatives. Cells 2 and 3 may be seen as intermediary cases, possibly resulting in the same intermediary degree of dependence on functional alternatives for need satisfaction.

		environmental possibilities to find satisfaction in a given way:	
		satisfactory	non-satisfactory
individual possibilities to find satisfaction in a given way:	satisfactory	1	2
	non-satisfactory	3	4

Figure 1 Typology of possibilities to satisfy a given need in a given way

As an example, let us take the need for social interaction, which we trust to be fairly general, demanding some capacities of the individual (e.g. a certain degree of extroversion, empathy and socialization) and of his environment (e.g. someone to interact with). Also, there is a 'natural' way of satisfying the need: face-to-face interaction with real, living human beings; and there are functional alternatives for the satisfaction of the same need, for instance, writing letters, reading books, or attending to such mass media as radio, television, newspapers, magazines.[3]

A well socialized person, high on extroversion and empathy, has satisfactory individual possibilities to satisfy his need for social interaction in the natural way, way 1, i.e. by means of interaction with real human beings. If he also has partners and other prerequisites (time, for instance), his environmental

3. 'There is good reason to consider this *basic drive for contact* the most important factor in keeping all communication in operation' (Nordenstreng, 1969, p. 254).

possibilities may also be said to be satisfactory, and, by definition, his dependence on such functional alternatives as reading books or listening in will be low (cell 1).

The highly introverted person, on the other hand, low on empathy, whose socialization leaves much to be desired, may be said to have non-satisfactory possibilities on the individual level to satisfy his need for social interaction in way 1. If his environment is equally lacking in this respect, he will be very dependent on such functional alternatives as may be offered, for instance, by the mass media (cell 4). And now let us continue our theoretical argument.

When we considered the suggested typology from the point of view of the individual and his relations to the functional alternatives, we arrived at the variable 'degree of dependence'. But one might equally well look at the typology from the angle of the functional alternatives and their relations to way 1. These relations may be seen as defined by the possibilities to satisfy the given need in way 1. That is, for each of the four cells of the typology of possibilities presented in Figure 1, we will get a special relationship of the functional alternatives to way 1. In this way some of the terms used in the debate may be given a somewhat more precise meaning.[4] This is done in figure 2.

1 supplement	2 complement
3 complement	4 substitute

Figure 2 Relations of functional alternatives to way 1, as defined by possibilities of satisfying the given need in way 1 (see Figure 1)

Figure 2, then, implies a suggestion for a more precise terminology. The terms themselves, of course, are mere labels, and

4. An excellent overview of the literature on mass media as substitute, supplement, escape, etc., may be found in Lundberg and Hultén, 1968, ch. 9. Lundberg and Hultén refer to well-known works by, for instance, Bailyn, Berelson, Hemmelweit, Riley and Riley, Schramm, Steiner, and also to some less-known pieces of research.

could be changed without much ado. Nevertheless, it seems to us that when there are satisfactory individual and environmental possibilities to use way 1, a functional alternative is precisely a supplement. (See Webster's *Dictionary of Synonyms:* '*Supplement* implies an addition to something relatively complete'.) When neither of these possibilities is satisfactory or even existent, the functional alternative may with some justification be called a substitute for way 1. (See Webster's *Dictionary of Synonyms:* '*Substitute:* . . . surrogate, makeshift, stopgap'.) A complement is what a functional alternative is when there are individual but not environmental (or environmental but not individual) possibilities of satisfying the need in way 1. (See Webster's *Dictionary of Synonyms:* '*Complement* . . . implies a completing'.) It should be pointed out that the labels are by no means intended to be evaluative, although, because of the paucity of the language, we have had to choose labels some of which sound nicer than others. This is in spite of the fact that all functional alternatives may serve in each of the four cells; that is, one man's substitute may very well be another man's supplement. Thus, the same functional alternative to actual social interaction – say, a TV play – may be either a supplement, a complement, or a substitute, depending on the circumstances.

1 change	2 compensation
3 escape	4 vicarious experience

Figure 3 Motives for seeking functional alternatives, as defined by possibilities of satisfying the given need in way 1 (see Figure 1)

The functional alternative may be sought by the individual for various reasons or motives. We believe that these motives should also preferably be defined in terms of the individual's possibilities to use way 1 for need satisfaction. So again we use the four cells of the typology of Figure 1, this time to distinguish between four types of motives (that is, here we find it meaningful to differentiate between the two intermediary cases). This is done in Figure 3.

Like Figure 2, Figure 3 implies a suggestion for a more precise terminology. Again the terms are but labels and could be changed without much consequence to our argument. But all the same we find them meaningful, at least to a degree. It is meaningful, we think, to assume that the man who has large individual and environmental possibilities to satisfy a given need in a given way is motivated by a wish for change when seeking functional alternatives to the first way of satisfaction. A man, on the other hand, who as an individual perfectly well could avail himself of the given way of finding satisfaction but whose environment offers no possibility to do so, such a man may with some justification be said to seek compensation in a functional alternative for what society denies him. The less talented or gifted, without individual possibilities for need satisfaction in the given way, but living – as far as our way 1 of satisfaction is concerned – in a world of plenty, may be seen as seeking escape from his frustrating situation. And the individual, finally, who has no possibilities of his own and is offered none from his environment either, his experience in this respect obviously will be vicarious. (To stick to our interaction example: this is the poorly socialized youngster without friends, who turns to the mass media, seeking a substitute – vicarious experience – for what his individual and environmental situation denies him.)

Starting from a typology of possibilities for need satisfaction (large and small individual and environmental possibilities for satisfaction in a given way), continuing by way of a new variable with three or four values (degree of dependence on functional alternatives) and a typology of functional alternatives (supplement, complement, substitute), we ended up with a typology of motives for seeking functional alternatives (change, compensation, escape, vicarious experience). How do we use all these concepts, the reader may rightly ask.

In principle they could be used whenever a social scientist is investigating individuals with needs that may be satisfied in a way that demands individual and social or societal resources of some kind, at the same time as there are other ways of finding satisfaction – the functional alternatives. In this paper we will apply the argument to the need for social interaction, which we have already used a couple of times for illustrative purposes.

This is hardly the first paper that has been devoted to the problem of mass media and the need for interaction. What one experiences, approaching the subject, is rather a feeling of *embarras de richesses*, and the embarrassment is caused not least by the richness of the terminological florilegium of the subject. There is hardly a dearth of terms like escape, substitute, compensation, fantasy, vicarious experience, etc. Before trying to express some of the thoughts hidden behind the terms, let us, however, introduce still another typology, pertaining to the special need on which we have now focused our attention: the need for interaction.

Interaction is a special type of relation between individuals. Another one is identification. If the first may be roughly determined as mutual stimulation and response, the other may be equalled for our purposes with the act of imagining oneself to be in the place of another person.[5] Stretching these somewhat elastic definitions, both relations may be said to exist also between a real human being and an individual – an 'actor' – of the mass media world: the hero or anti-hero of the TV play or the magazine story, the well-known columnist of the newspaper, the disc-jockey of the radio programme. At least this is what has been contended in more than one investigation about uses and gratifications of the mass media. Identification, of course, in these cases may be highly temporary and shallow, existing, perhaps, only during the fleeting moments of a mass media scene of heightened tension or relief. Interaction must be imaginary (the audience partaking only imaginarily in the action), one-sided or mutual only in a very special way (for instance, an entertainer tells a joke and then pauses, to let the far-off audience laugh).

The two kinds of relations – identification and interaction – may be used to construct a typology of relations between a real individual and one or more 'actors' of the mass media (Figure 4).

This fourfold Table gives us four types of relation. We label them from the point of view of the public and call the relation contained within cell 1 *detachment*. (From the point of view of the 'actor' we might have called it 'lack of rapport', for instance.) This is the case when the individual neither identifies

5. See Theodorson and Theodorson (1970) and also, among others, Emery (1959), Kelman (1961) and the literature cited by these authors.

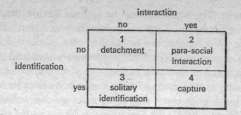

Figure 4 Typology of relations between audience and actors of mass media

nor interacts with any actor of the mass media content he is consuming.[6]

The relation of cell 2 we call *para-social interaction*, borrowing the term from an imaginative and insightful paper by Horton and Wohl (1956). This type of relation is treated at some length later in this paper. In short it denotes the interaction with somebody of the mass media world more or less as if he were present in person, without losing even momentarily one's identity. The mutuality of this type of interaction is of a very special sort.

The relation of cell 3 we believe is very rare or virtually non-existent in reality. We feel it is rather difficult to identify with somebody of the mass media content consumed, without at the same time interacting with the rest of the cast. But especially in the case of a one-man show, or when one person or role is very dominating, identification without interaction may, of course, occur. We have named this type of relationship *solitary identification*.

The relation of cell 4 we call *capture*. This is the opposite of the relation of cell 1: the individual both identifies with one or more of the 'actors' and also interacts with one or more other actors of the mass medium he is attending to. The interaction, of course, is imaginary.

The four types of relationship may be seen as forming the values of a new variable, which we prefer to call *degree of*

6. Note the related concept of 'adult discount', introduced in Dysinger and Rucknick (1933) and Blumler, Brown and McQuail (1970, p. 31).

involvement. The variable may be seen as having three values, that is, we prefer to collapse as before the two intermediate cases into one. We suggest the possibility of a positive correlation between degree of dependence as defined above and degree of involvement. The more dependent one is on one or more of the mass media as purveyors of functional alternatives to real inter-action, the higher one's degree of involvement would tend to be (see Turner, 1958). We also hypothesize a positive correlation between degree of involvement and amount of consumption: the higher the degree of involvement, the larger the mass media consumption. In both cases the relationship probably is mutual or interdependent (see Zetterberg, 1965, pp. 72 ff.).

We believe that irrespective of degree of dependence on the mass media, irrespective of motives and degree of involvement, the need for interaction (and, indeed, all needs that may be satisfied, in one way or another, by the mass media) may be satisfied by almost any type of media content. But this does not mean that we must expect no correlation at all between prefer-ence for, and consumption of, certain types of media content on the one hand, and degree of dependence, motives for seeking the functional alternative of the news media, or degree of in-volvement, on the other. Therefore, our argument should be connected with a typology of content.

Again, we resort to a fourfold typology, obtained this time by cross-tabulating the two concepts of fictitiousness and informa-tiveness (Figure 5). We take it for granted that it is possible to distinguish between fictional and non-fictional media content, although we are of course aware of the fact that there must be borderline cases. Informative media content to us means such media content that by the communicator (yet another tricky concept!) is intended to convey explicit and concrete information of some sort.

The figure shows what types of content items we feel should be placed in the various cells, and we do not have to enlarge upon that any more, although we freely admit that the typology is primitive indeed and needs elaboration. We think that a better version of a media content typology of this kind (i.e. content seen from the point of view of the medium or the communicator) should ultimately be correlated with a typology of the kind suggested by Emmett (content seen from the point of view of the consumer) (1968). However, in this paper we will have to let suffice with the typology just offered.

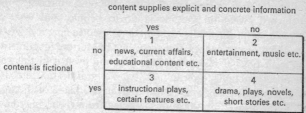

content supplies explicit and concrete information

		yes	no
content is fictional	no	1 news, current affairs, educational content etc.	2 entertainment, music etc.
	yes	3 instructional plays, certain features etc.	4 drama, plays, novels, short stories etc.

Figure 5 Typology of media content

In analogy with our previous strategy we may now see our four types of media content as values of a new variable, *degree of reality proximity of media content*. Content in cell 1, being non-fictional and supplying explicit and concrete information, is closer to reality, we feel, than content in cell 4, being fictional and non-informative, the contents of cells 3 and 4 coming in between these two extremes.

Let us remark here, parenthetically, that we are not unaware of the fact that we have not defined 'reality' at all. Starting from another set of explicit or implicit evaluations than those that form the implicit platform of this paper, it is very easy to arrive at a different conception of reality and consequently at a differ-ent ordering of the cells on the variable 'degree of reality proximity'. Thus we would not quarrel if anybody suggested that at least some dramas and novels are very close to reality indeed – 'reality' in a certain sense of the word, and 'close' in a certain sense of the word, that is.

Accepting our definition of the variable 'degree of reality proximity' we could correlate it with the variable 'degree of dependence' and 'degree of involvement' as earlier defined, and our hypothesis would be that high degree of dependence and involvement would tend to go together with preference for and consumption of media content with a low degree of reality proximity, both identification and interaction being easier to establish with this type of content. As before, we believe that the hypothesized correlations probably represent a mutual or inter-dependent relationship.

Finally, a word or two should be said about the effects of mass media consumption. As a rule, effect studies and functional studies are seen as belonging to two different approaches. The catchword 'what do the media do to people, and what do people do with the media' is sometimes used to characterize the two different approaches. But according to Merton, functions are a certain type of effect (1963, p. 51), and even if in this case one takes functions to mean uses, types of gratification, etc., it is quite possible to ask what effect a given use made of the mass media, or a given gratification obtained from them, may have. Thus we are convinced that sooner or later the two traditions must merge.

Waiting for such a merger it is urgent that effect arguments be as sophisticated as possible. However, it seems that it is not possible to be very sophisticated at the present stage of mass communication research. A minimum requirement would be to distinguish between long-term and short-term effects, and between effects on the individual and on society or parts of society. It is to be expected that effects of mass media consumption should vary not only with amount of consumption, but also with degree of dependence, motives for seeking the functional alternatives offered by the mass media, degree of involvement and degree of reality proximity of the content consumed. Consequently, one should try to heed variables such as these. Also, evaluations should be kept out of the argument as much and for as long as possible, so that they may be made with greater precision, and perhaps, greater weight, when at last they really are made.

Having covered within the narrow frames of a few pages the ground from degree of dependence on the mass media as func-tional alternatives to possible effects of mass media consumption under a series of varying circumstances, we are perhaps wise in trying to make our suggestions somewhat more clear. We will do this by means of expressing earlier results and arguments in terms of the typologies presented in the paper. We will choose three examples: the concept of para-social interaction presented by Donald Horton and Richard Wohl, the concept of escape as clarified by Elihu Katz and David Foulkes, and Wilbur Schramm's and his associates' two twin concepts of deferred and immediate reward, fantasy and reality-oriented content. It is obvious that in a page or two we can do less than full justice to all these concepts. Our aim is not an assessment or a review of earlier work in the field, but only to make our own contribution better with the help of earlier works that have proved to be pathbreaking, in one way or the other.

More than twenty years ago Wilbur Schramm presented his idea of immediate and deferred reward by means of mass media content, especially the news, and twelve years later he and his associates refined and developed the conception to encompass also the notion of fantasy and reality-oriented content (Schramm, 1949; Schramm, Lyle and Parkes, 1961; Pietilä, 1969).

Referring to Freud's 'pleasure' and 'reality' principles, Schramm and his associates maintain that there are two 'main strands of mass communication', which they 'label . . . with the terms *fantasy* and *reality*' (Schramm, Lyle and Parker, 1961). Fantasy makes for immediate, reality for delayed, reward.

In general, westerns, crime drama, popular music, and variety shows belong chiefly with fantasy, whereas news, documentaries, interviews, public affairs programs, and educational television are chiefly in the domain of reality materials (1961, p. 64).

The strands, then, are made up by differential content offering differential rewards. Fantasy-oriented content may be expressed in the terms of our content typology as non-informative, fictional or non-fictional content, i.e. content with a low to medium reality proximity. According to our arguments, the consumption of such content tends to go together with a high degree of dependence on the mass media as functional alternatives and with a high degree of involvement. Such content, then, tends to be sought as complement or substitute, for the compensation, escape or vicarious experience it may offer, under relations that may be described as para-social interaction, solitary identification, or capture, all these terms being used as defined earlier in this paper.

Reality-oriented content, on the other hand, in our terms, may be expressed as informative, usually non-fictional content, i.e. content with a high degree of reality proximity. To some – unknown – extent, of course, such reality-proximate content is not at all used for interactional purposes, as a functional alternative to real-life interaction. Rather it is used as a source of information, i.e. it is used just for what it is probably intended. We do not know to what extent this is so, but the empirical material accumulating over the years suggests that very often reality-proximate content is used for quite other purposes than the one for which it is said to be communicated.

Using results from other investigations than that of Schramm and his associates, Schneider and Lysgaard have generalized the concepts of deferred and immediate rewards into two different life-styles, assumed to be characteristic of the working and middle classes respectively: immediate and deferred gratification (1953). Without denying at all the validity of this generalization we are content here to make clear the four motives or functions suggested by us to be operative at various levels of dependence on the mass media, as functional alternatives should all be thought of as immediate rewards. Deferred gratification is obtained from the mass media not when their content is seen as a supplement, a complement, or a substitute and consumed for a change, for compensation, for escape or vicarious experience, but as a source of knowledge or information, i.e. when informative, non-fictional content is consumed, not as an alternative but for its own sake.

If we had more pages at our disposal, it would be possible, we believe, to express the more detailed empirical results reached by Schramm and his associates concerning television in the lives of our children in terms of our chain of typologies. For instance, it would be tempting to spell out chapters six and seven of that interesting book in such a way. It is probable that this would lead to a refinement of our typologies, and maybe also to a better understanding of the empirical results. But we refrain from this exercise, since we have already shown that the two 'strands' of Schramm and his associates may be explicated in terms of our typologies. Such an explication may seem only to make the argument more detailed and, perhaps, less elegant and more pedestrian. If so, we can only hope that it also makes it stand out in greater clarity, so that the insights into the complex phenomenon that it represents may be made still better use of. Now, let us turn to other outstanding contributions in the uses and gratifications tradition.

Expressing the arguments of critics of popular culture, Katz and Foulkes present a chain of key concepts within the area of mass communication:

Everyday roles in modern society give rise to tensions or *drives* (stemming from alienation or felt deprivation) which lead on to *high exposure* to mass media with its characteristic *context* (e.g. the movie palace) and its characteristic *content* (e.g. fantasy) from which, via *psychological processes* – such as identification, one can obtain compensatory gratification and, perhaps as an unanticipated *consequence*, 'narcotization' of other role obligations (1962, pp. 379 ff).

The key concepts of this explication are roles, drives, exposure, context, content, psychological processes, compensatory gratification and consequence. They fit in neatly with our own chain of typologies and variables. As a matter of fact, the latter may be seen as an attempt at explication of these and similar arguments, which, of course, form one of the starting points of this paper. Presenting the key concepts of the Katz and Foulkes paper and our own typologies and variables side by side gives a clear picture of the close parallellity of the two paradigms.

Katz and Foulkes:	Rosengren and Windahl:
Roles	Note: degree of dependence, further down the list
Drives	Need for interaction
—	Degree of dependence on functional alternatives for need satisfaction, e.g. mass media
—	Typology of functional alternatives
—	Typology of motives for seeking functional alternatives
Exposure	Amount of consumption
Context	—
Content	Degree of reality proximity
Psychological processes	Degree of involvement
Compensatory gratification	Note: typology of motives, above
Consequence	Effects

It will be seen that we have only neglected context, while on the other hand we have filled in some lacunae between drives and exposure in the Katz and Foulkes schema. We have not been able to relate the concept of context to our line of argument. As a matter of fact, we are not sure it is very relevant to it, although we recognize the possibility that in other arguments it may be of importance.

Continuing the comparison between the two columns, one notes that according to Katz and Foulkes, roles are seen as coming 'before' drives, while we have preferred to place our partly corresponding variable, degree of dependence, somewhat further down the list. This is due, among other things, to the fact that such dependence is to be seen as a characteristic of an individual, not of a role. The individual, of course, is acting within the frames of his bio-psychological and social possibilities, part of which is made up by the roles he is enacting. Thus, the degree of dependence is seen as determined by social variables, such as roles, *and* by biological and psychological variables. In fact, that is the way degree of dependence is defined.

One also notes a further difference between the two columns in that Katz and Foulkes have placed 'compensatory grati-fication' towards the end of their list, while we have our cor-responding typology of motives nearer the beginning. This differential location of partly identical concepts – compensatory gratification may be encompassed in our typology, and equated with compensation – is a reflection of a dilemma to be found in every study of goal-oriented behaviour: the goal, at the end of a chain of acts and processes, is one of the initiating factors of that chain.

It may be inferred from this confrontation that we do not agree with Katz and Foulkes 'that the ultimate referent of the term "escape" should have to do with the consequences of media usage' (1962, p. 380). On the contrary, we think that Katz and Foulkes have themselves made quite clear that escape is preferably to be seen as something of a goal, a value or a motive. This is in line with our typology of motives, where 'escape' is one among the four types of motives. The consequences, or effects, of having or seeking such a goal, value or motive may be various. They may be anticipated and intended, or unanticipated and unintended.

They may be anything but escape. They may be 'good' or 'bad'. They may be so in a short- or a long-term perspective, for the individual and/or for society, as Katz and Foulkes themselves tell us.

One potential, possibly 'bad' effect for the individual we may aptly call, with Katz and Foulkes, narcotization.[7] Thus the pursuit of escape may result in narcotization. It should not be forgotten, however, that sometimes narcotization may be the best of several 'bad' solutions to a difficult problem. Thus it will be seen that these are not only terminological questions. Terms are not always unimportant; sometimes they may be leading our thoughts in the right or in the wrong direction. On the whole we feel that the paper of Katz and Foulkes is potentially fruitful in this respect. We also feel that it is only by explicit confrontations between these and similar paradigms that the study of uses and gratifications may hope at long last to reach some sort of a take-off stage leading into faster growth and consequently into the cumulation of valid and relevant knowledge about the gratifications sought in and obtained from the use of the mass media.

One of the pieces of research quoted with explicit approval by Katz and Foulkes is that of Horton and Wohl (1956).[8] What Horton and Wohl call para-social interaction (PSI) is a special case of interaction, a 'similacrum of conversational give and take', between a certain type of mass media communicators, called *personae* (mainly entertainers) and their public. The give and take is said to be characterized on the part of the *persona* by an anticipatory adjustment to the supposed response of the public, and on the public's part, by actually making the supposed response something more than mere observation, namely,

to benefit by his / the *persona's* / wisdom, reflect on his advice, sympathize with him in his difficulties, forgive his mistakes, buy the products that he recommends, and keep the sponsors informed of the esteem in which he is held (1956, p. 219).

In short, the public is supposed to interact with the *personae* – the quiz-masters, the announcers, the interviewers, etc. This quasi

7. Katz and Foulkes (1962, p. 380). The term 'narcotization', of course. has been used in various ways, e.g. Lazarsfeld and Merton (1957, pp. 457–73).

8. See also Horton and Strauss (1957).

interaction is called para-social interaction, distinguished from the relationship that may sometimes exist between the performers of a drama and their public mainly by the lack of identification with any of the roles performed on the stage or on the screen. The public all the time maintains their identity, necessarily so, for now and then it is 'called upon to make the appropriate responses which are complementary to those of the persona' (1956, p. 219).

Horton and Wohl have many interesting things to say on the subject, and the reader is referred to their stimulating paper for further information. We must stay content here by observing that what Horton and Wohl have so eloquently described is the intermediary value of our variable degree of involvement, being characterized by interaction but lack of identification with one or more of the actors in the mass media. This value is conveniently labelled para-social interaction, in accordance with the suggestion made by Horton and Wohl.

According to our hypothesis, this degree of involvement should tend to be found when degree of dependence is intermediate and mass media are used as a complement to real interaction, in order to obtain compensation for or escape from a societal or individual situation characterized by certain, sometimes mild, sometimes strong, deficiences.

Thus the concept of para-social interaction as introduced by Horton and Wohl fits excellently into our various typologies, and that is no coincidence, for actually it was this concept that set us to work.

Having by now confronted our conceptual outline or paradigm with the arguments, concepts and paradigms of Schramm and his associates, of Katz and Foulkes, of Horton and Wohl, we proceed to another confrontation of no less importance, the confrontation between our theoretical constructions and empirical reality.

II

The empirical work connected with this paper was carried through while we were working out the theoretical approach we have just presented. Consequently, when collecting the empirical data, we could not take the later developments of our theoretical work into consideration – actually, some of these developments came after the data collection was finished. Therefore, we have sometimes spun too fine a web of theories for the data at hand. Nevertheless, we do not hesitate to combine data and theory; the whole field may be said to be in a preliminary stage, characterized less by systematic testing of hypotheses than by an exploratory search for fruitful hypotheses.[9]

Our data come from two surveys made on random samples from the adult population of two middle-sized towns in southern Sweden, Helsingborg and Växjö. The samples were drawn by means of systematic sampling from the population registers of the two towns. The surveys were carried out by trained interviewers (students of sociology) in 1969 and 1970, respectively. The proportions of interviews actually made were 69 per cent and 86 per cent, the number of interviews three hundred and sixty-five and four hundred and thirty-six respectively. There is no reason to suppose that there is any significant bias in the two materials at hand. Besides, our aim is not to make a description.

The two materials were differently used. The earliest one, the Helsingborg material, was used to find out which of several variables were related to the variable of para-social interaction. The relations found were then investigated also in the second material. Relations found in both materials we assume to be worth looking closer at in further research.

In the theoretical part of our paper we arrived at the following hypothesis. There is a positive relationship between degree of dependence on functional alternatives on the one hand, degree of involvement, amount of consumption and degree of reality proximity of media content consumed, on the other. The last variable we did not measure empirically, for the general reason already touched upon. Each of the three other variables may be operationalized in several ways. We proceeded as follows.

Degree of dependence was theoretically defined as individual and environmental possibilities to interact face-to-face with real human beings. By individual possibilities we meant personality

9. When this paper was all but finished we got into our hands an excellent paper by Blumler, Brown and McQuail (1970). The operationalization of para-social interaction and related concepts used in that paper sometimes bears close resemblance to ours, which may be seen as an indication that further work along these lines may be fruitful.

traits and/or types like empathy, extroversion, etc. Unfortunately, we did not include any such measures in our empirical materials, for the simple reason that when we collected the data our theory did not encompass personality variables.

However, if our hypotheses stand a test using only part of the independent variable, *a fortiori* they should not be falsified, were the other part also included.

We decided to build a simple interaction potential index, a high value on which would correspond to a low degree of dependence. (If one has a high potential for real interaction, one is less dependent on functional alternatives.) Anyone wanting to interact, we feel, should possess a minimum of status, means and opportunity, and also a partner. The status is necessary to attract somebody willing to interact, the means and opportunities are necessary to be able actually to carry through the interaction, and a partner, of course, is the real *sine qua non*. Our index of inter- action potential, therefore, should be composed of three sub- indices, measuring status, means and opportunity for interaction, and partner availability. The actual operationalizations of status, opportunities and means and partner availability are admittedly crude, limited as they are by the available data. Here they are.

Status: sex and education. Men or educated (secondary education or more) are taken to have a higher status than women or un- educated.

Means and opportunities: having a car, or having more than average leisure time. People having a car, or having more than average leisure time we take to have means and opportunities for interaction.

Partner: being gainfully employed, or being married. (We equalled 'going steady' etc., with being married, while widows, widowers, divorcees and those unmarried who did not 'go steady' were lumped together in the other category.) If you are married or if you have a job you also have at least someone to interact with. Also, having one partner often leads to having more.

Each of the three sub-indices may vary between 0 and 2, since they are made up by the simple addition of two qualitative variables, each given the values 0 and 1, or of a qualitative and a quantitative variable, in which case we dichotomized the quantitative variable as close to the median as possible, and gave it values 0 and 1.

The final interaction potential index, then, composed of the three subindices added to each other, may vary between 0 and 6. The higher the value, the higher the interaction potential, and the smaller the degree of dependence on functional alternatives to real-life interaction. This is our main independent variable operationalized.

(We also considered for inclusion such variables as having relatives in the same town, having a heavy workload, having small children, but since these variables were not found to be related in any meaningful way to our main dependent variable, para-social interaction, we decided not to include them. Such a procedure, of course, would be meaningless, were our aim to test hypotheses. But it is not – it is to find suitable operationalizations of some concepts of the hypotheses presented in the first part of this paper.)

The dependent variables of our theory are three: degree of involvement, amount of consumption, and degree of reality-proximity of media content. The latter was defined too late to be included in our material, so it had to be left out. The other two we treated in the following way.

Degree of involvement according to our theoretical definition has three values: (a) detachment, (b) para-social interaction or solitary identification, and (c) capture. When collecting the data we distinguished only between two degrees of involvement, which we called detachment and para-social interaction.

We assume that the category of detachment as operationally defined coincides roughly with the theoretical value of detachment, while our operationalized PSI covers roughly both PSI, solitary identification and capture as theoretically defined.

Operationally, we proceeded as follows. For each of the four mass media of newspapers, radio, television and weeklies the respondents were asked what kind of media content they preferred. If they answered in personal terms (for instance, David Frost or Chief Ironside) or in terms of various question-and-advice columns or programmes, they were taken to belong to the

PSI category. If they answered in terms of types of programme or content (westerns, quiz-programmes, cartoons, debates, etc.) they were taken to belong to the detachment category. The reliability of the coding was measured and found to be satisfactory (98 per cent agreement).

Since the coding was done for each of the four mass media that we covered, we could construct a simple additive index of degree of involvement varying from 0 to 4, 0 being given to those individuals who on all media were classified in the detachment category, 4 to those who on all the media were classified as PSI.

This operational definition of degree of involvement does not fit in too badly with the theoretical definition, especially considering the fact that the latter was developed after the former. All the same, we are not very satisfied with the operationalization. Especially we are embarrassed by the fact that it is based partly upon the respondent's avowed preference for a certain type of media content, partly upon his tendency to answer in personal terms (a tendency which we suppose to be indicating a certain degree of involvement during the actual consumption of mass media content). In future research we hope to be able to present a better operationalization.

Amount of mass media consumption we measured in hours per week for each of the four media. Since the average number of hours spent per week varied strongly from medium to medium, it would not make much sense simply to add them, for that would have meant that radio, with its high average, would dominate heavily. Instead we gave each individual on each medium a value of either 0 or 1, depending upon whether his amount of consumption fell below or above the median. Then we added these values, ending up with an index of mass media consumption giving equal weight to each of the four media and varying between 0 and 4.

Thus we were equipped with at least provisional operationalizations of the three variables of degree of dependence (index of interaction potential), degree of involvement (index of parasocial interaction), amount of mass media consumption (index of total consumption).

This would be enough to cover our hypotheses, but we also

included a fourth variable, only implicitly contained within our hypotheses, namely, amount of actual interaction. The respondents were asked how many people they had a personal contact with (i.e. not a formal contact only) at their job during an average working week, Monday to Friday, and also how many personal friends they met outside work during an average working week. On each of the two variables, the respondent was classified as falling within quartiles 1–4, and when added, these values gave us an index of actual interaction varying from 2 to 8, or, as we prefer to express it, from 0 to 6, 6 standing for a high amount of actual interaction. (We also included in the questionnaires similar questions about interaction during the weekends, but on second thought we decided not to include them among our data. Presumably interaction during the weekend is less sensitive to such factors as leisure time, car ownership, being gainfully employed, etc. Therefore, one may expect less variation in actual interaction during the weekend.)

We have now presented the operationalizations of our key variables. Let us see how we can use them.

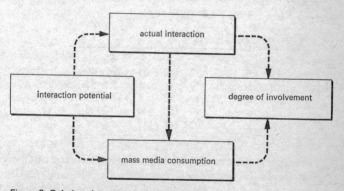

Figure 6 Relations between the four key variables

The assumed relations between the four variables of interaction potential, amount of actual interaction, amount of mass media consumption and degree of involvement may be visualized as in Figure 6 which may be used as a specification of our hypotheses from the theoretical part of the paper. The arrows stand for supposed causal relationships. At least some, possibly all, arrows should point in both directions, implying a mutual causal relationship, but we feel the directions indicated are dominant.

Table 1 Interaction potential and degree of involvement
(a) The Helsingborg material

| | | Interaction potential index | | | | | | |
		0–1 %	2 %	3 %	4 %	5 %	6 %	Total %
Degree of involvement index	0	17	15	28	35	43	58	30
	1	24	33	27	32	32	27	30
	2–4	59	52	45	32	25	15	39
	Total	100	100	100	99	100	100	99
	N	41	81	71	77	69	26	365

(b) The Växjö material

| | | Interaction potential index | | | | | | |
		0–1 %	2 %	3 %	4 %	5 %	6 %	Total %
Degree of involvement index	0	32	42	32	41	63	79	46
	1	31	29	40	41	29	7	35
	2–4	37	29	27	18	8	14	19
	Total	100	100	99	100	100	100	100
	N	19	41	102	141	119	14	436

The simple graphic model may be used to explicate some of the earlier theoretical arguments. For instance, the concept of narcotization, suggested by Katz and Foulkes and accepted by us as a possible effect (see p. 181), would be marked in the figure by a reversal of the arrows, indicating that a high degree of involvement might lead to increased mass media consumption, decreased actual interaction, and, ultimately, also to a decreased interaction potential, or, in the terms of Katz and Foulkes, to a 'negative feedback to one's everyday roles' (1962, p. 380).

Our crude empirical data do not allow even the illustration of such a complicated process, but they do highlight some of the relationships indicated by Figure 6. Let us start with the overall relationship between the two endpoints of the figure, interaction potential and degree of involvement. It may be studied in Tables 1(a) and 1(b).

Table 2 Interaction potential and actual interaction
(a) The Helsingborg material

| | | Interaction potential index | | | | | |
		0–1 %	2 %	3 %	4 %	5 %	6 %	Total %
Actual interaction index	0–1	85	77	52	44	30	31	54
	2–3	5	14	20	26	22	23	19
	4–6	10	9	28	30	48	46	27
	Total	100	100	100	100	100	100	100
	N	41	81	71	77	69	26	365

(b) The Växjö material

| | | Interaction potential index | | | | | |
		0–1 %	2 %	3 %	4 %	5 %	6 %	Total %
Actual interaction index	0–1	47	29	27	17	13	14	20
	2–3	42	49	37	45	39	29	41
	4–6	11	22	36	38	48	57	38
	Total	100	101	100	100	100	100	100
	N	19	41	102	141	119	14	436

The two tables express a clear relationship between interaction potential and degree of involvement. Among those who have a low interaction potential, it is much more usual also to have a high degree of involvement than it is among those who have a high interaction potential. The latter usually have a low degree of involvement. Also, the proportions rise (or fall) more or less continuously as we move from left to right along lines 1 and 3 of the two Tables. The relationship obtained is the expected one and may be seen as a first preliminary validation of the two crude indices. Thus the Table may be taken as an indication that a continued analysis may be worthwhile.

Table 3 **Various relationships between the key variables***

x	y	C_{xy}	
		Helsingborg material	Växjö material
1. IP	AI	0.31[+++]	0.23[+++]
2. IP	MMC	0.42[+++]	0.21[+++]
3. IP	I	0.24[+++]	0.25[+++]
4. AI	MMC	0.16[++]	0.09
5. AI	I	0.07	0.00
6. MMC	I	0.22[+++]	0.26[+++]

* As a measure of association between the various variables, we have used C (see Siegel, 1956, pp. 196–202). Note that C is a measure of association. It does not tell anything about the direction of the relationship. To obtain comparability, all Cs have been calculated on the basis of fourfold tables. Maximum C-value for a fourfold table is 0.71. This means that the correlations between the variables are stronger than the impression one may get from the figures of the table (the generally high levels of significance obtained in spite of the relatively small materials). A comparison between lines 3 and 1 on the one hand, Tables 1 and 2 on the other, may give a more detailed notion of the nature of the relationships expressed by the association coefficients. The plus-signs mark level of significance as given by the X^2-test: $+ = 0.05$, $++ = 0.01$, $+++ = 0.001$.

```
  IP = Interaction potential index
  AI = Actual interaction index
 MMC = Index of mass media consumption
   I = Involvement index
```

Now, let us look at interaction potential and actual interaction. Are the two variables related as they should be, according to our hypotheses? Tables 2(a) and 2(b) show that again there is a clear relationship, thus supplying further validation of the interaction potential index to the one obtained from Tables 1(a) and 1(b).

The rest of the relationships between the four key variables are presented in the form of association coefficients in Table 3, together with the corresponding coefficients for the two relationships of Tables 1 and 2. It will be seen that the two materials give much the same picture, although generally, the coefficients of the Växjö material tend to be somewhat lower than those of the Helsingborg material. (Note that our research design has made us exploit more chance variation in the Helsingborg material, see p. 183.)

A graphic representation of the results of Table 3 is given in Figure 7. The main difference from Figure 6, it will be seen, is that the arrow from actual interaction to degree of involvement has disappeared, while instead there is a new arrow from interaction potential to degree of involvement.

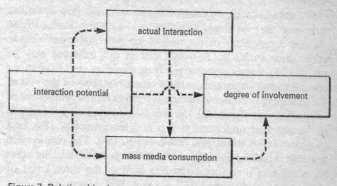

Figure 7 Relationships between the four key variables as obtained from Table 3

Let us take the relationship actual interaction–degree of involvement first. There seems to be no simple relationship between the two variables (Table 3, line 5). If we make various breakdowns – for instance, keep interaction potential or mass media consumption constant – and then calculate coefficients of associations for the partial tables thus obtained, the pattern is not consistent for the two materials. As might be expected, there seem to be various intricate patterns of interaction between the variables, but the two materials tell different stories as to the nature of this pattern. Probably this means that we have carried the analysis too far for our crude indices, simple measures and relatively small materials. Regardless of the differences between the coefficients of the two materials, however, the results suggest that the two variables of actual interaction and mass media consumption in a complicated interaction pattern relay part of the influence from interaction potential to degree of involvement. The further explication of the exact nature of these relationships must wait until we have better indices of at least some of our four key variables (see below).

From the relationship between actual interaction and degree of involvement, we have already moved to that between interaction potential and degree of involvement. We have said that part of the relationship that is found between these two variables (line 3, Table 3) may be seen as relayed by actual interaction and mass media consumption, although our two materials give dissimilar data here. But we would also like to know the influence of the various components of the interaction potential index on the other three variables. A rough idea of this influence may be obtained by keeping one of the three components of the index constant while investigating the relationship between the rest of the index and the other variables. We did so for the component of status (sex and education), i.e. interaction potential was reduced to 'means and opportunity' (car and leisure, see p. 184), and 'partner' (civil status and work, see p. 184). The relationship between this reduced index of interaction potential and the other variables was then investigated at each of the three levels of status that was discerned (0–1–2, see p. 185).

In both materials, the coefficients of association were heavily reduced, which indicates that status is an important, perhaps the most important, component of the interaction potential index. As a matter of fact, only scattered significant relationships remained, and these were not the same in the two materials. Again we concluded we had carried our analysis too far, and again we discontinued it. However, the reduction of the relationships was clear enough and must be heeded. Does interaction potential equal status – the rest of the index having practically no effect of its own? We can see two possibilities here.

One alternative is that the relationship between interaction potential and degree of involvement presented earlier in this paper is at least partially an artifact, caused by a tendency of high-status people (especially, perhaps, educated men) to express themselves in abstract, non-personal terms (see Schatzmann and

Strauss, 1955). This tendency would contaminate our index of degree of involvement, composed in part, it will be remembered, from the respondent's having answered in personal terms when asked about his mass media content preferences (see p. 186). This means that we may have to cleanse our degree of involvement index from this source of contamination.

Another alternative is that there may be qualitative as well as quantitative differences as to interaction. With status you have the option to initiate interaction. Without status, interaction to a large extent is imposed upon you. Imposed interaction probably is not as satisfactory as is self-initiated interaction. This would mean that our index of actual interaction, too, would have to be refined.

Thus, to continue our research, we need two conditions in the first place:

1. A better index of degree of involvement, not contaminated by a possible tendency to express oneself either abstractedly or in personal terms – or, alternatively, an index of this very tendency.

2. A better index of actual interaction, differentiating between imposed and self-initiated interaction.

As suggested in the theoretical part of the paper (see pp. 168, 183), we also need a third condition, namely,

3. An index of individual possibilities to interact face-to-face (empathy, extroversion, etc).

Provided with these indices, one might continue research into mass media consumption as a functional alternative to actual interaction.

References

BLUMLER, J. G., BROWN, J. R., and McQUAIL, D. (1970), *The Social Origins of the Gratifications Associated with Television Viewing*, mimeo.

BROWN, J. S. (1968), 'Acquired drives', *International Encyclopedia of the Social Sciences*, vol. 4, Macmillan.

DYSINGER, W. S., and RUCKNICK, C. A. (1933), *The Emotional Responses of Children to the Motion Picture Situation*, Macmillan.

EMERY, F. E. (1959), 'Psychological effects of the Western film: a study in television viewing, *Hum. Rel.*, vol. 12, pp. 195–229.

EMMETT, B. P. (1968), 'A new role for research in broadcasting', *Pub. Opinion Q.*, vol. 32, pp. 654–65.

HORTON, D., and STRAUSS, A. (1957), 'Interaction in audience-participation shows', *Amer. J. Sociol.*, vol. 62, pp. 579–87.

HORTON, D., and WOHL, R. R. (1956), 'Mass communication and para-social interaction', *Psychiat.*, vol. 19, pp. 215–29.

KATZ, E., and FOULKES, D. (1962), 'On the use of the mass media as 'escape': clarification of a concept', *Pub. Opinion Q.*, vol. 26, pp. 379 ff.

KELMAN, H. C. (1961), 'Processes of opinion change', *Pub. Opinion Q.*, vol. 25, pp. 57–78.

LAZARSFELD, P., and MERTON, R. K. (1957), 'Mass communication, popular taste and organized social action', in B. Rosenberg and D. M. White (eds.), *Mass Culture*, Free Press, pp. 457–73.

LUNDBERG, D., and HULTÉN, O. (1968), *Individen och Massmedia*, Stockholm, Norstedt & Soner (in Swedish).

MERTON, R. K. (1963), *Social Theory and Social Structure*, Free Press, pp. 34 ff.

MÜLLER, P. (1970), *Die Soziale Gruppe im Prozess der Massenkommunikation*, Ferdinand Enke Verlag, pp. 60–70.

NORDENSTRENG, K. (1969), 'Consumption of mass media in Finland', *Gazette*, vol. 15, no. 4, pp. 249–59.

PIETILÄ, V. (1969), 'Immediate versus delayed reward in newspaper reading', *Acta Sociologica*, vol. 12, pp. 199–208.

ROSENGREN, K. E., (1971) 'Diffusion of news, the case of Sweden and Apollo 13', *Psykologiskt Forsvar*, vol. 51, Stockholm, Beredskapsnamnden for Psykologiskt forsvar, pp. 67–9, (mimeo).

SCHATZMAN, L., and STRAUSS, A. (1955), 'Social class and modes of communication', *Amer. J. Sociol.*, vol. 40.

SCHNEIDER, L., and LYSGAARD, S. (1953), 'The deferred gratification pattern: a preliminary study', *Amer. Sociol. Rev.*, vol. 18, pp. 142–9.

SCHRAMM, W. (1949), 'The nature of news', *Journalism Q.*, vol. 26.

SCHRAMM, W., LYLE, J., and PARKER, E. B. (1961), *Television in the Lives of our Children*, Stanford University Press.

SIEGEL, S. (1956), *Nonparametric Statistics*, McGraw-Hill.

THEODORSON, G. A., and THEODORSON, A. G. (1970), *A Modern Dictionary of Sociology*, Methuen.

TURNER, M. A. (1958), 'News-reading behavior and social adjustment', *Journalism Q.*, vol. 35, pp. 199–204.

WRIGHT, C. R. (1959), *Mass-Communication: A Sociological Perspective*, Random House.

ZETTERBERG, H. L. (1965), *On Theory and Verification in Sociology*, Bedminster Press, pp. 72 ff.

9 B. P. Emmett

The Television and Radio Audience in Britain

Published for the first time in this volume

Introduction

The Audience Research Department has for more than thirty years been undertaking scientifically designed research, mainly in the form of sample surveys, to provide the BBC with comprehensive information about the audience for broadcasting in the United Kingdom. The most familiar of its activities is the estimation of audience size, i.e. the provision of listening and viewing figures – what are often known as 'the ratings' – but at no time has it restricted itself to this. The BBC has consistently emphasized the equal importance it attaches to other forms of 'feedback' from its listeners and viewers, to studies of the way in which listeners and viewers react to the programmes they see and hear, to explorations of the effects produced by programmes, to surveys of the interests and tastes of the population, and so on. This article is restricted to audience-size statistics and closely related topics simply because this aspect of audience research lends itself to summarization in statistical form, whereas much of the other work, being concerned with individual broadcasts or with studies of particular categories of output such as 'the news' or 'serious music', does not.

Most of the statistics that follow are derived from the BBC's continuous Survey of Listening and Viewing in which, each day, some 2250 persons aged five and over, spread throughout the United Kingdom, are asked about their listening 'the day before'.

How many listeners and viewers?

In order to understand the way in which listening and viewing patterns have changed over the years, it is necessary to consider the extent to which the population of the United Kingdom has been equipped with radio and television sets to receive the various transmissions.

Throughout the twenty years covered by Table 1, virtually everyone in the United Kingdom has had access to a radio set – increasingly often more than one, though this is not shown in the Table. Listening on VHF is still confined to a minority, only a little over one person in three having a VHF set, and this proportion appears to be increasing only slowly. Stereo radio receivers are a rarity.

Television began its rapid spread early in the 1950s, reaching virtual saturation by 1965. Few of today's young adults had television when they were very young – it arrived as they were growing up. It is *their* children, today's toddlers, who can be considered the first true television generation in Britain.

The 'first generation' receivers, used by the earliest wave of British viewers, started becoming obsolescent towards the end of 1955, when Independent Television began its transmissions in 'Band III', for which new sets and aerials were required. The next technical development requiring new (or adapted) receivers was the beginning of transmission in the ultra high frequency (UHF) band, coinciding with the start of BBC-2 in 1964. The proportion of the population equipped with UHF sets and aerials and who can receive BBC-2 has been increasing steadily, reaching 60 per cent by mid-1971. More recently, since January 1968, the UHF transmissions of all three television channels have increasingly been made in colour. The spread of colour receivers is only beginning, the proportion able to view in colour reaching 5 per cent of the population in mid-1971.

What kinds of people acquire new kinds of sets first?

Since all innovations in transmissions have necessitated buying new sets, often at considerable expense, it is not surprising that the financially-advantaged 'middle class' should be the first to buy. In 1952, 26 per cent of the 'top 10 per cent' of the population in terms of income had television sets, compared with only 9 per cent of the 'bottom 68 per cent', and even by 1954 the gap had not narrowed greatly, the comparable figures being 41 per cent and 25 per cent respectively. There was, it seems, never much

Table 1 How many listeners and viewers?

October/ December	Proportions of the population of UK					
	With Band I (BBC only) %	With Band III (BBC and ITV) %	With UHF (BBC-1, BBC-2 and ITV) Monochrome %	With UHF (BBC-1, BBC-2 and ITV) Colour %	All with television %	With radio but not TV %
1952	14·0	N/A	N/A	N/A	14·0	73·9
1953	21·8	N/A	N/A	N/A	21·8	67·0
1954	30·6	N/A	N/A	N/A	30·6	57·7
1955	35·1	4·5	N/A	N/A	39·6	48·9
1956	30·3	17·7	N/A	N/A	48·0	41·0
1957	31·0	25·3	N/A	N/A	56·3	33·0
1958	19·8	45·0	N/A	N/A	64·8	23·5
1959	13·7	60·7	N/A	N/A	74·4	16·4
1960	9·9	71·9	N/A	N/A	81·8	13·3
1961	4·8	80·2	N/A	N/A	87·4	11·2
1962	3·7	83·7	N/A	N/A	88·8	10·0
1963	2·3	86·5	N/A	N/A	90·8	8·2
1964		87·6	3·2	N/A	90·8	7·2
1965		83·9	7·9	N/A	91·8	6·6
1966		80·5	11·8	N/A	92·3	6·1
1967		70·3	22·5	N/A	92·8	5·7
1968		60·8	32·4	N/A	93·2	5·4
1969		42·7	48·3	3·2	94·2	4·8
1970						

Note: from 1952 to 1959 the figures refer to the population aged sixteen and over, from 1960 onwards to the population aged five and over

truth in the story that television was 'the working man's preroga-tive' or that the middle class regarded it as 'the idiot's lantern'.

'Band III' sets also appeared first in middle-class homes but the appeal of ITV programmes to working-class viewers soon redressed the balance. By 1958, two years after the start of ITV, there was little difference in terms of occupation or educational background between those who could receive BBC television only and those who could receive ITV as well. BBC-2, on the other hand, offered material that, in the main, found its greatest follow-ing amongst the middle class. At the end of 1966, 20 per cent of the numerically small upper-middle class had UHF sets, compared with 10 per cent of the working class. Even by the end of 1970 – six years after the start of BBC-2 – the gap remained, 63 per cent of the upper-middle class being equipped to receive the new service compared with 49 per cent of the working class, a fact that seems likely to owe as much to lack of interest as lack of money. The few colour sets are predominantly a middle-class luxury and it is too soon to predict their spread with any reliability.

A less-expected finding is that the presence of children in the home has also proved to be a spur to getting 'the latest thing' in television. For example, in 1954, amongst households that con-tained no five to twenty-year-olds the proportion with television was 19 per cent, whereas amongst those that included at least one five to twenty-year-old the comparable figure was 28 per cent. Similarly, a survey made in 1958 showed that the number of children in households that could receive ITV exceeded the number in equivalent households that could *not*; whilst recent analyses have shown that 63 per cent of five to fourteen-year-olds can view all three channels on UHF sets compared with 57 per cent of their elders.

The amount of listening and viewing

Though the amount of listening and viewing that people do is inevitably affected to some extent by the durations of the radio and television transmissions available to them, the effect of in-creases in transmission hours over the years has not been very great. Provided 7a.m. to 11p.m. for radio and 5–11p.m. (plus weekend afternoons) for television are included, further extensions make relatively little difference, it seems. This emerges from Table

2, even though it has not been possible to produce directly comparable statistics year by year. Small amounts of listening and viewing have had to be excluded in *all* years, in an attempt to achieve limited comparability by restricting the statistics to specified hours.

With the spread of television, radio listening in the evening rapidly decreased, but daytime listening (i.e. before 6p.m.) has changed little, even increasing slightly during the 1960s despite the increasing frequency of encroachment of television into the afternoon.

Viewing increased in step with its spread throughout the population, but the amount of viewing by those with television proved to be little affected either by the increases in transmission hours or by the introduction of new channels in 1955 (ITV) and 1964 (BBC-2).

At present, viewing works out at an average of sixteen hours twenty-seven minutes per head per week; listening at eight hours twenty-seven minutes per head per week. These averages of course conceal enormous individual variations, from virtually nil to over forty hours a week of viewing and to over eighty hours a week listening.

Peak listening and viewing times

As the preceding section showed, evening listening is nowadays comparatively rare. More detail of the way audiences vary throughout the day on weekdays will be found in Figure 1 which shows that the largest radio audiences (Monday to Friday) are found in the 7a.m. to 2p.m. period. Thereafter they fall steadily to no more than 2–3 per cent throughout the evening. There is very little late-night listening, after television programmes end, or in the early mornings.

Viewing audiences on weekdays rise steeply and steadily from 4p.m. to 7p.m. and fall even more steeply after 10.30p.m. There is a 'plateau' between 7.30 and 10p.m. but the viewing levels just before and just after this are not very much lower. As far as weekends are concerned, *evening* viewing levels do not differ greatly from those of Monday to Friday. Afternoon audiences are much smaller, with Saturday's exceeding Sunday's. Listening and viewing audiences (particularly the latter) also vary between

Table 2 The amount of listening and viewing

| October/ December | Listening per head of population per week | | | Viewing per head of population per week | Approximate transmission hours per week | Viewing per head of persons with television | |
	7a.m.–6p.m. hours.minutes	6p.m.–11p.m.	Total			with Band I	with Band III
1952	7-50	7-05	14-55		17-30	7-20	
1953	6-25	5-55	12-20		17-30	7-40	
1954	6-25	5-15	11-40		22-50	9-40	
1955	6-10	4-30	10-40	4-25	28-00	10-55	10-50
1956	6-05	4-20	10-25	6-00	30-00	11-20	11-45
1957	5-55	3-20	9-15	6-50	35-00	11-50	11-50
1958	5-45	3-05	8-50	8-25	35-00	11-50	12-25
1959	5-55	2-30	8-25	9-10	35-00	11-45	12-00
1960	6-05	1-40	7-45	13-35	47-00	16-20	
1961	6-25	1-20	7-45	13-20	47-00	15-35	
1962	7-20	1-15	8-35	13-55	47-00	15-40	
1963	7-30	1-10	8-40	13-55	47-00	15-30	
1964	7-05	0-55	8-00	14-05	47-00	15-25	
1965	6-45	0-50	7-35	14-50	47-00	15-35	
1966	6-45	0-50	7-35	14-50	47-00	15-35	
1967	7-55	0-55	8-50	14-25	47-00	15-55	
1968	7-30	0-55	8-25	14-25	47-00	15-55	
						with UHF	without UHF
1969	7-31	0-58	8-29	16-20	58-00	17-35	17-37
1970	7-16	1-11	8-27	16-27	58-00	17-30	17-39

Note: from 1952 to 1959 the figures relate to the population aged sixteen and over, from 1960 onwards to the population aged five and over

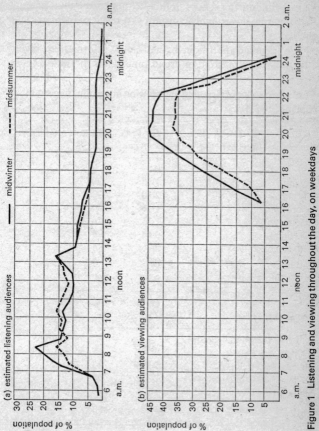

Figure 1 Listening and viewing throughout the day, on weekdays

winter and summer, the overall drop from mid-winter maximum to mid-summer minimum being of the order of one-fifth.

In addition, listening audiences in the early morning – before 9a.m. – fall during school holidays; though the total amount of listening remains roughly constant as a result of increases later in the day.

The detailed half-hour-by-half-hour information given in Figure 1 is summarized in broad time bands in Table 3.

Table 3 **Amount of listening and viewing in certain time bands** (Spring, 1971)

Amount of listening between	Per head hours.minutes	Share of total %
5.30–7a.m.	0·09	2
7–9a.m.	1·53	20
9–noon	2·30	28
Noon–2p.m.	1·56	20
2–5p.m.	1·23	14
5–7.30p.m.	0·44	8
7.30–10p.m.	0·26	4
10–1a.m.	0·24	4
	9·25	100

Amount of viewing	Per head hours.minutes	Share of total %
Saturday and Sunday before 4.20p.m.	0·54	5
All days 4.20–7.30p.m.	5·39	33
All days 7.30–10p.m.	7·37	44
All days 10–11.45p.m.	3·12	18
	17·22	100

Channel choice

As will be seen from Table 4, nearly half of all listening is to Radio 1, despite the fact that it is on the air for a shorter time than all the other three national BBC radio services. However, the times when it is *not* on the air are the ones when there is little listening (before 7a.m. and after 7p.m.). Next comes Radio 2 with somewhat more than one-third of all listening, then Radio 4 with about one-fifth. Radio 3 – which is deliberately designed for

Table 4 **Amount of listening and viewing by channel Spring 1971** (nationally available services only)

	Amount of listening per head per week hours.minutes	Share of total %
Radio 1	3·55	41
Radio 2	3·12	34
Radio 3	0·11	2
Radio 4	1·53	20
All national BBC services	9·11	97
Radio Luxemburg	0·15	3
Total	9·26	100

	Amount of viewing per head per week (a) Total population hours.minutes	Share of total %
BBC1	8·03	46
BBC2	0·59	6
ITV	8·20	48
Total	17·22	100

	(b) Those with UHF sets, during BBC2 hours hours.minutes	Share of total %
BBC1	8·25	45
BBC2	1·42	10
ITV	8·25	45
Total	18·32	100

minorities and which does not seek to encourage continuous listening – contributes about 1 per cent of all listening.

The only other nationally available radio service,[1] Radio Luxembourg, transmits in English for English audiences from 7p.m. to 2a.m.; its share of total listening is about 3 per cent.

Turning to television, BBC-TV and ITV are running virtually neck-and-neck, and have been doing so for a decade – with occasional swings one way or another. BBC-2's contribution has always been much smaller than BBC-1's; and still is, though it is growing steadily as more people equip themselves with appropriate sets and aerials. Those who *have* done so, nowadays spend about one-sixteenth of their viewing time watching BBC-2; though if the comparison is restricted to the hours when BBC-2 is continuously on the air, its share rises to one-tenth. The balance between BBC-TV viewing and ITV viewing is much the same in the early-, mid- and late-evening periods.

Listening by sex, age, and social class

The most striking finding yielded by analyses of the listening of various sub-groups of the population (see Table 5) is the very high level amongst the fifteen to nineteen, and twenty to twenty-nine-year-old age groups – despite the fact that in this age range the proportion in full-time employment is greatest. Their ability to listen so much has clearly been facilitated by the spread of portable and 'personal' radios, but must also owe something to the willingness of employers to permit listening at work. As would be expected, the great majority of the listening of these age groups is to Radio 1. Children under fifteen listen very little to the radio, and when they do it is almost always to Radio 1. Listening to Radios 2 and 4 increases with age.

'Availability' clearly plays a part in determining the amount of listening, the 'unemployed females' (who are mainly housewives) and 'unemployed males' (who are mainly retired) making much greater use of the radio than do adults who are in full-time employment.

The expected relationship between 'taste' and 'class' also

1. The BBC's twenty Local Radio stations (introduced progressively over the past two-and-a-half years and so far restricted to VHF) bring a fifth BBC service to some 20 per cent of the population. In the areas served by the stations opened before the end of 1970, listening to their output (by those who have VHF sets) rivals that to Radio 4.

Table 5 Listening by age, sex and social class (nationally available services only)

	Age groups					Males		Boys	Females		Girls	Adults over 15		
hours.minutes	5–14	15–19	20–29	30–49	50 and over	in employment	not in employment	under 15 (still at school)	in employment	not in employment	under 15 (still at school)	upper-middle	lower-middle	working-class
Radio 1	2-15	9-49	8-19	4-24	1-55	4-09	1-10	1-50	5-54	4-50	2-40	1-45	3-29	5-09
Radio 2	0-47	1-50	3-09	4-05	3-57	2-46	2-46	0-39	3-02	5-16	0-55	3-09	3-49	3-41
Radio 3	—	—	0-14	0-14	0-14	0-14	0-14	—	0-07	0-14	—	0-55	0-21	0-07
Radio 4	0-14	0-29	1-12	1-55	3-07	1-33	1-33	0-14	1-41	2-52	0-14	3-43	3-07	1-41
All BBC	3-16	12-08	12-54	10-38	9-13	8-42	5-43	2-43	10-44	13-12	3-49	9-32	10-46	10-38
Radio Luxembourg	0-06	1-37	0-33	0-03	—	0-22	0-11	0-03	0-30	—	0-08	—	0-14	0-17
Total	3-22	13-45	13-27	10-41	9-13	9-04	5-54	2-45	11-14	13-13	3-57	9-32	11-00	10-55

shows up strikingly. Middle-class listeners show a much greater than average appetite for Radios 3 and 4 than do the much more numerous 'working class'.

Viewing by age, sex and social class

The pattern of viewing by age (see Table 6) is in some respects the opposite of listening by age. The under-fifteen's listen least and view most; the fifteen to nineteen's listen most and view least. Close examination shows that, of the under-fifteen's, it is the twelve to fourteen-year-olds who are the heaviest 'consumers' of television programmes, the viewing of eight to eleven-year-olds and even more of five to seven-year-olds being limited to some extent by parental insistence on reasonable bed-times. Even so, five to seven-year-old viewing after 9p.m. is by no means rare, whilst of eight to eleven-year-olds as many as 18 per cent are viewing as late as 10–10.30p.m. on the average weekday.

The dip in viewing in the late teens has sometimes been mis-interpreted as evidence that, as children grow up, they lose interest in television. They certainly *do* for a few years whilst interests outside the home are dominant – but every study made during the past twenty years has shown that as soon as they themselves become settled, they view as much as do their elders.

Another noteworthy finding is that the numerically small upper-middle class views considerably less than does the far more numerous 'working class'. This in part reflects a greater 'choosiness' and in part the fact that they have more extensive and more varied interests both in the home and outside it.

Programme audiences: radio

There are so many programmes every day and so many are ephemeral that it would be convenient to be able to present audience statistics in terms of programme types. Unfortunately many programmes are *sui generis*. What is more, audiences depend as much on factors such as timing, service, surrounding programmes, season of year, etc., as on 'type', so that few generalizations are possible.

Perhaps the most important thing to note from Table 7 is that the range of size of radio audiences is extremely great – from little more than 20,000 to not far short (on exceptional occasions) of

Table 6 Viewing by age, sex and social class

	Age groups					Males		Boys	Females		Girls	Social class of adults (15+)		
	5-14 hours.minutes	15-19	20-29	30-49	50 and over	in employ-ment	not in employ-ment	under 15 (still at school)	in employ-ment	not in employ-ment	under 15 (still at school)	upper-middle	lower-middle	working-class
BBC1	9.51	7.31	7.31	8.47	8.52	7.58	10.29	10.18	7.26	9.19	9.19	8.52	9.35	8.04
BBC2	0.43	1.13	1.16	1.21	0.59	1.16	1.05	0.43	1.13	1.08	0.43	1.29	1.32	1.02
All BBC-TV	10.34	8.44	8.47	10.08	9.51	9.14	11.34	11.01	8.39	10.27	10.02	10.21	11.07	9.06
ITV	10.06	7.51	8.12	8.17	9.04	7.05	8.07	10.27	8.17	10.37	9.51	3.38	5.42	10.01
Total	20.40	16.35	16.59	18.25	18.55	16.19	19.41	21.28	16.56	21.04	19.53	13.59	16.49	19.07

20 million. 'Being broadcast' is not synonymous with 'being heard by millions'. Practically all 'types' of programme can, and on occasions do, attract both large and small audiences – plays, light entertainment, news and comment, record-request programmes, commentaries on sporting events, etc., – though nowadays, with daytime being the peak period for listening, programmes that are suitable as an accompaniment to doing other things will generally be the most widely listened to. However, even some forms of 'serious music' – unquestionably a minority taste – can be presented in such a way that their audiences number 1,500,000; as for example when it has a well-known 'presenter' and is placed on a Sunday morning on Radio 2.

Table 7 Estimated audiences for selected radio series

	1000s
News bulletins	
8a.m. (R.4)	4000
1p.m. (R.4)	3500
10p.m. (R.4)	1250
Current affairs	
Today (8.10a.m. Mon.–Fri. R.4)	2500
From Our Own Correspondent (9.05a.m. Sat. R.4)	550
Letter from America (9.15a.m. Sun. R.4)	900
Analysis (9.15p.m. Fri. R.4)	200
Specialist magazines	
Woman's Hour (2–3p.m. R.2)	1500
You and Yours (12–12.25p.m. R.4)	650
Motoring and the Motorist (11.15a.m. Sun. R.4)	300
In Touch (for the blind) (5.0p.m. Sun. R.4)	150
Sport	
Sport on 2 (2–6p.m. Sat. R.2)	550
Test Match Special (ball-by-ball coverage of cricket R.3)	250–750
Horse racing in 'Follow the Favourites' (3p.m. R.2)	550
Record-request programmes	
Family Favourites (Sun. 12 noon R.2)	11000
Junior Choice (Sat. 8.30a.m. R.2)	6000
Jazz record requests (Sat. 5.30p.m. R.3)	

Readings
Morning Story (11a.m.   R.2) — 1500
Story Time (4.30p.m.   R.4) — 50

Religion
The People's Service (11.30a.m. Sun.   R.2) — 1460
Morning Service (10.30a.m. Sun.   R.4) — 710
Sunday Half Hour (8.30p.m. Sun.   R.2) — 660

Drama
Afternoon Theatre (3p.m. Mon.–Fri.   R.4) — 650
Saturday Night Theatre (8.30p.m.   R.4) — 500
Plays on R.3 — 50

Serials
Waggoners' Walk (11.15a.m.   R.2) — 750
The Archers (1.30p.m.   R.4) — 1300

Popular music
Jimmy Young (10a.m.–Noon   R.1) — 4000
Open House (9a.m.–11a.m.   R.2) — 2750
Pick of the Pops (5–7p.m. Sun.   R.1) — 4500
John Peel (3–5p.m. Sat.   R.1) — 850

Jazz
The Best of Jazz (7p.m. Wed.   R.2) — 450
Jazz Today (5.55p.m. Wed.   R.3)

Light music
Melodies for You (10a.m. Sun.   R.2) — 2200
Friday Night is Music Night (8.45p.m.   R.2) — 700
All Kinds of Music (10.30a.m. Mon.–Fri.   R.4) — 300

'Serious' music
Orchestral concerts, recitals and opera on R.3 — 20–200

Comedy
Does the Team Think? (7.30p.m. Thurs.   R.4) — 500
The Navy Lark (2p.m. Sun.   R.2) — 1250

Panel games
Twenty Questions (6.15p.m. Wed.   R.4) — 860
Just a Minute (12.25p.m. Tues.   R.4) — 860
My Word (7.30p.m. Mon.   R.4) — 450

Indeed, the influence of the presenter or disc jockey on radio audience size must be emphasized. He is not all-important but since one of the principal functions of radio has been found to be 'providing pleasant company', the style of presentation will obviously do a great deal to attract or repel listeners.

Programme audiences: television

Television programmes are as difficult to classify as are radio programmes, but an attempt has been made to do so in Table 8.

Major events, be they public occasions or sporting fixtures, will always dominate any list of large audiences, e.g. nineteen million for Prince Charles' investiture as Prince of Wales (despite its timing on a Tuesday afternoon), thirty million for the Apollo 11 moon-landing, twenty-eight million for the 1966 World Cup Final, etc.

Another clear fact stands out, *viz.* the attraction for viewers of films originally made for the cinema. Virtually any film, placed at any time in the evening, on either BBC-1 or ITV, can be expected to draw an audience of between ten and twenty million. The best-known example of the soap-opera genre in British television is *Coronation Street*, which – of all the *regular* series – is still the most consistent contender for a place in the 'top ten'.

The News has always been an ingredient of evening television schedules on all channels. Almost three-fifths of the population see one or more of the five main bulletins on the typical day, the choice depending on surrounding and competing programmes. On average, however, the *Main News* at 9p.m. on BBC-1 and *News at Ten* on ITV have very similar-sized audiences.

The middle ground is held by a wide range of light entertainment, drama series and current affairs, whilst the more serious informational and cultural programmes, together with those aimed at minority tastes, not surprisingly come at the foot of the list.

Variations in audience composition

Radio and television audiences differ not only in size but in composition. As far as daytime radio is concerned, the figures given in Table 5 are sufficient to indicate the make-up of the audience. The small evening radio audiences are predominantly elderly, at

Table 8 Estimated audiences for selected television series *

	1000s
News bulletins	
News at 10 (ITV)	9500
The Main News (9p.m. BBC-1)	9500
The News (5.50p.m. BBC-1)	9000
The News (5.50p.m. ITV)	6000
Newsroom (7.30p.m. BBC-2)	500
Current affairs	
World in Action (8.00p.m. Mon. ITV)	6000
This Week (9.30p.m. Thurs. ITV)	5500
Panorama (8.00p.m. Mon. BBC-1)	4000
Twenty-Four Hours (c.10.20p.m. BBC-1)	3000
Documentaries	
The Tuesday Documentary (9.20p.m. BBC-1)	5000
The Documentary (c.10.30p.m. ITV)	2500
Specialist Magazines	
Omnibus (Arts) (c.10.30p.m. Sun. BBC-1)	2500
Horizon (Science) (9.20p.m. Mon. BBC-2)	2000
Wheelbase (motoring) (8.50p.m. Tues. BBC-2)	1250
Chronicle (history) (7.25p.m. Sat. BBC-2)	750
Sport	
Professional wrestling (4p.m. Sat. ITV)	4500
Grandstand (1.30–4.30p.m. BBC-1)	2750
Match of the Day (c.10p.m. Sat. BBC-1)	9500
Wimbledon tennis (6.15–7.30p.m. BBC-1)	6000
Sunday afternoon cricket (1.50–6.50p.m. BBC-2)	1500
Horse-racing (weekday aft. BBC-1)	1000
Show-jumping (weekday eve. BBC-1)	8590
Films	
Sunday night (8.10p.m. BBC-1)	10–20,000
World Cinema (10.15p.m. Thurs. BBC-2)	2000
Cartoons	
Tom and Jerry (6.50p.m. Thurs. BBC-1)	6620
The Pink Panther Show (5.20p.m. Sat. BBC-1)	4240
The Magic Roundabout (5.45p.m. Mon.–Fri. BBC-1)	3080

* Comparatively few ITV series are included because few are nationally networked. Further examples of audiences for BBC programmes will be found in the BBC's Annual Handbooks.

Table 8—*continued*

Drama – single plays and short series

Play of the Month (8.10p.m. Sun. BBC-1)	3000
Play for Today (9.40p.m. Thurs. BBC-1)	3500–8500
Armchair Theatre (Tues. 9p.m. ITV)	7500
Thirty-Minute Theatre (Mon. 10.10p.m. app. BBC-2)	850
The Six Wives of Henry VIII (8.15p.m. Sun. BBC-1)	12,930
The First Churchills (Thurs. 9.20p.m. BBC-1)	5000

Drama – series

A Man Called Ironside (9.10p.m. app. Sat. BBC-1)	10,500
Public Eye (9p.m. Wed. ITV)	10,500
Star Trek (7.25p.m. Wed. BBC-1)	9500
Kate (9.00p.m. Fri. ITV)	7000
Take Three Girls (9.20p.m. Fri. BBC-1)	5500
The Borderers (c.10.30p.m. Sun. BBC-2)	2000

Drama – serials

Coronation Street (Mon., Wed. 7.30p.m. ITV)	9000
Owen M.D. (Wed., Thurs. 7.00p.m. BBC-1)	4600

Drama – serializations

The Forsyte Saga (7.25p.m. Sun. BBC-1)	15,630
Cousin Bette (8.25p.m. Sat. BBC-2)	1060
The Canterbury Tales (9.20p.m. Wed. BBC-2)	1000

Light entertainment
Situation comedy:

Steptoe and Son (10.10p.m. Mon. BBC-1)	9900
On the Buses (7.25p.m. Sun. ITV)	11,500
Up Pompeii (9.20p.m. Mon. BBC-1)	11,720

Variety:

The Morecambe and Wise Show (7.25p.m. Sun. BBC-1)	12,500
The Andy Williams Show (7.15p.m. Mon. BBC-1)	6500
Monty Phython's Flying Circus (8.20p.m. Thurs. BBC-1)	7420

Quizzes and contests:

It's a Knock-out (9.20p.m. Fri. BBC-1)	11–15,000
Opportunity Knocks (6.40p.m. Mon. ITV)	9000
Golden Shot (4.45p.m. Sun. ITV)	7000
Call My Bluff (8.50p.m. Mon. BBC-2)	2500
Animal, Vegetable, Mineral? (7.30p.m. Sun. BBC-2)	250

least until 10.30p.m. Then the stay-up-late youngsters predominate, nearly 60 per cent of the audience between 11p.m. and 2a.m. being between fifteen and twenty-nine years of age, a group that constitutes little more than one-fifth of the total population.

The sub-group of the population to whom *viewing* has always been of greatest concern is 'children'. As has been shown they view *more* than do any of the other age groups, and their appetite for television appears to be catholic as well as voracious. Admittedly news, current affairs and documentaries figure less prominently in their viewing than in the smaller 'consumption' of their elders but, this apart, they view 'everything'. Even five-to seven-year olds see more of the television programmes designed for their parents than of the programmes designed for them, older children having an even greater adult-programmes component in their viewing diet. Admittedly some children's programmes, e.g. *Blue Peter* (BBC-1) invariably attract large child audiences (35 per cent of eight to eleven-year olds and 25 per cent of twelve- to fourteen-year olds on each edition) but so too do *Coronation Street* (ITV), films, *Top of the Pops* (BBC-1), *Mannix* (ITV), etc.

Mannix provides a thought-provoking example. In all the public concern that has been expressed in the United States over television violence, this has been one of the series most frequently condemned. A number of the ITV contractors have been showing *Mannix* in recent months, the series being broadcast by London Weekend Television at 8.00p.m. on Fridays and by Yorkshire and ATV, first of all on Saturdays at 9.00p.m. and later (by ATV only) at 10.10p.m. on Saturdays. The mid-evening placing by LWT resulted in there being a very high proportion of children in the audience – about one child between the ages of five and fourteen in every five in the coverage area watching the programme, compared with one adult in every seven; and the same appears to be true of the 9.00p.m. Saturday placing. Even when placed at 10.10p.m., about 11 per cent of all children in the coverage area watched it, the audience amongst eight- to eleven-year olds being particularly high (17 per cent).

Another example of children's voraciousness concerns *Blue Peter*'s 'Royal Safari' (a film of Princess Anne's East African game-reserve visit), which attracted its expected large number of

Table 9 Viewing audiences and social class – some examples of differential appeal

	Audience amongst		
	upper-middle class %	lower-middle class %	working-class %
Max Ophul's film 'The Sorrow and the Pity' (8p.m.–12.20a.m. Friday 10 September 1971, BBC-1)	17	7	3
Play for Today 'Sovereign's Company' (9.20–10.35p.m. Thursday 15 April 1971, BBC-1)	23	11	9
Kenneth Clark's 'Civilisation' (BBC-2 originations 8.15–9p.m. Sundays, March/May 1964)	5	3	1
(BBC-1 Repeats 9.20–10.15p.m. Tuesdays, March/May 1970)	16	11	6
Panorama (8–9p.m. Mondays, February 1971, BBC-1)	21	13	9
'The Six Wives of Henry VIII' (8.20–9.45p.m. Sunday 24 January 1971, BBC-1 Repeat)	45	30	17
Elvis Presley film 'Tickle Me' (7.30–9p.m. Tuesday 7 September 1971, BBC-1)	10	19	25
This Week (7.30–8p.m. Thursday 15 April 1971, ITV)	5	7	11
Coronation Street (7.30–8p.m. Mon. and Wed., March 1971, ITV)	9	11	26
Doctor at Large (7.25–7.55p.m. Sunday 18 April 1971, ITV)	12	24	32
The Andy Williams Show (8–9p.m. Thursdays, February 1971, BBC-1)	10	19	20
Top of the Pops (7.15–8p.m. Thursdays, January 1970, BBC-1)	9	20	23

eight- to eleven-year olds, 40 per cent of them viewing the broadcast on Easter Sunday afternoon. But exactly the same proportion of them viewed *Miss United Kingdom* broadcast from 9.20 to 10 p.m. (also on BBC-1) a few days later!

Social-class differences in viewing patterns are largely determined by the greater interest of the middle-class than of working-class viewers in current affairs and 'high culture', though the fact that they view rather less in total can, on occasions, tend to cloud the picture. Examples of programmes for which the middle class following considerably exceeded that amongst the working class, and of others for which the reverse was true are given in Table 9.

Listening and viewing 'continuity'

As has been shown, the average amount of viewing per head of population works out at about two hours per head per day. On weekdays (Monday to Friday), the figure is a little lower than this. Table 10, which refers to a typical weekday in the summer of 1971, shows how this average is made up. Thirty per cent of the population did not view anything at all, whilst one in four of those who *did* do some viewing, watched more or less continuously for between three and seven hours. The remainder viewed for shorter periods, still – in the main – continuously or with only short breaks.

Table 10 **Distribution of the population (aged five and over) according to amount of viewing on a typical weekday evening (Summer 1971)**

	%
Did not view	30
Viewed for	
up to 1 hour	14
1–2 hours	19
2–3 hours	15
3–4 hours	9
4–5 hours	7
5–6 hours	4
6–7 hours	2
	100

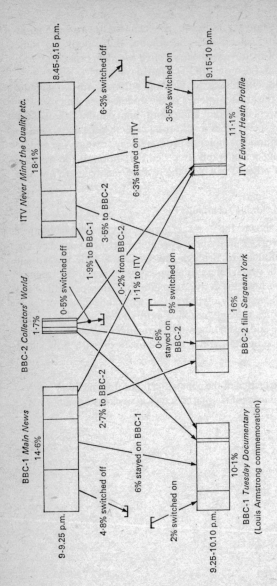

BBC-1 Main News
14·6%

9-9.25 p.m.

4·8% switched off

6% stayed on BBC-1

2% switched on

2·7% to BBC-2

BBC-2 Collectors' World
1·7%

0·5% switched off

1·9% to BBC-1

3·5% to BBC-2

0·2% from BBC-2

1·1% to ITV

0·8% stayed on BBC-2

9% switched on

ITV Never Mind the Quality etc.
18·1%

8.45-9.15 p.m.

6·3% switched off

3·5% switched on

6·3% stayed on ITV

9.15-10 p.m.

ITV Edward Heath Profile
11·1%

BBC-2 film Sergeant York
16%

BBC-1 Tuesday Documentary
(Louis Armstrong commemoration)
10·1%

9.25-10.10 p.m.

A Tuesday 3 August 1971

Figure 2 Examples of 'audience flow'

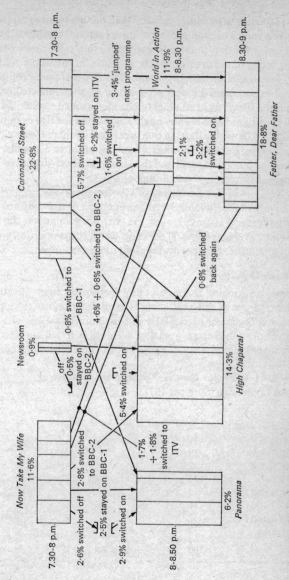

B Monday 27 September 1971

7.30-8 p.m.

Coronation Street -22.8%

7.30-8 p.m.

3.4% 'jumped' next programme

6.2% stayed on ITV

5.7% switched off

1.6% switched on

World in Action 11.9% 8-8.30 p.m.

2.1%

3.2% switched on

Father, Dear Father 18.8% 8.30-9 p.m.

0.8% switched to BBC-1

4.6% + 0.8% switched to BBC-2

0.8% switched back again

Newsroom 0.9%

off 0.5% stayed on BBC-2

5.4% switched on

High Chaparral 14.3%

Now Take My Wife 11.6%

2.6% switched off

2.8% switched to BBC-2

2.5% stayed on BBC-1

2.9% switched on

1.7% + 1.8% switched to ITV

Panorama 6.2% 8-8.50 p.m.

7.30-8 p.m.

It appears to be widely believed that, though virtually all viewers have a choice of channel, few of them exercise this choice, at least on any given day, thus leading to the maxim 'catch a viewer at the beginning of the evening and he is your's for the whole evening'. It is certainly true that, in general, most viewers of one programme continue to view the next programme on the same channel and that the 'flow' from channel to channel is much smaller than the viewing figures themselves might suggest. As the two examples in Figure 2 show, the illusion of a great deal of channel-switching is created by the large number switching off after a popular programme on one channel and the large number switching *on* for a popular programme on another channel.

Analysis of a wide variety of viewing situations suggests that 'the inheritance' factor, i.e. the proportion of the audience for a programme that stays on for the next programme on the same channel averages some 60 per cent, whilst the proportion switching to another channel averages no more than 6 per cent.

Channel loyalty

Though switching channels at any given programme junction is rare, the use of different channels at different times throughout the evening is *not* particularly uncommon. About one viewer in three, on the average weekday evening, is found to view programmes on more than one channel, as Table 11 shows. Indeed, a

Table 11 **Television channels 'patronized' on a typical weekday evening** (Summer 1971)

	%
None	30
BBC1 only	19
BBC2 only	2
ITV only	23
BBC1 and BBC2	3
BBC1 and ITV	18
BBC2 and ITV	2
All three	3
	100

small proportion, 4 per cent, viewed all three channels – a practice that will almost certainly increase as more people acquire UHF sets.

Looking at longer periods than a day, few viewers do *not* use any of the channels (two *or* three) available to them – at least occasionally in the course of a week. Taking an even longer view still, only a small minority claim that they stick almost entirely to one channel. 'Channel loyalty' is, it seems, low.

10 V. A. Piramidin

Evaluative Attitudes Towards the Newspaper

V. A. Piramidin, 'Gazyeta kak obyekt tsenostnovo otnosheniya', *Vyestnik Zhurnalistiki*, no. 1, 1970, pp. 39–47.

This article is presented in a new translation by Denis McQuail.

In our time the idea of the 'far depths' has become more and more relative. The storms of scientific and technical progress, the powerful whirlwinds of economic growth, have taken over yet more of the 'haunts of bears' and included them in the social and productive processes of modern times. Such a fate has, in particular, overtaken the old village of Turinskaya Sloboda, which lies close to the eastern border of the Sverdlovsk oblast. From there, by the most direct route, it is three times nearer to Tyumeni than to its 'proper' regional centre, Sverdlovsk, and it is eighty and one hundred kilometres respectively to the railway north and south. The region of Turinskaya Sloboda is devoted to farming, of which there is little in the vicinity of the industrial Middle Urals. Here there are six collective farms and five state farms.

The readers in the said village of Turinskaya Sloboda became the object of some new sociological research which formed a logical continuation of a questionnaire survey undertaken a year earlier in the town of Kamyshlov. The results of the Kamyshlov research were published in the booklet *The Reader and the Newspaper* (Piramidin, 1967) and in other publications.

The research in Turinskaya Sloboda was carried out according to the same plan, and using the same methods. It had as its aims: 1. To clarify the scale and particular characteristics of the audience for certain central, regional and local newspapers; 2. to shed light on the motives according to which the reader (subscriber) chooses between one paper and another; 3. to measure the breadth of reader interest in different sections amongst the total content of newspapers; 4. to define precisely the ways in which the interests of readers are dependent on their social and demographic characteristics; and 5. to obtain data about the ways in which the newspaper acquires authority and about the effectiveness of newspaper presentations.

The researchers were also interested in other questions arising from the interrelationship between reader and newspaper. And since on this occasion the rural reader was under examination, a comparative analysis of data received from two different groups of readers was added into the programme – groups whose social and demographic characteristics were very different.

Particular attention was paid to the selection of participants in the survey, and they were chosen primarily to assure a high level of representativeness in the results. The comparatively small size of the population under study allowed this question to be resolved without any special difficulty. There are 4100 inhabitants in Turinskaya Sloboda and of these the adult population consists of 2530 persons, amongst whom are to be found the newspaper readers. It was decided, therefore, to interview 843 persons (i.e. 33 per cent of the adult population) known to be representative in terms of sex, age, education, social position and other characteristics. In this way the model corresponded maximally to the social-demographic structure of the population of the village as recorded in the statistics of the regional inspectorate.

What interests the rural reader and how much do his sympathies vary between this or that publication? The data collected suggest that the village reader is more active in relation to the periodical press. The average index (number of replies divided by the number of respondents to the questionnaire) stands at 2·7 – greater than in Kamyshlov by 0·25. Evidently these results reflect the separation of Turinskaya Sloboda from large centres, in particular from Sverdlovsk. It is not possible, for example, to receive broadcasts here from Sverdlovsk television. Apart from this, the cultural life of this village is less intensive, it is poorer in events (visits from touring artistic companies, general travel to town to see theatre performances, etc.) than in the town. Consequently the leisure time of the village dweller is more often taken up with reading newspapers and magazines than is the case with the town-dweller.

A tendency, noted in the early survey, for young men (the first, male age group) to be less active in relation to the press than young women, showed itself less markedly in the village sample.

At the same time, if we take particular newspapers, then for the majority of central publications, the rural subscriber as a rule lags behind the town-dweller. An essential difference can, for example, be observed in subscriptions to the papers *Pravda*, *Izvyestiya*, *Komsomolskaya Pravda* (see Table 1).

Table 1 'Which newspaper do you take regularly?'
(as a percentage of the numbers of answers to the question)

Newspaper	Kamyshlov	Turinskaya Sloboda
Pravda	10·6	6·0
Izvyestiya	7·2	3·4
Sovyetskaya Rossiya	5·2	3·0
Komsomolskaya Pravda	10·7	6·7
Ekonomicheskaya Gazyeta	1·4	0·1
Syelskaya Zhizn	3·2	19·4
Trud	1·5	0·5
Uralskii Rabochii	14·1	13·0
Smyenu!	5·5	3·2
Uchityelskaya Gazyeta	2·8	1·9
Meditsinskaya Gazyeta	2·5	1·6
Town or regional newspaper	26·4	29·1

In the country, as in the town, demand is highest for local newspapers – in Kamyshlov *Za Kommunizm* and in Turinskaya Sloboda *Kommunar*: more than a quarter of subscribers in the town and just less than a third in the village. It is curious to note that the interests of the town reader are spread out rather more evenly amongst the proferred list, while the village reader confines his attention essentially to three publications. These are the local *Kommunar*, *Syelskaya Zhizn* and *Uralski Rabochi*. In these cases, the indices, high in themselves, markedly outstrip those of the town.

All this obliges one to comment on the much more narrow range of interest of village readers, since they seem to lack the kind of strong and many-sided motivation which would lead to the active use of other central publications. And we have noted above that the general activity of the village reader is much more specific and directed to a limited circle of publications.

But one way or another, each periodical publication attracts and strengthens its own intended audience, the scale and particular character of which is affected by many circumstances and factors. The most important of these include the age of the reader, his education, profession, party standing, engagement in work for society, place of residence. On the other hand, a large if not decisive effect is produced by the character of the newspaper and the level of its professional, literary and printing attainment.

But what sort of mechanism is it that interrelates these and many other causes and factors? It is certainly the case that the attitude of choice which the reader has towards a newspaper is formed as a result of some such interaction. What is the secret which leads one to be chosen rather than another? In our view, we can take a notable step forwards towards answering this question, if we look upon the newspaper as an object of evaluative orientation.

We have already emphasized that it is a mistake to see the reader as some kind of passive object, subject to the massive influence of the press. In the face of the enormous scale and seeming irresistibility of its methods, the individual reader retains great firmness of choice. Moreover, the press in general cannot ignore the opinions, tastes, demands and responses of the reader.

In our view, the analysis of the evaluative element in the system of relationships between reader and newspaper should proceed from the fact that the press appears to be one of the important elements of the immediately perceived social environment, or the microenvironment, in which the personality and world-outlook of the individual is formed. Similarly, the press as a factor in the spiritual life of society, and the newspaper as a case in point, is able to satisfy a known part of spiritual needs, and thus finds itself the object of interests directed at it. That is, it is a link to the real world and is encompassed within a system of evaluative attitudes.

The practise of a systematic relationship between people and the press transforms each newspaper for any given person into an object of value for his family. Thanks to this he develops preferential and selective attitudes to newspapers, choosing amongst them whatever things are most meaningful for his own life. Thus a given person, along with all those for whom a newspaper represents a particular and indeed, exclusive, interest comprise in a manner of speaking a kind of social community, united by common interests and having also at some level a common attitude towards the publication in question. It can be asserted with some confidence that the most important condition for the existence of such a community is a value system, to a large extent emerging from, and in particular coinciding with, attitudes taken up towards the press. Evaluative attitudes of the reader to the majority of periodical publications are highly diverse and rarely taken into account. But, as the data presented below show, they can be systematized on the basis of statistical material.

The activeness of a reader's attitude to a newspaper takes on a distinct meaning when a person makes a definite choice by opening a subscription. Evaluative orientations show themselves at this time in the form of motives, which lead a reader to subscribe to one or another publication. It is clear that most subscriptions are based on extended past experience of interaction between the reader and his chosen newspaper. As a rule, this experience is strengthened by tradition and habit. Amongst the complex of motives determining choice traditional reasons occupy, according to our data, second place. But it is important to note that in the village they are more noticeable (25·2 per cent) than in the town (11·7 per cent). This circumstance explains why the village reader is rarely led by other motives, and why he is more resistant to propaganda and advertisement for the press. For example, such potentially powerful stimuli as attempts to achieve a wider circulation for the press in society, or the appeal or advice of a party, komsomol or trade-union activist to subscribe to a paper receives a lower response in the village than in the town (see Table 2).

One of the most important reasons for taking out a subscription originates in the sphere of cognitive interests of the personality. This conclusion is well supported by the rural indices which, as in the town sample, constitute more than a third of replies to the question 'Why did you begin to take this particular newspaper?'. In this connection we must draw attention to the rather heavy endorsement (about 11 per cent) of the motive connected with the chance reading of newspaper materials. Evidently, however, curiosity and the wish to receive new information – that is, an aim dictated by the cognitive interests of the personality – are also motives which compel people to a regular reading of a given newspaper.

And when we see people standing at glass-cased newspapers while waiting for the tram, or reading through the files in the foyers of cinemas, in the reading room of libraries, in the 'red corner' of workplaces or in dormitories, we can with reasonable certainty see them as future subscribers. As our data bear witness, it is just such an unsystematic, chance contact with the newspaper which frequently leads a person into the ranks of regular readers and firm fans.

Table 2 'Why did you begin to subscribe to this particular newspaper?'
(as a percentage of the number of replies to the question)

Motives	Kamyshlov	Turinskaya Sloboda
As a result of campaigns for a wider press circulation in society	9·9	4·7
Through the example of a comrade	5·5	5·4
Because of advice from a party (or komsomol or trade-union) worker	8·1	4·0
After chance reading of interesting articles	10·9	11·2
After joining the party (or komsomol)	8·6	5·5
Following exposure to advertisements for the paper	3·0	2·2
Through tradition (or habit)	11·7	25·2
To satisfy internal needs	35·0	34·3
For other reasons	4·2	3·4
Difficult to reply	3·1	4·0
Total	100	100

In the village, as in the town, advertisements for the press constitute the weakest stimulus. Everywhere we saw 'for sale' notices, placards, appeals, notifications, announcements – on the streets, in the tram, in the newspapers, etc. And all the time we remember that these advertising productions are far from perfect: they are often boring and indifferent, lacking in any lively thought, un-expectedness, energy, persistence or interest. The advertisement has yet to become an art form.

However, the determining factor in the formation of an evaluative attitude of the reader to his newspaper appears to be its contents and the literary and professional level of published materials. The content of the modern press which deals with society is both extensive and varied and the press is rightly regarded as a faithful reflector of life. But for this very reason, it is a daunting and complex task to try to examine, and account for, the interests of the reader with respect to particular types of subject matters.

But if we concentrate attention on the broad categories of material which are most fully represented in the majority of leading newspapers, then it is possible to obtain a fully representative picture. For example, such themes as party life, international relations, questions of economics, problems of morals, satire and humour, physical culture and sport are prominent and elaborated in all general-political publications. The preferential, selective attitudes of the reader towards a particular section (and through this to the newspaper) are formed, likewise, on the basis of a determinable complex of value judgements, arising in the practise of a relationship between the person and the newspaper.

There is yet a further set of valuations which reflect the spiritual interests of the personality and correspond to the level of his moral and idealistic development; these relate to questions of a scientific and professional kind and also to a person's everyday inquiries, demands and inclinations. Namely, those values of the individual and his consciousness which in the final result programme his character and determine the intensity with which his attitudes as a reader will be expressed.

What, from the point of view of content, does attract the town and country readers as between the mass papers which are published? The question 'What subjects in newspaper articles interest you most?' stimulated fifteen variations of response. It was clear, however, that a reply to such a question could not be simple, because the modern reader is an educated person with a wide range of spiritual interests and inquiries. The replies do, nevertheless, indicate the character of value gradations at the time of choosing a paper to subscribe to. The readers in Kamyshlov gave on average five variants of reply, and in Turinskaya Sloboda, four – yet again illustrating and emphasizing the existence of known differences between the interests of town and village dwellers.

We discovered that the highest level of reader interest attaches to articles, correspondence and paragraphs concerned with events and processes of international life. At almost the same level is located interest in family and daily life, about which village readers are even more keen. Two final peaks are shown in relation to satirical-humorous publications and material about 'people of unusual or heroic destiny'. It is not without interest to observe that the latter section attracted, above all, younger readers – thus providing very convincing evidence of the socializing function of the press, especially for the young (see Table 3).

Table 3 'What subjects in newspaper articles interest you most?'

Themes	Kamyshlov %	Turinskaya Sloboda %
Theoretical articles about philosophy, economics, scientific communism	3·3	1·2
Party life	4·1	3·2
Practical, economic and industrial problems	2·9	1·2
Practical economic and farming problems	2·6	3·5
International life	12·5	14·4
Progressive propaganda	3·2	3·7
Daily life, family, upbringing of children	10·7	13·0
Problems of morals, conscience, duty	7·4	7·5
Poems, short stories, reviews, articles about art	7·0	6·9
Satire and humour	8·5	8·8
History of the country and native region	6·2	7·1
About people of unusual or heroic destiny	8·3	9·5
Physical culture and sport	6·8	4·3
Practical advice	7·2	6·0
Events 'from the courtroom'	9·3	9·7
Total	100	100

Lower down on the list comes material published under such headings as 'Events of the day' or 'From the court-room'. In our view this fact should be viewed in a positive light, and not interpreted as a display of narrow-minded curiosity about harsh experience. The truth is that these and similar published items in soviet newspapers contain a high potential for moral education. As a rule it is only at second or third level that an element of sensationalism shows itself in them.

Readers in town and country, men as well as women, demonstrate a unanimous restraint in relation to material of an economic-production character, together with questions of advanced experience. The evidence on this point clarifies the degree to which, as we have already pointed out, the newspaper in the first instance satisfies the cognitive interests of the reader. If he is attracted by articles concerning matters in the factory or in the sovkhoz or kolkhoz, then it will be those articles which concern people or life or work in the collectives. In addition, some interest is shown at the moral-ethical level, in the sphere of human work relationships. Questions concerned especially with production, together with those to do with economics, technology, the organization of work, are attractive above all to specialists or farm managers. In any case these questions are more fully and basically dealt with in branch publications. Therefore the evaluative meaning of such themes in newspapers is relatively restricted in scope. But there is one additional circumstance worthy of note: it is evident that journalists consistently write about production and about economic problems in ways which lack interest and fascination. In this respect one can speak with some certainty of the growth of a certain degree of reader resistance, which it is up to the workers of the press to master.

A large proportion of readers judge a newspaper according to its effectiveness. The more often a person is convinced that an article in the press has a real effect, that press criticism helps to remove some failing, then the greater the authority of the press organ, and the higher its evaluative meaning in the eyes of the reader.

Generally, the creative, transformative power of the printed word was not doubted by anyone. But many readers did not regard it as having any absolute character, and a much more correct appreciation was the following: that it reflects the actual position of things. It is true that the editor cannot, when publishing items of varying degrees of completeness in terms of factual content, and varying in direction, guarantee 100 per cent results each time. Besides, the valuation placed on either an undesirable occurrence or on a newspaper report about it cannot be expressed in terms which are absolute or unambiguous.

A reflection of this dialectic of interaction and interrelationship can be seen in data obtained in answer to our fourth question 'Do critical presentations in the newspaper attain their aims?'. An unconditionally positive reply is given by the majority of respondents – 59·2 per cent. A little under a third of respondents (28 per cent) consider that criticism is 'partially' effective. More than 11 per cent of readers 'don't know' whether criticism in the press is effective and a bare 1·4 per cent of readers say 'no, it is not effective'.

But the effectiveness of the press is not only confined to the sphere of negative reporting. The overwhelming majority of things published in our newspapers have a positive character and help to forward some desirable objective. The newspaper helps its readers in all their productive, social and personal affairs. The formation of a reader's attitude to his newspaper depends very much on the level of this kind of 'participation'. His evaluative position in relation to the press will be just one amongst other value judgements.

In what ways does the 'positive' help given by the press show itself? Under the influence of the convincing, stimulating and authoritative source provided by the printed word the reader reflects upon and judges his own actions, collates his plans and actions, orients himself towards events, choosing what for himself is the optimal course of behaviour. We are, of course, far from supposing that in this respect the press is the sole, or determining, factor. But that it does have a role, and participates in these processes and in the action of the individual conscience cannot be disputed.

But what sort of concrete examples of this do we have? Amongst the replies to such a question we have chosen a few typical statements to which, in one way or another, the majority of participants in our survey could respond. The results enable one to see a certain pattern of practical involvement on the part of the press in the thoughts and affairs of the reader. Numerically the most prominently acknowledged element in this pattern is the reply 'The newspaper helps in taking a correct decision in work or social affairs' (28·1–30·4 per cent). Next, the newspaper helps a person to 'convince someone of his own correctness' (24·2–17·9 per cent) or to 'recognize one's mistake' (12·3–12·7 per cent). That is to say, the authority of the newspaper as the voice of public opinion, and as its powerful representative, lends its convincing weight on the side of those actions, stands, judgements and aims which correspond most to societal interests, to the norms and principles of communist morality, and to the objective logic of life (see Table 4).

Table 4 'Has the newspaper helped you?'
(as a percentage of replies to the question)

The newspaper has helped	Kamyshlov	Turinskaya Sloboda
to take a correct decision at work	28·1	30·4
to take some important step in personal life	17·0	20·9
to convince someone of one's own correctness	24·2	17·9
to recognize one's mistake	12·3	12·7
to resolve doubts, change one's views	18·4	18·1
Total	100	100

In the maintenance of high standards of personal behaviour, an important place is held by such intellectual-psychological processes as the resolution of doubts, perplexities and mistakes; we sometimes term this 'a revision of values', or 'a breaking with illusions' – in effect the move from a former point of view to a new and more complete one. This refers, in turn, to the levels, stages, moments of advance in the process of learning about reality, mastering it, arriving at the limits of individual consciousness. These underlie the cognitive interests of the personality which are, in an important part, satisfied by the means of mass information, according to the law of synthesis and struggle against contradictions. In particular, a negative moment of interaction in a given instance achieves realization as a positive fact of cognition – a person rejects a prior estimation of some thing or event, and is persuaded (with the help of the newspaper) that it was mistaken; a new point of view is adopted which leads the person in his aim of uncovering truth, and will fix his new, more complete, and more mature position in relation to a given aspect of reality. The role of the newspaper as a 'helper' in the resolution of doubts and as a factor influencing the outlook and estimation of the personality can be seen equally distinctly in town and village (in both around 18 per cent of replies).

Table 5 'How would you define your relationship to the newspaper?' (as percentage of replies received to the question)

	Kamyshlov	Turinskaya Sloboda
As a source of information about issues of the day	14·2	11·5
As a means of widening horizons	35·0	36·1
As helper in work or study	20·0	18·1
As adviser in societal matters	14·1	11·7
As a means of participating in public opinion	7·7	6·6
As a means of participating in political life	9·0	7·0
As a source of information about progressive experience and the achievements of science	3·1	9·6
Total	103·1	100·6

Finally, it remains to note that the newspaper helps people to 'undertake an important step in personal life'. Such a judgement is made in 17 per cent of replies given by townsfolk and 20·9 per cent of replies of village dwellers. Members of the younger age group are in large part inclined to adopt such an opinion.

The attitude of the reader to his newspaper also expresses itself in the form of definitions, formulated in answer to the question 'What does the newspaper mean to you?' Some account of the main types of definition is the more necessary since they have the character of evaluations.

In town, as in the village, the question drew a quantity of replies, exceeding by a factor of two the number of participants who were questioned. That is to say, each of them on average gave two variants of reply. In actuality, the distribution of replies was far from even (see Table 5).

Again, we are convinced that the reader's attitude to his newspaper is formed, above all else, in the sphere of cognitive interests. The newspaper is evaluated most highly as a means of widening the general horizon of a person. Indeed, education is not completed with the receipt of a diploma or a leaving certificate. Throughout his life a person continually supplements his knowledge so as to be able to cope with the demands life makes on him. And it would seem that the newspaper constitutes the most accessible source of knowledge. It allows the reader who has an unspecialized occupation to acquire sufficient information to orient himself freely to questions far from his profession or specialism but which happen to attract his attention from time to time. For example, the metal worker, systematically following press content about farming questions, art, or morals, can in the course of time become sufficiently informed over a wide field of knowledge to be able to interpret facts independently, come to his own conclusions, have his own opinions. Of course, the demand that the newspaper should act as a source of facts is unequally distributed: in this respect it is more important for a reader with incomplete secondary education, for people outside work collectives (housewives, pensioners), than for highly educated specialists in the productive sphere. On this point the questionnaire material speaks very clearly.

A significant proportion of readers value the newspaper highly as an aid to work and study. In deciding about this or that question of work in a shop, section, at a place of work, or about personal relationships in the work collective, in efforts to acquire knowledge, people are drawn to the newspaper and acquire from it answers to many questions bearing on their own lives. This is what binds many people to the newspaper, and elevates its role in the life of working people.

The very diversity of societal goals in our time makes the newspaper an indispensable participant in all events of party, komsomol and trade-union life. Agitators and political propagandists, lecturers, activists of popular control, of comrades courts, of betterment committees, of women's soviets, of social construction bureaux, of voluntary artistic organizations – all who give their free time, energy and knowledge in fulfilling social duties, always and inevitably turn to the newspaper for advice, for fresh facts and figures, for some persuasive example, for some better experience. We can judge, on the basis of our questionnaire data, not only who amongst the readers most need the newspaper as a source of advice in societal matters, but also how numerous our social activists are and how they are composed as a group; this means that we can learn something of the scale and depth, about the intensity of the action, of the press as a champion of societal interests amongst the reading masses.

The cognitive value of the newspaper is manifested also in the significant role which it plays as a source of everyday information. This role is reflected directly in that meaning attributed to the newspaper which refers to its ability to widen horizons.

The recorded answers of readers reveal considerable insight in showing the newspaper to be valued as a means of linkage to the political life of the country and to public opinion. This is evidence of the great significance and authority of the internal and external politics of the Communist Party and the Soviet government, and also evidence of the reinforcing and regulating role played by the principles and norms of communist morality.

The sum total of replies discloses an extensive and complicated world of readers' interests. They also reveal enough for some conclusions to be drawn about the existence of an autonomous world of readers' judgements, forming a system of evaluative orientations in relation to the press and to what it presents. A positive pattern of valuations seems to result from a complicated process of 'learning' about the newspaper, from its increasing meaningfulness for the reader and a growing sense of its meeting the spiritual needs of his personality. Such a perspective, in our view, opens new possibilities for strengthening the action of the press and enlarging its role in the process of building communism.

Reference

PIRAMIDIN, V. (1967), *The Reader and the Newspaper*, Sverdlovsk.

Part Four
Mass Communication Organizations

A frequently remarked upon characteristic of mass
communications is the fact that they typically originate in
specialist, complex and often large organizations. In recent
years there has been a growing realization of the important
implications which follow from this. Mass communication as a
social process cannot be properly understood without some
knowledge of the internal structure and dynamics of
communication organizations. The three pieces which follow
can be seen either as additions to our knowledge of complex
organizations or as sources of hypotheses about the independent
effect which organizational factors may have on the flow of
media content. The reader interested in media organizations
is also referred to the contributions by Hood and by
Nordenstreng, in Part Six of this volume.

11 Philip Elliott

Mass Communication—A Contradiction in Terms?

Excerpt from Philip Elliott, *The Making of a Television Series: a Case Study in the Sociology of Culture*, Constable, 1972.

One aim in case-study research is to move from the particular to the general. This Reading presents an account of the production process for television abstracted from a case study and drawing on other studies to show how they contribute to the overall argument. It looks forward to further research on other types of programmes to fill out the general picture. The more speculative parts of the analysis presented in this article are included in the hope they will stimulate such research. Meanwhile, however, there is no need to wait for such work when that already completed suggests some extremely important propositions about the nature and scope of communication possible through a mass medium like television. These raise specific questions about the type of content which can be expected from a medium of mass communication, as well as wider questions about the modes of communication possible within societies dominated by such mass media and the possible consequences of these for social structure and process.

This Reading will extend the view of the mass media and the professional communicators who work within them as crucial intermediaries between the society as source and the society as audience. This intermediary role cannot be seen simply as a passive channel of information flow, as implied by the 'gate-keeper' model and its derivatives. Nor are the intermediaries purposive communicators in the terms suggested by the persuasive models of the communication process. But the actions of such communicators do result in the creation of an image of social reality which includes both cognitive and evaluative elements. The cognitive elements are drawn from a limited range of sources in society, processed through occupational and technological routines and presented to add to a separated and self-supporting media culture. It acquires an evaluative dimension through the elaboration of symbols and definitions within it, identifying particular social groups and their positions on particular social issues.

The concept of media culture suggests support for McCormack's argument that in modern society the output of the mass media can be seen as drawing on and reinforcing a collective, integrative gestalt (McCormack, 1961). But there are important limitations on the communicator's ability to elaborate and communicate substantive meaning through television. On the account of television production developed through the case-study material, it seems likely that the output of the medium will lack the planning and the integration implied by McCormack's phrase. An essential feature of media culture is its ability to embrace confused and contradictory positions. It could be suggested that television does not provide society with an homogeneous integrative gestalt so much as with a variety of ways of managing and assimilating knowledge and opinion, in some cases by presenting and reinforcing established perspectives, in others by challenging or cancelling particular points of view.

The limits on communication in television documentary production

A variety of factors inhibit communication through television. They may be grouped under four main headings – relationships with sources, the division of labour at different production stages, the relationship with the audience, and institutional or communicator control. The central position of the producer as leader of the production team has emerged from the analysis of the production of the documentary series, *The Nature of Prejudice*. To an extent he created the final output. One of the three chains which generated and supported ideas for the programmes – the subject chain – was firmly based on the producer's ideas and past experiences. However, the other two chains – the presentation and the contact chain – placed two limitations on the producer's creative role. Material had to be suitable and available for television presentation. These two chains did more than limit what the producer could achieve. They themselves generated ideas and items for programme content. The contact chain shows one way in which the professional communicator is dependent on the society in which he works. The presentation chain emphasizes the requirements of the medium and the development of particular methods and standards of production within it.

The three contact mechanisms subsumed within the contact chain played a particularly important part in limiting the range of material available for television production. The range of material is heavily skewed towards ideas about a subject, previously elaborated through the culture of the mass media. Television, the press and other media played a large part in making a particular set of people, events and previously prepared material available for the *Nature of Prejudice* series. The case of Programme 6 [not included here] provides a particularly clear example of the way in which the production team was forced to use media channels and to draw on their experience of a general media culture to find the people they wanted to appear in the programmes. These various mechanisms show the way in which a new production draws on the established culture of the media, thus ensuring similarity and continuity in the view of the world presented. Nevertheless, they also show the large part which chance plays in the process. Change occurs within a bounded system.

This picture of the media culture as a largely separate and self-contained system is further supported by the use made of the other two contact mechanisms, personal acquaintance and organizations. The personal acquaintances of production personnel are built up through working in the medium and through contacting sources for other productions. Organizations, especially representative ones such as were used in *The Nature of Prejudice*, are outside the media culture but available for use by it. In many cases these organizations have a view they want to put across. They are likely to want to be purposive communicators in terms of the Westley-Maclean model (1957). But their ability to be purposive or persuasive is limited by the intermediary role of the professional communicator. Occasionally, through constant contact and exposure, their view is incorporated as an accepted part of the conventional wisdom of the media culture. Such examples are comparatively rare, however, because the purpose of many organizations is to put forward views in sensitive areas. These cannot be accepted as they stand because the communicator and the institution in which he is employed are required to be impartial. At this point the factor of *institutional or communicator control* appears.

A more usual process than the incorporation of the views of a particular group and one which was illustrated in *The Nature of Prejudice*, is the incorporation of publicized expert opinion on issues too global to be directly subject to the rules of political partiality. The 1967 Reith Lectures had the effect of elevating Edmund Leach, the lecturer, to the status of 'global thinker'. Suddenly he was in great demand throughout television as a guest-speaker. Similar processes on an even larger scale can be seen in the treatment given to Desmond Morris following the publication of *The Naked Ape*. Clearly these processes of cultural change require much more detailed investigation than is possible here. The main conclusion to be drawn from the present study is the way in which the situation of television production tends to ensure cultural repetition and continuity. On many subjects which might be treated by television, and on most which are continually regarded as news, there seem to be standard perspectives available within the media culture which are likely to be reinforced and repeated in the process of gathering material for a new programme.[1] The question we are left with is what are the conditions a new perspective has to meet in order to be taken up by the media?

The problem of partiality is only one of the hurdles such a new perspective would have to clear. A second is the desire of the production personnel to avoid control or influence from outsiders, including sources. This can be demonstrated from the findings of another study of a television documentary, this time on cancer research. In the study research scientists and doctors specializing in the treatment of cancer with radiotherapy were interviewed for their views on television publicity for cancer research and for their reactions to the particular programme.[2]

1. For an elaboration of a similar argument in another case study see Halloran, Elliott and Murdock (1970).

2. The programme was *Men Against Cancer* made by Associated Redif-fusion and networked on ITV in September 1967. The study of cancer professionals was carried out by Philip Elliott. A study of a sample of the general public was also conducted by Roger L. Brown. Reports are forthcoming.

The scientists and doctors held two rather different views of cancer research. The scientists stressed the need for basic scientific work, the doctors the more immediate returns to be expected from empirical manipulation of treatment techniques. These can both be seen as professional ideologies, in the terms used by Strauss and others, based on and justifying the different features of their professional work (Strauss *et al.*, 1964). But both groups, and especially the leading scientists and doctors in their public capacities, also subscribed to an over-arching ideology which stressed that cancer was not the terrifying, unknown killer of popular imagination. They pointed to the way in which education and diagnosis facilities might breach the vicious circle of public fear which kept death rates high. These three ideologies and especially the third, which was used widely for public consumption in other fields, show the way in which television's potential sources made sense of the field of cancer research.

The television documentary, however, did not adopt any of these views. Instead it presented a picture of cancer research in which a variety of points of view were reflected but none presented or developed as a coherent view of the subject. The final section of the programme, for example, consisted of statements from prominent research scientists on the likely rate of progress in research. These varied wildly, but they were simply laid side by side in the programme with no attempt to judge between them. Another feature of the content of the programme – the number of sequences picturing research with animals – shows the way the selection criteria of the professional communicators were superimposed on the views of their sources. The use of animals in research was one aspect of a complex scientific problem which the audience could be expected to understand and react to. Further, the scientists, although they did not attempt to restrict the material available to the communicators, tried to discourage the portrayal of animals as they feared repercussions from an emotional public. This type of material therefore both fitted the communicator's idea of 'good television' and enabled them to assert their independence from their sources.

This study also shows the important difference between presenting a picture of a subject through television and making sense of it, by providing a coherent account. Many of the scientists, some of whom had experience in giving public talks or lectures on research, criticized the programme for not giving simple, developing accounts of the research problem and the way it was being tackled. Conversely, they approved of one section of the programme which did 'tell a story' about a particular cancer and the attempts which had been made to control it. The use the professional communicators made of the medium, showing animals and complex research machinery for their visual appeal, and because they fitted a special musical score, seem to have inhibited the development of a coherent story approach such as the scientists advocated. Moreover, the professional communicators were not expert in the field which they proposed to cover. They could hardly be expected to become conversant with a complex subject in the space of time it took to make a television programme. This is another form of the dilemma discussed in the adult education phase of *The Nature of Prejudice* – the choice between a subject expert, and an expert in the television medium. The communicators' non-expert status, their production criteria, the nature of the medium, their desire to keep their distance from their sources, and their beliefs about audience reactions, all inhibited an account of the subject emerging through the television programme.

Such factors are reinforced by others following from the basic legal structure within which the communicator operates. Two which have been illustrated in the analysis of *The Nature of Prejudice* are the need to avoid libel and to ensure balance and impartiality. One common technique for handling the requirement of impartiality is to ensure that any view is matched by its opposite. The non-expert status of the communicator may also make him anxious to avoid assertions which might be faulted, or he may simply be unsure which assertions are correct. Another technique for handling such problems is to attribute views to outside parties, thus absolving the communicator from responsibility. This technique of attribution to an outside source is one commonly used in news bulletins where there are differences of opinion over the facts of a case.[3] A producer seems more likely to adopt a particular point of view when it has been previously put forward by others in the media and so sanctioned as part of the

3. See Halloran, Elliott and Murdock (1970, pp. 185–6) for a discussion of this point.

conventional media culture. The evidence needed to support a known perspective will be much slimmer than that required to support a new and different point of view.

Table 1 **Producer, intermediaries and sources**

	Production team	Contact mechanisms	Other intermediaries	Sources
Producer	Director	Press	Organization leaders	People in society
	Researcher	Organizations		Events in society
		Personal		
			Controllers of material e.g. librarians	Previously prepared media material

But as well as working through sources, the television producer has to work through a variety of other intermediaries who stand between himself and the society as source. This is the problem identified above as *the division of labour inherent at different stages of television production*. On *The Nature of Prejudice* it was always possible for the producer to deal directly with a source, though, as Table 1 demonstrates, contact mechanisms and other intermediaries were usually necessary for the producer to reach a source of useful material. 'Vox pops' provide perhaps the best example of a direct approach to 'people in society', and they show the inherent inadequacy and fortuitousness of this method of finding material. The production personnel, recognizing the editorial control which could be exercized by intermediaries and sources, tried to get as close to their material as possible. It can be argued that the more distanced they were from the source, the more likely they were to use material already accepted within the media culture because they were dependent on other people's understandings of their ideas and purposes.

The producer had to work through others not only to collect

ideas and material but also to realize those ideas on the screen. Each separate specialist involved in this process had his own set of standards for judging and selecting material. These were based on their own particular skills and so might vary from those of the producer. The way in which this could contribute to a reduction in the meaning of the programme content is best illustrated in the role played by the programme presenter. On occasion the presenter 'took the role of the audience' in order to suggest cuts, simplifications and adaptations to make the content more appealing to an average audience member. His knowledge about such an average audience member was necessarily tenuous and speculative. But regardless of the characteristics attributed to the imagined audience, for example their level of intelligence, the concern in this process seemed to be not with simpler and so more effective communication of meaning, but with simplification in order to ensure that audience attention was not lost. In other words, the aim was to establish a relationship between production and audience based on audience satisfaction rather than the communication of meaning. Of course audience attention is an essential precondition to the communication of meaning and the producer of *The Nature of Prejudice* thought that realistically he could only hope to put across a few simple points to an audience varying greatly in intelligence and educational experience. The contrast, however, rests on whether production decisions were made to facilitate communication of such ideas or to attract and hold an audience in front of the set.

The use of 'live' studio discussions in television programmes illustrates another way in which the actual process of television production tends to reduce the meaning contained in the output. Some of the points already made generally apply specifically to 'live' discussions – for example, the tendency to challenge guest opinion and to use a panel rather than a single guest. A panel both ensures variety of view and insures against a guest who does not come over well on television. But a panel discussion is liable to limit the scope allowed to any guest to develop an account or an argument. The presenter in such a discussion has a difficult role to play, drawing out the views of a guest but at the same time representing the viewer and summarizing or simplifying on his behalf. Discussions also aim to be attractive spectacles in which the participants challenge each other or engage in conversational repartee. The premium on brief, simple expression makes for a reliance on conventional points or illustrations in the argument. In *The Nature of Prejudice* this was again well illustrated in the case of the combative interviews in Programme 6. The presenter's reference to 'the way Hitler used to talk about the Jews' or Lady Dartmouth's claim that she would 'fight to the death for the freedom of the individual' are two particularly clear examples of participants using conventional phrases with wide cultural and symbolic overtones. They are further examples of the general perspectives available in the media culture which are associated with evaluative reaction as well as cognitive meaning. The general tendency, whether in explanatory or combative discussions, seems to be towards encounters which follow a simple and predictable form, as if each side was making moves in a game. This tendency is more likely the more the subject recurs in the media and so the more it is embedded in the media culture.

A typology of televisual communication

These various processes through which meaning is controlled and reduced in television documentary production all suggest important ways in which the medium and its output is managed and assimilated within the social structure. But before considering that problem further it is worth trying to widen the horizons of the discussion from documentary production to include other types of production for television. In documentary production the professional communicator has a part to play as a creative intermediary between source and audience. In the course of the study of *The Nature of Prejudice* this type of production was contrasted with the system used to produce Adult Education programmes. This was a system through which material was funnelled into the visual and verbal forms necessary to make a television programme. 'Funnelled' seems the best word to describe a system in which the material was taken from sources outside television and then passed through a series of specialized processes to fit it for presentation on the screen. Although the television personnel still retain authority over their sources in this case it seems qualitatively different from the documentary production system in which the television producer takes his own view of the subject matter, albeit in interaction with the material available to him.

The contrast between these two production systems suggests that one continuum underlying different types of production for television is the varying scope of the producer's role.[4] This continuum is set out on the left hand side of Table 2. Party political broadcasts and 'one-shot' plays are examples of programmes which might be expected to come at opposite extremes of such a continuum. In the first case the role of the television producer is limited to making technical facilities available to communicators outside the medium, in the second the terminology of production and source ceases to be relevant and we are dealing with a case much closer to the high cultural model of artistic creativity. Compared with these two, both documentaries and adult education programmes come towards the centre of the continuum. News programmes can also be fitted into this framework. Newsmen do not recreate their view of a subject in the same way as a documentary producer but they do have important decisions to take on selection and presentation. A recent study of the television news coverage of a particular event, the Anti-Vietnam war demonstrations of 27 October 1968 showed that bulletins produced some time after the event were more like television programmes made to retell the story as the newsmen had seen it than those which were put out while the event was still going on (Halloran, Elliott and Murdock, 1970, especially Ch. 6). This had important consequences for the way the story was structured and interpreted in later bulletins. In other words, even with a single type of production, there is likely to be some variation in its place on the continuum, in this case according to the time and resources allowed for making the programme. It should be clear, however, that this continuum, based on the scope allowed to television production, has important implications for the relationship of the medium to the society as source. A parallel continuum based on this is shown on the right of the Table 2. The more limited the scope of television production the more direct the access of the society as source to the society as audience. Party politicals are a

4. In this context and throughout the rest of this Reading, producer is used as a general term to include all those involved in production within television.

Table 2 A typology of mass communication

Scope of production	Production function	Example programme type	Access of society as source	Audience relationship
Limited	Technical facilitation	Party political	Direct	Persuasive effectiveness
	Facilitation, selection	Adult education	Modified direct	Informative effectiveness
	Selection, presentation	News bulletin	Filtered	Informative, satisfaction
	Selection, compilation	Documentary	Remade	Satisfaction, informative
	Realization, creation	'Realistic' serial	Advisory	Satisfaction, entertainment
Extensive	Creation, origination	'One-shot' plays	Uncontrolled	Artistic, satisfaction

comparatively rare example of direct access being allowed to persuasive communicators outside the medium. Other examples of direct access include sports programmes and outside broadcasts, neither of which usually deal with purposive communicators or persuasive subjects. Programmes designed to deal regularly with a specific subject for a minority audience or to cater for a particular audience need, such as religious programming or adult education broadcasts, offer the purposive communicators in each field -- the clerics and the educators -- a more modified form of access. In both cases special institutional machinery has been set up to link television production with interested parties in the particular field. But in both cases television producers have retained ultimate control over programme production. In the field of religious broadcasting, for example, there has been a continual search for programmes which would fill the religious 'closed period' on Sunday evening but which at the same time would not be branded with a religious label, which would have a wider appeal than to the committed religious audience. This seems a particularly good example of the professional communicator trying to develop the mass characteristics of the medium and the potential of his own role, even in an area which had been to some extent insulated for a minority audience.

These examples suggest that there are comparatively few cases of direct or modified-direct access through television to the audience for purposive or persuasive communicators. It is also interesting to note that, with the exception of party political broadcasts, there seems to be an inverse relationship between access for outsiders and the amount of resources and the size of audience made available in television. Adult education programmes, for example, are generally given a small budget and placed in unattractive time-slots. This point can of course be argued both ways. Programmes allowing direct access are likely to be less attractive to viewers than those made by professional communicators because they are attempts to use the most mass of media for minority purposes.

Proceeding along the continuum the greater the scope of the television producer's role the more limited the access available for the society as source to the society as audience. In news bulletins, information about people and events in society comes filtered through the selection and presentation decisions made by television newsmen. Their ideas on what makes news decide which people and issues will receive publicity through the medium. Purposive communicators often supported by public-relations specialists can attempt to manipulate the news media by trading on these criteria or by bringing pressure to bear on the newsroom to change the criteria in their favour. Some politicians, *par excellence* Senator Joseph McCarthy, have been outstandingly successful at news management. This is a danger of which newsmen themselves are very well aware.[5] They are also aware of attempts by politicians to pressure them into changing the rules of the game. The central point, however, is that access through this type of programme is allowed on the media's terms. At another level it is then possible to explain the terms offered according to the occupational and institutional situation of the journalists and of their place with the news media in the social structure.

Most research on mass communication which has dealt with problems of production and process has concentrated on non-fictional output. The data reported in this study has been no exception. The attempt made to extend the two continua in Table 2 into the field of fictional programmes and dramatic productions is even more speculative than the rest of this discussion. The typology outlined in Table 2 probably suffers from a phenomenon familiar to social scientists in other fields – that it is easy to make fine discriminations when dealing with subjects on which information is available and to fall back on more general categories when the subject matter is less familiar. The types of dramatic programme shown in Table 2 – realistic series and 'one-shot' plays – are included to give an example of the type of discrimination which it might be possible to make in this area. A more comprehensive typology must await further work on these and similar programmes.

The term 'realistic series' is intended to include programmes based on known communities or occupations. Such series are often equipped with an expert adviser whose task is to keep creative imagination within realistic bounds. Moreover, the community or occupation concerned is likely to take an interest in

5. See for example the various recent accounts of the 'making' and the 'selling' of a number of potential figures.

how it is portrayed in the programmes. Its success in influencing the production personnel and the television organizations will depend on a variety of factors such as the strength of any representative organizations and the social standing of the group concerned. In contrast 'one-shot' plays seem to be more simply a matter for the writer and the television production team to originate and create as they think best. It is a moot point whether the author of such plays should be regarded as inside or outside the medium.

Media, audience and society

It should be clear that although this typology of different programme types has been presented as if each type was a distinct, homogeneous category, considerable variation is to be expected between different programmes in each type. Drawing on the contrast between communication and satisfaction or communication and attention which has been made on several occasions above, it is possible to introduce another set of terms to explain some of the differences between and within the programme types outlined in Table 2. To do so the concepts of communication, attention and satisfaction need further consideration.

The aim of the persuasive communicator, the party political broadcaster or the advertiser, is to change or confirm attitudes and behaviour. The principal criterion against which their communications should be judged is persuasive effectiveness. Although we have suggested that various features of the production process in television militate against it, it is possible that professional communicators working on non-fictional programmes will be concerned with informative effectiveness, that is in using the medium for the effective communication of meaning. In the case-study, although there were elements of such an approach behind some production decisions, these appeared to be over-ruled by a contrasting orientation towards audience attention. The difference between these orientations can be highlighted as a contrast between interest in the meaning of the content and in ensuring an audience regardless of content. Stated so baldly it is clear that any production team is likely to have a mixed orientation, but the aim of this study has been to isolate the main tendencies inherent in production for the medium.

Discussion of the relationship between fictional programmes and the audience is subject to the same reservations already made above. Nevertheless Hall and Whannel's contrast between high art, popular art and mass media art shows sufficient similarity to the contrast between communication and attention to provide some grounds for the claim that related conceptual distinctions are available in this area (Hall and Whannel, 1964). Hall and Whannel stress the close relationship between artist, art and audience in popular culture. They suggest that such culture depends for its popularity on the continuing reaffirmation of known attitudes, values and opinions among the audience. The audience respond by recognizing familiarity. This is in sharp contrast to the traditional claim on behalf of 'high art', that it enables the audience to 'see the world afresh'. In this case the audience responds to new perspectives and unfamiliarity. Hall and Whannel have no doubt that mass art is a corruption of the conventions of popular art. It is brought about mainly by the mass media's need to be sure of a large audience. Various processes of standardization remove those particular references appealing to specific audience groups which are to be found in popular art. The new art form becomes available to an undifferentiated mass audience. Mass art has to rely primarily on universal emotional reactions. The result is a form of art which is available to everyone but has nothing to say to anyone. The parallels with the account of nonfiction television advanced earlier in this Reading are, first, between the repetition of a conventional media culture and the continuing reaffirmation of values and opinions found in popular culture, and, second, the focus on audience attention rather than communicative meaning.

It seems likely that the different types of art distinguished by Hall and Whannel will be the result of rather different production orientations. 'High art' is believed to be the product of individual creative genius. In W. H. Auden's words, 'the interests of a writer and the interests of his readers are never the same and if, on occasion, they happen to coincide, this is a lucky accident'. Such work is often spoken of as something which the artist had to create, regardless of audience and critical reaction. It seems doubtful whether this type of individual artist can even be said to be working for himself in a complementary role as audience. Although it may be possible to develop such an orientation in the newer media the closest approach to it commonly found seems to be to put oneself and/or one's immediate colleagues into the role of audience. Colleagues are readily available and moreover they share many of the perspectives and assumptions which are held in common within the media culture. On occasions the *Nature of Prejudice* production team worked for themselves as their own audience. An example was the inclusion of the film clip showing riotous fans after one of the 'prejudiced' interviewees had suggested that Englishmen were traditionally reserved and restrained. It was open to the audience to recognize the intentions behind this insert and to react in the same way. But the important feature of the audience relationship to this type of production orientation is that it depends on coincidence between the interests of the producers and the audience.

This point may be illustrated by the results of another case-study carried out on two programmes, in a series of topical, satirical, entertainment programmes produced by Danish Radio for a youth audience (Halloran and Elliott, 1970). These programmes, called *Peppermill*, were produced by a group of young journalists and television personnel. Production of each programme took place within a week and was centred on a series of production meetings. In these meetings the producers used each other as a sounding board for their ideas and to test reaction to the completed material. The producers made little reference to the audience except to assume that they would respond in the same way as themselves. Audience research carried out as part of the study suggested that the programmes were not strikingly popular. Young people critized the programmes mainly on the grounds that they could not understand them, that they were too boring or that they dealt at too great a length with serious political subjects. But within the general *Peppermill* audience there was a small group of 'devotees' who followed the series regularly on television and radio. These devotees liked the programmes and generally recognized the production intentions which lay behind them. The socio-economic indices available from the surveys were fairly crude but the minority group of devotees appeared to be more like the production team than the rest of the target youth audience. They were older, more intelligent and, among the girls, more likely to be middle-class. They tended to live in or around Copenhagen, the metropolitan centre, and they appeared to share, however loosely, the production team's political sympathies. The result was a form of minority, 'special-public' communication within the setting of a mass medium.

No doubt one of the skills in production work for a mass medium is the ability to empathize with audience groups of which one is not a member. Some producers seem to have favourite target audience groups. They use their imagined reaction as a yardstick against which to judge a production. There seems to be a chance with producers using this type of production orientation that they will hit on a programme that strikes a chord for a large audience group and becomes in Hall and Whannel's terms popular culture. There is also the chance that they will miss their audience and end up in the situation of the *Peppermill* producers, working only for a minority of 'devotees'. Comparable conclusions could be drawn from the world of newspaper publishing where some publishers, and to a lesser extent editors, have succeeded in creating papers with definite identities which have appealed to large but distinctive audiences. Others have developed papers with distinct identities which have failed to find a large market, while others have sought to increase audience size and advertising revenue by abandoning rather than creating such identities.

But the reference to audience size and advertising revenue suggests that this production orientation is likely to be under continual pressure. It is inherently uncertain. Such pressure shows itself in, for example, the repetition of standardized genres, the avoidance of material which might provoke offence and generally in the attempt to be all things to all men. At the production level it is reflected in a third orientation towards what we have termed audience attention. The disparity between high art and standardized genres has generally been explained in terms of conflict between artistic creativity and the commercial and administrative concerns of large-scale media organizations. So far in this Reading discussion has been confined to the production level within the medium. Such concentration is justified by the relative autonomy which appears to be enjoyed by those working at this level in British television. Nevertheless, it is important not to lose sight of the over-arching commercial and institutional structures within which the production teams operate. These structures, just as much as the production personnel within them, can be seen as mediating between society as source and society as audience.

The society as source influences the media institutions by setting the conditions for their survival and growth. Clearly some groups in society are in a better position to influence these conditions than others. In Britain there has also been some variation in the requirements which the two broadcasting institutions have been expected to meet. This study was carried out within commercial television but it is useful to consider briefly some of the changes which have occurred in the situation of the BBC. The institutional structure of the BBC was explicitly designed to provide some insulation between communication and commercialism. Throughout the period during which the BBC had a monopoly in broadcasting it was able to play a considerable part in defining its own role. This established some independence for the BBC from the immediate demands of the mass audience. Instead the BBC had support from various custodians of the cultural heritage. Ironically the most recent activities of members of this group, in the form of the Campaign for Better Broadcasting, have been directed against the BBC, specifically against changes in BBC Radio. The introduction of commercial television gave fuller expression to the mass characteristics of the television medium and changed the situation in which the BBC operated. To safeguard its case for future increases in the licence fee it had to set about competing for the audience as a mass. A further irony is that the BBC has since been blamed for succeeding in this endeavour, often by the same people who supported, or who now claim to have supported, its previous role as cultural custodian. Some have even gone so far as to stand the case against the BBC as a monopoly on its head, claiming that there is now no difference between the two popular television channels so that the continued existence of the BBC as a separate institution cannot be justified. Such an argument begs a variety of questions, not least whether the two channels are really so similar. The argument has mainly been advanced for political purposes, but even so it provides an apposite illustration of a shift in the conditions under which one television organization has operated. Another example, drawn from the present study itself, shows how the institutional structure of ITV may on occasions temper the dictates of commercialism. At the time *The Nature of Prejudice* was in production the prospect of the reallocation of contracts made documentary production especially advantageous to the companies as a means of impressing the Authority. Both British television systems show how variations in organization structure can modify the simple equation between mass audience and mass medium. The ability to judge consumer demand is one, but only one way of ensuring the survival and growth of the television organizations. It is also necessary to bear in mind the conditions set by other constituents.

The traditional dispute between creative personnel and administrators in the media can be seen as a special case of the problem of reconciling professional authority and consumer demand. Professional expertise may suggest a course of action which would not be that preferred by the customer. In some professions, notably medicine, professional expertise is presumed to be sovereign, in other fields it may still be accepted that the customer is 'always right'. An additional problem in the case of the mass media however is that both communicators and administrators are distanced from their clients or customers. They have to make guesses about their needs and tastes on the basis of inadequate information. Administrators are likely to be guided in the guesses they make by the view they take of the organization's other constituents and their demands. On the other hand the creative personnel are likely to adopt one of the three orientations towards the audience outlined above. They may hope that the audience will follow them, in Auden's words that 'their interests will coincide'; they may work for themselves or their colleagues as a notional audience; or they may concentrate on audience attention. Although it is a common answer to problems of media organization to advocate more professionalism, more creative autonomy for the programme producer, a distinction needs to be drawn between professional autonomy in developing standard procedures for dealing with recurrent work tasks, and creative autonomy, which in the high cultural sense would lead to individuation rather than standardization of output. Professionalism may take the form of a concentration on routine procedures for handling problems posed by television production. The occupational group may develop its own routines, criteria and standards and become even more enclosed within them as a separate system intervening between source and audience.

Earlier in this Reading we suggested that such occupational specialization is one of the factors tending to inhibit communication through the medium of television. Our model of the mass communication process consists of three separate systems, society as source, mass communicators and society as audience. Each of these systems takes from the other what is necessary for its own needs. The mass communicators draw on society for material suitable for their purposes, the audience is left largely on its own to respond to the material put before it. Each system has its own set of interests and its own ways of bringing influence to bear on the others. This model is in direct contrast to those which link the different parts of the communication process directly, conceptualizing it as a process of influence or communication flow. The model can be clarified by substituting the term 'spectator' for the audience. The analogy is with the spectators at, for example, a tennis match. They sit outside the court and watch the game. If mass communication was a process of direct influence or transmittal of meaning the players would turn round and hit their balls into the crowd. This is an over-extreme case to argue from the present study. More comparative work is needed before it can be said to have been established. But if communication is defined as the transference of ordered meaning, the paradox suggested by the present study is that mass communication is liable not to be communication at all.

This claim, that the dominant means of communication cannot be used for communication, raises wider issues about the relationship between the media and society which can only be touched on here. First, it seems inevitable that if the main focus in programme production is on audience attention and satisfaction, the main dimension of possible audience reaction will be emotional response to familiar symbols. McCluhan has argued that the electronic, visual media are about to change the whole sensory and cognitive style to which we have become accustomed through the literary media. The argument suggested here is that a shift towards emotionalism and symbolism is not just a consequence of the different inherent qualities of the different media. It is a result of the gradual progression towards media showing more and more mass characteristics in content and organization. C. Wright Mills had a phrase for it. In mass society, he argued, the public have become 'mere media markets'; a phrase which reflects not simply the spread of commercialism but also the change in the relationship between people and society from the nineteenth-century view of a community of publics (Mills, 1959). A second issue is that although the professional communicator has gradually emerged as a new-style intellectual in society, the tendency is for him to be preoccupied with the form rather than the content of communication. On the other hand those who are preoccupied with content are not likely to achieve access to the form. The factors which inhibit the broadcasters' opportunities to communicate through the media, also ensure that they will be unlikely to provide society, in Mannheim's terms, with any 'free floating' intellectual challenge.[6] Like other professionals, the communicator works within a particular occupational milieu and organizational structure.

Together these two issues contribute to a third which is best expressed in the familiar question – does the output of the media necessarily maintain consensus and the *status quo*? The first argument about the relationship possible between the audience and the media seems to support a Marcusian view of a mass population available for manipulation. However, the second argument suggests that those working in the media are not able to exercise sufficient direct control over its output to engage in such direct manipulation. In this chapter it has been argued that it is difficult for a communicator in the mass media to say anything. This does not mean however that nothing is said, that no effect is produced. What is said is the unplanned product of following accepted production routines within established organizational systems. As a result it must be expected that what is said will in the main be fundamentally supportive of the socio-economic structure of the society in which those organizations are set.

Nevertheless, the argument that mass communication is not communication is an extreme one, designed not as an absolute assertion but to focus attention on a tendency. Among the variety

6. Mannheim (1936). Anyone who cherishes a belief that academics can fill such a role, or who suspects that I hold such a belief, should read Gouldner (1971).

of programmes on television today there are some which seem to have more communicative meaning, to be less conventionally reflective than others. One of the commonsense arguments which appears to contradict the view of the media as system-maintaining is that in most sections of television at least the predominant ethos continues to be liberal-progressive. But such an ethos, and even occasional programmes which seem to be a direct reflection of it, cannot by themselves refute the argument of this book that the more mass the media the more inhibitions are placed on a direct communication process. It may seem paradoxical to argue that the dominant means of communication in society is tending more and more to be controlled and operated by people who have nothing to say, or if they have, cannot use the media to say it. It does suggest however that the mass media illustrate the contradictions rather than the conspiracies of capitalist society.

References

GOULDNER, A. (1971), *The Coming Crisis of Western Sociology*, Heinemann.
HALL, S., and WHANNEL, P. (1964), *The Popular Arts*, Hutchinson.
HALLORAN, J. D., ELLIOTT, P., and MURDOCK, G. (1970), *Communication and Demonstrations: A Case Study*, Penguin Books.
HALLORAN, J. D., and ELLIOTT, P. (1970), *Peberkvaemen*, Danish Radio.
MANNHEIM, K. (1936), *Ideology and Utopia*, Routledge & Kegan Paul.
McCORMACK, T. (1961), 'Social theory and the mass media', *Canad. Rev. Econ. polit. Science*, vol. 27, pp. 479–89.
MILLS, C. W. (1959), *The Power Elite*, Oxford University Press.
STRAUSS, A., SCHATZMAN, L., BUCHER, R., EHRLICH, D., and SABSHIN, M. (1964), *Psychiatric Ideologies and Institutions*, Free Press.
WESTLEY, B. H., and MACLEAN, M. S. JR. (1957), 'A conceptual model for communication research', *Journalism Q.*, vol. 34, pp. 31–8.

12 Jeremy Tunstall

News Organization Goals and Specialist
Newsgathering Journalists

Published for the first time in this volume

Newsgathering for whom?

Sociologists have played only a very small part during the last decade in public debates about the collection of news for, and its
dissemination through, the press and broadcast media. Clearly
this debate is part of the broader continuing debate about the
nature and purposes of 'democratic', and other, forms of government. But central to the debate are fundamentally different
assumptions about the journalists who gather the news. Some
criticisms imply that journalists belong to an autonomous occupation, and are controlled only by other journalists. Secondly, it
is argued that journalists are controlled by their news sources –
such as the government officials whose activities they report.
Thirdly, quite a different assumption is that journalists are under
the control of their employers; sometimes the partisan political
aims of the employer are emphasized, sometimes his supposed
subservience to advertisers, and sometimes the employer's subservience to the mass audience.

The purpose of this paper is to consider three relevant roles of
specialist newsgathering journalists:

1. The *employee* role
2. The *newsgatherer* role
3. The *competitor-colleague* role

The *competitor-colleague* role refers to the specialist newsgatherer's membership of a 'group' of correspondents who cover
the same 'news-source area', but who work for separate, and
competing, news organizations; the other correspondents are
thus both competitors and colleagues. The *newsgatherer* role
refers to the specialist correspondent's active pursuit of, and

gathering of, news from a specialized news source area (such as Aviation or Education or a foreign country). The *employee* role refers to the specialist correspondent's employment by a news organization – such as a newspaper or a news department in a radio/TV organization.

News organizations are seen in turn as having a mixture of three types of goal.

1. Audience-revenue goal
2. Advertising-revenue goal
3. Non-revenue goal

The audience-revenue goal refers to the goal of gaining (or maintaining) readers (or buyers), viewers, and listeners (or switchers-on). The advertising-revenue goal refers to the partly, but not wholly, related, objective of gaining advertising revenue. The non-revenue goal refers to any other objective – such as gaining political influence, furthering cultural or educational objectives, or merely increasing general prestige.

Previous research and the present study

Of the large quantities of published social research on the mass media, a substantial proportion deals with various aspects of the flow of news, and the audience for news. The great majority of such studies have, however, been conducted at the local, or American-state level – where the competitive position is radically different from that at the national level. One such local study has relied primarily on content analysis to measure the importance of pressure exercised by newspaper publishers as against the pressure of the audience and its socio-economic characteristics (Donohew, 1967). Despite the unusual empirical rigour of this study, its findings are somewhat limited by its concentration on newspapers in the state of Kentucky – as well as its focus on a single political issue (medicare).

Some studies of newsgathering at the national level are studies concerned primarily with foreign news; one deals with mainly newspaper reporters of foreign news based in Washington (Cohen, 1963), while another deals with the internal operations of the national network news operations in New York City – primarily as these relate to foreign news (Warner, 1968). A third study deals with a broader range of political newsgathering in Washington (Nimmo, 1964). All three studies were carried out by political scientists. But to a sociologist interested in a wider range of news – included 'non-political' news – this is a serious weakness. By concentrating on overtly political areas of news, the revenue goals of news organizations – more apparent in areas such as sport or fashion – are excluded; these political scientists have ignored the complexity of news, or journalism and of news organization goals. Cohen, Warner and Nimmo all regret what they regard as the excessive commercial emphasis in political and foreign news. They ignore the point that from a revenue point of view political, and especially foreign political, news is already subsidized by the overall news organization.

Although it lacks national newspapers (in the French, German, or British sense) the United States does have national *journalism* – the networks, newsagencies, the newsmagazines, and the whole national syndication phenomenon. Nevertheless, the more complex arrangement of national journalism, plus the presence of *two* national news centres, Washington and New York (in contrast to Paris or London), creates special difficulties for conducting a comparative study of national specialist journalism in the United States.

The present study focused on London – where British national journalism is very heavily concentrated. Only newsgathering specialists employed by twenty-three national news organizations were included:

Ten national daily newspapers (including the *Financial Times* and the communist *Morning Star*)
Seven national Sunday newspapers.
Two London evening newspapers.
Two national broadcast news departments (BBC-2 and ITN).
Two national news agencies (Reuters and Press Association).

These twenty-three national news organizations dominate the dissemination of news in Britain, to an extent not known in any other major country, with the possible exception of Japan. BBC and ITN at the time accounted for *all* broadcast news. The national newspapers accounted for over *two-thirds* of daily newspaper sales in Britain, and almost all Sunday newspaper sales.

Specialist correspondents supplied information in two rounds of data gathering. Firstly, an unstructured interview in or around their place of work (median 1 hour, 45 minutes); secondly, in summer 1968, two hundred and seven specialists completed a mailed twenty-two page questionnaire. The successful response rate for London-based specialists was 76 per cent. The response rate for foreign-based correspondents was 58 per cent; although visits were paid to all four foreign centres (including New York, Washington, Bonn, Rome); nevertheless, a lower proportion of these correspondents were interviewed face-to-face.

National 'specialists' are here defined as journalists who:

1. Are employed full-time by one of the twenty-three national news organizations.
2. Spend over half their working time covering a single specialized 'news source area'.
3. Actively *gather* and pursue news. (This excludes literary and other critics, and other chairbound reporters – of political debates, court cases.)

This definition excludes all columnists, and all radio/TV journalists who do not work for daily news bulletins. It excludes all news executives and their staffs, all newsprocessors (subeditors, re-write men, etc.), all photographers; and it also excludes general reporters, feature writers and editorial leader writers.

In 1968 a representative British national daily newspaper employed about three-hundred journalists. Of these only about 16 per cent came within this definition of 'specialist' newsgatherers. The specialist fields selected for this study included roughly half of these specialist newsgatherers.

News organization: the goals of a non-routine bureaucracy

News organizations are here defined as that part of a media organization which carries on journalistic work. The overall media organization is concerned with various additional functions of a more industrial and commercial kind. In the case of newspapers, the 'news organization' is the editorial department; only about one-tenth of total personnel work in this department. The other nine-tenths are printers, advertising salesmen, etc.

The produce of a news organization is 'news'. A study of foreign news suggests a number of aspects which make some events more likely than other events to become news. Frequency, amplitude, lack of ambiguity, meaningfulness (culturally relevant), unexpectedness within predictability, composition – all these aspects make events more likely to become news. Events connected with elite individuals, groups or nations, events which can be personified, events which are sudden and negative – these also will more probably become news (Galtung and Ruge, 1965).

These characteristics which predispose events to become news ensure that news can never be a standardized industrial product. The kind of work which journalists do is 'non-routine'. The number of exceptional cases encountered in the work is high. The nature of the *search* process, undertaken when exceptions occur, cannot be systematic, logical or analytical (Perrow, 1967). Instead the 'personal' is emphasized, and 'experience' of an uncodified sort is highly regarded.

Nevertheless, the overall media organization with its industrial production and marketing characteristics is much more routinized and pre-programmed. Within the news organization itself there are strong pressures in both directions. The media organization exerts pressures towards routinization in various ways; a notable example are the rigidly fixed deadlines of news bulletins and newspaper editions. The nature of journalistic work exerts pressures in the opposite, non-routine, direction. This continuing counter-pressure can be summed up in the term 'non-routine bureaucracy'.

Within the news organization's non-routine bureaucracy some elements are more bureaucratic or routine; one example is the whole *newsprocessing* phenomenon in which material is processed, arranged and shaped for insertion in the end product – the bulletin or edition. Newsprocessors (called sub-editors in Britain) are more hierarchically organized than are gatherers; newsprocessors are the organization men of the news organization – they align themselves with the overall (revenue) goals.

Newsgatherers in general, and specialist correspondents in particular, are involved in the news organization's most non-routine work. Specialist newsgatherers are strongly oriented towards establishing and maintaining personal relationships with individual news sources. Newsgatherers are less inclined to align themselves with the overall revenue goals, and are more inclined to support non-revenue goals.

Clearly this perspective implies that there is no single unambiguous organizational goal; on the contrary it implies a more flexible, bargaining usage for the concept 'organizational goal'. Yuchtman and Seashore (1967) have argued that the goal concept should be retained 'as a specification of the means or strategies employed by members towards enhancing the bargaining position of the organization'; and 'as a specification of the personal goals of certain members or classes of members within the organizational system'.

The tripartite division of news organizational goals outlined above is to be seen in this light. The three types of goal – audience revenue, advertising revenue, and non-revenue – result from the unusual commercial situation of news organizations (especially dependence on advertising revenue from publications). We argue below that some types of news output give special emphasis to one of the three goals. But there is usually some element of at least one other goal; there is always ambiguity.

The goals of specialist newsgathering

In the present study, on the basis of preliminary investigation and the unstructured interviews specific newsgathering fields were classified under predominant goals as follows:

1. *Non-revenue*: Foreign correspondents in New York, Washington, Bonn and Rome.

2. *Audience revenue*: Football (soccer) and Crime correspondents.

3. *Advertising revenue*: Fashion and Motoring correspondents.

A further category of 'mixed goal' was included; one of these – the Political Lobby correspondents – is the leading group of British political journalists and has a number of unique characteristics (Tunstall, 1970); for the latter reason the Lobby is listed separately, giving two more goal categories:

4. *Mixed goal*: Aviation, Education, Labour correspondents.

5. *Mixed goal*: Political Lobby correspondents.

'News values' not only predispose certain types of events to become news, but are also a main criterion by which it is decided to allocate specialists to some areas and not to other areas. For instance, Aviation – which is strong on elite individuals, sudden negative events and so on, is covered by specialists, whereas Shipping (which now has less of such attributes) has declined as a specialist field. News values are also relevant within each of the goal categories; for instance many sorts of editorial content can be related to the advertising goal, but only some of these fields (such as Fashion and Motoring) are also regarded as satisfying general news values.

General 'news values' are most closely allied to the audience goal; this audience goal in turn tends to become the predominant coalition goal of the news organization. The audience goal receives the greatest all-round support; it is accorded legitimacy by the occupation of journalism; and it is vigorously supported by sales-oriented managers in the overall media organization, as well as by advertising-oriented managers (since appealing to the audience is a *sine qua non* of advertising activities).

In view of this coalition goal, of the mixed overall goals of news organizations, and the continuing bargaining between different sub-occupations within the organization, one would not expect to find absolute empirical proof of the goal classification outlined here. Nevertheless, four separate kinds of evidence were collected and these in general support the classification:

1. The views of specialists as to the prevailing goal in specialist fields other than their own. This evidence comes, of course, from specialists who work within role-sets parallel to those of the other specialists about whom they are questioned.

2. The views of the specialists about the interest taken in their own field by the sale/circulation department and the advertising department within their own media organization (see Table 1).

3. Unstructured interviews were also conducted with senior editorial, sales and advertising executives. These views were broadly in line with the goal classification. The editors of fifteen of the twenty-three national news organizations were interviewed; of these editors two-thirds expressed views in line with the classification – at least in relation to news organizations other than their own.

4. Impressionistic evidence of two other sorts supports the general classification: Firstly, the editionizing phenomenon

(which involves late and expensive changes, especially in the case of newspapers with regional editions) concentrates heavily on Sport and Crime. Secondly, the juxtapositioning of advertising and related editorial appears to concentrate on certain fields such as Fashion and Motoring.

Table 1 **Goals of specialist newsgathering fields**

	Non-revenue Bonn, Rome, New York, Washington	Mixed Political lobby	Mixed Aviation, Education, Labour	Audience Crime Football	Advertising Fashion, Motoring	All Selected Specialists
Percentage of specialists employed by *quality* newspapers	35	28	40	24	52	35[b]
Percentage of specialists claiming active *audience circulation department* interest	22	18	30	90	79[a]	42[c]
Percentage of specialists claiming active *advertising department* interest in own field	11	6	19	29	43	18[c]

a excludes fashion
b N = 207
c N = 153

These four sorts of evidence suggest the following points:

Advertising-goal fields (Fashion and Motoring) are seen as having the strongest revenue goal of all – since they combine audience and advertising appeal.

Audience-goal fields (Crime and Football) both have a strong audience appeal – although in the case of Crime this may be declining.

Mixed-goal fields vary somewhat in the mixture of other goals. For instance Aviation is seen as having a somewhat larger element of advertising goal than have Education and Labour.

The Political Lobby is seen, compared with other mixed goal fields, as having a particularly low advertising goal element. But it is strong in non-revenue goal.

Non-revenue Foreign correspondence is seen as low on both advertising and audience goal elements. Senior executives (editorial, sales and advertising) are especially emphatic about the very high costs of maintaining foreign correspondents in distant capitals. It is the high level of expenses (transmission charges, travel, rent, etc.) of employing *staff* correspondents – as opposed to using newsagency material – which makes Foreign correspondence so impossible to justify in revenue terms.

If, then, the goals of these fields do differ so sharply, one would expect major differences in the social characteristics of specialists in particular views – and further differences in their experience of work roles.

Career background and status

British journalism lacks any clearly defined career structure. Nevertheless, marked differences exist between different fields and prevalent goals. Some of these differences are shown in Table 2.

Foreign correspondents with their non-revenue goal have an elite career pattern. Half are university graduates; more of them have upper-middle class parents than in other fields; most of them enter journalism either in London or overseas. Despite entering journalism late, foreign correspondents are likely to have precocious careers.

Audience goal specialists (Crime and Football) by contrast are very much less well educated; their parents are much more working-class. There is a much longer time gap and more job moves between entering journalism and national specialization.

The elite foreign correspondence career provides a sizeable career ladder and further opportunities for senior executive posts in the news organization. The Crime or Football correspondent's career provides only a short career ladder and little in the way of other career opportunities.

There is a marked correlation between the amount of non-revenue goal within a field and the status of the field among specialists overall. Specialist opinions about other fields were scored; there was little variation between fields in the general tendency to place the fields in this order: 1. Foreign correspondents, 2. Political, 3. Other mixed (with Labour leading), 4.

Audience, 5. Advertising goal fields. Every other field reserved its lowest opinion for Motoring correspondents.

When specialists gave these opinions of their own field there was a general tendency to push it up one or two places in the pecking order. But, with this exception, self-perceived status was very consistent with the opinions of specialists in other fields.

Table 2 Specialist correspondents' career backgrounds

	Non-Revenue Bonn, Rome, New York, Washington	Mixed Political lobby	Mixed Aviation, Education, Labour	Audience Crime, Football	Advertising Fashion, Motoring	All Selected specialists
Percentage of specialists in field aged 45 and over	42	44	22	41	16	34
Percentage of specialists with terminal age of education, aged 20+	52	30	42	6	19	33[a]
Percentage of specialists whose first journalism job was on weekly or provincial newspapers	42	86	74	64	39	62[b]
Percentage of specialists whose first journalism job was in London or overseas	62	39	55	50	60	55[c]
Percentage of specialists in present specialization at least five years	66	66	43	82	42	60[d]

a N = 196
b N = 195
c N = 193
d N = 179

Specialist correspondent as employee

Table 3 shows that there are major differences according to the goal of the field on several dimensions of the employee role. On pay there is a sharp distinction between the non-revenue Foreign and the mixed-goal Political correspondents as against all the rest. The Washington correspondents are the highest-paid single field, the Crime correspondents the lowest-paid.

Table 3 Specialist correspondent as employee

	Non Revenue Bonn, Rome, New York, Washington	Mixed Political lobby	Mixed Aviation, Education, Labour	Audience Crime, Football	Advertising Fashion, Motoring	All Selected specialists
Percentage of specialists in 1966 General Election						
Voting Conservative	32	34	19	54	67	39[a]
Voting Labour	38	31	55	31	13	36
Percentage of specialists spending less than half working time in news organization office	19	97	37	50	34	46[b]
Percentage of specialists saying at least 80% of output used	57	73	56	97	87	71[c]
Percentage saying space given by news organization to their field is very satisfactory	38	54	23	29	22	34[d]
Percentage saying that 80% or more of stories are own idea	41	51	40	36	60	45[e]
Percentage paid annual salary over £3000	64	67	31	31	39	48

a N = 170
b N = 194
c N = 159
d N = 201
e N = 191
f N = 176

One of the most striking differences is in the political partisanship by goal. Foreign and Political correspondents were fairly equally balanced between Conservative and Labour – as were the selected specialists overall. But the other mixed-goal specialists

(Aviation, Education, Labour) favoured Labour against Conservative by nearly three to one; in contrast the advertising goal specialists (Fashion, Motoring) favoured Conservative against Labour by five to one. Despite these major differences in the partisanship of correspondents there was a general lack of serious conflict between correspondents and news organizations along politically partisan lines. Although British national newspapers do have fairly explicit partisan positions in national politics, these positions tend to have relatively little impact on news reporting.

The most strongly pro-Labour in politics are the Education correspondents and the Labour correspondents. News organization executives place a great emphasis on specialist newsgatherers establishing compatible personal relationships with such news sources as trade-union leaders and teachers' leaders. In some cases there is a positive preference within a pro-Conservative news organization for a pro-Labour correspondent; but since both news executives and specialists have internalized the same broad view of news values, conflict along partisan lines is relatively unimportant. The strong preponderance of pro-Labour specialists in such 'social' areas as Education and Labour and the strong preponderance of pro-Conservative specialists in such 'business' areas as Fashion and Motoring is in line with the markedly different goals of all news organizations within different news areas.

The great majority of specialists see problems of political partisanship as much less important than autonomy and control issues in general. Different parts of the specialist newsgatherer's work present different problems for news organization surveillance. Specialists spend a fair amount of working time physically outside their news organization's office. The Political Lobby correspondents, for instance, work out of special offices at Westminster. But even while physically within his employers' office the specialist spends much time on the telephone.

The major areas where the news organization executives can attempt to establish control over specialists are:

1. In choice of stories to be covered.
2. In processing, altering, or not using stories after the specialist has gathered them.

Table 3 shows Foreign correspondents apparently less autonomous in both these areas than are specialists overall. Political Lobby correspondents are roughly similar to the general level; other mixed-goal specialists appear less autonomous in both areas. The audience goal specialists appear to have low autonomy in story-choice but very high autonomy in story-use. However, the advertising-goal specialists appear most autonomous on story choice and story use combined. This high autonomy for advertising goal correspondents within the news organization is consistent with 'control' being exercised elsewhere – by advertisers and by advertising executives within the media organization.

Specialist correspondent as newsgatherer

News value is so defined that search procedures in newsgathering cannot be systematic; one obvious type of search is travel. And the amount of travel varies greatly by field. Of the London-based fields the most travelling abroad in 1967–8 was done by these fields:

Motoring 42 days abroad (mean)
Fashion   36 days
Aviation 34 days
Football 26 days

The least foreign travel was reported by the Political Lobby men (mean nine days). Foreign travel is expensive and news organizations allow much more of it to fields which bring in revenue.

But in the non-routine work of journalism, the newsgathering 'technology' consists primarily of a telephone and a contact book of news-source telephone numbers. These tools, of course, reflect the overwhelming emphasis on personal 'experience' and 'personal contact' with individual news sources. The only other form of newsgathering technology – shorthand – also focuses on individuals and their words. Foreign correspondents (who rely heavily on surveillance of the local press and agencies) use shorthand less (Table 4).

'Writing and sending stories' is, not surprisingly, the most time-consuming single activity, but here are the next most time consuming for the selected specialists overall:

2. Telephoning sources

3. Dealing with documents
4. Face to face interviews with sources
5. Talking to other journalists

Three of these four involve talking to people.

Basic to any specialist newsgathering field are the news-source area's general structure and its publicity stance. Once again the revenue goal fields are different from the other fields. In the other newsgathering fields there is little in the way of single news sources which have a monopoly control of information over a broad area. Even in national politics the British Prime Minister only has a very limited area of monopoly control – and other Cabinet Ministers (in contrast to the US system) talk freely, and competitively, to journalists. But in the audience fields there are monopolies of relatively wider areas of information – especially Scotland Yard's monopoly of much Crime information. In the advertising goal fields (in Britain) source monopolies again exist – especially in the case of car manufacturers. Car and fashion organizations operate both as news sources and advertisers in relation to the same news organizations. This ensures that advertising-goal specialists are to a great extent controlled by news sources.

In general, specialists believe that news sources prefer dealing with 'quality' rather than with 'popular' newspapers. But this varies according to the predominant goals in differerent fields, in revenue-goal fields specialists think that sources prefer popular newspapers – presumably for revenue reasons.

Payment by journalists to news sources in most fields is regarded as rare. But in Crime and Football such payments are said to be much more common (Table 4). The audience goal predominant in both fields leads news organizations to regard such payments as worthwhile in simple terms of audience/sales revenue.

Structured arrangements for publicity also vary according to the predominant goal. Public-relations activity is least evident in the audience-goal fields in Britain; it is most evident in the advertising-goal fields. The lack of public-relations provision is illustrated in the audience-goal fields by there being very few press conferences or briefings. The Political Lobby's uniqueness

Table 4 Specialist correspondent as newsgatherer

	Non-revenue Bonn, Rome, New York, Washington	Mixed Political lobby	Mixed Aviation, Education, Labour	Audience Crime, Football	Advertising Fashion, Motoring	All Selected specialists
Percentage of specialists spending at least 10 hours a week on each of:						
(a) Face-to-face interviews with news sources	6	59	20	39	13	25[a]
(b) Telephoning sources	32	19	52	61	30	37
(c) Dealing with documents	39	34	43	12	26	33
Percentage of specialists who use short-hand	45	74	79	68	59	64
Percentage saying in their field fair amount or much payment to sources	6	0	11	58	0	15[b]
Percentage saying these demeanours with news sources sometimes necessitate						
(a) Deference	65	33	56	65	59	56
(b) Toughness, aggression	75	78	69	91	70	76
Percentage saying the sources help journalists more than journalists help sources	51	46	44	24	27	40[c]
Percentage saying there is a small number of key news-source individuals	40	84	60	51	73	59[d]
Mean number of press conferences and briefings per 30 days						
(a) 'Not for attribution'	1·2	20·7	2·2	0·1	0·5	4·5[e]
(b) Total per 30 days	10·4	27·7	10·0	1·6	11·1	11·7

a N = 186   c N = 196   e N = 190
b N = 192   d N = 200

emerges here – it has more than twice as many such meetings as the other fields; these are the famous daily Downing Street briefings.

The Political Lobby also has the highest proportion of specialists (84 per cent) saying that there are a small number of key *individuals* in their news-source area. Lowest here are the foreign correspondents – which is consistent with their surveillance activities. But 59 per cent of all specialists believe there are key individuals. This belief, which is consistent with broad 'news values' is in turn consistent with the lack of newsgathering technology or systematic search procedures.

Specialist correspondent as competitor-colleague

Specialists seek and gather news from news-source individuals and organizations in conditions of competition with other specialists. These specialist competitiors are usually referred to as 'colleagues'. A typical group of national specialists consists of between fifteen and forty correspondents. Most fields have some kind of correspondents' association with elected office-holders. Such associations arrange some off-the-record briefings with news sources; they may issue lists of correspondents to sources which want to mail handouts; associations may also consider complaints.

Much more important, however, than such occasional association activity is the day-by-day personal interaction of the correspondents within a particular field; they visit source organizations, attend press conferences and become work colleagues.

Nevertheless, they are also *competitor*-colleagues. Competition is basic to the ideology of the journalism occupation and to production and marketing arrangements of media organizations; especially perhaps in a nation like Britain (with a substantial number of national news organizations), 'news' is defined in terms of competition. Specialists express ambivalent views about 'exclusives'; but reputation with the occupation and status in the news organization depend heavily on successful competitive performance. Within the occupation the hallmark of competitive success is to be 'followed up' by one's competitors. Competition within a group of specialists takes on a strong interpersonal element.

Competition takes two main forms:

1. To get stories the competitors do not have
2. To get stories the competitors do have

On most days the second kind of competition is more important; most specialists are less often trying to get 'exclusive' and more often trying to cover all the stories most of the other competing specialists are likely to have. In such circumstances it is easy to predict that competitors will cooperate.

Table 5 shows that 42 per cent of specialists will hand on any piece of information which other specialists are 'bound to get before the next deadline'. This is general group exchange. There is, however, a more specific 'partnership' type of exchange – usually between just two or three competitor-colleagues. 50 per cent of all specialists were 'aware of competing against two or more specialists who cooperate in a partnership'. Twenty-three per cent of specialists said they themselves belonged to such a partnership (although since many regard this as a sensitive question, the true proportion is probably higher).

Table 5 Specialist correspondent as competitor-colleague

	Non-revenue Bonn, Rome, New York, Washington	Mixed Political lobby	Mixed Aviation, Education, Labour	Audience Crime, Football	Advertising Fashion, Motoring	All Selected specialists
Percentage saying 'I will hand on any piece of information which other specialists are bound to get before next deadline'	26	59	49	47	27	42[a]
Percentage saying they compete *against* a cooperating partnership	14	74	67	71	27	50[b]
Percentage saying they belong to such a partnership	14	39	22	29	12	23[b]

a N = 191
b N = 192

Once again there are major differences – in both general group exchange and partnership exchange – between correspondents in fields with different goals. Both kinds of exchange behaviour are much less common in the non-revenue and advertising revenue fields. In Foreign correspondence the surveillance of local media makes for a different competitive position. In Fashion and Motoring, the unusually strong control by news sources has a similar result.

The most cooperating behaviour is in the mixed-goal and audience-goal fields. Here the full weight of competition – and its resulting uncertainty – is to be found. It is not possible to demonstrate that more competition produces more cooperation; but impressionistically the Political Lobby and Football appear to be two of the most fiercely competitive fields – and these both have an unusually high proportion of specialists admitting that they have exchange partners.

Specialist correspondent autonomy

Within each of the three major work roles – employee, newsgatherer, competitor-colleague – it is possible to point out elements both of autonomy and control. The whole issue of autonomy and control is very complex because within each major role there is great variety.

Within the employee role there are the conflicting news organization interests of the editorial, audience/sales and advertising. Within the newsgatherer role there are the differing pressures which can be executed by prominent news-source organizations (perhaps with monopolies of certain types of information) by less prominent source organizations, as well as by different news source individuals. Within the competitor-colleague role there are the conflicting requirements of competition, general exchange colleagueship and the more specific exchange partnerships.

The very great variety between the news stories of one day and the next, the lack of pattern within a non-routine type of work, and the major differences between news organizations – all of these make any general statements inevitably tentative. Nevertheless, differences by the predominant goals of fields are sufficiently great for broad contrasts to be drawn. This will now be done by summarizing the data under five main headings.

1. *Careers* and the prevalence or otherwise of elite and precocious specialist careers.
2. *Status* within the overall occupation of journalism.
3. *Employee* role autonomy in relation to (a) story use, and (b) story choice.
4. *Newsgatherer* role autonomy
5. *Competitor-colleagueship* and the prevalence of exchange partnership.

Non-revenue goal Foreign correspondents. Elite careers are common and status is high within journalism. Within the employee role the level of story-use is low and level of story-choice only medium. It is in the newsgatherer role, however, that autonomy is very high – since, at least in countries like USA, Italy and West Germany, news sources lack effective sanctions or control over Foreign correspondents. There is a low level of exchange partnerships.

Mixed goal Political Lobby correspondents. Career backgrounds are very varied; but status within journalism is high. In the employee role Lobby correspondents have greater autonomy than Foreign correspondents – notably in a higher level of story use. Autonomy in the newsgatherer role is high – although it is much higher in relation to most politicians, parties and organizations than it is in relation to the Prime Minister. Within the competitor-colleague role the high level of competitive pressure is matched by a very high prevalence of exchange partnerships.

Mixed goal aviation, education and labour correspondents. The elite-precocious career element is medium. Status within journalism is also medium, with Labour correspondents having markedly higher status than the other two. Within the employee role autonomy in story choice is medium; but story-use is fairly low – reflecting competition for space against the news organization's 'general' reporters and other newsgatherers. In the newsgatherer role these specialists have medium autonomy; their prevalence of exchange partnerships is also medium.

Audience goal crime and football correspondents. The elite career element is very low indeed. General status within the occupation is also low. Within the employee role the situation is paradoxical; these correspondents have low autonomy in story-choice but high autonomy in story-use (reflecting the importance of late news and editionizing in these fields). The prevalence of exchange partnerships within the competitor-colleague role is high.

Advertising goal fashion and motoring correspondents. The elite-precocious career element is high among Fashion and low among Motoring correspondents. Status within the occupation is low (reflecting general antagonism among journalists towards the advertising-goal fields). Within the employee role autonomy is higher than in any of the other fields; for advertising goal correspondents both story-use and story-choice autonomy is high. However, this high employee autonomy is matched by very low autonomy in the newsgatherer role. The salience of competition is also low within the competitor-colleague role, and there is a low prevalence of exchange partnerships.

In all specialist newsgathering fields there are, then, some areas of autonomy and some of control. But there are very considerable differences in autonomy and control in particular roles between fields with different predominant goals.

Conclusion

An unstated assumption of previous research has been challenged in this paper. News organizations are here categorized as having not one but three goals – an advertising-revenue, an audience-revenue and a non-revenue goal. In the goal-bargaining perspective adopted, organizational goals are the result of changing coalitions and pressures. News organizations were seen as having an overall coalition goal of audience revenue. It was hypothesized that some particular specialist fields would have a predominant non-revenue goal. Data about selected specialists fields were then presented. These data broadly support the classification of goals adopted.

Sweeping assertions on the subject of either the control of, or the autonomy of, newsgatherers are – in the light of these data – extremely unlikely to be of general validity. Firstly, there are major differences between fields of newsgathering which have different predominant goals; although news sources may maintain substantial control in one area such as Motoring (with its advertising-revenue goal) it does not follow that news sources can control, for instance Foreign correspondents; indeed Foreign correspondents (with their non-revenue goal) appear to be very largely free of news-source control.

Secondly, these data suggest that it is misleading to regard any group of specialist journalists as either 'autonomous' or 'controlled'. Specialist journalists have three major work roles – and substantial autonomy in one role tends to accompany substantial control in another role.

This approach and these data have several implications for further research on the mass media and the communicator occupations:

1. The mixture of goals present in news organizations is likely to exist in other sorts of mass communication and with large organizations involved in a variety of mass media output.

2. Studies of one type of news output (such as foreign news) one type of entertainment output (such as large budget feature films) or one type of broadcast output (such as TV drama) are unlikely to be of general applicability. Comparative studies are likely to be more remunerative – in particular studies which compare different categories within one type of output; more studies are required which systematically examine different types of 'news' output, different types of 'drama' and so on.

3. Studies of the 'flow of news' appear to have a number of weaknesses. These studies have concentrated too much on certain types of news (such as foreign and political news), certain types of news organization (such as news agencies) and on certain stages in the news flow (especially the *processing* of news). More studies are required of the *gathering* of news.

The kind of study reported here will in the future be most remunerative if it can be incorporated into an overall research framework which includes not only communicators and communication organizations, but which also incorporates those traditional mass media research areas – the content and the ultimate audience.

This study has attempted to incorporate the perspectives of other areas of sociology – such as organizational sociology. The mass media touch society at so many points that the sociology of the mass media badly needs to incorporate the insights of a number of other fields in sociology and in social science.

References

COHEN, B. (1963), *The Press and Foreign Policy*, Princeton University Press.

DONOHEW, L. (1967), 'Newspaper gatekeepers and forces in the news channel', *Pub. Opinion Q.*, vol. 31, pp. 61–8.

GALTUNG, J., and RUGE, M. (1965), 'The structure of foreign news', *J. Peace Res.*, vol. 1, pp. 64–90.

NIMMO, D. (1964), *Newsgathering in Washington*, Atherton.

PERROW, C. (1967), 'A framework for the comparative analysis of organizations', *Amer. sociol. Rev.*, vol. 32, pp. 194–208.

TUNSTALL, J. (1970), *The Westminster Lobby Correspondents*, Routledge & Kegan Paul.

WARNER, M. (1968), 'Decision making in TV news', *Television Q.*, vol. 7, pp. 60–75.

YUCHTMAN, E., and SEASHORE, S. E. (1967), 'A system resource approach to organizational effectiveness', *Amer. Sociol. Rev.*, vol. 32, pp. 891–903.

13 Tom Burns

Commitment and Career in the BBC[1]

Excerpts from 'Cultural bureaucracy', a study of occupational milieux in the BBC undertaken in 1963/4.

'The BBC is full of dedicated people who care more for the job than for getting on. The trouble is, they see other people around them getting on faster.' This revelatory utterance puts succinctly two of the conflicting pulls of interest which affect a great number of members of the Corporation. It shows the individual to be faced with the dilemma of the BBC itself, and is, I believe, largely a reflection of it. It seems that the personal dilemma has become more explicit and acute during the recent past; the personal moral issue hinges, like the Corporation's, on the continued validity or the hollowness of a traditional ethos; and the

1. This contribution is made up of excerpts from a lengthy 'working paper' presented in April 1964 as a draft final report to the Administration Division of the Corporation after the completion of a study of the Corporation carried out in the early months of 1963. The study involved interviews with some two hundred people, attendance at a number of meetings and rehearsals, and some time spent in television studios and control rooms. The interviews, and the study generally, were confined largely to four sections of the Corporation. While these departments differed greatly from each other in many respects they could not, of course, be considered a representative sample of the Corporation's activities or staff. So while, to avoid the annoyance of perpetual qualification, reference is made in this excerpt to 'the Corporation', it should be borne in mind that the reference is always as it appeared in, or to, those departments the author got to know and the people he met.

Financial support for the study was provided by the Committee on Cooperation and Research in the Social Sciences of the University of Edinburgh. It was undertaken on the understanding that nothing would be published without the consent (which need not necessarily mean approval) of the Corporation.

The prefatory statement to the draft report contains the following passage:

To acknowledge my indebtedness to the people I met in the BBC requires and means more than the usual polite gesture. Without saddling them with responsibility for the ideas contained in this essay or their arrangement and presentation, I have nevertheless

individual is split between rival interests as much as the Corporation is.

There are other divisions of commitment. At a rather more sophisticated level it is now possible for someone to declare that he thinks it immensely worth while working for the Corporation and at the same time to say that he has 'no time for the kind of stuff the BBC broadcasts in sound and television'. Again, there is the distinction drawn by engineers between the communications system they have created and now maintain – the best there is available – and the vulgar or tedious uses to which some of them say it is put.

Remarks like these specify the array of commitments in which the individual members of the Corporation become involved: commitments, loyalties, or, so to speak, investments of psychosocial capital. Most people I met seemed to feel themselves confronted with conflicting commitments – although it was only in a minority of cases that the personal conflict seemed to reach serious dimensions.

The mildest form of conflict may yet perhaps be of most enduring significance for the Corporation at large: the widespread distinction made between the Corporation as it is and a platonic

to make it clear that their part in this study is much more considerable than is usual in such affairs. The text of this report makes it even clearer. In addition, earlier versions of this essay have been presented and discussed with senior members of the departments in which the study was, for the most part, carried out. Their comments and criticism have of course been of the greatest value. In no case have I been asked to remove or dilute passages which have seemed to them to be hostile or unjust, although where I have thought what I had written was wrong, I have corrected it.

In the event, the Corporation felt it impossible to consent to the preparation of the report for publication, a decision which the writer was informed was imposed largely by their view of outside circumstances.

The passage of time since 1964 has altered conditions outside and inside the Corporation, and this excerpt is published with the permission of the BBC. However, we are asked to draw readers' attention to the judgement of the Corporation that the period during which the study was undertaken:

coincided with certain major changes in the BBC, including the development of a second television channel (BBC-2) with a consequent rapid increase in technical and production staff. As a result, conditions and strains were experienced which could not be regarded as typical.

This is the second excerpt from the report to be published. The first appeared in Sociological Review Monograph no. 13, *The Sociology of Mass Media Communicators* (ed. P. Halmos) 1969 under the title 'Public Service and Private World'.

idea of the BBC which shows in depreciatory references to 'the way the BBC does things', 'Broadcasting-House mindedness' and 'the kind of line being taken by the people on top now' by the same people who see 'what the BBC stands for' and 'the public service idea in broacasting' as altogether admirable.

Commitment within the administration

Only in the higher reaches of the administration was this distinction not apparent, and an almost complete identification with the Corporation achieved. Their role obliges them to speak with the voice of the Corporation. They must appraise the deserts of individuals who apply for assistance or for special concessions, advise or influence heads of departments so as to ameliorate working arrangements or relationships, act in certain circumstances as watchdogs of the Corporation's interests *vis-à-vis* departments. They also represent the Corporation as employer in dealing with staff organization, categories of employees, and individuals.

It is not surprising, therefore, that senior members of the administrative staff often seem to assume the persona of the Corporation. 'My job is to adapt the old ethos of the Corporation to the needs of the 1960s.' 'As soon as I came into the Corporation I saw the place acted as a team. I see this as a strength we must fight to keep.' As against this, however, there is an acute and perpetual awareness of the output departments, especially producers, as the 'business end' of the Corporation.

Each attitude is, in fact, complementary to the other. To see production as 'the coal-face', to be occupied with the precise arrangement of the organizational environment of the producer so as to 'optimize his working conditions', to seek to relieve him of just enough administrative chores and routines to allow his creative impulses free play without endangering the structure of the Corporation, to watch so anxiously for signs of failing powers and to strike a balance between the established and short-term producers which will 'maintain vitality' and not endanger commitment to the job, all bespeak a degree of protective regard for the situation of producers and an involvement in fostering highly valued personal qualities which demands some defensive or self-assertive reflex. This role-reversal becomes evident in a slightly adult–child tone in observations about producers or, more firmly, in a manipulative, organizing attitude. With this there went what can only be described as a strong departmental *esprit de corps*. Hardly an interview with administrative officers did not contain passages of willing admiration for superiors or subordinates, in fairly marked contrast with the critical detachment apparent in other sections of the Corporation in the infrequent sessions when people discussed seniors or juniors. [. . . .]

Vocation and career

It would be obviously absurd to represent administrative officials as career-minded, as against the vocationally dedicated staff of output and other departments. There are, perhaps, ambitious men among administrators, although no more than elsewhere. What is more to the point, however, is that they appear to be free of the fundamental ambivalence which affects these others, a perpetually unresolved choice between commitment to the professional role of producer, technician, designer, or engineer, and furtherance of a career in terms of rank, power and money.

Preoccupation with career, with the standing of one's present post in relation to others, and with one's prospects of advancement, bulks larger in people's lives when the organization is growing or changing unusually fast; preoccupation in such cases shows itself most generally as a perpetual watchfulness on developments which affect relative status and promotion criteria, but it varies from this towards a conscious abdication from the 'rat-race' on the one hand, or a troubled, self-doubting anxiety on the other. Obviously, different areas of the Corporation have very different rates of growth and change and therefore different possibilities for movement and promotion, and therefore different levels of preoccupation with career. An engineer in Television Centre saw this clearly, but as a rather puzzling aspect of life in an organization which went to very great lengths to ensure that promotion opportunities were equally distributed throughout its entire staff.

x: People are very concerned here about promotion prospects. . . . When you get changes interfering with the structure, you see, you get people thinking, well, it's up to them to put a case. You've got to look after yourself, to look sideways and see what the other chaps are doing.

т.в.: Exactly, yes – and see how you're doing in relation to others?

x: It's a matter of keeping your end up. We've expanded so much, and people have got used to a perpetual state of expansion. . . . Even as far as our lower levels of staff are concerned it's been steady growth in the staff and now there's a great increase. Cameramen, for example, have come to see life as a succession of expansions, with upgrading and promotions and so on. And they'd be very disappointed if ever things became stable.

т.в.: I don't know. These changes make themselves visible long before-hand and people can get used to the fact that life has become stable. . . .

x: I must say that just after the war I was at a place where stability was the order of the day. . . . As far as I know the total staff there now is very much what it was in 1946 and the individuals are practically the same individuals.

т.в: How do they take it?

x: They're very happy – because they've never seen any other kind of existence.

Again, one becomes conscious of the way in which changes in the external circumstances of an organization impose organic changes on the structure and processes within it, of how these latter changes alter the life-situation of people working in the organization, and of how, finally, the attitudes, aspirations, pre-occupations and direction of effort of people are affected.

This is not a simple mechanical chain of cause and effect. The presentation of the dilemma between commitment to one's job as vocation – as '*Beruf*' – and as a step on a career ladder in the terms used by the man quoted in the opening sentence of this chapter is a gross oversimplification. The choice is not between devotion to the public interest or to artistic or professional values on the one hand, and to self-interest on the other. A man may feel that his own selfish interests impel him towards absorption in his professional role while it is the needs of his family, the social pressures exerted on him to attain a style of life commen-surate with what he and his wife see as their rightful social setting, which impel him to seek promotion. He may feel guilty about not seeking promotion, and relieved when he finds sufficient reason for not competing. This was made evident with the utmost clarity, honesty and indeed poignancy in the course of one interview with a producer:

T.B: When you questioned what I said about careerism, what did you mean?

x: I don't really question it. There is a tremendous career sense in here. The trouble is, I think, that one comes into the BBC thinking there is a career here, thinking 'I'll start as a floor manager, I'll go to PA, I'll become a producer' – that's as far as it goes.

I enjoy doing what I'm doing here and I don't see it as a career. I don't see where I'm going from here, I don't 'hope I'll go into pictures' – I'd love to go into pictures and now and again I think, 'why don't I do something about it?' But I don't think that way and I think very few producers here do, and plan for it. We're far too occupied in the here and now. . . .

I never have time. I shall have time in a month when this programme's off the air, and I shall grumble. I shall grumble for a whole month, and then I'll go for a month's holiday, and then I'll come back and say 'Come on, let's get on with this programme'. The Programme! [. . .]

The changing balance of commitment between
vocation and career

Nevertheless, there are people who are wholly committed to the present job – not only because of its intrinsic interest and rewards but also because of the sheer richness of the working environment – the attractions of working in studios with well-known actors and television notables, the satisfactions of doing a reliable, or competent or imaginative job in a complex operation, and receiving recognition for it, the pleasurable sense of being an essential part of a world which nightly attracts millions of people, the privileged membership of a glamour world which comprises the elites of the West End, Westminster, Fleet Street and the City, with occasional incursions from international celebrities. All this in itself can provide a large, if immaterial, increment to one's style of life. In addition for studio staff, the shift system provides either three or four free days a week and the opportunity for extensive leisure activities denied the great majority of occupied people, or for moonlighting on a grand scale.

Many people who have made the move out of this world into a higher paid management job are often filled with regrets.

It's supposed to be a step up, but you might as well be working in a cheese factory as work up here. I can't get used to working an ordinary five-day week. And you find yourself travelling at the rush-hour times. The best job in the world is on the studio floor. Up here, the biggest pleasure you have is being right on a personnel move – and even that's not the same as knowing you're right when it comes to making a suggestion in a production.

The fact that such moves are made, and indeed are competed for, is evidence of the strength of the pressure which the career system exerts – of the overwhelming value placed in contemporary society on the rewards of career advancement as against vocation. One comment demonstrated the nature of the pressure and the judgement of self, as of others, in which it finds expression.

You don't get many people – very few really – opting out of the rat-race, which is what it's called, and what it is. We tend to think that they're people who've reached the limits of their capacities.

In some parts of the Corporation, to have 'reached the limits of one's capacities' may be a judgement applied to people who, for their part, feel that they have served the Corporation best by a whole-hearted devotion to a professional or specialist job during the most productive years of their lives. The realization that this judgement was in fact being passed on them seems to have been a considerable shock to the older members of Schools Broacasting, Sound.

In a sense, they felt they had been tricked. They were recruited as among the brighter members of the teaching profession, and as people with the right ideas and with enthusiasm for the job of producing programmes for schools. In the Corporation they would be able to make a worthwhile contribution to education, and one for which there was positive demand. Professional commitment for them, therefore, was double-decked – to broadcasting production and to education. They became involved in developing their own creative expertise, and in the techniques and methods appropriate to this particular broadcasting function, they immersed themselves as thoroughly as any other producer in the world of production. Sometimes, they thought, they achieved a professional competence as radio producers as good as that of any other output department. Yet they saw this involvement in the job of production as somehow deeper than what prevailed elsewhere, because this professional role was itself incorporated in that of an older profession external to the BBC.

Yet, the more professionally committed they had become, and the longer they stayed committed, the more they ignored, missed, or even lost sight of, opportunities for advancement which were seized by other people, less qualified perhaps, less committed certainly. The years in which they had done the jobs which, after all, constitute the Corporation's *raison d'être*, had driven them into an occupational *cul-de-sac*, so far as career was concerned. And they were horrified to find, as one or two of them did find – and indeed, had been told – that they were now regarded as 'part of the problem of ageing staff'.

There is, therefore, in some sectors of the Corporation, no longer a choice between commitment to professional specialism and to career advancement, a choice which may have been a more or less uncomfortable dilemma. As the Corporation has grown, and become more administratively self conscious, or as the ethos of the world of broadcasting has shifted esteem away from broadcasters and towards the controllers of broadcasting, those who have committed themselves to professional broadcasting, or who have taken at face value the admonition 'The BBC exists to broadcast, not to offer careers' have found themselves devalued. Now that this realization has come to them – or has been forced on them – they find they are classed among those who 'have reached the limit of their capacities'. As a younger member of the department put it:

We tend to feel that we got the rough end of the stick both ways. Promotions go to people from outside the department. Anybody who's been in Schools quite a long time gets looked askance at. So really it's a bit of a bottleneck.

T.B: Do people here feel strongly about this?

x: I think so, yes. The older people in the department do, I'm sure.

T.B: Well, why is this so? Because you're not the only place which is slightly cut off from the hubbub of Television Centre, or the centres of Broadcasting House –

x: No, no.

T.B: – and the people at Broadcasting House think they fall over themselves to meet this particular problem – of providing escape-hatches, if you like, out of the top of departments. In fact, if I'm right, they see their problem as one of places where people have stuck, where there isn't enough turnover. They are doing something to remedy this, they say. So in one place you have people who feel they have a problem in that their legitimate expectations about careers are frustrated, and, in another, the people who are in a position of being able to do something about this feeling themselves obstructed by people's unwillingness to move. This is a curious impasse.

Without entering too far into the special problems of the Schools Broadcasting Department, one may point to two further features of the situation which have general implications. First, that when people suspect that they have attracted the label of 'stick-in-the-mud', or that they are 'looked at askance', or that in some indefinable, unspoken, but significant sense they are perceived as having reached the limits of their capacities, i.e. to have fallen behind – to have failed – they look around for corroborative evidence. So senior appointments in the department which to others appeared to have been given to men with, perhaps, wider experience of educational broadcasting were regarded by the staff in the department as given to 'outsiders'; the limitation of the slightly senior producers' posts to six was seen as an adverse reflection on the number of older men with *prima facie* claims to seniority; the rise in teachers' salaries until many teachers had the scales higher than that of the basic producer's grade in the department was evidence of some kind of betrayal by the Corporation.

Secondly, there is the relationship between commitment to the professional role of producer and age. For the most part, it is the younger members of the department who are most clearly involved in the job of producing; they are anxious to acquire competence and range, they are much more alive to their tenuously-known audience; acquiring and practicing the technical grammar of production and the social skills which are needed to control studio staff and performers is interesting; they have no time or inclination to think of their future careers. It is the older people – who have proved themselves, who find their work interesting still, and worthwhile, but do not face an all-round challenge with every programme – who have to find a new balance between commitment to their occupational selves and commitment to their external, domestic situation. Nevertheless, there are younger people in the department who are manifestly not committed to Schools Broadcasting in the sense traditional in the department, and who look forward to moving elsewhere, and certainly upwards, just as there are older people who are as devoted to their professional role as ever they were and who merely deplore the elements in the situation which have aroused hankerings after change or promotion in others. [. . .]

Age-grading

There seems to be a fairly clear age-grade structure within the Corporation – groups differentiated not so much by chronological age as by the period they entered the Corporation, manifested in their attitude to, and beliefs about, other age grades. Older people, on the verge of retirement, say that they 'can't think what will happen' when they retire.

A war-time recruit said,

I always feel that people who joined the BBC when I did – we regarded working for the BBC as a vocation. There was a tremendous aura of this during the war. Nowadays they'd just as soon work in an ice-cream factory if the promotion prospects and the rates of pay were the same. This is quite true. Therefore they have a different outlook from me.

There are four distinguishable age-grades: the pioneers of the 1920s; a second group who are associated with the years of expansion and the establishment of the BBC as a nationally and internationally important institution during the 1930s; the war-time group, who identify themselves with the Corporation as it was in that time of emergency and triumph; and those who came in with, or after, television. Members of each group have an inescapable feeling that 'our lot has what it takes'. They also have the feeling either that the others (or many of them) are, in some ineluctable but important sense, wrong-headed or not quite up to the standards which their group set – or that the peculiarly different standards, qualifications and values of the other groups are now more highly valued than theirs.

This interpretation was set off by the impression that the different sections of the Corporation I have encountered seem to be dominated by one or other age-grade. This is most strikingly apparent in the television service, the 'young man's world', in which the age-grading structure which prevailed in the Corporation has been dislocated. As elsewhere, the forceful rationalization which is a necessary lubricant of such changes in social structure has generated a number of beliefs about age and ageing, about the 'creative years' of life, and about the finite, exhaustible nature of such qualities as inventiveness, imagination, and enterprise. The measure of the dominance of the younger age-group is the extent to which such beliefs are shared by older men.

The abnormality of the age-structure in television, where seniority in age is not related to seniority in status even within the same occupational order or career progression, adds another classificatory system to the social structure itself. Thus to be younger is to have a kind of social edge on others, even if they are senior in grade.

There is also a fourth kind of systematic differentiation in the cultural affinities which divide people. This derives from the implication of the whole occupational community in the world of the theatre and of social sophistication. So people are divided into professionals and amateurs, and, more significantly, into camp, butch (terms now used without any hint of their nineteenth-century origins as homosexual cant), or square. Individuals can be 'camp' – i.e. act habitually with an edgy elegance or sophisticated charm – or 'play it camp' for a special occasion; groups, occasions or whole departments can be 'campish'. 'Butch', which carries an equal connotation of being sophisticated and on the inside, allows of an alternative mode of acting – plain or coarse-spoken cynicism or directness. Both terms clearly denote, again, not personality types but a manner and style of conduct which can be assumed, and relate to traditional characters or humours in the English theatre as old as the seventeenth-century stage, in which both types are clearly discernible. To reject both, and to be square, is, in this milieu, an equally positive choice, equally a style which has to be cultivated from models and consciously maintained. These three humours cut across the other structures of economic status, rank, authority and age.

In the enclosed single space of the studio, and in the closed, concentrated world of the production, the simultaneous and coordinated interplay of all these systems creates a small, exotic plural society.

There are two material circumstances which support this peculiarly enriched social world. First, every person present – actor, vision mixer, electrician, scene shifter, technical-operations manager – contributes and represents an essential resource, or is in control of essential technical equipment. They are present as of autonomous occupational right, and there is no organizational hierarchy; the three kinds of authority – one derived from the possession of skill or information, another from the attributes of office, the third from prestige – are all clearly distinguished, are invoked on distinct occasions by producer, floor manager, or lighting supervisor, or fireman, and have well-defined limits.[1] The overriding authority of the producer comes, ideally, from his exercise of all three kinds of authority, but even here there are command areas defined by other people's competence and responsibilities which he must not invade or seek to amend. What exists – again, ideally – is a fully articulated organic system of cooperative action, in which the leadership role is properly that of defining aims and other contributors are fully involved in working towards their realization, within limits of feasibility which they themselves lay down.

Secondly, almost everyone is necessarily unemployed for periods of varying but unpredictable length; there may be forty or more people in the studio, and for the most part less than half a dozen may be actively engaged in rehearsal.

The mental clock in everyone present which is ticking off the minutes left before the terminal point of recording or transmission introduces the kind of multiplier into the relevance and significance of one's own and everybody else's conduct familiar in crises. On such a basis, in the sealed remoteness of the studio, people can, if they choose, free themselves from the more unsuccessful and duller aspects of their conduct and recompose models of demeanour, style of action, and level of sophistication out of a range of possibilities offered by ascriptions, age, status, membership, interests and affiliations, and ground what they affect to be in the virtually unchallengeable authority of their technical role and commitment to the production task.

1. It is, in fact, the floor manager's job to see to the maintenance of these limits and to resolve any friction or problem arising from ambiguity about their definition.

The effectiveness of the total system varies. Almost universally, it is thought to vary with the effectiveness of the producer. Occasionally the complexity is dissolved into a simple relationship of command and compliance at transmission time, or, more rarely, is disrupted into a single antagonism between producer and an individual or group. But in general, a television studio at work represents an extraordinarily refined system of human and technical organization, effective in its ability to produce what it was designed to produce, and efficient in providing a satisfying array of rewards for the people concerned in the production. To run such a system obviously requires organizing, administrative, managerial skills of the highest order. It is a curious commentary on the way in which industrial society has developed that it is firmly believed that good producers make poor administrators, and even more curious that this is almost certainly true.[2]

Even so far as this study has taken me, there is a much wider variety of commitments into which individuals enter than the simple trio of work, department and career. There is the distinction between 'working in the BBC' and working for the Corporation as it is in reality. There is the attraction of the world of broadcasting with its own distinctive prestige and glamour and its links with the elites of every sector of sport, entertainment, art and public affairs, and the involvement in a technical or specialist job which is usually unique to broadcasting and often novel. There is the 'political' sense of loyalty to people doing the same kind of work and at the same grade, and therefore representing the same kind of human resource and sharing the same self-interest, and the devotion to 'getting the show out' and to serving the public. There is commitment to the studio, and to producers, or to others to whom one is engaged in a working relationship, and commitment to one's own career. There is affiliation with people of the same age or date of entry, and with

2. The present Director General of the BBC, Mr Charles Curran, has commented on this passage as follows: 'The validity of this statement is open to question: many of the most senior administrators in BBC Television first made their reputations as television producers, e.g. Huw Wheldon (Managing Director, Television), David Attenborough (Director of Programmes, Television), Paul Fox (Controller, BBC-1), Robin Scott (Controller, BBC-2), Ian Atkins (Controller, Programme Services, Television) and Alasdair Milne (Controller, Scotland) etc.'

people who share the same models of behaviour, and there is attachment to these people scattered about the Corporation who represent what is felt to be television production, or sound broadcasting, or engineering, or simply the BBC 'at its best'.

Finally, there is a balance between occupational and outside commitments, a balance which fluctuates through life (as the balance between occupational commitments fluctuates) but which is of the utmost importance to the individual to hold constant with his aspirations and his conception of what he is. It is in the disturbance of this balance, the knowledge that a balance struck has been upset by the relative devaluation of one or other of these commitments, that personal problems originate, and discrepancies arise between the needs of the individual and the needs of the organization. To disturb the balance produces, instead of a 'pluralistic' (and therefore, by implication, an 'integrated') organization, a segmented one.

The individual and involvement

'My job', said one senior member of the Corporation,

is to encourage attitudes which will pull out of the staff more than you could justify getting out of them by any of the usual criteria which exist in, say, the business world. [Further,] what you have in mind when setting conditions of services is to set them so as to get the best out of people. This is an increment you don't pay for, and because of that, it's invaluable. Management is really entitled to so much but what we have to do is to stimulate people into giving all they're capable of.

Almost any manager would subscribe to such sentiments. They are echoed in public pronouncements on the education and selection of managers, and are implicit in the talk of leadership which is part of the currency of business psychology. What is unusual about the quotation is the clear perception it reveals of the distinction between the commitment of engagement and commitment of dedication, and the task of management as expanding the latter, and using it.

The social norms which apply to conduct in paid employment of all kinds now contain an element of involvement beyond the contractual engagement. Such involvement tends to increase with rank within the same organization, and with the rate at which circumstances change in the market or in the supporting techniques. Both are different instances of demands for personal involvement increasing with uncertainty, or, what amounts to the same thing, of the thrusting of the onus of defining and redefining ultimate ends or mediate goals on to the members of the concern.

Public service and the Corporation

But to be involved in this way presumes that the individual identifies the values implicit in the ends of the concern as his own. This is, in fact, what one means by involvement. A direct and simple identity of personal and organizational goals is reserved for a small minority – political leaders, owners and directors of business concerns, for example, or those whose total dedication to the social, spiritual or intellectual purposes of institutions in which they have found a place shelters or absolves them from attention to other purposes. More common is a stoic dedication to keeping a system going at all costs or furthering its growth merely because to do so is better than any alternative, and offers the best chance in a hostile or deplorable world for the survival of oneself and what one values. The distinction, familiar enough among civil servants, and raised to the level of a political ideology by the Milnerites in this country and a social ethic by Ernst Jünger in Germany, is visibly present in a number of professional contexts.

The distinction, in fact, emerges as a consequence of the surrender by the specialist of direct professional commitment to the individuals or groups he serves. For him to yield the direction and application of qualities and talents which are as intrinsic to his character as those of the professional must, by definition, be to control by senior officials in a bureaucratic hierarchy means not only that he resigns his relationship with the public to be 'taken care of' by the organization; it also means that the notional matching of professional performance with its full requittal in client or public satisfaction or applause is never attained, or is lost in anonymous membership of the organization. There is an inevitable discrepancy between what the professional envisages as his true relationship with the public and the proper uses which an organization finds for him. Thus one finds a 'para-dedication', a commitment to the BBC as a public service together with a critical dissociation from the Corporation as it is.

The distinction is implicit in the situation of the professional specialist. It was articulated in a number of interviews in which the public-service image of the BBC was distinguished from 'the system' or the 'policy' or 'the way things are done' by the 'people on top'. This is not to say that active dissociation from policies as they were in practice, or depreciation of the senior members of the Corporation was widespread, but that loyalty to one's superiors, and dedication to the BBC's purposes, are not necessarily dedication to the purposes which they saw explicitly or implicitly pursued.

This distinction seemed to be held particularly clearly and irreconcilably among engineers.

The public-service conception of the Corporation is simpler and more prominent in Engineering Division, largely because engineers bear no responsibility for the content of programmes and can dissociate the ideal image of the BBC from what is actually done in its name. The dissociation is also made easier by the contrast between the precision and reliability of the complex technical apparatus which the engineers provide and maintain, and the procession of minor vicissitudes – with occasional breakdowns – which afflict studio programmes and which have to be handled either by the staff of the Central Control Room or by the Presentation Editor who works among them.

The criteria by which this contrast is established between the technical equipment of television and the material actually broadcast are in terms of moral and intellectual codes and of practical efficiency. So, for engineers, professional identification may be said almost to require dissociation from the actual BBC and its replacement by a 'public-service' image. This image remains unformulated since it is there as a negation of actuality rather than a definition which it is possible to aspire to and work for, a *quid pro quo*, in critical detachment, for the engagement of one's professional qualities to the organization.

These elements in the situation of the professional engineer are perceptible most clearly in the working style of the group of engineers in the Central Control Area. Talk inside the room, over the multiplicity of telephone connections, with the rest of the building, with other studios in London and the regions, and with transmitters, is couched in a flip, offhand, joking style, with a heavy loading of technical terms, jargon and initials. An intense 'insider' feeling is built up in this way. Through this interplay runs an intermittent commentary on what is appearing on the monitors before them. The patter both contributes to and expresses the feeling of the group's enclosure within the walls of a room which is the communication centre of the whole of the BBC Television Service. It consists again of 'inside jokes', sardonic or cynical repartee aimed at the studio performers, and highly critical discussion of the evening programmes. This particular group was among the most outspoken of the critics of audience-catching policies.

Corporate professionalism

In other cases, which may constitute a majority, what happens is that the individual devotes himself to values and ends which are consistent with the ends of the concern without being identified with them. There are needs of the concern which cannot be presented in a formal contractual undertaking. These needs can only be met through the achievement of personal goals and the realization of personal values which are consistent with those of the organization, or rather through which the organization's own ends and purposes are deployed. In the Corporation, where this has been done with very considerable success, one encounters a formidable hierarchy of ends to which individuals dedicate their occupational careers and to which they bring their whole intellectual and intuitive capacities. The central matter of human organization lies at this point, where deeply-felt concern in the attainment of best results emerges out of the elements of organizational requirements.

New industries and the new specialisms which technical development and the rationalizing of management functions have introduced into industry provide general indications of the way in which involvement is created out of organizational purposes. Personnel management, methods study, production control have all, to some extent, grown their own vocational appeal and professional interest. But the fact and character of this process of motivation manufacture reveal themselves most clearly when one finds committed individuals baulked of those immaterial, inner rewards which psychologists in the past labelled 'job satisfaction'.

Situations in television production reveal organization as the script-writer of roles to which individuals find themselves emotionally committed.

x: In this case the producer was never giving the operators time to rehearse and build the thing up into a proper performance. When they eventually came to do the telerecording, half of the stuff had been unrehearsed and they couldn't remember what to do properly. Then they got terribly exasperated because they said, well, 'look at the telerecording – it's lousy; and it wasn't really our fault. It looks as if we didn't do this pan properly or this move properly, but we never rehearsed it.'

T.B: I suppose what the producer is looking for, inevitably, is the same kind of emotional identification with his production as he gets from his cast.

x: He's looking for this, and in fact he gets it. . . . And again: you only get an emotional kick out of a production when it begins to work. A lighting supervisor can really get a tremendous thrill out of something really beautifully lit. He thinks 'Did I really do this? Isn't it marvellous?' . . . . But, you see, you can spend hours and hours and hours gradually building this up, and you can get a tremendous amount of frustration if the producer is always occupied with something else. You're saying, 'I know there's a light in the corner there. I wish he'd come to that shot so that I can just see what happens:' you never come to it, and just as he's going to come to it, he decides on something else.

Broadcasting requires the combined efforts of a multiplicity of departments and groups, each representing a specialist function. It is customary for any difference in function to develop swiftly and naturally into a job for specialists. The development we have been discussing takes place more effectively, more quickly and more completely because of the widespread cultivation of professionalism through the Corporation. However, as soon as one can call a job one for professionals, it becomes associated with a professional ethos, even perhaps a mystique, but in any case a unique set of qualifications either obtained by technical education and training, or derived from qualities of sensibility, flair, intelligence, or skill. One of the central notions of professionalism is unique qualification for a particular kind of job, and with this goes the disqualification of outsiders not only from the job, but effectively, from competence to evaluate performance.

'Only a specialist', as one man said, 'can judge the work of a specialist.'

Leadership and loyalty

Pseudo-charisma. It is in the television studio that the distinction between the two kinds of commitment, engagement and involvement, is most obvious, and where the contrast between monitoring contractual engagement and creating involvement is most vivid. Monitoring the performance of individuals, in the terms used in a previous chapter [not included here] is, in fact, largely the task of technical supervisors and managers, many of whom are not present in the studio. Involvement is the producer's affair.

The television producer, in organizing a production, is faced with a heterogeneous *ad hoc* assemblage of individuals and groups. While they acknowledge his authority so far as the direction of their efforts is concerned, he has none over the definition of their functions, powers or responsibilities. Nevertheless, the success of a production depends largely on his success in persuading them not merely to act, to operate cameras, to design sets, to plan a lighting plot, in ways which will fit in with the scheme of production, but to exploit their special capacities to the full in the interests of the programme, and in the development, expansion and improvement of his ideas. He has to generate as full an involvement in the success of the production as possible, and an equal commitment to himself as the leader of the whole organization. To do this, most producers work up an odd, fictive kind of charisma, something we can perhaps best call pseudo-charisma.

The development of involvement is critically important at the early stage of planning meetings and first meetings with cast, and it is at this point that the producer exercises to the full what social skills he has to fabricate the temporary bonds of commitment. Pseudo-charisma, in this context, denotes the finished explication of one or the other recognized models of theatrical demeanour and conduct – 'camp' or 'butch' – together with effective devices to achieve empathy – jokes, host display, and a curiously common feature, a 'cockney' voice. All these appurtenances of a producer's appropriate persona are almost consciously donned at the commencement of meeting or rehearsal; there is an observable moment of bracing. Significantly, there is room for only one such performance in any setting; when a planning meeting for a production was interrupted by the executive producer of the series, liveliness and temperamental quality at once transferred to him, the director assuming a rather flat, business-like tone.

Compliant involvement. Even in the most rigorously ordered system of management and supervision, many of the items which enter into the definition of jobs, and the way they are to be done, are worked out by a common consent arrived at by work groups in the face of precedent, the demands of the job as acknowledged by them and the direct instruction as requests delivered by superiors. 'Work norms', if the phrase may be used in this connection, thus present a shifting balance of feasible demands for time and effort, a balance which has limits of oscillation and a 'true level'. Subordinates, no less than superiors, have to be perceptive about the balance and the limits.

In the reaches of the Corporation where it is possible to speak of professional and quasi-professional specialists – the monthly staff grades – the ability to appraise the correct balance without explicit appeal or order is essential. To make an explicit rule about lateness, for example, would indicate ignorance of the importance of the system of consent or an outright betrayal of it.

I remember some years back, when I was in the studio this was, we used to have one chap who was always turning up late.... It was always this one man. Well, eventually it was decided that something had to be done, so everybody was told that they had to show up on time at ten. Well, there was a lot of cribbing about this, but the people who created most – as you'd expect, really – were just the people who nearly always turned up fifteen minutes early.... If we went by rules rather than by conscience, the Corporation would lose out. But this can only come from being brought up in the atmosphere of the Corporation.

With so much dependent on the ability of superiors to perceive the boundary between explicit specification of the needs of a particular job and tacit recognition that the engineering specialists or technical operators or designers or production assistants working under them see these needs as written into their roles, people acting as superiors have to rely on their own ability to read the extent to which behaviour and demeanour complies with requirements. This must mean that they look for compliance with their own view of the requirements of the work situation – with their own appraisal of 'conscience' and 'atmosphere'.

You get youngsters falling into traps – not understanding the way things go in this place. The biggest trap, I suppose, is the matiness. Some youngsters get deceived by this, youngsters with no real discipline. I had one of them in here only recently. We had a very interesting conversation, really – because after a time we got to talking quite openly. He said he saw no reason why his opinions about things outside work weren't just as worth saying as his boss's. I said there's lots of opinions I have which I don't parade in front of my bosses. After all, I said, people fifteen or twenty years older are entitled to some deference. . . . He was one of the chaps – you know – he kept looking out of the window when I was talking to him. I took him up on this – he said he'd always done that at school – used to play with his pencil, look miles away, while the teacher was speaking. Then they'd jump on him with a question and he'd always know the answer – make them furious! ·

Outside the fairly prescribed boundaries within which specific instructions are given, therefore, jobs have to be carried out in compliance with the needs of the particular situation, in compliance with one's superior's reading of those needs, and, what is more, in compliance with some code of deferent behaviour which indicates to that superior that his reading is accepted.

Optimally, a superior's reading of the requirements of the situation allows for discussion of them and of ways of meeting them. But this is not always so, and the tact on which the system of compliance rests is replaced by a positive demand for obedience. Again, this is behaviour which implicitly distinguishes commitment to one's specialist task from commitment to the organization as it is.

'Wearing one's rank' seemed to run so much counter to the obvious egalitarianism of manner which prevails in many aspects of the Corporation's world that I had some difficulty in accepting it as a substantial element in management. That this is so, that 'doing things my way' can be insisted upon as a matter not of the argued rationale of a situation but of superior rank, was maintained by people in very different parts of the Corporation.

T.B: Do people wear their rank? There are said to be occasions when a junior having some mild – or serious, for that matter – difference of opinion about the way a thing should be framed, can be told, 'Look,

I'm two grades above you, or one grade, I'm senior man here, and we'll do it the way I want it.' When I first heard this, I thought this was probably a peculiar situation – untypical. Would you agree?

X: I haven't come across it in exactly that way.

T.B: Nobody above you . . . ?

X: But the situation exists. Definitely. Even half a grade. You know; 'I'm in charge of this part of the organization, and I want it done this way. We may have discussed it beforehand, but this is what's got to be.' This is no exception.

So far, what was under discussion in this instance was the devolution through the management hierarchy of the Corporation's authority to direct the effort of individuals under contractual engagement to it. But commitment at this level is not enough in the Corporation, where management is everywhere conscious of the need to involve people in their work over and above the measure of their contractual engagement.

T.B: There's no feeling that you have to carry people with you, whatever the cost?

X: This varies from situation to situation, and person to person. I'd say it goes with the organized part of the labour force, when chaps are very, very sensitive, and very delicately treated. There are many occasions when people have to be 'carried' with you in this way. I'd say there was an equal number of occasions – more often when dealing with individuals or small numbers of fairly closely graded people, that you get the senior person finishing things by saying 'It's got to be done my way, and now you will support my policy', and not only that, I'm conscious on certain occasions when I'm one of the people having this kind of thing imposed upon me, of it not being satisfactory just that you concede this point, that the senior, confronted with a conflicting view, has the right to make the decision, and I, as a loyal member of the staff, will support it. This is not enough. You have to subjugate your own opinions completely, and accept that this is the right way to do it – as far as that. And there's a feeling of antagonism there if you don't.

The pressures on senior people to act in this fashion were said to arise from the insecurity attached to lower – or lowered – technical competence among older people and to the compelling need to maintain or raise the department's 'professional' standing. There were also said to be a few personal tragedies occasioned by lapses from professional standards; enough to make this a matter of constant preoccupation which would lead to an over-anxious dominance of subordinates' activities. While it may be true (and it is a familiar aspect of higher rank in large organizations) that compelling subordinates to swear their faith in the rightness of decision is evidence of doubt about their rightness, it may also be seen as an attempt to escape from the 'loneliness of command', which mechanistic (bureaucratic) forms of management thrust on people, into shared responsibility.

Involvement and the values displayed by the organization as it is

Since the Corporation is a career system as well as other things, the men who have reached the highest positions represent a kind of showcase of the characteristics of success. If intellectual capacity, technical information, local experience of the resources available, and managerial skill in the ways in which they may be employed to the best effect, can be taken for granted as the main criteria of success, there are, nonetheless, other considerations which are, in the Corporation as elsewhere, taken into account. Indeed, it has been argued that, above the ranks in which vacancies are filled by Appointments Boards, these extraneous considerations carry more weight. While the Appointment Board system, it is said, imposes its own discipline on selection procedures, in that all considerations other than those related to choosing 'the best man for the job' are ruled out:

. . . very senior appointments are not made with the same discipline as those which come under the Appointments Boards system. If you are a member of an Appointments Board, you cannot exclude the possibility of somebody else on the Board coming out with exactly the opposite opinion. You are under the discipline of controversy. Every time somebody says, 'If only we take candidate A and promote him then that means I can promote B in that department and that will mean he will cease to quarrel with C, because he'll no longer be dealing with him' – there's always a chance that there'll be somebody there – it's part of the job – to say, 'Look, I'm sorry, I realize it's desperately important to you as Head of Department, but it's totally irrelevant to the Board'.

But with senior appointments which are not conducted by a Board, but by somebody saying, or agreeing with somebody else that this is the best man to put in, not only are you not subjected to this discipline, but you follow all your inclinations over these extraneous things. Such as – you don't, as a Board has to, have to try and determine who is the best candidate. With your senior appointments it's always possible to have appointments of convenience – very understandable convenience – not necessarily the best man. He's not forced on you. There's always a difficulty about top appointments – there's every inducement to think up these other points.

As the balance of power shifts at the top of the Corporation, or of its divisions, or of its major departments, as the need to redress the balance alters, and as policy considerations themselves alter over time and call for different arrays of talent and kinds of commitment, so the line between relevant and extraneous considerations, and their relative importance, will alter. Yet, over time, the people occupying the top fifty or more positions may be taken – indeed, must be taken – as the preferred models of effective performance, conduct and demeanour, thrown up by the perception among the directorate of the Corporation's needs. This basic assumption of the career system is carried into the basic assumption of the generality of staff about preferred behaviour which will lead to their own success.

Involvement develops, therefore, through the operation of the career system itself, which serves to demonstrate both the degree and direction of dedication which are prerequisites of success and the qualifications, the social skills and qualities of character which impersonate the ethos of the Corporation. Any diversity of view about ethos is, of course, reproduced in the models which are presented by the people at the top.

There are also other assumptions which have the appearance of the insurance against, or reassurance about, failure which has to be generated in any career system. These assumptions about the values implicit in the system are, like the others, grounded in – or at least related to – observable facts or people. For instance, in Engineering, professional and career commitments also presented themselves as a dilemma, if not more strongly, then to far more people than in other departments. Ascent of the career ladder tends to mean, for most people, losing touch with the technical expertise on which their occupation is founded. With the high premium placed on professionalism in the division, as elsewhere in the Corporation, and the idiosyncratic conception of the management role as largely a matter of monitoring, there is an inescapable feeling that as people ascend the ladder of power and responsibility they lose the authority which comes from superior professional skill and knowledge.

This has some bearing on the otherwise curious suggestion, made or corroborated by several people independently, that formal professional qualifications – university degrees, associate membership of professional institutes – were becoming more and more insisted on as essential for promotion to higher posts in Engineering. The power hierarchy, it was argued, would thus be reinforced by educational qualifications. That this insistence was not made explicit by the Corporation made it more suspect still, and linked it, in some people's minds, with the equally suspicious growth of a university graduate freemasonry in Engineering Division.

None of these circumstances prevented there being a far greater preoccupation with promotion, and with grading, than appeared in any other department I visited. At the very outset of this study, the announcement of a number of new appointments to the highest posts in the division was discussed largely in terms of their meaning for career prospects, and the kind of qualifications or personal qualities or Corporation experience which might be most favoured.

There are a few men in the Corporation who not only attach the personal loyalty of their immediate work group to them, but whose influence seems to extend through large sections of the Corporation. Some do so because they represent at their best and most effective the professional values cultivated in different departments, and carry with them a prestige which subordinates wish to share. Thus the successful television producer, at the end of a series, will be approached by the cameraman, floor managers, and others who worked with him and asked to keep them in mind for his next production.

A less familiar instance of the natural desire to catch some reflection of the light shed by prestige is the regard paid to a few isolated senior individuals who are felt perhaps to represent the ethos of the BBC, as a powerful and beneficient institution, but, more certainly, to give some assurance of the power, value and beneficience of the BBC because of their presence in it. They are known as intelligent, humane and honest men, and dedicated to their work in the Corporation. To some extent, therefore, they stand as guarantors of the moral value of the BBC's existence and aims; they underwrite, too, the unearned and therefore slightly embarrassing increment of prestige derived from membership of the Corporation; they represent the ethos of the Corporation and of the professionalism it has generated.

More importantly, perhaps, their presence in the senior ranks offsets the ultimately depressive effect of the scandal-mongering which circulates in the main centres of Corporation gossip in the Saville, the 'George', the BBC Club and at parties. This is not a matter which would ordinarily engage attention in a study of the present kind, least of all in 1963, but it apparently has contributed in the past to what are described as 'crises of confidence in the leadership of the BBC'. Clearly, the implication of the Corporation in the theatre and the entertainment industry, and the power of the patronage exercised by many of its officers are themselves enough to provoke a sizeable and constant stream of malicious anecdotes and witticisms. However, the circulation of this kind of stuff through the very large, formally organized, working organization of the Corporation gives it a totally different significance from that which commonly attaches to theatre gossip. That this feature of Corporation life is not more disruptive may be due to the presence of individuals whose conduct and demeanour act as a counterpoise. [. . .]

Policy and professional involvement

For the unstable and complex system of organizational purposes to be realized and pursued by individuals and groups there has to be a superstructure of involvement, or dedication, added to the contractual engagement which binds people to the concern. Because involvement in this sense means the assumption by the individual of aspirations, values and purposes which are private to him – as well as implicit in the ends and functions of the organization – involvement is personal, autonomous and, except in special circumstances, distinct from attachment to the organization as it in fact presents itself to him. In the last few pages, we have been examining the way in which such involvement, while in general consistent with organizational ends, may yet generate rivalries which are not in accordance with the purposes and effectiveness of the organization, in the same way as the contractual form of commitment carries with it consequential engagements to sections and grades, and so provides a foundation for internal politics.

Nevertheless, despite its apparent independence of organizational needs and requirements, the involvement which is so essential an element in the contribution required of the individual is still rooted firmly in the simple business relationship with the concern in which membership itself is founded. This is best demonstrated by reference to television producers, whose involvement and professionalism carries the highest value. For, in this case, there are alternative basic business relationships between the individual and the Corporation. One can be either established as a permanent member of staff, or be engaged on short-term contract for a couple of years. The very existence of the alternative has interesting implications.

The advent of short-term contracts in television is, in some ways, yet another symptom of the changed social situation of the Corporation. Television broke the BBC monopoly in broadcasting in more ways than one. The forms, the conversations, the dramaturgic skills, the machinery and the design resources of stages and films became more immediately relevant to broadcast production. As television developed, a little of the traffic began to move the other way. Today, television is much closer to the genre of the theatre and cinema than ever sound radio was.

Producing television programmes is interesting in its own right, the medium offers its own problems, challenges and opportunities, it is no longer a freak, and less of a stand-by in bad times or a haven for the frustrated. Nevertheless, BBC Television, although a very *special* part of the world of cinema, theatre and entertainment, is perceived very much as part of it, not only by performers, but by producers and their aides, and by many floor managers.

This breaching of the occupation and cultural barriers has been acknowledged concretely by a new kind of business relationship between the Corporation and staff in the departments – Television Drama and Light Entertainment – most directly affected. In the theatre, in films and in the entertainment industry, work is traditionally insecure, unpredictable in its rewards or, at best, subject to specific contract for a limited period. In the Corporation, work is traditionally secure, established and – virtually, if not contractually – for life. But in Television Drama and Light Entertainment, the Corporation now offers a proportion of short-term contracts for producers.

This has all the appearance of a sensible, indeed, a necessary, shift of policy. It introduces a useful ambidexterity into the difficult task of recruiting suitable people for the crucially important function of producing television shows. But the two kinds of engagement appear to have encouraged the belief that these are two quite different kinds of people whose personalities, or expectations, or ambitions, square with each kind of contract. Interviews with producers under either kind of contract moreover, give almost the impression of a package of values and beliefs which are associated with the two types of engagement.

First, a television producer on the established staff:

T.B: What brought you into the BBC?

X: I wanted to continue working in the entertainment industry, I wanted a higher salary and more security than I thought the theatre offered me – by this time I was married, with two children, and a third on the way – and I think it's true to say that almost everyone in the entertainment industry wants to work in the BBC at some stage or another in their careers.

T.B: What do you think they want to do this for? One can see that 'a good, steady job' is attractive – is there anything beyond this?

X: Oh, yes. Bascially, the entertainment industry is run by thugs, and there's a general feeling that the BBC isn't – that it's a civilized organization. And this is perfectly true. It enables someone who wants to do something creative to do it without feeling that the pressure of profit motives is going to disturb everything he wants to do. . . . I'd think there's a certain prestige . . . to say to people I work for the BBC carries something – some weight. It carries weight even with one's bank manager!

No other kind of employment in the entertainment industry offers anything like comparable advantages; every producer, whether established or on short-term contract, was well aware of them, and they counted overwhelmingly with most.

There are some important qualifications and corollaries to be made, but for the present it is sufficient to point out that what is under discussion is a kind of social contract between producers and the Corporation which extends well beyond the business contract and the monetary considerations which undoubtedly do cement people to their jobs in the Corporation, and which do bulk large in discussions – because they are the only considerations which can usefully be discussed, because, in turn, they can be changed arbitrarily and effectively.

Nevertheless, it is this social contract, with all its implications, which some people reject, and not a settled income.

x: If you've got something else to hand on – if you've got another life – if you've been meeting writers and artists, as I have, a different world altogether – so much the better, because it gives you something to set against the BBC.
t.b: What does this mean, exactly? Does it mean that you don't really want to commit yourself to something which is an organization?
x: No, I don't. It's a personal opinion, but the idea of being on long-term contract, signing away maybe ten, twelve, twenty years of my life, is complete anathema.

This reads almost like a bachelor's rejection of the idea of marriage. The very existence of short-term contracts gives established posts the appearance of life-long, unbreakable, indentured service. The conception, indeed, is not very far removed from the idea of marriage:

x: I would never want to work for the Corporation except on short-term contract. But I'm not married, and maybe that's a lot to do with it.
t.b: Yes, though not every marriage leads to a semi-detached house and a car.
x: But I think marriage, to a bachelor, does.

Marriage to the BBC meant, in this case, having to settle permanently in London, only four weeks off a year, a whole-hearted commitment to television – to name only the more obvious drawbacks.

The producers I have quoted were a year or two on each side of thirty. One can presume that they were either actually or potentially valuable members of their department. One can more certainly presume that each was aware of the existence, and of the benefits, of the other kind of relationship. Neither really conceived the choice as between security and constraint on the one hand, and insecurity and freedom on the other.

Each kind of reaction, each set of valuations, is, in fact, a crystallization of beliefs around the two kinds of contract offered by the Corporation. Both reactions were feasible because both relationships are possible; a decision one way or the other precipitates and forms the values attached to them – or rather, attracts and organizes them into a coherent confession of beliefs. The upshot is two alternative arrangements of commitment, and ultimately, two sets of life-chances and careers, one institutionalized in terms defined by the Corporation and its activities, the other in terms of the traditions of the independent professional artist, writer and actor. The difference between the two, as members of the Corporation, is that overriding loyalty will go, in the first case, to the notion of the BBC, and in the second case to the notion of the artist, writer or actor to which the individual devotes his life.

Part Five
Structural Analysis of Mass Communications

The Readings by Burgelin and Lovell (14 and 15) both serve to remind us of the existence of modes of thought and traditions of inquiry which may, too often, be unknown to, or undervalued by, students of mass communications (especially if they are English or American). The two authors open up questions of great theoretical and substantive interest which might otherwise not seem amenable to investigation in any rigorous way. By way of additional recommendation we may note the particular relevance of these contributions to the study of the cinema which, since the advent of television, has tended to suffer an undeserved neglect at the hands of sociologists.

14 Olivier Burgelin

Structural Analysis and Mass Communication

Revised and shortened version of Olivier Burgelin, 'Structural analysis
and mass communication: tendency of French research on mass
communications', *Studies of Broadcasting*, no. 6, 1968, pp. 143–68.

This article is presented in this volume in a new translation by Susan Bennet.

We should begin by saying a few words about the linguistic
tradition from which the method described here as structural
analysis or semiological analysis derives.[1]

The linguistic model

Structural linguistics is undoubtedly one of the first of the
human sciences, with economics, to deserve to be called a
science, not only for its aims, but for the results it has obtained:
the discovery of necessary relations. This achievement came
about in the 1930s with the work of the linguistic circles of
Prague and Copenhagen, but the basis for it was laid thirty
years earlier by Saussure (1960). Saussure held that language
should not be considered as a substance but as a form, that is to
say, as a pure system of differences, in which the value of each
linguistic unit is not determined by an absolute relationship with
some other, non-linguistic unit, but by its place within the system
of language. This means that the first object of linguistics ought
to be to discover the set of relations forming that system – what

1. Since this article was written (1966) there has been a considerable
development in semiological studies throughout the world, accompanied
by incessant and sometimes feverish theoretical activity, with the result that
many basic assumptions have been challenged. Consequently it was
impossible to bring the article up to date in anything but a very incomplete
fashion. There is not one of the problems which the author would not
formulate in different terms today. In addition, at that time it was natural
to assume that the vast majority of readers would be unfamiliar with the
problems of semiology, and so simplicity of exposition seemed more
important than detail. Under these conditions, the reader should be fore-
warned not to expect a summary of the latest developments in semiology:
at the very most this article should be regarded as an introduction to the
semiological analysis of mass communications.

Saussure called 'language' as opposed to 'speech' (an antithesis very similar to the one, more frequently used today, of 'code' and 'message'). The essential moment of the linguistic process is that of *immanent analysis*, in which we take into account only the internal relations of the system, and exclude all those between the system and man, culture, society, in short the outside world, and in which we attempt to discover the code by analysing the structure of the 'messages' alone, without being influenced by any other considerations, whether physiological, psychological, sociological or historical. This does not mean, of course, that no relationship should ever be established between linguistics and other disciplines – which would be absurd – but that no such relationship should be established until it can have a stable foundation, which will not be achieved until linguistics, using nothing but its own resources, has firmly determined the structure of its object.

Further, these principles are applicable not only to linguistics, but also, as Saussure himself perceived, to all the human sciences, or, to use his expression, all the disciplines which are concerned with *values*. Since then the anthropologist Claude Lévi-Strauss has proved their fruitfulness in various domains related both to ethnology and to communication: kinship, economic exchange, myths (1963). There is no reason why these principles should not prove equally applicable to the study of mass communication. Like the linguist, the student of mass communications is surrounded by a universe of messages. Certainly, not all these messages are coded linguistically: the mass media include a vast amount of visual matter, music and non-linguistic signs generally. But all these messages appear nonetheless to relate to a general science of signs, the principles of which were laid down by Saussure and which he christened *semiology*. Mass communications studies might well provide a favourable opportunity for developing other branches of this science.

The immanent universe of mass communications

The transition from linguistics to semiology of course demands a certain number of transpositions.[2] Mass communications study

2. On these transpositions, and methodological problems generally, see Barthes (1969).

is a case in point. The prime object of interest for research in this area is not the purely linguistic properties of the messages conveyed by the mass media, but rather, in a more general sense, the *meaning* of those messages, and the universe which they constitute. This leads naturally to the study of what could be called the 'vocabulary' of the mass media. By this we do not, of course, so much mean a vocabulary of words, but rather of units which are in some way larger than words: the 'things' or symbols (in the sense in which the term is frequently used) which are the stock-in-trade of the mass media: stars, politicians, gangsters, cowboys, fashion, beauty products, love, youth, etc.

However, it would be to misunderstand the nature of structural analysis to suppose that its immediate aim is the interpretation of such symbols (for instance, by sociological or psychoanalytic means). This would be a contradiction of the principle of immanence, for such interpretation essentially entails seeking a key to the symbols *outside* the universe under consideration. Structural analysis consists, on the contrary, in attempting to reconstitute the organization of symbols *within* the system in which they are situated.

So, the aim of the semiologist must be to find how units of the type described above relate to each other within larger units, for instance those of the type resembling what linguists call the 'sentence'. By 'sentence' we mean something broader than the linguist: a unit of meaning of a certain size, within which a certain number of relations can be distinguished. The linguistic sentence conforms to this definition in that it has (at the very least) a subject and a predicate and so fulfils what logicians call a 'propositional function'. But, in the area we are studying, this role is not confined to the linguistic sentence. The pictures we find in the mass media, advertising photographs for instance, also fulfil a propositional function by placing various elements of the vocabulary of the mass media in a relation to each other within a specific framework. Moreover, if we asked somebody without prior warning to tell us what was depicted by a certain advertising photograph, he would probably reply with a sentence, this time in the strictly linguistic sense of the term 'It's an elegant lady dressing', or 'It's a young girl drinking a cup of coffee', etc.

Such 'sentences' are of great interest for the semiologist because it is through them, and them alone that he can hope to work his way back to the *meaning* of their constitutive elements. The crucial problem is always to know *who* is to define the meaning of any given element. Evidently it cannot be the person doing the analysis, because his ideas on meaning will vary according to his culture (a sociological bias will produce different results from a psychological bias, for example). Nor can he look it up in a dictionary, for what dictionary could tell us the meaning of the 'gangster' as he appears in the mass media? The transmitter of the message (supposing he could be identified and questioned) and its intended recipient (supposing a 'typical' or 'statistically average' recipient could be found) might well be perfectly able to manipulate the symbols contained in the mass media without being able to specify the meaning of those symbols: they might be partially unconscious of it themselves. In short there is nobody, and nothing, outside the message which can supply us with the meaning of one of its elements. So we have no choice but to turn to the message itself and to admit that the only rigorous definition of the meaning of an element of the 'vocabulary' of the mass media is the one implied by the contexts (or 'sentences') within which it is used. This is why the first aim of the semiologist must be to describe the immanent universe of meaning in the corpus he is studying (in this case, the mass media). In this way he can hope to work his way back to the cultural 'code' governing the meaning of all individual elements.

It might well be objected that such a project must result in an extremely flat and trivial description of the universe of the mass media, which would not bring to light any of the things which it might appear most 'interesting' to discover, such as ideological motivation or hidden meanings. To take an example: if we look at French advertisements for coffee we shall see that in almost all cases text and pictures associate coffee with images of repose: a break at work, restful evenings, relaxation in the family circle. Now it is perfectly obvious that coffee is, above all, a stimulant, and if the advertisers seek to link coffee with repose it must be with the intention of concealing, or at the very least *neutralizing*, whatever might be alarming to the consumer in the idea of coffee as a stimulant. But as the only authentic association that immanent analysis can reveal from the contexts under consideration is that between coffee and tranquillity, is it not missing the essential point?

We should draw attention, here, to the fact that the essential point (that is to say, the one which really adds to our understanding of the mass media) is not, in this case, that coffee is a stimulant, nor that it should be associated with the idea of repose in advertising in the mass media, but simply that there is a relationship between these two facts – one of which was brought to light *by immanent analysis*. In other words, if immanent analysis is not perhaps adequate on its own to reveal the type of *repression* (in the quasi-psychoanalytic meaning of the term) being brought to bear on the fact that coffee is a stimulant, it is nonetheless necessary. But is it not adequate in itself? Here two hypotheses are possible. One: that an attentive study of a sufficient number of contexts, even drawn from advertising alone, ought to permit us to reconstitute the 'repressed' meanings by following indications present in the contexts themselves. Two: that a second stage of analysis is needed, in which immanent analysis of the contents of the mass media would be integrated into a general analysis of the culture under consideration. There is nothing particularly radical about this hypothesis: after all, the mass media clearly do not form a complete culture on their own: in other words, they do not form an entirely closed system, like a language, but simply a fraction of such a system, which is, of necessity, the culture to which they belong. In either case immanent analysis would always be needed to reveal the problems, even if it would not necessarily be adequate within a strictly defined corpus to resolve them.

Moreover, examination of certain contextual elements can bring to light facts about the structure of the material in question involving wider and more profound levels of meaning. This we shall find to be particularly true of those units whose dimensions exceed those of the 'sentence': films, newspaper stories, songs, etc. These forms also consist of a framework, with certain clearly defined relations operating within it. Take, for instance, the mass of anecdotes which appear in the French press, particularly the non-pictorial section, in the form known as 'faits divers' (news in brief) (Barthes, 1962). We shall discover that, in France at any rate, almost all these items are constructed on one or other of two models, either emphasizing a paradoxical or extraordinary relationship: 'Englishman joins the foreign legion – he didn't want to spend Christmas with his mother-in-law', or 'She went for her lover with a knife – they didn't agree on politics', or else emphasizing an extraordinary coincidence such as the repetition of an event: 'Robbery in a jeweller's shop – it was the third time', or the assortment of two very disparate terms: 'Icelandic fishermen net a cow'. It will be seen there that a whole story appears to have been constructed by the journalist, or at any rate reported to the reader, with the sole purpose of fulfilling what we have termed a 'propositional function'. Moreover, if we examine a number of such units we shall see structural constants emerging which form elements of the very phenomenon which it is the chief purpose of structural analysis to uncover: a code.

Structural analysis and content analysis

Structural analysis, then, takes a very different line of approach to the texts under consideration than content analysis. This difference centres upon three points: firstly, the problem of quantifying the different elements of the content; secondly, that of taking account of the 'form' or style of the communication; and finally the problem of the latent content of the communication.

The problem of quantification

Traditional content analysis is essentially quantitative. Whatever its aim may be, its method is always to itemize and enumerate. Behind this attitude, whatever the arguments may be in its favour, lurks an old behaviourist prejudice: we may not be able to ascertain with absolute certitude what the text means, but we can ascertain with absolute certitude that the item 'Stalin' appears ten times more often than the item 'Lenin' or (if we are studying a comic strip) that the item 'yellow hair' recurs ten times more often in heroes than villains. Structural analysis, on the contrary, only rarely enumerates. Why? It would be pointless to deny that it is sometimes possible to draw certain inferences from the fact that the word 'Stalin' occurs more frequently or less frequently in a text. But in itself this fact is unintelligible if we do not take account of what the text says each time about Stalin. If we do, enumeration becomes more and more difficult, even impossible; it is highly probable that the text never says the same thing twice about Stalin. But above all there is no reason to assume that the item which recurs most frequently is the most important or the most significant, for a text is, clearly, a *structured* whole, and the place occupied by the different elements is more important than the number of times they recur. Let us imagine a film in which the gangster hero is seen performing a long succession of actions which show his character in an extremely vicious light, but he is also seen performing one single action which reveals to a striking degree that he has finer feelings. So the gangster's actions are to be evaluated in terms of two sets of opposites: bad/good and frequent/exceptional. The polarity frequent/exceptional is perceptible at first sight and needs no quantification. Moreover, we clearly cannot draw any valid inferences from a simple enumeration of his vicious acts (it makes no difference whether there are ten or twenty of them) for the crux of the matter obviously is: what meaning is conferred on the vicious acts by the fact of their juxtaposition with the single good action? And only by taking into account the structural relationship of this one good action with the totality of the gangster's vicious behaviour in the film can we make any inference concerning the film as a whole. In more general terms, one could say that the meaning of what is frequent is only revealed by opposition to what is rare. In other words, the meaning of a frequently-recurring item is not essentially linked to the fact that it occurs ten times rather than twenty times, but it is essentially linked to the fact that it is placed in opposition to another item which occurs rarely (or which is sometimes even absent). The whole problem is therefore to identify this rare or absent item. Structural analysis provides a way of approaching this problem, which traditional content analysis does not.

'Form' and content

The distinction between content and 'form' is generally thought of as being that between 'what one wants to say' and 'the way one says it' or between the 'anecdote' and the 'style'.[3] This is a perfectly real distinction, and at a certain level of analysis it is impossible to do without it. If, for example, we find a man wearing glasses in an advertisement, and the context tells us they are meant to signify competence, not short-sightedness, we can regard 'competence' as the content of the message and 'glasses' as a stylistic element, a figure of rhetoric used to express this content. The style of advertising (as opposed, for instance, to that of the weather bulletin) is characterized by the frequency of such figures of rhetoric. But however real this distinction between style and content may be, it should not lead us to overlook a fundamental fact: they are two levels of meaning, which must, therefore, be studied within a common framework. Both the fact that a certain type of man is presented to us as 'competent' and the fact that glasses are used to signify his competence embody meaning within the ideological universe of the mass media. So it follows that at a certain level of analysis we should be able to integrate both of them. This is another problem that content analysis, which rarely goes beyond the enumeration of stylistic devices, has not been able to resolve. Unlike structural analysis, it has never evolved a common framework for these two levels of analysis. The answer proposed by structural analysis is that style should be regarded as the level of integration of content within the code. Consequently stylistic analysis and in particular analysis of figures of rhetoric are regarded as the best means of access to the code. Figures of rhetoric are, in a sense, the moment at which the code (of which we are normally unconscious) gives itself away and comes out of hiding. For if competence is replaceable by glasses (or a woman by a flower, etc.) there must be a code authorizing these transformations.

Manifest content and latent content

According to Berelson, the goal of content analysis is to describe the manifest content of the communication. This description is

3. The word 'form' is ambiguous. It is often used rather loosely, as we are using it here (hence our inverted commas) to mean 'style'. It is quite clear that when Saussure says language is a form, he is not referring to style, but to something higher, a pure totality of relations which we have generally designated here as the code.

not necessarily devoid of interest, especially where very factual, non-dreamlike communications are concerned. But it is precisely this type of communication which appears relatively infrequently in the mass media. When it comes to analysing songs, novels, fiction, anything that is dreamlike to some degree, it is evident that we should be missing the most essential part of the communication if we left out the latent content. But how are we to get at the latent content? There is no one better qualified to answer that question than the man who devoted his life, his writings and his genius to understanding the latent content of communication: Sigmund Freud. If we turn to those sections of his work in which he examines the transition from manifest content to latent content, particularly in reference to dreams, we shall see that 'condensation' and 'displacement', which according to Freud are typical modes of transition from one level to another, are quite plainly figures of rhetoric analogous to those which appear at the stylistic level of communication. The antinomy of manifest content and latent content is really just another expression of the reality that we have been trying to understand in the form of the antinomy of 'form' and 'content'. In any case, if we talk about the 'latent content' of communication, are we not implying that manifest content is a sort of metaphor, the real meaning of which is the latent content? It must be obvious that a genre like the Western owes its success to the fact that all its defining elements (the hero, the badmen, the fight to establish the rule of law, violence put to the service of good, etc.) are metaphors for content of another kind, and problems of another kind: those of the societies which consume Westerns. In adopting the principle of analysing everything which has meaning in the communication (that is to say, everything that can be altered without altering the meaning) structural analysis, like Freud – and incidentally for the same reasons as Freud – provides itself with a means of understanding the whole structure, and thus the whole 'depth' of the communication.[4]

4. Roman Jakobson in particular has made a study of the similarity between figures of rhetoric and the patterns of development of the dream as described by Freud. See Jakobson (1956). This text has had a considerable impact in France, particularly via the psychoanalytic teaching of Jacques Lacan. See in particular Lacan (1957).

Towards the audience

The structural approach should enable us to reformulate the terms in which we discuss the audience and the effects of mass communication.

Traditional mass communications study claimed to devote equal attention to the message, the transmitting group, the audience and the effects of the message. But this was only in theory: we have seen that its techniques turned out to be rather inappropriate to the study of messages; and the difficulty of conducting inquiries about the transmitting groups – plus the not inconsiderable fact that it is often the transmitting groups which sponsor the inquiries – resulted in a paucity of work in that area also. Consequently audience research and research into the effects of the mass media have been carried out on a much larger scale and in greater depth than research of the other two types.

Structural analysis, however, concentrates on the message itself on the presupposition that problems concerning the audience and the effects of mass communication (and indeed those concerning the transmitting groups) cannot be correctly posed except on the basis of a thorough analysis of the message. There are a number of facts which seem to justify this method.

In the first place, it is a remarkable fact that in 1966, despite the enormous amount of work that has been done in the area, we still know very little about the effects of mass communications, or to put it more precisely, the 'knowledge' acquired in this field can scarcely ever be put to use because it cannot be integrated into a sound theoretical framework.[5] A very clear example of this fact is to be found in what is without doubt one of the most frequently researched of all the problems: the effect on children of violence in the mass media. It is notoriously difficult, even today, to formulate any precise theory on this question which does not have a marked ideological bias (Glucksmann, 1971). And yet there is no reason to believe that the research was not conducted with the necessary care. So we have to ask ourselves whether the question was posed in such a way that it could be answered.

5. As is very clearly demonstrated by Klapper (1960).

In fact, over the last ten years, many researchers have been led to modify the question itself, and have sought to investigate what children do with a communication rather than what it does to them – to paraphrase Schramm's formulation (Schramm et al. 1961). This new way of formulating the problem forms the basis of research of the 'uses and gratifications' type which has been very widespread in the United States in the last few years (Klapper, 1963).

Nonetheless mass communications are plainly not just so much raw material, of which the consumer, child or adult, can make absolutely anything he likes; they are products which have already been extensively pre-structured (as Meyersohn puts it) by the conditions under which they were manufactured. They resemble many modern industrial products in being, as it were 'pre-stressed', i.e. in having many of the conditions which they will encounter in use already built into them (Meyersohn, 1961). So it would seem as though our first priority ought to be to analyse the stresses to which the 'pre-stressed' product is subject at the moment of distribution. These stresses form elements of a code, and it is the prime objective of structural analysis to get a detailed picture of that code.

Naturally it remains to be discovered, as a second stage of the process, how the product fits into the totality of the culture, and also whether the universe constituted by such products is not purely and simply identical to the cultural universe of the consuming public. For instance, in France at any rate, it is a fairly striking fact that the consumers very often evince an extremely critical attitude towards certain elements of mass culture (for instance the star cult) (Barthes, 1963). Does this mean that the mass culture which people object to is in some sense a foreign body imposed on them from without by the small minority who hold the strings of power in the mass media, and that it is not what they really want at all? The hypothesis is naive – rather in the same way as the school of thought which criticizes Freud for attributing such importance to sexuality, when most people disapprove of sexual motivation. All that we can conclude from this situation is that any definition of the cultural universe of French consumers of mass culture must encompass both mass culture and criticism or censure of it.

In these circumstances, structural analysis is inevitably drawn sooner or later to reformulate the problem of effects. No direct approach is possible to the problem of knowing what consequences the communication (considered as a cause) will have on the behaviour of the audience (considered as an effect). The problem must, essentially, be viewed in the light of the more fundamental one from which it is derived: how does the communication fit into the cultural universe of those who consume it? This is another problem which can only be posed in structural terms. For here again quantitative analysis is not an adequate method. We shall not learn anything important from the fact that children see ten rather than twenty violent episodes on the screen a day, or that the public hears ten rather than twenty times a day that product X is best, or political party Y will lead the country into a prosperous future. What we need to know is how such statements fit into their cultural universe. Everyone must by now be aware that the same propaganda can have a radically different effect on different populations. It has been proved over and over again; the French experience in Algeria is a classic recent example.

Special problems

In conclusion we should like to touch upon certain special problems which have traditionally been left to one side by communications research, but which structural analysis has been attempting to tackle in the last few years.

The image

Everything to do with visual images and music is particularly inaccessible to the human sciences, doubtless because they are communication but not language. So talking about images and music (and however scientific our discourse may be, it is still 'talking') always implies translating material into words which is not of the order of words – a particularly brutal operation which can never be more than partly justified. However, we must admit that the difficulty is less great in the field of mass communications than elsewhere, simply because images and music are rarely, in this field, unaccompanied by words. So the analyst has an invaluable extra tool at his disposal, for if he cannot arrogate the right to divide up and delimit the meaning of musical and plastic units, he can legitimately admit a division and meaning resulting from a confrontation between such units and their verbal context. In addition, there are two lines of approach which we can use: analysis of the 'formal' properties of the image (space, light, colour, etc.) as practised by theorists of the plastic arts; and, more important still, analysis based on the eminently figurative character of the images found in the mass media. For in these images we find 'symbols', elements of a specific 'vocabulary' being manipulated in a way that closely resembles the process we have observed in the written part of the mass media. Thus in any newspaper or magazine photograph, we are liable to find a certain number of contextually-determined elements of a specific 'vocabulary': a teenager, long hair, a guitar, jeans, a sunset, etc. By referring to these elements and the way they are organized on the one hand, and to the written context on the other, we can begin to make a semiological analysis. But semiological analysis of the image does not consist in trying to reduce everything to one single code, since in this area it is patently obvious that there are any number of codes intersecting each other. Thus in a drawing, of whatever kind, elements of a code, or codes, appear at the level of the graphic style itself, and in the features which the artist chooses to portray. In photography such elements are less evident, because they are, as it were, built into the way the camera operates; but there are levels at which they become manifest, for instance in the choice of angle, focus, etc.[6]

The cinema

The cinema poses different problems from still photography. In the first place, the film is not only composed of images, in general moving images, but also of words and music. Our 'text' therefore is an extremely complex, multi-dimensional one. For one thing, the fact that the image is moving completely transforms its properties. The framework within which characters and objects have their existence becomes a temporal one, and thus they become integrated into a new dimension which is, broadly speaking, that of narrative. And so the first problem which we

6. There is a bibliography on the semiological analysis of visual material in *Communications* (1970a).

have to solve, if we apply the structural analytic method to the cinema, is that of discovering the processes whereby characters and objects become integrated into this new dimension, and the type of units determined by these processes (Metz, 1971).

The narrative

As is to be expected from a fully self-conscious method, semiological analysis determines its own problems without regard to how the material has previously been divided up by other disciplines or other specialized branches of knowledge. The narrative is a broad structure of integration which we find in all language and all cultures, in literature and in everyday life, in traditional folklore and in the modern mass media. So it will be seen that structural analysis, in examining such problems as the structure of the narrative, broadens out the range of mass communications study from the psycho-sociological field of effects-studies in which it had become confined into the field of general culture studies. Structural analysis seeks to determine elements of the code which governs sequences of the narrative genre in whatever medium they appear: folk tales or films, comic strips or newspaper stories (Bremond, 1964; *Communications*, 1966).

Fashion

Fashion is a 'total social phenomenon', relating to the fields of aesthetics and psychology as well as economics and sociology. But it is in an equally fundamental way a phenomenon embodying meaning: if we say that an item of clothing, a colour, or a certain type of behaviour is fashionable, we are above all attributing a certain meaning to it. And that is precisely what fashion magazines do: the function of this type of magazine is, precisely, to introduce a signifying discourse as a mediation between the supply of clothing (embodied in our society by a vast economic network) and public demand. This we could call the discourse of fashion. Roland Barthes has made a structural analysis of this discourse which we should like to quote as an example of method. His first step is to make a list of what he calls 'commutative classes', meaning classes which interreact in such a way that any change in one brings about a corresponding change in another.

The existence of such classes is demonstrated by certain statements in fashion magazines, such as: a cardigan which is casual with the collar open, formal with the collar closed. This amounts, in effect, to saying that in the context of fashion as it is at present, a change from the open-necked cardigan to closed-necked cardigan within a certain class (which could be called clothing) produces a corresponding variation within another class (which could be called the world): a change from the casual to the formal. In the remainder of the book Barthes explores each of these classes and their relationships in detail, with particularly fruitful results (1967).

Rhetoric

We have already encountered the problem of figures of rhetoric in our discussion of the antithesis of 'form' and content. It is a remarkable fact that these figures, which were named and enumerated by the classical rhetoricians have all turned up again in the mass media, in every type of message: advertising, film titles, life-stories as told in popular magazines. The same can be said of all the procedures of rhetoric, which are far from being confined to figures, but cover the whole composition of the discourse. By an apparent paradox it seems as if the old discipline of rhetoric, which had been abandoned as an academic subject and discredited as a technique by the end of the nineteenth century (i.e. when the mass media first came on the scene) is particularly well suited to the analysis of works produced for a mass audience. For instance, the informational discourse of the mass media fits perfectly into the Aristotelian category of 'that which appears true', i.e. a discourse which is not founded on scientific truth, even if it takes scientific truth as its justification, but on public opinion, on what people believe to be possible. So semiological analysis has much in common with the old system of rhetoric, but it should be stressed that their aims are very different. The point of Aristotelian rhetoric is to ensure the efficacity of the message, and so its sphere is the fundamentally sociological one of communication. The point of semiology is to reveal the meaning of the message, and so its sphere is basically that of cultural studies as they relate to the mass media. Semiology is not concerned to produce a new version of classical rhetoric, but simply to show the profound congruence existing between rhetoric and the contemporary mass media.[7]

7. Durand (1970, pp. 70–95). *Communications* (1970b) surveys the contemporary relevance of rhetoric from a semiological viewpoint. There is a bibliography.

References

BARTHES, R. (1962), 'Structure du fait divers', *Essais Critiques*, Éditions du Seuil, Paris.

BARTHES, R. (1963), 'La vedette, enquêtes d'audience?', *Communications*, vol. 2.

BARTHES, R. (1967), *Système de la Mode*, Seuil.

BARTHES, R. (1969), *Elements of Semiology*, trans. Annette Lavers and Colin Smith, Cape.

BREMOND, C. (1964), 'Le message narratif', *Communications*, vol. 4, (special number), pp. 4–32.

Communications (1966), 'L'analyse structurale du récit', (special number), vol. 8.

Communications (1970a), 'L'analyse des images' (bibliography), vol. 15.

Communications (1970b), 'Recherches rhetoriques', (entire issue), vol. 16.

DURAND, J. (1970), Rhetorique et image publicitaire', *Communications*, vol. 15, pp. 70–95.

GLUCKSMANN, A. (1971), *Violence on the Screen*, trans. Susan Bennett, British Film Institute.

JAKOBSON, R. (1956), 'Two aspects of language and two types of aphasic disturbances', in K. Jacobson and M. Halle, *Fundamentals of Language*, Mouton.

KLAPPER, J. T. (1960), *The Effects of Mass Communication*, Free Press.

KLAPPER, J. T. (1963), 'Mass communication research: an old road resurveyed', *Pub. Opinion Q.*, vol. 27, no. 4.

LACAN, J. (1957), 'L'instance de la lettre dans l'inconscient', *La Psychanalyse*, vol. 3. Reprinted in *Écrits*, 1966, Édition du Seuil, pp. 473–528.

LÉVI-STRAUSS, C. (1963), *Structural Anthropology*, trans. Claire Jacobson and Brooke Grundfest-Schrepf, Basic Books; Allen Lane The Penguin Press, 1968.

METZ, C. (1971), *Language et Cinéma*, Larousse.

MEYERSOHN, R. (1961), 'A critical examination of commercial entertainment', in R. W. Kleemeier (ed.), *Ageing and Leisure*, Oxford University Press.

SAUSSURE, F. de (1960), *Course in General Linguistics*, trans. Wade Baskin, Peter Owen.

SCHRAMM, W., LYLE, J., and PARKER, E. D. (1961), *Television in the Lives of Our Children*, Stamford University Press.

15 Terry Lovell

Sociology of Aesthetic Structures and Contextualism

Published for the first time in this volume

Introduction

Although our chief interest is in the sociology of film, many of our remarks relate to either *media sociology* or *sociology of aesthetic structures* in general, and are not specific to film.

Media studies commonly distinguish three phases of the communication process; source system, message system and receiver system. They have concentrated on the latter, while analysis of message systems has proved relatively intractible, and has been neglected. Berelson (1952) gave a remarkably pessimistic account of the state and prospects of 'content analysis', a judgement confirmed by Janowitz (1968–9), who speaks of 'intellectual stagnation' in this field. More promising developments have come from outside sociology, notably the 'structuralism' of Lévi-Strauss, which draws nothing from the techniques of sociological content analysis.

Lacking sophisticated theoretical orientations (Tudor, 1970), media sociology makes many 'commonsense' but questionable assumptions. The commitment to content analysis itself is a case in point. In the sociology of science there is no equivalent, and any such suggestion would be greeted with derision. If this approach seems appropriate to the arts and the media, then it can only because these stand in a different relationship to society than does science. The exact nature of this assumed relationship must be specified theoretically, so that the appropriateness of content analysis follows.

Content analysis – the categories of analysis being drawn from the categories of social life itself – is biased in favour of the representational arts. We have little in the way of sociology of music (Weber, 1958). Sociology of 'pop' music is uniformly restricted to analysis of the lyrics. (Rosenstone, 1969; Carey, 1969). Where there are no lyrics, we may yet get trivial results. (Hamburger, 1967, tells us that the fragmented structure of Thai music reflects the fragmented structure of Thai society). We need a sociology whose categories are more broadly applicable, drawn in the first instance from categories immanent to the works themselves. The question of the societal function of art may be raised, but only after the work has been placed and understood in its primary aesthetic context.

This plea for *contextualism* in media sociology and sociology of art alike, is not new (see Glucksmann, 1971). The argument that items of the work belong to a structured whole, from which they gain their significance, entails that any social or psychological function is mediated by that relationship.

In the absence of an alternative method incorporating contextualism, this plea would have fallen on deaf ears; as long as the alternative was merely the old 'Eng. Lit.' methods, intuitive, qualitative and unreliable, however much theoretical sense the plea made.[1] With the advent of structuralism, the situation changes. We may forecast increasing application of this method in sociology of art–media.[2] The coincidence of a prestigious new method with the self-confessed lack of success of the old, makes this development inevitable. This 'crisis' of the old methods is amply demonstrated by Glucksmann (1971), using the simple but effective expedient of juxtaposing the major theories and empirical studies of the effects upon the audience of screen violence. Every imaginable hypothesis has been advanced at some time, and each adduces supporting evidence.

The 'internalist' or contextualist movement in the study of cultural phenomena is not so militant as its counterpart in philosophy of science. Natural scientific knowledge has been handled by the sociologist with a caution not always extended to other cultural phenomena. Any attempt to relate scientific knowledge to social or psychological antecedents immediately

1. Warshow's (1962) justly famous essay on the Western illustrates to strength and weaknesses of his approach.
2. In an unpublished MA dissertation, Slater (1970) applies this method to the analysis of newspaper reports of the October 1968 demonstration in Grosvenor Square.

falls foul of what Martins (1970) calls 'the philosophical blows of anti-sociology of knowledge'. The arts–media have available no equivalent to the scientist's epistemological defence against intruders, nor are they organized into professionalized and tightly knit 'social systems', jealous of and able to defend their autonomy. Kuhn (1969) remarks that the general public may react with dismayed incomprehension to both science and the more esoteric products of art, but only in the latter case with incredulity and dismissal. The scientist's self-evaluation is authoritative; that of the artist open to question.

The success of anti-sociology in relation to science resulted in the elimination of scientific creativity from the problematic of sociology of science (Martins, 1970). Although there is a similar 'sacred' area in artistic creativity, the arts have always been more vulnerable to 'externalist' explanations. At times, a Freudian, a Marxist, and various sociological theories of art have been advanced. But in general, sociologists have been happy to concur in the judgement that 'hack art' is more amenable to sociological analysis than great works, presenting less distorted reflections of social currents, and being unaffected by personal marks of genius. 'High' art is thus marked off, and granted autonomy, to be explained by the personal, creative, vision of the author, or by the immanent development of an artistic tradition or style. It is interesting to see that the revaluation of the American cinema, instigated by *Cahiers du Cinema* in the 1950s, was under the rubric of 'authorship', and it was thus assimilated to the aesthetic categories of the established arts (see Wollen, 1969).

Martins (1970) proposes a less crude typology as substitute for the 'external-internal' dichotomy used so far, and here it is suitably adapted for the present context.

Most writers use a mixture of variables in their explanations. Their appropriateness depends on the aspect of the phenomenon to be explained, and its description. Danto (1965) points out that our explanations only explain under some description of a phenomenon. Under others it may be inexplicable. Part of our inquiry, then, must be directed towards uncovering appropriate descriptions of aesthetic phenomena, if our explanations are to be sociological.

Few sociologists would hazard an attempt to isolate sufficient conditions for almost any aspect of art, and their explanations may cite necessary conditions only in the weaker sense of 'background conditions'. There is a danger of triviality. But there is a precedent in Weber's famous 'Protestant ethic' thesis. Weber did not claim that the religious factor was either a necessary or a sufficient condition for the rise of capitalism. This does not so much throw doubt upon the value of his explanation as upon the practice of assessing explanations in terms of 'necessary and/or sufficient conditions' (Mackie, 1965).

Table 1 **Sociologies of art and the media**

	Cultural variables	Social Structural variables
Internal variables	e.g. Kroeber (1947)	e.g. Macherey (1970) e.g. Crozier (1964)
External variables	e.g. Goldmann (1964) e.g. Williams (1958)	e.g. Vulgar Marxism

The 'anti-sociologists' who wish to protect aesthetic phenomena from sociological contamination are not so modest in the claims they make for the status of their explanations of those phenomena. For if they are to exclude 'external' factors, then they must leave no room for them. Typically, the claim is that, under all interesting or relevant descriptions, works of art may be fully explained by factors immanent to art itself, thus preempting any other explanatory factors.[3] Alternatively, artistic creativity is supposed to elude explanation altogether, being ineffable, undetermined and altogether mysterious. The implication of the first of these arguments is to relegate sociology to the secondary task of analysing the reception of innovations which it can have no part in explaining; to what Martins (1970) has called 'selectionism'. It would be a retrograde step were 'contextualism' to remove artistic creativity from the purview of the sociologist, because of unjustified fears of reductionism.

3. MacIntyre (1971) offers this argument against sociological explanations of rational beliefs and actions, and in passing, of art styles.

Structuralism and ideology

In so far as contextualism takes the form of structuralism, anti-sociology may be contained. Lévi-Strauss, being an anthropologist, has always been concerned with the relationship between two structures, one of which pertains to society, (e.g. kinship structures). Myths are seen as attempted resolutions of various kinds of contradiction contained in social theory and practice. The union of structuralism with Marxism reinforces this effect. The societal reference should not be lost.

It has been noted (Goldthorpe et al, 1969), that the current 'return to Marx' has concentrated on the theory of super-structures. Althusser's (1970) structuralism allows the ideological component of the superstructure 'a certain autonomy' in relation to the infrastructure, via his concept of *overdetermination*. In the Marxist as opposed to the Hegelian dialectic, it is not permissable to reduce all contradictions to a single determining contradiction located in the economic infrastructure. He draws attention to the existence of contradictions at all levels, and argues that in a given juncture, each one may add its determination as it were, to the final outcome, which in the short run, is contingent, rather than necessary.

For Marxists, film belongs to the ideological superstructure – it is defined as 'ideological practice' (Fargier, 1971). This irreducible interest in its ideological function ensures that Marxist, like sociological, film theory, retains an interest in the societal relationships of film. Their theories of that relationship differ of course, although the Marxist category of 'false consciousness' may be considered functionally equivalent to the sociologists' 'consensus', via the theory of socialization (see Mann, 1970, for an account of the conceptual and empirical differentiae of 'false consciousness' and 'consensus'). In the union of Marxism and structuralism, the formula that ideology has 'a certain autonomy' may open a path between the Scylla of economic–social determinism, and the Charbydis of immanentism.[4] This particular theoretical orientation has found expression in an important debate between two leading French film

4. Although the formula leaves wide open the question of *how much* autonomy. Perhaps this is variable. See Slater (1970) for an interesting attempt to specify this relationship.

journals, *Cahiers du Cinéma* and *Cinéthique* (Fargier, 1971), a circumstance which reflects the more highly politicized nature of French culture as well as the seminal influence of structuralism in diverse fields. If ideology can no longer be dismissed as *mere* ideology, if its variety of form and function is appreciated, more perceptive analyses may ensue than are possible within the undifferentiated category of 'bourgeois ideology'. *Cahiers* started more promisingly than *Cinéthique* in this respect with a typology of the modes of relationship between capitalist society and its ideological presentation of itself, to itself, in film (Comolli and Narboni, 1971).

Yet despite its ties to a theory of society via the concept of ideology, there is evidence of a residual distrust of the sociological intrusion, in the light of which the response to Goldmann's contribution to the Johns Hopkins colloquium on structuralism of 1965 (Macksey and Donato, 1970; Brewster, 1971) may be understood. For Goldmann, structures are defined in terms of their functions,[5] which relate to the situation of some specific group, and its social experience. Goldmann seeks homologies of structure between the mental categories with which the group orders its experience, and the imaginary universe of the creative writer. In one of his best known studies, he relates the works of Racine and Pascal to the mental categories of the Jansenist world-view, and thence to the situation of the *noblesse de robe* in seventeenth century France (Goldmann, 1964).

In his paper to the colloquium, Goldmann briefly outlines his 'genetic sociological' approach to literature. In the ensuing discussion, Hyppolite and Vernant take issue with him over the postulated relationship of structures to functions, arguing for the primacy and autonomy of structures. Vernant suggests that it is the internal aesthetic function of literary structures which is relevant, not their social function. Goldmann, in his reply, argues that these structures exist within a number of encompassing 'totalities', to each of which they are functionally related. Yet despite his disclaimer, the suspicion remains that he is forcing

5. Goldmann: 'La *structure* existe par sa charactère significatif qui résulte de son aptitude à remplir une *fonction*. Ses *fonctions* ne sauraient être remplies que par des *structures*, les structures sont *significatives* dans la mesure où elles sont aptes à remplir une *fonction*' (Macksey and Donato, 1970, p. 324).

the works into preconceived categories external to them, resulting in blindness to other aspects. Glucksmann (1969) makes this point most forceably. She dismisses Goldmann's sociology of literature as addressing itself only to problems of genre, rather than to the multiple levels and referents of the works. She remarks that 'Analyses of genre are patently insufficient for a total conception of literature'. Although the problem she raises is a very real one, it may be said in his defence that Goldmann is not proposing a 'total conception', but only a *sociology* of literature.

We may accept Goldmann's account of the multiple significance of aesthetic structures according to the context in which they are being considered – the different structured 'totalities' in which they participate. What is unclear is whether these structures remain the same in the different contexts. It seems more likely that when they are related, e.g. to 'the libidinal problems of the individual' (Goldmann, 1970), different structurations will be revealed from those of a sociological context. We cannot determine by fiat whether a sociological or some other point of reference – psychological, intentional – will give 'the best' reading. Yet Goldmann wishes to establish the priority and necessity of a sociological reading.[6] He postulates a continuum, along which all the phenomena of consciousness may be placed. At one extreme, the 'transindividual' group consciousness is placed, at the other 'individual libidinal problems intervene so forcefully that they completely deform social logic' (Goldmann, 1970, p. 105). At the former extreme he places great aesthetic achievements; at the latter, dreams. If great works embody social logic, then only social logic can decode them. A sociological reading becomes 'the only possible reading' (p. 105) because it can decode '80 per cent or 90 per cent of the text' (p. 105). The prejudice that mediocre art is more sociologically relevant is reversed. Indeed, great works are *assessed* in terms of the purity and coherence they exhibit in transposing socially given categories into imaginative structures. Goldmann has a sociological aesthetic.

6. 'Dans la plupart des cas, la mise en lumière de ces structures n'est accessible ni à une étude littéraire immanente, ni à une étude orientée vers les intentions conscientes de l'ecrivain ou vers la psychologie des profondeurs, mais seulement à une recherche de type structuraliste et sociologique' (Macksey and Donato, 1970, p. 333).

If we add the principle of multiplicity of structures according to context, to Goldmann's multiplicity of functions, then different interpretations are not mutually exclusive. We are not forced to choose between, say, Lévi-Strauss' and Douglas' interpretations of the Oedipus myth (Lévi-Strauss, 1963; Douglas, 1969). Yet *as sociologists* a choice may be necessary, whose control is *significance for a given audience*. But to speak of controls in this matter is perhaps too sanguine. We have stumbled upon one of the most pressing problems of 'interpretive sociology', that of circularity. We take our interpretation from the text – it is not given. If we use our reading of social reality to make this interpretation, then there is a danger that we discover homologies only because we impose one structure upon another.

This problem closely resembles the one faced by Weber when he sought to relate the 'Protestant ethic' to the 'spirit of capitalism'. Each of these ideal types was extracted from a context which allows of alternative renderings, many of which have been offered in the history of one of sociology's most protracted controversies. The 'control' of subjective meaning for the participants, is no control at all when we have no access to it other than via our interpretations of their actions and the texts. The suspicion is frequently voiced that Weber defined his ideal types in relation to each other *before* he found that they were mutually supportive.

Such circularity is difficult to escape (Gellner, 1970). Yet the enterprise is not without value. We have no viable alternative, and in any case, some interpretations and hypotheses are more plausible and valuable than others, even when they cannot be decisively validated or refuted. The aim should be to search for interpretations which stand up most strongly to such circumstantial evidence as can be adduced, and which are able to reveal hitherto unnoticed patternings in the forms and themes of the works examined. Goldmann significantly defends his method by his claim to have made an original contribution to Pascal scholarship which only a *sociological* analysis could have revealed. Perhaps this mode of assessment is parallel to Lakatos's (1970) 'progressive problem-shift' in science?

Goldmann is exclusively concerned with the social genesis of aesthetic structures, and therefore with the source–message complex. Sociological studies of 'effects' examine the message–receiver complex. Given this interest, the 'significant structures' of the works may be different, yet no less significant. The meaning of the works cannot be held constant between source and receiver, nor between one audience and another. We may assume that Pascal and Racine were not the exclusive property of a Jansenist circle. For other publics, different aspects of the works may have salience. An important part of the sociologists' task is the location of sociologically defined audiences and the nuances which the works had for them.

Paradigms and creativity

Kuhn's (1962) highly influential theory of science, centering on the concept of a 'paradigm', has been transposed to other disparate fields. (Feyerabend, 1970, even suggests that professional crime has all the defining characteristics of a paradigm-bonded activity). The discontinuities and lack of progress of the arts having long been recognized it was to be expected that the concept would be applied here also. Kuhn himself has recorded some brief remarks on this possibility, in a comment on two papers (Ackerman, 1969; Hafner, 1969) in the sociology of art which use a Kuhnian frame of reference. Using Kuhn's 'paradigm' and 'puzzle-solving', Hafner tries to show that art and science cannot readily be differentiated by any of the categories. This Kuhn denies, and he attempts to differentiate them within the terms of his theory of science. While both engage in 'problem-solving', this is the end of 'normal science', while for art, it is merely a means to an aesthetic end. Similarly, while aesthetic criteria are not lacking in science (elegance, simplicity and the like), for the scientist these are means, for the artist, ends. He relates the fact that each has a different type of public to this difference in goal. Puzzle-solving, in art or science, is esoteric, addressing itself only to the peer-group. Aesthetic objects may be appreciated, however, without technical understanding of the puzzle-solutions which they represent ('I don't know anything about art, but I know what I like').

Kuhn distinguishes between the norms of the two communities somewhat paradoxically. He argues that while creativity is a paramount value for the community of artists, such an explicit commitment would actually be counterproductive to the cause of scientific creativity. Science has, he claims, built-in mechanisms which signal the need for innovation in science (puzzle-solving within a paradigm – crisis – new paradigm – puzzle-solving). In art there is no equivalent, so commitment to creativity must be specific.

It is clear at once that Kuhn is making contradictory assertions – that creativity, at the same time, both is and is not a value for the scientist. For if high valuation of innovation is not needed because creativity and innovation are built in, then manifestly innovation is valued, if implicitly. Kuhn shifts without warning from the participant's point of view, where innovation is allegedly not valued, to the observer's, where it is. His argument begins to look like a variant of the 'cunning of history' thesis – conservatism and dogma having the latent function of guaranteeing periodic radical change, and progress.

It is evident from Kuhn's own strictures, and in view of the various criticisms of his theory in its application to science, that we should be cautious about making any uncritical applications to art, although it remains to be seen whether it has any heuristic power at a metaphoric level.

Social system of the cinema

Goldmann relates aesthetic structures to a single context – the social class of the author, and the mental categories of its world-view. For him, social class is *the* point of reference for explanations of men's thought and action. For Weber, class was only one such point. Another was social status. One membership group which must have high presumptive salience for the creative artist is the community of peers and sponsors, within which he works. Sociology of science concentrates its attention exclusively on 'the social system of science' – the scientific community, its organization, norms and sanctions (Merton, 1957; Storer, 1966; Hagstrom, 1965, etc.) Surprisingly, in the case of media sociology, this perspective has been relatively neglected. The production context has given precedence to the audience context. How, then, should a concept of 'the social system of art–media' be articulated? Kuhn's value in this respect lies in his creation of a single theory of structure, process and change in science, and this should also be our aim.

Kuhn might have noticed another differentiating characteristic of art in the fact that in a market economy, its product has exchange value. It thus belongs in two sectors, the cultural and the economic. The mass production 'leisure industries' which are currently enjoying a boom, exhibit this dual character prominently, and in the cinema this duality pervades the whole enterprise. Different people, at the same and at different parts of the production process, may be systematically differentiated in terms of goals, motivational commitments and definitions of the situation.

The exigencies of the cinema in this respect have often been noted by those who bemoan the evils of 'the system'. Film, especially in its Hollywood zenith, has been a lucrative source of investment, and depends on such investment because of its high costs. The social structure of film exhibits little normative consensus. Even where there is minimal consensus on goals (to produce films which are intrinsically interesting and also profitable), it is only the latter which yields a standard measure of success. Film aesthetics is underdeveloped in the extreme, and thus is no source of authority. Criticism largely reduces to the assertion of personal taste. There is no peer group consensus on aesthetic achievement in this field; no 'paradigm' or 'paragon' films which may be used as standards, only competing schools, competing pantheons. If scientists exchange ideas for 'competent appraisal' (Storer, 1966), the cineaste is in the position that everybody and nobody may claim such competence. He is appraised by conflicting and heterogeneous groups (peers, critics, producers, public). While he might choose to be judged by selected peers the peer-group has no sanctions, while those available to other groups are particularly severe.

If the definition of the situation of the various actors within this 'social system' differ, so does their power to enforce their own definition, which is largely determined by access to and control over scarce resources – money, equipment, personnel, technical training, distribution and exhibition facilities, etc. (Lovell, 1968). In this power line-up, neither the director nor any other creative artist *in his professional role* features very prominently. (They may amass sufficient resources, if they are successful in those roles, to be able to set up their own production companies, but that is another matter).

The French 'New Wave': a case study[7]

The above remarks apply more or less generally to capitalist film production. To go further, we must be more specific. The phenomenon which we shall examine is an example of a *film movement*, the so-called French 'New Wave.' It will be analysed from a sociological point of view, in order to try to meet the criteria above (reference to structure, process and change), and in order to illustrate the manner in which, in a specific uuncture, the different types of variables combined to effect a certain result.

The term '*Nouvelle Vague*' was a convenient journalistic label, probably originating in *L'Express*, used to acknowledge the fact that the French cinema was undergoing rapid change on several fronts, rather than to refer to any well-refined, unitary phenomenon. During the period roughly 1958–61, an unprecedented number of young directors made their film debut. Between 1958–60, the number was over one hundred (Siclier, 1961).

It is always problematic to take a commonsense, or journalistic demarcation as the basis for defining a phenomenon for sociological purposes. We are concerned here with the work of three groups of directors: the nucleus of *Cahiers* critics turned directors, who, to the chagrin of the rival journal *Positif*, appropriated the 'New Wave' to themselves – Godard, Truffaut, Chabrol, Rivette, Rohmer and Doniol-Valcroze; the Left Bank group of Resnais, Marker and Varda; and that of Malle, Demy and Vadim. Considered individually, these directors are each very different, especially in the light of their subsequent development. Nevertheless, the 'New Wave' heralded recognizable innovations of style and theme.

It would be out of place here to attempt any adequate, rigorous analysis of the films. All that will be adumbrated is a rough sketch. (Ideally, we would need also to look in some detail at the movies against which the 'New Wave' directors defined themselves – the '*cinema du papa*'.) Two points must be made to avoid

7. This section is based on an article which appeared in *Screen*, March 1971.

misunderstanding. The following 'thumbnail sketch' is reductive in that it points up recurring themes common to the films in question. It represents the 'lowest common denominator', as it were, of analysis. Structural analysis is of course very different, looking not merely for repetitions, but also for 'systems of differences' (Wollen, 1969). It is open to all the objections to content analysis, with the additional disadvantage of being impressionistic and cursory. Its inclusion is justified only in that it establishes a *prima facie* case for treating the films of the 'New Wave' as marking a distinctive break with the past. This bring us to the second point, which is that this break is not absolute. Even revolutions, in culture and politics alike, exhibit 'massive cultural continuities' (Martins, 1970), and here we are looking only at a *movement*. Its achievement at best could not have been a *coup d'état* in which the old elites of the cinema were replaced, but the right to entry and peaceful coexistence was established. The diffusion processes here were complex. In the first case, many of the characteristics of the older tradition continue in the themes of the New Wave films. Some French cultural themes of considerable antiquity, common to other art forms as well as to film, can be found in these films (see Wolfenstein and Leites, 1950, for a comparison.) Secondly, those directors who survived the 'ebb tide' established themselves alongside their older colleagues. They did not replace them. Thirdly, the innovations which they inaugurated were easily imitated, and soon decorated the surface appearance of large numbers of films, in France and abroad.

The lack of any social dimension is one of the most notable features of the typical New Wave film. Its heroes are neither personally nor socially integrated, and are dissociated from their social roles. These are, in any case, difficult or impossible to identify. They are marginal men; disaffected intellectuals, students, and in one case (Rohmer's *Sign of the Lion*), a rather high-class tramp. Interest centres exclusively on immediate face-to-face relations. They have no family ties that are apparent, and on the whole, no political affiliations. Action is for its own sake, having no further end, arbitrary and motiveless. There are no social antecedents of action, only emotional and volitional. There is no point of contact between the individual and society, nor are these anomic lives placed in any broader context within which they can be understood. The *milieu* of the individual exhausts the film's compass.

The subjective and objective worlds are fused, also reality and fantasy. Cartesian epistemology, egocentric and individualistic, is here reduced to absurdity. Egotization of the world reaches the point of solipsism, where the ego submerges the world, and is in turn submerged in it. The interiority of the subject is paradoxically lost, the world depersonalized. Resnais and Godard are twin poles of this phenomenon.

This stands in marked contrast to the naive realism of the films of the 1940s and 1950s. Stylistic and technical innovations are equally marked. In addition to new cadres of directors and actors, certain cameramen and other technical experts emerged, and were specifically associated with New Wave films.

At the thematic level, the break which the New Wave represents, as well as some continuities, may be seen by comparison with Wolfenstein and Leites' (1950) profile of the post-war French cinema.

External-cultural bearings for an explanation of the French New Wave

We face the difficulty of knowing when the judgement that a whole national culture is 'in crisis' or exhausted, may properly be made. If there were any evidence of a subjectively felt crisis, this might suffice. It is interesting to note that Hughes (1966) marks the period 1930–60 as one of felt cultural crisis and gropings for new alternatives. He locates the emergence of promising new developments precisely at the period of the New Wave (marked on the political and economic front by the advent of Gaullism, peace in Algeria, and the post-war 'economic miracle'). Stuart Hughes's analysis rests on a rather jaundiced view of French cultural life, however, and we may not attach too much significance to this coincidence. Crozier (1964) makes a similar assessment, couched in terms of a crisis in the changing role of the intellectual in France. But his argument smacks of the 'End of Ideology' thesis, and to that extent, is also suspect. One phenomenon, to which Wollen (1969) has drawn attention, was the huge influx of American films upon the market immediatey after the war, in the circumstances in which the American allies were also liberators. This influx may have something to do with the near-obsession with all things American, and especially with American movies, which the New Wave evidenced so strongly in both its films and in its critical judgements.

At a different level of analysis, a word must be said about the relationship between the cinema and the other arts. In America the cinema is isolated both economically and culturally. In France, the cinema has achieved a degree of cultural integration which Anglo-Saxon film cultures lack. This is partly due to the fact that from the start, the French cinema was forced to differentiate from the American, with whose scale and technical brilliance it could not hope, on limited resources, to compete. The French staked out a place in the world market on the basis of the intellectual and aesthetic quality of their product, and hence cultural integration was easier and in line with French claims to cultural hegemony in all spheres. Cinematic references in the other arts, especially literature, are frequent (Chevalier and Billard, 1969). Simone de Beauvoir's biography similarly attests to this integration, recording an involvement with a cinematic as well as a literary culture. And the composition of the French audience has changed in recent years. It is on average more highly educated than its Anglo-Saxon counterpart, although here it may simply lead a general trend (Chevalier and Billard, 1969).

Internal-cultural bearings

Both Kuhn (1962) and Kroeber (1947), tell us to look for conditions of crisis prior to cultural change (although Kuhn's terms of reference do not strictly apply here as we have seen). Kroeber writes of 'cultural configurations' initiated by clusterings of innovations, which exhibit a certain pattern or plan. This pattern has certain inherent possibilities of development (Kroeber explains cultural change purely in cultural terms). A cultural movement ends either when it comes into conflict with the rest of the culture, or when the possibilities of that particular pattern are exhausted, a peak is reached, and subsequently, that particular cultural configuration goes into decline, or degenerates into static institutionalization.

It should be noted at once that on Kroeber's time scale, and given his aesthetic preferences, the French New Wave would hardly deserve notice. With that reservation, we may ask how far the French New Wave may be explained in terms of the 'exhaustion' of the tradition/style associated with the post-war era. There is an element of hindsight in making such a judgement. At the very least we may say that the emergence of a new style at that time was 'overdetermined'. More important than the validity of this judgement of degeneration is the fact that it was made, and made to stick, by the *Cahiers* critics and others, and that a new definition of the situation, a new style, was readily available at that time.

Internal-structural bearings

Production and finance. The French cinema is structured horizontally along functional lines in contrast to the American which contains major vertical cleavages. It is highly segmented lacking any monolithic power structure, or important bottlenecks, where systematic discriminations could be made in determining the fate of individual films.

The French industry is small and marginal. It has suffered endemically from a small turnover and underinvestment. It is not integrated with the industrial sector, on account of its size, but also because of features which pertain to the nature of film rather than to conditions in France. The film industry has a product which cannot be standardized. Each production is a *prototype*. Financial success is in principle uncertain and unpredictable. Yet large sums of money must be committed in advance. There is no possibility of trial and error, since error may prove fatal. But large profits accrue to the successful. The film is hired, so unit costs do not increase markedly with wide distribution. In sum, the norm of economic rationality could hardly flourish here. The ethos of *chance* and *luck*, rather than of the calculated risk, prevails. The Weberian 'spirit of capitalism', frugal, cautious, conservative, is less in evidence than a more primitive spirit of speculation – the ethos of the casino.

The risk taken is unevenly distributed. Foreign producers, distributors, and the state, bear much of the cost. Banks of course take no risks as they only lend against collaterals and not against the uncertain prospect of a 'best-seller'.

French film production is an occasional and sporadic activity.

In any one year, only about one-fifth of the number of registered production companies is active. The majority produce only one film. 'The producer makes a film in the manner in which one mounts a hold-up. Each one is different from the last, each time he must seek collaborators and creditors' (Chevalier and Billard, 1969) The average cost of film-making rose phenomenally between 1956–66. But at the New Wave period, it was still relatively low.

Distribution. Distributors play a key role in the French industry. A few large companies dominate the market. It is more highly capitalized than other sectors, and is an important source of film finance.

Exhibition. There are no large circuits. The overall ratio of exhibitors to houses is almost 1:1. This sector was heavily hit by the crisis of falling attendances.

State aid. The Centre Nationale du Cinématographie (CNC) controls everything to do with state finance and receipts of films. It grants authorizations to make films, issues professional cards, gives advances and subsidies, and organizes professional training. The amount of state intervention in film is greater than in any other non-socialist country.

Crisis. The above paragraphs describe the relevant background conditions obtaining in the French film industry. Such conditions, being relatively stable over time, cannot explain the emergence of the New Wave. More proximate causes relate to the crisis in the industry in the 1950s. The history of the French film industry is a history of crises. After the war the Blum-Byrnes agreement resulted in a flood of American films, with which a war-damaged indigenous industry could not compete. The 1949 Temporary Aid Law was ameliorative, but the situation remained precarious. Many well-established directors were unable to work, or did so at a much reduced rate. Clair, Autant-Lara, Becker, Duvivier and Carné had each directed only one film between 1946–9. The opportunity structure for film personnel was extremely poor. This situation was exacerbated from the point of view of new entrants by the policy of using well-known actors and directors, in adaptations of literary works for prestige productions, aimed at the foreign market. (It is interesting that it was precisely these films with which the New Wave competed. They tended to have a cool reception in France initially, followed by success abroad, and renewed interest at home.) Union regulations were formidable, although loosely enforced.

The crisis in the cinema traditionally and misleadingly associated with the advent of television, came late in France, and can be dated almost precisely at 1957. At the same time, 'quality films' were waning in their success. The old formula was failing, and the result was a widespread openness to innovation. The success of Vadim's *And Woman was Created* let loose the flood.

External-structural bearings

We do not find any variables of this category which were important in respect to the French New Wave. But by way of illustration, we may refer to the changes in the American film industry associated with the decline of the big studios. The development of *conglomerates* – large companies whose investments covered many different fields – took an interest in the possibilities of the 'leisure industry'. The existence of this source of finance has to some extent cut across the studio system which is geared to high-cost productions and hampered by union restrictions, and encouraged the emergence of independent companies and free-lance individuals who remain free from the traditional long-term studio contract.

Achievements of the French New Wave

This movement, especially in its contribution to film criticism, gave the French cinema a new paternity. It instituted a new, *cinematic* cinema, whose heroes included Renoir, Rossellini and Leedhardt. Above all it integrated the American cinema into its cultural heritage. It was almost exclusively American directors who featured on its pantheon. It shifted the locus of cinematic creativity from the writer to the director, with the concept of the 'auteur'. It represents in many ways the coming of age of the cinema, in which it could insist on the value of its own past, refusing to rely for legitimation on borrowings from literature and drama.

The French New Wave revitalized the French cinema. Its

effects are still being felt throughout the cinematic world, in 'the look' of films, and more importantly in the continuance of a critical and theoretical debate which it initiated. The contributions to the theory of André Bazin, and the critical judgements of the *Cahiers* team, remain a continuing point of reference in this debate.

At the structural level, it resulted in little change. Controls were if anything tighter than they had been previously. Initial capital requirements, for instance, for a film were raised out of all proportion to increased costs, in order to deter ill-considered ventures. Union requirements were more strictly enforced. The net result was merely that a generation of film-makers were able to force an entry into a moribund industry, without in any way changing its structure so as to make it any easier for future generations.

Conclusion

The account we have given of the French New Wave does not amount to an explanation so much as an explanation sketch. It maps out a research project of considerable proportions. Its function is to illustrate the theoretical considerations brought out in the first part of the paper. Even this limited aim is only partly achieved, since a large part of those considerations related to the message–audience complex, and this aspect of the New Wave has remained untouched in the present analysis.

References

ACKERMAN, J. S. (1969), 'The demise of the avant garde', *Compar. Stud. Soc. Hist.*, vol. 11, pp. 371–84.

ALTHUSSER, L. (1970), *For Marx*, Allen Lane The Penguin Press.

BERELSON, B. (1952), *Content Analysis in Communication Research*, Free Press.

BREWSTER, B. (1971), 'Structuralism in film criticism', *Screen*, March.

CAREY, J. T. (1969), 'Changing courtship patterns in popular song', *Amer. J. Sociol.*, vol. 74, pp. 720–31.

CHEVALIER, L. and BILLARD, P. (1969), *Cinéma et civilisation*, Paris.

COMOLLI, J. L., and NARBONI, P. (1971), 'Cinema/ideology/criticism', *Screen*, March.

CROZIER, M. (1964), 'The cultural revolution: notes on the changes in the intellectual climate of France', *Daedalus*, Winter.

DANTO, A. C. (1965), *Analytical Philosophy of History*, Cambridge University Press.

DOUGLAS, M. (1969), 'The meaning of myth', in E. Leach (ed.), *The Structural Study of Myths and Totemism*, Tavistock.

FARGIER, J. P. (1971), 'Parenthesis or indirect route', *Screen*, vol. 12(2), pp. 131–44.

FEYERABEND, P. (1970), 'Consolidation for the specialist', in I. Lakatos and A. Musgrave (eds.), *Criticism and the Growth of Knowledge*, Cambridge University Press.

GELLNER, E. (1970), 'Concepts and society', *Trans. Fifth World Congress Sociol.* Reprinted in D. Emmet and A. MacIntyre (eds.), *Sociological Theory and Philosophical Analysis*, Macmillan.

GLUCKSMANN, A. (1971), *Violence on the Screen*, British Film Institute.

GLUCKSMANN, M. (1969), 'A hard look at Lucien Goldmann', *New Left Rev.*, vol. 56.

GOLDMANN, L. (1970), 'Structure: human reality and methodological concept', in R. Macksey, and E. Donato (eds.), *The Languages of Criticism and the Science of Man*, Johns Hopkins Press.

GOLDMANN, L. (1964), *The Hidden God*, Routledge & Kegan Paul.

GOLDTHORPE, J., et al., (1969), *The Affluent Worker*, vol. 3, Cambridge University Press.

HAFNER, E. M. (1969), 'The new reality in art and science', *Compar. Stud. Soc. Hist.*, vol. 11, pp. 385–97.

HAGSTROM, W. (1965), *The Scientific Community*, Basic Books.

HAMBURGER, L. (1967), 'Fragmented Society: the structure of Thai music', *Sociologus*, vol. 17(1), pp. 54–71.

HUGHES, H. S. (1968), *The Obstructed Path*, Harper and Row.

JANOWITZ, M. (1968–9), 'Harold D. Lasswell's contribution to content analysis', *Public Opinion Q.*, vol. 32, pp. 646–53.

KROEBER, A. L. (1947), *Configurations of Cultural Growth*, University of California Press.

KUHN, T. (1969), 'Comment (on the relations between science and art)', in *Compar. Stud. Soc. Hist.*, vol. 11, pp. 403–12.

KUHN, T. (1962), *Structure of Scientific Revolutions*, University of Chicago Press.

LAKATOS, I. (1970), 'Falsification and the methodology of scientific research programmes', in I. Lakatos and A. Musgrave (eds.), *Criticism and the Growth of Knowledge*, Cambridge University Press.

LEBLANC, G. (1971), 'Direction', *Cinéthique*, no. 5., trans. in *Screen*, Summer.

LÉVI-STRAUSS, C. (1963), 'The structural study of myth', in *Structural Anthropology*, Allen Lane The Penguin Press.

LOVELL, T. (1968), 'An approach to sociology of film', in P. Wollen (ed.), *Working Papers on the Cinema: Sociology and Semiology*, British Film Institute.

MACHEREY, P. (1970), *Pour une Théorie de la Production Littéraire*, Paris.

MACINTYRE, A. (1971), 'Rationality as a sociological category', in *Against the Self-Images of the Age*, Duckworth.

MACKIE, J. L. (1965), 'Causes and conditions', *Amer. Philos. Q.*, vol. 2, pp. 245–64.

MACKSEY, R., and DONATO, E. (1970), *The Languages of Criticism and the Sciences of Man*, Johns Hopkins Press.

MANN, M. (1970), 'The social cohesion of liberal democracy', *Amer. Sociol. Rev.*, vol. 35, pp. 423–39.

MARTINS, H. (1970), 'Sociology of knowledge and sociology of science', unpublished. A shortened version appears under the title 'The Kuhnian "Revolution" and its implications for sociology', in A. H. Hanson, T. Nossiter, and S. Rokkan (eds.), *Imagination and Precision in Political Analysis*, Humanities, 1972.

MERTON, R. K. (1957), *Social Theory and Social Structure*, Free Press.

ROSENSTONE, R. A. (1969), '"The times they are a-changing", The music of protest', *Ann. Amer. Acad. polit. soc. Science*, vol. 382, pp. 131–44.

SICLIER, J. (1961), 'New wave and French cinema', *Sight and Sound*, vol. 30, no. 3, pp. 116–20.

SLATER, M. (1970), *Lévi-Strauss in Fleet Street*, unpublished thesis, Essex University.

STORER, N. (1966), *The Social System of Science*, Holt, Reinhart & Winston.

TUDOR, A. (1970), 'Film, Communication and Content', in J. Tunstall (ed.), *Media Sociology*, Constable.

WARSHOW, R. (1962), *The Immediate Experience*, Atheneum.

WEBER, M. (1958), *Social and Rational Foundations of Music*, S. Ill. U.P.

WILLIAMS, R. (1958), *Culture and Society*, Chatto & Windus; Penguin, 1961.

WOLFENSTEIN, M., and LEITES, N. (1950), *The Movies: a Psychological Study*, Free Press.

WOLLEN, P. (1969), *Signs and Meaning in the Cinema*, Secker & Warburg.

Part Six
Issues of Policy or Social Concern

A case has already been made out, in the Introduction, for paying greater attention than hitherto in studies of mass media to certain questions and issues which are both perennial and puzzling and which are not easily contained within what has been traditionally regarded as the proper area for academic attention. Such questions tend to be regarded with ambivalence because of uncertainty over the line which separates what should be a private matter between communicator and audience and what should be matters of wider public concern. And, as we have noted, they also straddle the boundary which marks off the sphere of 'objective' scientific discussion from the speculative, moralistic and political. There is, on both counts, a real dilemma, but it is not solved by regarding these lines as uncrossable. Our argument is that a social scientist can contribute to the growth of knowledge in his own science and help to solve important policy questions if he tries to cross the rather arbitrary boundaries established by the stance of objectivity. A similar case has recently been put by Nordenstreng (1968), one of the contributors to this collection. He writes:

Too many communicologists have chosen the convenient role of an indifferent observer in relation to the ethics and ideology of communication; and this has been done for the sake of 'objectivity of science' . . . In the current research tradition, normative considerations have been too much masked by factual documentation, thinking about the *goals* of communication in various situations has been replaced by experimentation with different *means* of communication.

Each of the contributions which follow could have been categorized under some heading other than the blanket one which has been chosen, and this in itself illustrates the ease with which normative and ethical considerations can be shelved. The pieces are, nevertheless, related by their explicit relevance to some current social issue. In one way or another the contributions also teach the lesson that no desired end is likely to be attained, or undesirable one avoided without informed and purposeful action. Similarly they remind us of the essential point that there are consequences for society inherent in existing structures and ways of doing things and that the purpose of inquiry should be to increase our awareness of such latent tendencies.

Reference

NORDENSTRENG, K. (1968), 'Communication research in the United States: a critical perspective', *Gazette*, vol. 14, no. 3, pp. 207–16.

16 Elihu Katz

Platforms and Windows: Broadcasting's Role in Election Campaigns

Elihu Katz, 'Platforms and windows: broadcasting's role in election campaigns', *Journalism Quarterly*, Summer 1971, pp. 304–14.

Election compaigns, for all their faults, may be the major learning experience of democratic polities. They deserve, therefore, to be better designed. That they are not is due to the fact that the manifest purpose of persuading voters is often at odds with the latent function of educating them. The tension between broadcasters and politicians over the use of the mass media during election campaigns mirrors this dilemma. The object of what follows is to reflect on the several functions of election campaigns and their implications for use of the media, especially in societies where the media are publicly owned.[1]

Three rather different sources prompt these reflections. Observing the Israel elections of 1969 is one source. Despite radical changes in the demographic structure of Israel since its establishment in 1948; despite the alignments, disalignments and realignments among the sixteen parties competing for votes; and despite the fact that television was used for political campaigning for the first time – the composition of the Seventh Knesset is remarkably like that of its six predecessors.[2] As in so many other campaigns

1. An earlier presentation of some of the ideas herein appeared in the Hebrew language monthly, *Molad*. I am grateful to the Editor for his permission to re-present some of the material in that article. I also profited from comments and criticism offered at a seminar organized by the Audience and Program Research Department of the Swedish Broadcasting Corporation.
2. When Mapam joined the Alignment recently, their combined strength in the outgoing Knesset totalled sixty-three (of one hundred and twenty) seats. The enlarged Alignment lost seven seats in the election, and thus lost its absolute majority (which had been very little noticed, anyway, prior to the elections). The decline is mostly accounted for by the three seats obtained by Ben-Gurion's rebel party which refused to re-Align when Moshe Dayan and most of the rest of the 1965 Rafi breakaway group decided to do so. In any event, with the four votes of the Arab satellite parties, the Labour

elsewhere, where noisy and expensive campaigning appears to have so little influence, one wonders whether the outcome alone justifies the huge cost – particularly in countries where the treasury pays most of the bill.

Unlike previous elections, the elections of 1969 were comparatively quiet. The issues were left virtually untouched, primarily because all of the major parties were members of the coalition government, which, in turn, reflected the national preoccupation with the delicate and difficult post-war situation. Except for the tiny groups campaigning for outright annexation of the occupied territories or for unilateral peace-making efforts, the parties all but ignored the major problem of the society and each other.

An important contributory factor to the lack of any real 'engagement' in the campaign was the tiptoe policy governing the use of radio and television. The electronic media are publicly owned by a BBC-like broadcasting authority. Only a year after the introduction of television, the predominant feeling in Government was that election politics should be barred completely from the TV screen, just as it is in movie commercials and movie news-reels. As the elections approached, however, there was mounting public pressure for the use of television in the' campaign, and the Knesset agreed.

But the role given to the electronic media is circumscribed, indeed. Campaign broadcasting in 1969 was limited to broadcasts produced by the parties themselves in the time periods alloted to them on the basis of their relative strength in the 1965 elections,[3]

Alignment has control of the Knesset – though, they cannot form a government without at least one of the middle-sized parties (Religious, Independent Liberals). Multi-party politics are not directly responsive to voting, and while major changes in the government may take place as a result of inter-party bargaining, there can be no doubt about the unchanging voting behavior of the Israeli electorate.

3. To provide for the smallest parties and for those unrepresented in the Sixth Knesset, a minimum allocation of twenty-five minutes of radio time and ten minutes on television was given to all parties. In addition, each party was alotted five minutes on radio and four minutes on television for each seat it held in the outgoing Knesset. Altogether there were more than ten hours of party television during the month-long campaign period which constituted a substantial proportion of total broadcasting (25 per cent) of the fledgling television system, and compares with Britain's three hours (in

and a late-at-night roundup on sound radio only of the day's election events and pronouncements. Otherwise, programs having anything to do with public affairs were declared out-of-bounds for the month-long period of the campaign, and candidates for the Knesset – including ministers – were not permitted to be shown on television in any capacity.

Thus, like Britain in the 1950s, but unlike it in the 1960s, there was no independent examination of the issues by professional broadcasters; there was no confrontation between broadcaster-journalists and party leaders; there were no spontaneous confrontations on the air between spokesmen for the public and party leaders; and there was certainly no confrontation of party leaders with each other. Of the mass media, only the press tried to sort things out for the voter.

A second source of inspiration for this paper is the recent publication by Blumler and McQuail, *Television and Politics* (1968). Thanks to this study of voters in two Yorkshire constituencies during the British elections of 1964, we have learned some new things about what campaigns mean to different kinds of voters. The book analyses the 'uses' to which political communications are put by different kinds of voters, and then goes on to consider 'effects'. Blumler and McQuail's emphasis on the functions of election campaigning for the voter is essentially different from the classical studies of election campaigns which see voters, primarily, as the *objects* of the persuasive attempts of the political parties and the mass media.

This points to the third source which enters into the present paper. We have just reached the twenty-fifth anniversary of the publication of *The People's Choice*, the pioneering study of the American presidential campaign of 1940 by Lazarsfeld, Berelson and Gaudet (1944). It seems appropriate to take ceremonial note of that fact. But beyond ceremony, it is relevant also to note that *The People's Choice* set the tone for subsequent studies of voter behavior during election campaigns. Although their subject is the voter – his predispositions, his response to influence-attempts on

1966). The parties produce the broadcasts by themselves and at their own expense, subject only to the approval of the Supreme Court Justice who is chairman of the Central Elections Committee, but broadcast time is provided free of charge.

the process of his decision-making – these studies are in a sense more concerned with the functions of election campaigns for the parties than for the voters. Neither the Columbia nor the Michigan studies ask, for example, whether the voter learned anything from the campaign, or whether he found it entertaining. It is in this sense that election research, at least until Blumler and McQuail, may be said to be concerned with the manifest functions of elections, that is, with the process of mobilizing support for a political party or parties.

Indeed, it seems useful to sort out the functions of election campaigns in terms of the individual voter, the political party, and society as a whole. Perhaps looking at the different ways in which election campaigns serve each of these will suggest ways of improving them. The next section, therefore, quickly reviews what has been learned from the empirical studies so far. It will not come as a surprise if we find some good explanations of why election campaigns are useful to *political parties* despite the small number of voters who change their minds. But we shall also be asking, with Blumler and McQuail, in what ways campaigns are useful to *voters*, and how they might be made more useful (if they could be better designed) both to the individual voter and to the *society* which pays the bills. Or, in the words of Blumler and McQuail, the challenge is to help make broadcasting less of a platform for election rhetoric and more of a window through which the voter can get a true view of the political arena.[4]

What election studies tell us

Since 1940, perhaps a dozen major elections have been studied intensively, mostly in the United States and England, but elsewhere as well.[5] Many used the method, first introduced in *The People's Choice*, of repeated interviews with the same sample of voters. This so-called 'panel' method is the only one that gives a glimpse of the sequence of changes that take place inside people's heads between the onset of an election campaign and its conclusion.

4. The metaphors are from Blumler and McQuail (1968).

5. Seven such studies (through 1952) are compared in Appendix A to Berelson, Lazarsfeld and McPhee (1954). More recent studies are cited in the bibliography to Blumler and McQuail (1968). Apart from specific citations in the text, no attempt will be made here to provide detailed documentation.

What has been learned?

1. Despite the many differences among countries and from election to election, typically about 80 per cent, or more, of the voters have made up their minds about their vote before the campaign begins, that is at least several months prior to the election. Some 70 to 85 per cent will vote for the same party as in the previous election. Some 10 per cent change their intentions from party to party and another 10 per cent make a decision (having previously been undecided) during the campaign itself. Of these shifters and doubters many will 'return' during the campaign to the party for which they voted last time. To the group of voters who participated in both elections must be added the 'new voters' who have recently come of age as well as those, who for one reason or another, did not vote last time. The young voter and the in-and-out voter are sometimes decisive elements in an election, and they contribute substantially to the ranks of the 'undecided' during the campaign itself.

2. The changers – those who shift from one party to another *during* the campaign – have been found to be relatively uninterested in the election and its outcome. The voter with a high interest in politics is much more likely to have made up his mind early, and to hold firmly to his intention throughout the campaign. Changers are also more likely to be 'inconsistent' in their positions—in disagreeing with their parties on certain issues, for example. The same holds true for changers *between* elections, though the chances are that these changers are rather better informed and more interested than those who switch during the campaign.

3. It follows from the fact that the changers are recruited from among those least interested in politics that they are not much exposed to mass communications about politics. On the other hand, however, although his overall level of exposure to mass communications is lower, the voter who changes his mind during the campaign, or who is trying to make up his mind, is more likely to be more *equally* exposed to the communications from the several parties than is the more staunchly partisan voter. The latter is likely both to be more exposed and to favor communications originating on his own side. Interpersonal persuasion is particularly effective with the changers.

Nevertheless, some voters do appear to be influenced by the mass media in making or changing their decisions during the campaign. The Yorkshire study of Blumler and McQuail documents the influence of Liberal party broadcasts on the small group of inter-party switchers and the as-yet-undecided in 1964. While this group of voters may be said to have had a higher level of political interest and sophistication than that characteristic of switchers in other elections, it is also clear that the viewing of Liberal party broadcasts was particularly effective in converting those who had only weak motivation for following the campaign. The irony in all this, however, is that the success of the Liberal party was essentially unimportant from the standpoint of the election as a whole. While the Liberal vote was doubled during the campaign, it remained the vote of a small minority. Those who switched to Labor apparently did so *before* the campaign, and they are the ones who made the difference.

4. Election broadcasting is often kinder to the opposition party and to the newcomer. Blumler and McQuail argue that the persistence of a third party in England may have been given a boost by television,

partly because of its high popularity and the heavy use made of it by the more vulnerable viewers, partly because the Liberals received a relatively generous share of TV time, and partly because of the sheltered status that politics enjoys in the programme schedules of British broadcasting (1968, p. 207).

Similar support for the underdog can be seen in John Kennedy's successful use of television in the 1960 presidential election in the United States. In the historic 'debates' with Richard Nixon, the less-well-known Kennedy apparently captured enough votes to assure his election (Katz and Feldman, 1962). Many of those votes – the studies imply – were actually 'recaptured', in the sense that they belonged to reasonably loyal Democrats who had 'strayed' to Eisenhower.

5. Indeed, there seems to be an underlying party loyalty on the part of most people in countries with reasonably stable political systems. This loyalty may be upset, occasionally, by situational pulls – Eisenhower's glory, Kennedy's Catholicism – but, over the long run, most people 'return' to their basic political al-

legiances. It has been shown for the US elections of 1962, for example, that the individuals most susceptible to change were those whose basic loyalties were weak enough to make them vulnerable but whose basic involvement in politics was strong enough to cause them to expose themselves to at least *some* election propaganda (Converse, 1966). This is essentially the explanation offered for the effectiveness of the Liberal party broadcasts in the British elections of 1964, according to Blumler and McQuail: 'the availability of a large group in the electorate who are prepared to tolerate political messages without being keen to receive them' (1968, p. 206).

6. The combination of a low degree of loyalty and yet some exposure to election communications has become a more probable combination in the era of television than ever before. Large numbers of people are watching election broadcasts not because they are interested in politics but because they like viewing television. When asked, they say that they dislike political broadcasts – especially those originating with the political parties themselves – but when there is no alternative, they watch. There is good reason to believe, moreover, that these are people who were *not* previously reached by any other form of election propaganda. Television has 'activated' them: they have political opinions, and talk to others about them. It can be demonstrated that they have learned something – even when their viewing was due more to lack of alternatives than to choice.

This role of television – which does not seem to be wearing off with its novelty – contrasts very sharply with the role of the press in political campaigns. While television is being credited, increasingly, for its impartiality, its trustworthiness and its contribution to assessing candidates and issues, the press is continually acknowledged as the source which provides the fullest account of political events. The press is the medium of the better educated and the more highly partisan voter. It is, in particular, the favored medium of the opinion leaders – the individuals who influence the opinions of others.

7. More than the mass media are able to convert, they reinforce vote intentions and the basic loyalties underlying them. Occasionally, as the Kennedy-Nixon debates demonstrate, the reactivation

of loyalties may be associated with actual changes of vote intention, as when Kennedy recaptured former Democratic loyalists who had voted for Eisenhower and were unsure, or still leaning toward the Republicans, in 1960. However, compared with those who are actively 'seeking guidance' (in Blumler and McQuail's terminology) those who are 'seeking reinforcement' are more politically interested, and more politically sophisticated. They are more selective in their viewing, and are often looking for ammunition for political arguments with others. They use the media to help adjust their political attitudes to those articulated by their party.[6]

8. Sometimes, as certain studies show, the media influence votes indirectly by focusing on an issue which, in turn, affects the frame of reference of the 'guidance seekers', and perhaps others. If problems of defense or of 'national honor' are made salient, for example, a voter may decide differently than if, say, the central issue is an economic one.

9. The mass media rarely work alone, whether to reinforce or convert. The mass media, rather, stimulate discussion, and the discussion clinches – or negates – the effect. The Kennedy–Nixon debates, for example, stimulated an extraordinary amount of political discussion. One study has shown that individuals whose vote intentions were shaken by the debating candidates tended to speak to another person whose opinion corresponded to the prior opinion of the potential convert, and the result was that he did not stray. Only when the discussion reinforced the newly-awakened inclination was a successful conversion likely (Deutschmann, 1962, pp. 232–52).

10. In explaining the attention paid by voters to the election campaign, and it is considerable, there are even more important motives at work than the manifestly political ones of 'guidance seeking' and 'reinforcement seeking'. People expose themselves to party propaganda, and to election communications, because they want to know 'what will happen' to them and/or to their

6. One of the key arguments of those who advocate the rationality of the average voter is that attitudes toward issues show a reasonably high correspondence with one's party's stand on the issues. But an important unsolved problem is, which came first? Studies that do not follow individuals over time cannot answer this question very well.

country. They want to see what their leaders look like. Blumler and McQuail call these functions 'surveillance'. People also want to judge how well their team is doing, and who is going to win the race. None of these motives can be discounted.

It is unlikely – after all the research that has been done on the dynamics of decision-making during election campaigns – that the classical image of the rational voter will soon be revived. The citizen who follows the campaign avidly, weighs the opposing arguments, and retires to the quiet of his study on election eve, there to make his decision – is non-existent, statistically speaking. On the other hand, the opposite image of the omnipotent media and the defenseless masses has also been dispelled. The twenty-five years of empirical research into the voting process has, on balance, probably enhanced the image of the voter. In the period prior to Lazarsfeld's initial study, the predominant image was that of a defenseless, rootless individual at the mercy of the media of mass communication. With Lazarsfeld's study there came a downgrading of the persuasive powers of the mass media together with the rising image of a relatively stable voter, influenced by basic commitments to class, religion, family and friends, but not much moved by the opposition arguments or by the issues. This image, in turn, has been succeeded by that of a more thinking voter, more attentive to the performance of government and the promise of the opposition, accessible – but not too easily – to campaign propaganda. The keynote of recent research is summed up much better by the title of Key's posthumous analysis, *The Responsible Electorate* (1966), than by McGinniss' *The Selling of the President 1968* which tells of the effort to remake Richard Nixon's image on television (1969).

It is difficult for a public-relations man or a professional communicator or a politician to believe that the time and money and effort invested in election campaigns are not usually responsible for their outcome. Even researchers themselves fall prey to self-doubt, occasionally blaming inadequate methodology or other scholarly failings for camouflaging what 'surely' must be a larger effect. One wonders whether one is not again giving the public more credit than it deserves, remembering how often the 'rational' public opinion of democratic liberalism has been victimized, how little accurate political information the public possesses and the low level of sustained interest in political affairs. Nevertheless, it is a fact that mass media campaigns – not just political campaigns – convert very few people.

The use of election campaigning

This rather cavalier summary of an extraordinary quantity of data and hard work gives a picture of the functions of election campaigns for the voter and for the parties; it only hints at their possible functions for the society as a whole.

It is evident, first of all, that even if election propaganda generally influences only an extremely small proportion of the voters (if 'influence' means converting them from one party to another, during the relatively brief period of the campaign), the investment of effort and money may be worthwhile, nevertheless *from the point of view of the political parties*, for small minorities may make large differences. This is obvious in two-party systems where a single vote may, theoretically, change the result: Kennedy's 1960 victory was by an extremely small margin. But even in multi-party regimes, a very small change in voting may make for major changes in the government: in the recent German elections, for example, the Christian Democrats lost only 1·5 per cent of their previous vote, while the Social Democrats gained 3·4 per cent over 1965. Ostensibly, these would appear to be very small changes – if it were not for the fact that they were sufficient to bring about a complete change of government: the Christian Democrats withdrew and the Social Democrats together with the Free Democrats (which had *lost* almost half of their 9·5 per cent following of 1965) came to power. Of course, these are *net* results, and do not reflect the extent of interparty switching which was mutually compensating. Net results cannot tell us either what proportion of the switching was concentrated during the period of the election campaign as compared with the proportion which 'floated' from party to party over the four-year period between elections. Nor do we know how much of the changing is a result of direct exposure to political communications transmitted by the mass media.

The parties, perhaps, have good reason to continue their traditional forms of campaigning to change voting intentions, even if one might expect more imaginative use of the information available to them from opinion polls concerning their most likely target audiences and the ways to approach them. They also have reason to provide their followers, particularly those who may influence others' votes, with reinforcement.

From the point of view of the voters who are actively seeking guidance or reinforcement – almost half the population, according to Blumler and McQuail – the functions of political campaigning are also clear. But these political motives for exposure to mass communications at election time are less important than other 'uses' which the voter finds for political communications. Thus, in reply to Blumler and McQuail's questions, those who intended to watch a party broadcast during the 1964 campaign (four-fifths of the population surveyed) said they would do so 'to see what some party will do if it comes to power' (55 per cent); 'to keep up with the main issues of the day' (52 per cent); 'to judge what political leaders are like' (51 per cent). The frequency with which these 'surveillance' functions were mentioned far exceeds the functions connected with decision-making.

These expectations of the electorate help to explain the high level of dissatisfaction with political broadcasting in the British elections of 1964 and 1966. While the dissatisfaction surely has a variety of causes – including the feeling of being imposed upon by the monopoly granted to party broadcasts – the politically-relevant reasons for the dissatisfaction of the voter-viewer appear to converge on the inherent inability of party broadcasts to satisfy his need for 'surveillance'. What the voter wants, in return for his investment of time, is the feeling that he has fulfilled his duty as a citizen by orienting and updating himself to the political situation. He wants to be able to identify the candidates and the issues; he wants the issues clearly and interestingly explained; he wants to know where the parties stand with respect to the issues, and how their stands are likely to affect him. If you ask him whether he knows where to get what he wants, he will tell you: in direct confrontation. The voter wants to see the candidates in action under stress, responding to challenge. He wants 'debates'.

This brings up the question of the functions of election campaigns *from the point of view of the society*, a point of view which is not identical either with that of the parties or even with that of the voter. Election campaigns are an integrative institution for the society. They focus all eyes on the center of political power at a time when the political parties are attempting to divide the society as best they can. From this point of view, election campaigns are a socializing institution, educating members of the society to the fundamental rights and obligations of the role 'citizen' at a time when the parties are simply trying to win. Moreover, to optimize their usefulness for society, campaigns must be designed so as to make change seem possible, to make evident that leadership may be replaced in response to the demands of changing situations. From the point of view of the social system, the campaign must underline the legitimacy of opposition and the acceptability of the 'other' candidates and parties even to those who opposed them. In other words, society must combat the individual voter's tendency to selectively expose himself only to his own side.

Perhaps the political parties have reason to be satisfied with the traditional forms of campaigning. The voter, for his part, is less well served. Society – the social system – benefits least of all.

A formula for political broadcasting

The question that must be asked, therefore, is how to employ television, and the other media, in a way which will maximize the unique educational opportunity as well as the societal functions of political campaigns. Even if the parties are out only for themselves, and even if the voter exposes himself to political communications for irrelevant reasons, it is up to the society to devise a system whereby the interested voter will be intelligently served and whereby the political consciousness of the uninterested voter will be aroused and channeled to the central issues which are at stake. In the final analysis, it is 'society' which pays the bills for election campaigns – particularly in societies such as Israel, where the Treasury pays the largest share of the parties' expenses. In other words, the society must strive toward a system of election campaigning which constrains the principal actors – even when it does not coincide with their perceived self-interest – to serve it in the best possible way.[7]

7. Recent proposals for redesigning election campaigns include Rose (1967), Kelley (1960) and Blumler and McQuail (1968, Part IV). The design of elections in Israel, and the legal basis therefore, is reviewed by Witkon (1970).

But how? The answer is not a simple or standard one – and it will surely vary from nation to nation – but in so far as public broadcasting is concerned, it involves two dimensions: the method of dividing broadcasting time, and the overall division of labor in the production of political broadcasts.

As far as the division of broadcasting time is concerned, officially, there are two formulae in operation in the western democracies: the 'equal time' formula and the 'proportional time' formula. The 'equal time' formula is particularly suited to two-party systems, though even in the United States there are more than two parties – the Prohibition party, for example – and these are entitled to 'equal time'. In other words, if the networks allocate half-an-hour to a Democratic party broadcast, the Republicans – as well as any other party – are entitled to half an hour at the same time of day. In practice, the tiny 'third parties' that have appeared on the American scene have not been able to take advantage of the time thus offered because, in general, the American system requires them to pay for the time. Nevertheless, the law is so strict on this point that when the proposal was put forward, in 1960, for the innovation that has come to be known as the Kennedy-Nixon debates, Congress had to agree to suspend the 'equal time' provisions (Section 315 of the Federal Communications Act) so that the Democratic and Republican candidates could confront each other, at the invitation of the networks without running the risk that some other candidate could demand 'equal time'.

In practice, however, the 'equal time' formula is a special case of the 'proportional time' formula for those societies which have two parties of nearly equal strength. The 'proportional time' formula allocates time differently to the different parties, usually on the basis of their past voting strength. Israel, as we have seen, uses the 'proportional time' formula rather strictly; England and other countries have given the opposition parties somewhat better treatment than their actual parliamentary strength would justify, thus creating a kind of compromise formula. No society has yet tried to allocate time (and money) in inverse proportion to a party's previous strength, though one can make a rather good case for such a system in a democracy.

If the money and effort invested by democratic societies in

their election campaigns are to be repaid, that is, if the campaigns are to serve the functions required of them by the social system, the issues must be *debated*. The 'proportional time' formula, strictly invoked, works against this kind of confrontation. Witness the Israel campaign of 1969 where one party had nearly half the time, the next largest party had only one quarter, and no other of the fourteen remaining parties had as much as 10 per cent.[8] On the other hand, the 'equal time' formula is an unrealistic solution in a multi-party situation. Obviously, some compromise formula is required, though it would probably help – for societies such as Israel – if the formula could be applied mechanically rather than by negotiation. A method might be considered, for example, where parties might be permitted to buy their time from the global sums placed at their disposal. But this formula is probably not the right answer either since, at one extreme, it would merely reflect the proportional allocation of funds according to previous voting strength, and at the other extreme, it would silence those parties whose attributes do not happen to include affluent supporters.

Although it may seem far-fetched, thought might be given to the idea of asking voters which parties they would like to see and hear. Employing a pre-election referendum, or even a publically-supervised opinion poll, one might ask voters to rank the parties according to their interest in hearing their spokesman. Such a poll would, of course, have to be preceded by an initial presentation – on television, and however briefly – of all the legitimate contenders. While the voter's initial tendency will be to name his own party as the one he would like to hear most, the object of the referendum would be to elicit the names of the *other* parties whose arguments are of interest.

However, even a completely ideal allocation of time to party

8. In spite of the consideration given small and new parties, proportional to its size the Labour Alignment was given over 40 per cent of the total television time alotted. Virtually every television evening 'starred' the Alignment. The Alignment presented its leaders answering invited and pre-taped questions; the Alignment presented tendentious quiz programs; the Alignment presented light entertainment; the Alignment presented documentary films about national achievements as well as about unsolved problems. The Alignment was practically a Program Contractor to Israel Television.

broadcasts is not a substitute for a better division of labor in the production and presentation of politically relevant broadcasts. There is no substitute for 'confrontation'. This is accomplished, first of all, by the intervention of journalist-broadcasters who know how to join the issues in documentary and discussion programs. The media themselves – not just the parties – must take an active share in presenting the candidates, introducing the issues, challenging the parties to take clearcut stands on the issues, and in general 'representing' the intelligent voter in trying to make sense of the campaign. And the public must be given what it wants – and almost never gets – direct confrontation among the leading candidates. This need not be an actual debate – as, indeed, the Kennedy-Nixon 'debates' were not debates – but rather the successive replies of each candidate to the same set of questions, one by one, as put to them by a panel of journalists. The better-known candidate – usually the incumbent – runs the greater risk in such a confrontation, hence this much-touted innovation in American politics has remained unused in the two presidential elections since 1960. It has been similarly praised, but avoided, in England – where the problem is additionally complicated by the question of fitting Liberal party leaders into the format of a 'debate'.[9]

One may object that a candidate's 'performance' on television – his showmanship – is not a good predictor of how he will perform in office where administrative skills and effective face-to-face diplomacy are more important requirements than gala appearance; but one may argue the other side with equal cogency. At any rate, observers of American and British elections who are concerned with designing a campaign context in which communications appeals are directed to the intelligence of the interested and rational voter and in which the marginally involved voter is aroused are convinced that the institutionalization of direct televised confrontation is one of the most important answers.

9. The Canadian elections of 1968 featured a four-way debate on all CBC networks. For an extremely thorough analysis of the Canadian situation, see Paltiel and Kjosa (1970). It is my understanding that debates were also featured in recent Swedish elections, and that audience research found these *less* satisfactory to the public than the analyses of the Swedish broadcaster-journalists whose freedom seems considerable.

Problems of bias and freedom

That does not mean that there are no problems in election broadcasting where the issues or the candidates are joined. From England, which took major steps in this direction in the 1960s, we have some idea of what may go wrong. Interestingly, there were apparently very few protests of unfairness: the intensive coverage of the campaigns of 1964, 1966 and 1970 in the major evening news; the analysis of basic issues by the television news-magazines; the series of Forum interviews with party heads on the several evenings before election – were all accepted as pro-fessional and non-partisan. The problem according to Harrison, has to do with one of the built-in conflicts between journalism, including broadcast-journalism and political campaigns, and centers on the broadcaster's or journalist's professional bias in favor of dramatizing the campaign (Harrison, 1966). Where it is usually in the interest of the party in power to keep the elections quiet, and to avoid the sharpening of issues or the stimulation of partisan feelings, the professional bias of the broadcaster is in the drama of conflict. This, as Harrison suggests for 1966, sometimes 'pushed [producers] by pure "news" criteria towards giving Conservative issues greater play,' because it was the opposition that was raising the issues. 'Equally questionable,' continues Harrison,

was the assumption implicit in some current affairs coverage that it is up to the parties to produce a steady succession of newsworthy themes – the issue-a-day approach to electioneering . . . . While all the fears and conjectures are highly questionable, at the core of Mr Wilson's com-plaint lay a plausible fear that the pressure of media coverage could distort campaigning patterns for the worse.

This concern is echoed in the reflections of British broadcasters on the coverage of the 1970 elections.[10] Jeremy Isaacs feels that broadcast-journalism is not free enough – to comment, to analyse, to personalize the issues – because of the fear of stepping beyond the boundaries set by the parties themselves for what is to be

10. Post-election discussion in *The Listener* are especially illuminating. The following draws freely on Isaacs (1970, p. 822), Blumler (1970, pp. 845–6) and Grist (1970, p. 4).

debated. John Grist sees no other way. 'Television journalism,' he says,

can only move a little beyond the areas charted by the parties in the general conduct of the campaign. Editors cannot produce a private electronic election.

All agree, however, that the case for greater freedom for broadcaster initiative during election campaigns rests on the journalist-broadcaster's ability to resist the temptation to overdramatize and oversimplify serious and complex issues. Yet, it is ironic to note, with Jay Blumler, that it is now the politicians who are increasingly guilty of this kind of irrationality and trivialization as they adopt the styles of television advertising and 'drama'. In this context, the case for giving professional journalism a more active role seems strong.

If the role broadcasters should play in issue-setting is controversial, there seems rather less disagreement over how the issues should be debated. The principle of proportional time – the allocation of broadcast time according to the parties' previous strength – seems undesirable; this is all the more evident where one party predominates. More generally, the party-produced broadcasts deserve to be curtailed, because they seem constrained to go to one extreme or the other: either to dry, one-sided talk or to slick dramatization. The citizen appears better served by the intervention of the professional broadcaster. The broadcaster-journalist should be free to explore the issues and to confront party leaders with his questions. He should be a catalyst for the confrontation of members of the public and of various interest groups with party leaders, and of course, of the leaders with each other. These are the things that are 'useful' to the voter and to society.

But the politician is very reluctant to agree, and understandably so, from his point of view. It is not simply that he is still afraid of television, as many writers argue, or that party managers do not trust their clients without a script. It happens to be true that persuasion – which is what the parties are after – is not abetted by 'arguing'.

Again and again, one is led to the conclusion that election campaigns are better designed to serve the political parties, particularly the dominant ones, than to serve society or the voter – if the liberal desiderata of optimizing rationality and participation are accepted. Campaigns *can* be better designed, but politicians will not do this voluntarily. As Grist (1970) writes of the recent British elections:

disquiet (was) felt by many people in broadcasting (over) the appearance of an agreement between the parties and the broadcasting authorities to restrict the ability of television journalism to cover the election, an agreement in which the public took second place. The representatives of the political parties are not perhaps the best people to decide the television coverage of an election campaign just as the campaign is starting.

Yet, despite this, the advances made in the 1960s in the actual freedom given British broadcasters to take initiative, were maintained in the 1970 campaign, it seems. And it may be that Grist is right in implying that progress will be made if broadcasters and politicians continue to 'bargain' with each other – though not on the eve of the campaign.[11] This is the way in which the laws governing broadcasting get written, and it is perhaps the only way out of this dilemma for democratic societies with publicly-operated broadcasting systems. In any event, technological innovation will soon make 'audience participation' a less empty concept. It would be well for all those concerned with election campaigns to take note.[12]

11. Grist (1970, p. 4). '. . . the television authorities will have to recognize the distinction between showmanship, which is an essential part of television journalism and gladiatorial spectacle at the expense of the issues. In return, the political parties must learn to be less restrictive about television.' Note, however, that Grist's thesis is based on the assumption that the parties are genuinely concerned about clarification of issues. Experience shows that they are often not so inclined – except with respect to certain highly selected issues of their own choosing.

12. This is not to underestimate the importance of between-election political broadcasting. Crossman (1968) rightly calls for more and better coverage of partisan issues. The fact that more voters change their intentions between elections than during election campaigns should even make the parties interested. Grist (1970) also sees the between-election period as the appropriate time for experimenting with new formats.

References

BERELSON, B., LAZARSFELD, P. F., and MCPHEE, W. N. (1954), *Voting: A Study of Opinion Formation in a Presidential Campaign*, University of Chicago Press.

BLUMLER, J. G. (1970), in the *Listener*, vol. 83.

BLUMLER, J. G., and MCQUAIL, D. (1968), *Television and Politics: Its uses and Influence*, Faber & Faber.

CONVERSE, P. (1966), 'Information flow and the stability of partisan attitudes' in D. Campbell (ed.), *Electors and the Political Order*, Wiley.

CROSSMAN, R. H. S. (1968), 'The politics of viewing', *New Statesman*, vol. 76, pp. 525–30.

DEUTSCHMANN, P. J. (1962), 'Viewing, conversation and voting contentions', in Sidney Kraus (ed.), *The Great Debates*, Indiana University Press.

GRIST, J. (1970), in the *Listener*, vol. 84.

HARRISON, M. (1966), 'Television and radio', in D. E. Butler and A. King (eds.), *The British General Election of 1966*, Macmillan.

ISAACS, J. (1970), in the *Listener*, vol. 83.

KATZ, E., and FELDMAN, J. J. (1962), 'The debates in the light of research: a survey of surveys', in Sidney Kraus (ed.), *The Great Debates*, Indiana University Press.

KELLY, S. Jr (1960), *Political Campaigning: Problems in Creating An Informed Electorate*, The Brookings Institution, Washington.

KEY, V. O. (1966), *The Responsible Electorate: Rationality in Presidential Voting 1936–1960*, Harvard University, Belknap Press.

LAZARSFELD, P. F., BERELSON, B., and GAUDET, H. (1944), *The Peoples Choice, How the Voter Makes Up his Mind in a Presidential Campaign*, Duell, Sloan and Pearce.

MCGINNISS, J. (1969), *The Selling of the President 1968*, Trident Press; Penguin, 1971.

PALTIEL, K., and KJOSA, L. G. (1970), 'The structure and dimensions of election broadcasting in Canada', in G. Leibholz (ed.) *Jahrbuch des Offentlichen Rechts der Gegenwart*, vol. 19, n.s. J. C. B. Mohr, Tubingen.

ROSE, R. (1967), *Influencing Voters: A Study of Campaign Rationality*, Faber and Faber.

WITKON, A. (1970), 'Elections in Israel', *Israel Law Rev.*, vol. 5, pp. 42–52.

17 Herbert J. Gans

The Politics of Culture in America: A Sociological Analysis

Herbert J. Gans 'La politique culturelle aux États Unis', *Communications*, vol. 14, 1969, pp. 162–71.

I

Culture is usually considered a form of spiritual expression, and is therefore thought to be 'above' such worldly concerns as politics. This view of culture is naive, however, for politics concerns the distribution of resources, power and prestige in society, and culture plays a role in determining that distribution.

My analysis of the politics of culture must begin by defining the term culture. As translated from the German word *Kultur*, the term refers to the aesthetic standards, activities and products of 'serious' artists and intellectuals who create for 'cultivated' audiences; but I use culture in a broader sense, to mean the aesthetic standards, activities and products of any human group, a definition that encompasses both high culture and popular (or mass) culture.[1]

Culture affects the distribution of resources, power and prestige in at least two ways. First, culture is transmitted by institutions such as television networks and schools, and such institutions participate in the governmental or party politics of almost every society. Second, culture provides people with symbols, myths, values and information about their society. Every cultural 'product', whether a serious play or a light novel, offers some social commentary about today's society, and often some political commentary as well. Because culture has influence on the members of society – although not as much as is often thought – the determination of what culture and what socio-political commentary is to be created and distributed has political implications. For example, even the most impartial television documentary

1. Many of the ideas in this Reading about the nature of culture are developed in more detail in Gans (1966).

about income redistribution would create some political support for this issue, partly because some viewers might now favor redistribution as a result of having watched the documentary, and partly because the mere fact that the subject is presented on a mass medium gives it some political strength. But even a light comedy about family life has some political implications, for it must inevitably comment on the rights and privileges of parents and children and can thus affect, however slightly, the struggle between the generations over the allocation of power within the family.

The question of what socio-political commentary is to be distributed is particularly important because in any modern society in which a number of classes, ethnic and religious groups, age groups and political interests struggle among each other for control over the society's resources, there is also a struggle for the power to determine or influence the society's values, myth, symbols and information. Every group seeks to persuade the mass media to transmit its values and to exclude competing ones, for whichever group can have its values legitimated as the values of the nation obtains considerable political advantage. For example, many working-class and lower-middle-class whites are attempting to persuade America of the values of 'law and order' to justify the repression of the protesting Negro population, and they – or their political representatives – would like to see the mass media present mainly their point of view.

This type of struggle is most intense in films and television, for because of the limited number of television channels and movie theaters, only a few of the potentially infinite number of cultural products can be distributed. Consequently, the decision as to what will be shown on the screen must inevitably be political, involving considerations that go beyond the merit of the cultural product in question. It should be emphasized, however, that the participants in these cultural struggles are rarely conscious either of the conflict or of its political implications, for the struggles are usually fought over whether a particular cultural product has artistic merit or commercial appeal. For example, I doubt that the producer and director of a recent Hollywood film (neither of them Catholic) which portrayed the happy life of a family with eighteen children ever realized that their film might be relevant to the public debate about birth control.

In Europe, where government plays an important role in the creation and distribution of culture, the politics of culture often takes place within the formal political institutions, but in America the politics of culture takes place largely in the world of commerce, although government officials are sometimes asked to regulate the commercial media on behalf of one or another class or interest group. Moreover, the major issues in the politics of culture are different in America and Europe. In Europe, where high culture has considerable power and prestige, the question of how much high and popular culture are to be distributed by the mass media is a major issue. In America, high culture is politically too weak to appear in the mass media, and the major cultural-political struggles take place within popular culture, particularly over erotic and quasi-erotic material. The producers of films, television programs etc. are under considerable pressure from older, conservative audiences and from their elected representatives and church and school officials to censor such material, but under commercial pressure to provide it – reflecting the demand for erotic material from younger, more liberal audiences. Since the assassinations of Martin Luther King and Robert Kennedy, the reduction of violence in television entertainment and the role to be played by Negroes as performers and characters in popular culture have also become major issues.

Formal censorship plays only a minor role in America's politics of culture. The United States Supreme Court has severely limited the power of the federal government to censor, although it can still refuse permission for the import of foreign culture, as it did recently for the film *I Am Curious*. Most formal censorship is practiced by local governments, particularly in the conservative rural areas of the country, but the Supreme Court decisions have also reduced it in recent years. Informal censorship and precensorship still abound however; church and civic group pressures impose a taboo on overt eroticism in Hollywood films, and films with a left-wing point of view have been persecuted so harshly by right-wing 'patriotic' organizations that they had practically disappeared until the recent wave of 'underground' films – but these are shown only in a handful of cities and on college campuses. There was no censorship, formal or informal, of violence until the recent political assassinations.

II

An analysis of the patterns of cultural politics in America is best carried out by comparing it with governmental or party politics. Since American party politics is rarely concerned with questions of culture – the political parties do not have ideological positions on culture – and since government plays such a minor role in the creation and distribution of culture, the politics of culture takes place largely in commercial institutions devoted to culture, and in the complex relationship between the distributors (the owners and managers of the media which distribute culture, high or popular), and the artists, writers, directors, etc., who are the creators of culture, and the audiences who consume it. For purposes of comparison, the distributors and creators may be described as cultural politicians; the audience, as their cultural constituencies. The cultural politicians are engaged in providing culture for their constituencies with the purpose of achieving their own goals and also satisfying their constituencies. Thus they face the same problem as the governmental politician – how to appeal to a constituency whose wants cannot easily be predicted in advance, and which actually consists of a number of sub-constituencies with conflicting or different wants.

These subconstituencies are not organized groups; they are aggregates of people with similar tastes, and may therefore be called taste constituencies or taste publics, who share a taste subculture or taste culture. A society as heterogeneous as America contains many taste publics and cultures, each culture having its own preferred types of art, music, literature, theater, architecture etc., its own media, distributors, creators and critics, and of course its own definitions of beauty and aesthetic standards. For the purpose of this analysis, I will describe only the most important taste publics and cultures: high, upper-middle, lower-middle and low.

High-taste culture (or high culture) needs little discussion; it is the culture of 'serious' art, music, literature, etc., and its public is made up largely of affluent, university-educated persons, many themselves creators or critics of culture.

Upper-middle-taste culture resembles and often borrows from high taste culture. It is 'sophisticated' but not 'serious', for its aim is to provide appreciation and enjoyment rather than the intellectual and emotional insight sought by high culture. Its public is the American upper-middle class, the college-educated professionals, executives and managers. They are rarely creators of culture; they are consumers, which is why the culture seeks to provide enjoyment. Among its more important media are the *New York Times*, *Harper's Magazine*, Broadway theater, 'educational television' and the national symphony orchestras – whose products differ significantly in content and tone from such high-culture media as *Partisan Review*, *The New York Review of Books*, the off-Broadway theater, and chamber music groups.

Lower-middle and low-taste culture are generally described as popular or mass culture; they shun both seriousness and sophistication, and perhaps their main identifying characteristic is literalness and concreteness. Lower-middle-taste culture appeals to middle-class people in semiprofessional and white-collar jobs, who have graduated from high school and have perhaps attended a state or community college. The major media of this taste culture are Hollywood movies, commercial television, magazines such as *Look* and *Reader's Digest*, the Broadway musicals, and today, the pseudo-realistic novels, for example, *Valley of the Dolls*, which become best sellers.

Low-taste culture is pursued by people with less than a high-school education: the white factory workers and the black poverty-stricken residents of the ghetto. Low-taste culture differs from lower-middle-taste culture by its yet greater literalness and by its emphasis on 'action', as found in adventure stories, melodramas, and violent sports like boxing and football. Because the low-taste public is not affluent and is therefore unattractive to advertisers, it has to obtain much of its culture from the media that cater to the lower-middle-taste public; comic books, confession and fan magazines and tabloid newspapers are about the only purely low-culture media still in existence today.

These descriptions are quite superficial, and a more detailed analysis would have to indicate subdivisions and factions within each taste culture and public.[2] For example, each culture has traditional, progressive and avant-garde factions, and age-graded subdivisions as well. In almost all taste cultures, adolescent

2. For a more detailed description of the taste cultures and publics see Gans (1966, pp. 579–98).

publics have vastly different tastes in music from adults; today the former prefer 'rock and roll', 'acid rock', 'folk-rock', and folk music with social-protest lyrics, which are rarely popular among adults. Moreover, the boundaries between taste cultures are very diffuse, and much popular culture tries to appeal to several taste publics at once. For example, some parts of *Life* magazine are written for upper-middle-taste publics, others for lower-middle publics. The recent film *Bonnie and Clyde* was successful partly because it appealed to many publics, although for different reasons; the lower-taste publics viewing it as a crime adventure film, the higher publics as a commentary on violence in American society. Some forms of culture cater to just one taste public; formal literary criticism is found mainly in high culture, boxing appeals almost entirely to the low-taste public, and TV is created mainly for lower-middle-taste publics, although 'educational TV', which is not really educational, seeks out educated audiences, i.e. the upper-middle-taste public.

The hierarchy and characteristics of taste cultures and taste publics are quite similar to the hierarchy and characteristics of the American class structure. This is not coincidental, for the kind of taste a person develops depends very much on his class origins and particularly on the amount and quality of education he has received. In general, it is accurate to say that the better a person's education, the 'higher' his cultural taste.

Moreover, the taste cultures often express the class concerns of their publics. For example, a considerable amount of high culture writing, fictional and non-fictional, consists of thinly veiled attacks on the middle and working classes for holding too much cultural power, and much lower-middle and low-taste-culture fiction tells of heroes with traditional sexual norms who unmask other characters with avant-garde sexual norms as villains. The taste cultures do not, however, often express the class interests, in the Marxist sense, of their publics. Since the media of all taste cultures are owned by businessmen, these media are generally more conservative, at least on domestic policies, than many members of their publics. For example, low-culture news media, which appeal to a working-class public, are probably even more opposed to socialism than middle- and high-culture media.

Because the taste hierarchy reflects the class hierarchy, taste conflicts occur which are similar to class conflicts, with every taste culture critical of the standards and products of all others. Generally speaking, each taste culture criticizes those 'above' it in status as being snobbish and dull, and those below it as being superficial or vulgar, and high culture, of course, rejects all other taste cultures as being spurious and inauthentic. Indeed, the theory of mass culture has been developed as a major ideological tool with which high culture defends itself against the other, more powerful and popular taste cultures.

Since the various taste cultures and publics rarely meet on a common battleground, the conflicts between them are fought out by the critics, reviewers and commentators who represent specific taste cultures. For example, a book reviewed favorably by high-culture magazines may be criticized harshly by upper-middle-culture critics as being too abstract or scholarly and it will probably be ignored entirely by low-middle-culture reviewers as uninteresting. Conversely, high-culture reviewers normally ignore all popular books as too superficial to deserve attention, and no one reviews low-culture books, for they are thought to be so violent, erotic and poorly written that they cannot even be found in public libraries and regular book stores.

III

The politics of culture exists at every level of society, ranging from governmental conflicts over censorship to adverse comments people make about the cultural tastes of their neighbors. The most interesting phenomenon in America, however, is the political struggle between taste cultures over whose culture is to predominate in the major media, and over whose culture will provide society with its symbols, values and world view. This struggle is fought not only over the merits of each culture, but also involves the political and economic power of the various taste publics in the American class system and power structure.

High culture has the greatest prestige, of course, but because its public is numerically small – too small to justify even one television program that caters to it – the culture is relatively powerless. Low-taste culture is also quite powerless because its public lacks purchasing power and political influence. As a result, the mass media rarely provide information or entertainment about working-class people. Indeed, although Negro characters have recently been introduced into movies and television entertainment, so far all of them are middle- and upper-middle-class in status; characters modeled on typical ghetto residents have not yet appeared on the screen.

Most of the cultural power in America is held by the upper-middle and lower-middle-taste publics. The former includes many of the affluent corporate decision-makers, and is therefore most powerful in public cultural activities; members of the upper-middle-taste public obtain government grants to establish cultural centers, and architects who reflect the style preferences of upper-middle-taste culture design many of America's public buildings (other than in Washington, where Congressmen, most of whom come from and represent the lower-middle-taste public, vote for the traditional architecture still favored by this public). The power of lower-middle-taste culture is of course most visible in the mass media, which cater mainly to it. Its power is also enhanced by the public schools, which are run largely by lower-middle-class administrators and teachers, although they tend to favor a highly traditional, almost Puritan form of the culture, whereas students prefer a much more progressive form of the same culture. Indeed, as I have already noted, perhaps the major conflict in the culture of politics today is a power struggle between the traditional and progressive wings of lower-middle-class culture over the question of how much erotic material should be permitted in the mass media.

Another power struggle is now developing between traditional lower-middle-taste culture and progressive upper-middle-taste culture over the political content of the news media: whether or not news should express nationalistic and ethnocentric values, and whether events should be explained by a 'morality play' theory of national and international heroes and villains or by a more 'naturalistic theory based to some extent on social-science concepts'. For example, conservatives from lower-middle-taste culture have recently attacked the news media for 'unpatriotic' reporting of the war in Vietnam, and for describing the causes of the ghetto rebellions of 1966 and 1967 as poverty and segregation rather than as the work of villainous revolutionaries.

Although these cultural-political issues are attracting a lot of attention, the most typical and frequent processes of the politics of culture take place within the media of the various cultures, particularly between the distributors and creators of culture. The creators are usually recruited on the basis of their ability and willingness to create for the particular publics to which a medium appeals, so that one rarely finds high-culture advocates in television or low-culture advocates in museum staffs. Because of this recruitment pattern, the creators of culture are normally free to create what they consider good; they are professionals who are allowed to use their professional judgement and their own aesthetic standards in their creative work.

Because creators are usually free to create what they consider best, what they create reflects their own taste culture, and as a result, their products generally promulgate the values of their taste culture. For example, high-culture creators are very much concerned about their position in a society in which popular culture is politically and culturally dominant, so that much recent high-culture fiction has dealt with the relationship of the alienated individual to society. Similarly, adults of all taste levels are currently upset about adolescent youth culture, and as a result, there are many films, television programs and popular novels about adolescents, most of them reflecting their adult creators' misgivings about the 'hippies', and other forms of youth culture.

Although distributors and creators for any given product tend to come from the same taste culture, they often have conflicting ideas. Creators have what might be called a producer-oriented view of their culture, while distributors are more consumer-oriented.

Creators want to create good or important or entertaining or tradition-breaking products; they are primarily concerned with improving their aesthetic techniques and with 'educating' their audiences, trying to go to the fore of public demand, both in the mass media and in high culture. Distributors, on the other hand, are concerned first with attracting and satisfying not the largest possible audience, but the largest possible audience from those taste publics which they define as their 'market'. Conflict takes place when the distributors demand changes in the creator's work that would make it attractive to an additional audience, for example, by inserting youthful characters into a screenplay to attract young audiences, and creators object because such a change would violate their creative purpose, and destroy the unity of what they have created. If the creator has enough prestige and a record of having created financially successful cultural products in the past, he is likely to be victorious in this conflict; if not, the distributor will win.

As I noted earlier, ideological or other political issues rarely enter into this process explicitly; the conflict between creators and distributors is usually about questions of artistic merit and commercial appeal. Even so, if distributors argue that a film should have a happy ending to make it commercially more attractive to lower-middle and low-taste publics, they are also arguing by implication that in the end society and individuals can solve their problems, and that the *status quo* can be preserved.

The constituents play an important but largely passive role in the political process by which culture is created. Their main role is to choose from among the cultural products available, and this choice, reflected for example in box-office results and television ratings, is their 'vote' for or against the distributors and creators. The outcome of this vote determines the prestige, power and in fact, the career of the distributors and creators; the director of a successful film is overwhelmed with job offers; the director of an unsuccessful film may have difficulty in obtaining another job.

Because the careers of creators and distributors depend on their ability to attract their constituents, they try to create products which they think will appeal to their constituents. Distributors may do this deliberately, but creators usually create cultural products that appeal to them personally, hoping that the audience will feel as they do. Even so, both creators and distributors 'represent' their taste public in the creation of cultural products, much as politicians represent their constituencies when they create legislation. In fact, some of the conflict between creators and distributors is over the question of which taste cultures and publics are to be represented in a cultural product.[3] When creators and distributors come from different taste cultures, or from opposing factions of the same culture, the conflict may end

3. For an example of this conflict see Kael's description of the filming of *The Group* in Kael (1968, pp. 65–100), Ross (1952) and Gans's sociological reanalysis (1957, pp. 315–24).

in the replacement of the creator by someone who shares the cultural allegiances of the distributor. Film directors are often replaced in the middle of a film for this reason.

Neither creators nor distributors have much direct contact with or knowledge of their constituents, and because past audience choices cannot predict future choices, culture is created amidst great uncertainty about its ultimate acceptance. If a creator or distributor does not know whether his next effort will be a success, and whether he can maintain his power and prestige, he tries to find ways of reducing the uncertainty, and of obtaining a base of power that is independent of his creative efforts. Like government and party politicians, creators organize cliques that will support them in instances of failure; they put their friends into positions of power for the same purpose, and they even try to obtain 'patronage', establishing jobs in their own organizations or elsewhere whose holders will be indebted to them and will support them.[4] The 'literary politics' of high culture and the internal bureaucratic struggles within the mass media are therefore quite similar; in both instances, creators (or distributors) use many of the same methods as the politician in government to stay in power.

These observations about the culture of politics apply to all taste cultures, high or low, for in America, at least, the 'serious' artist of high culture must concern himself with distributors and constituents as much as the mass media artist and perhaps more, because the high-culture audience is so much smaller than the mass media audience, and the occupational opportunities to work as a creator of high culture are so much scarcer.

Moreover, what I have written about the culture of politics applies not only to the arts and entertainment, but also to news and other 'informational culture', for each taste culture has its own *Weltanschauung*, which affects the kind of news and non-fiction it prefers, and even its attitude toward the social sciences. For example, lower-taste publics are more interested in local news and 'human interest' stories than in national and international news, and as already noted, upper-middle-taste culture is at least mildly interested in social-science explanations of events. High

4. For a recent description of literary politics in New York see Podhoretz (1967).

culture still prefers to get its social analyses from literary sources, while the more progressive factions of lower-middle culture are beginning to be interested in 'popular sociology', although this is often created by journalists, with concepts and methods that bear only a slight resemblance to academic sociology, and with findings and generalizations that are often completely different from those of academic sociology.

The news media function much like the other media, with every newspaper or magazine appealing to only one or two taste publics. As already noted, the *New York Times* appeals largely to upper-middle-taste publics; tabloid newspapers to low-taste publics. Although the style and complexity of news writing also varies depending on the educational level of the taste publics in a particular publication's audience, news reporting tries to ignore cultural differences by seeking 'objectivity' through a highly logical-positivist philosophy of what facts are deemed to be news, and by 'balanced' reporting which tries to provide information about all sides of every controversy. The complexity of reporting is adjusted to taste-culture considerations, however; high- and upper-middle-taste culture news media attempt to analyse and explain events as well as describe them, while the other news media place more emphasis on pure description.

IV

My analysis of some aspects of the politics of culture has proceeded from the perspective of cultural relativism, an anthropological doctrine which assumes that all taste cultures are of equal worth. This perspective has some obvious normative implications, for it questions the traditional belief of high culture that it is superior to all other taste cultures.

My own normative position is close to the position implicit in the analysis. I do not believe that all taste cultures are of equal worth, but that they are of equal worth *to their publics*. Indeed, I would agree with the advocates of high culture that their culture is superior in quality because it provides greater, more intense, more diversified, and perhaps even more permanent aesthetic gratification.

Taste cultures are chosen by people, however, and therefore cannot be evaluated without taking their publics into consideration.

The choice of taste culture is, however, a function of the class and educational level of the person who is choosing, and the ability to create and consume high culture requires an education of the highest quality and almost always, a high income as well. Consequently, it would be unfair to expect or demand that people of lower educational levels and incomes choose high culture. Rather, I would argue, every person should be expected to choose the taste culture that accords with his educational and class status, and conversely, every taste culture should be considered as having equal worth in relation to the people who choose it, simply because all people are of equal worth, regardless of their class position. From this point of view, high culture cannot be considered as having superior worth unless and until society provides everyone with the education and income prerequisite to participation in high culture.

Until then, I would advocate the desirability of cultural democracy and cultural pluralism; the co-existence of all possible taste cultures in accordance with the distribution of taste publics in society, so that everyone may enjoy the kind of culture for which his education and class background has trained him. This does not prevent anyone from participating in any other taste culture, and it does not discourage political efforts to increase educational levels and change the class system so as to change the quality of taste cultures. (In fact, this has already happened in America on a *laissez-faire* basis; improvements in public education over the last twenty-five years have significantly reduced the number of people who prefer low-taste culture, and they have also increased the aesthetic and intellectual level of lower-middle and upper-middle-taste culture.) I would limit cultural democracy only to the extent of excluding any taste culture, or elements thereof, that can be *proved* to be harmful to the individual or to the society, but so far I have seen no reliable evidence which proves that any culture is harmful, despite the claims by high culture that popular culture is intellectually and emotionally damaging.

The role of government in the politics of culture ought to be to maximize cultural democracy, to enable all taste cultures to exist, grow and develop. This means that government should not censor or otherwise restrict any taste culture because politically powerful members of another taste public demand censorship; instead, government should aid the growth and development of taste cultures which are held back by economic and class inequality. In America, governmental efforts should not concentrate solely on subsidizing high- and upper-middle-taste culture as is now the case, for their publics are affluent, and many private foundations are already providing subsidy. Instead, these subsidies should go primarily to low culture, for it cannot attract foundations or advertisers to finance the growth of the culture and the recruitment of more creative talent. The most needy group in America is probably the black community; until recently, Negro culture has been discouraged and even suppressed, and black people have had to choose among films, television, fiction and art created by, for, and about white people. Only Negro music has flourished, but because it has been popular with whites as well. Greater cultural democracy in America could best be achieved by aiding black creators and distributors financially and politically, to develop culture in all forms of art and entertainment that is relevant to the needs and wants of the black community, and particularly of the poor blacks in the ghetto.

References

GANS, H. J. (1957), 'The creator-audience relationship in the mass media: an analysis of movie making', in B. Rosenberg and D. White (eds.), *Mass Culture*, Free Press, pp. 315–24.

GANS, H. J. (1966), 'Popular culture in America', in H. S. Becker (ed.), *Social Problems: A Modern Approach*, Wiley, pp. 549–620.

KAEL, P. (1968), *Kiss Kiss, Bang Bang*, Little Brown & Co.

PODHORETZ, N. (1967), *Making It*, Random House.

ROSS, L. (1952), *Picture*, Harcourt, Brace & World.

18 Kaarle Nordenstreng

Policy for News Transmission

Kaarle Nordenstreng, 'Policy for news transmission', paper presented in
the general assembly of the International Association for Mass
Communication Research, Konstanz, Germany, 1970. Reprinted in
Educational Broadcasting Review, Autumn 1971.

Just a few years ago discussions around television and mass
communications in general were dominated by the medium's
technical characteristics and the journalist's daily problems in
taking advantage of them. A typical example of such debates
centered on the role of television in demonstrations – whether or
not the TV camera has a stimulating effect on the happening
itself. Now it seems that the governing theme in the debate is the
role of the media as communications institutions of the greatest
social and political importance. For instance, television is today –
after Spiro Agnew has spoken – viewed more as an institution
operating within the framework of other institutions; the level of
discussion begins to be sociological and political rather than
psychological and practical.

I see this as a significant indication of the direction taken by the
debate and research around the mass media in general: the emphasis is shifting from practical journalistic problems to general
societal problems. Of course this does not – and should not –
mean neglecting practical considerations; it only means that the
societal considerations so far largely neglected will be given
proper attention.

The central issue in the present debate around the mass media,
according to my diagnosis, is whether a mass medium should act
as a mirror reflecting the community, the society and the world
as a whole, or whether it should take an active part in changing
them. The prevalent opinion among the media people as well as
social scientists, as I perceive it, is that the media should not be
used as channels for the active promotion of social change but
that they should instead be used as an accurate mirror reflecting
events in the world. Accordingly, their relation to the rest of

society should be service-oriented, or to use an illuminating term 'parasitic'.[1]

I disagree with this concept of mass communication as a passive mirror, at least with regard to the broadcasting media. My point is that the adoption of a 'parasitic' mirror role does not necessarily make the medium impartial or objective, however carefully it covers everything that happens around – it only makes it impartial and objective in relation to those whose actions have been covered ('those' being persons, institutions, etc.). Reporting what happens – and only that – does not guarantee accurate coverage of the world. The event must be 'placed in perspective', as the function of background commentaries and current affairs programs is usually expressed.

It is not difficult to see how little of passive reflection is present in commentary programs and how much of an active element they unavoidably contain. No doubt it is these programs of 'perspective' that have recently raised pressures against the networks all over the world: the tendency of broadcasters to give as complete a picture of the world as possible has not appealed to everybody. Those who have become used to being 'objectively' covered by the mirror media are now annoyed by being presented 'in perspective', which is likely to be perceived as 'biased' however balanced it may be.

This anger is an indirect indication of the fact that a mirror medium tends to support the *status quo*, i.e. that it is likely to be partial to those interests which dominate the prevailing 'balance of power' in society. Or to use a term introduced by Antonio Gramsci, the mirror practice works in favor of the material and mental *hegemony* in society.[2]

What we are faced with here is not only the problem of the

1. I pass here the vital problem concerning the character and control of a service medium: should it reflect a monolithic majority point of view or should it follow a model of parliamentarism by sharing the contents according to relative size of various audience subgroups, etc.

2. Unfortunately these statements, purely empiric by their nature, cannot be documented by solid pieces of empirical research (in a positivistic sense), which in fact is an indication of the inadequacies of the mass communication research tradition (see Nordenstreng, 1968). Some empirical evidence (together with a general description of cultural and political conditions of a society) is included in a paper by Littunen and Nordenstreng (1971).

freedom of the press but also another dilemma: the more comprehensive a picture of the world we want to present in programs to our audience, the less we can function as a plain mirror. In fact, it is the whole principle of journalism and the ultimate aim of broadcasting which is at issue. The traditional concept of journalism as reporting the truth and the idea of mass communication as a non-biased mirror of the community and the whole world simply will not work any longer. Typical of the ambivalence of this new situation is the fact that journalists, while sympathizing with the mirror concept of broadcasting, at the same time firmly react against intimidation of the medium by governmental or other pressure groups.

At this stage there is an urgent need for specifying the role of broadcasting – and the concept of journalism in general. What is needed is not only empirical research into the practical aspects of broadcasting at different stages of the communication process (production, programs, audience) but also theoretical advance toward a *systematic explication of the ultimate goals of activity*, i.e. a careful re-evaluation of policy. This can be carried quite far without any new data, merely by means of systematic discussion and thinking. Such a clarification of meanings and aims does not imply esoteric speculation in an ivory tower far removed from practical problems, for which social scientists have often been criticized by practical workers, and on good grounds. It should also be remembered that a theoretical emphasis by no means rules out the importance of accumulating empirical evidence of the operation in practice.

Finnish broadcasting research has tried to advance systematically at both of these levels, empirical and theoretical. To ensure a balance between them – and especially to make sure that theoretical research into the aims of broadcasting does not lag behind – research has been incorporated with planning activities in a single unit for long-range planning. An example of the kind of work done in the Finnish Broadcasting Company in this field will be given below, in the form of excerpts from a report on the principles of news transmission prepared as part of long-range planning activity.[3]

3. A closer description of the research organization in the Finnish Broadcasting Company will be found in Nordenstreng (1971).

This news report has been drawn up following an assignment given by the Board of Directors to the Section for Long-Range Planning in September 1969, which says, among other things, the following:

In general, the foundations of news activity should be considered, all the way from the way in which news is chosen to the language used in news broadcasts. Only when the objectives of news activity have thus been made clear can we begin to plan the practical aspects of news and current affairs activity in a meaningful way (increasing the number of editors, expanding the correspondent network, etc.).

The LRP section then set up a special working group to carry out the actual work. The working group consisted of nine persons: five practitioners (the heads of the Finnish and Swedish TV news services, the head of provincial broadcasting, an editorial secretary of the radio news service, and a foreign news editor), two who were both practitioners and researchers (a radio news editor with a degree in the social sciences and experience in audience research, and a former researcher now working in the LRP Section as an expert on program activities), together with two research experts of the LRP Section, Professor Yrjö Ahmavaara and myself (I have also been involved in practical work). The working group was chaired by myself, while one of the practitioner-researchers (the radio news editor, Mr Pekka Peltola) acted as secretary. The group worked for over four months, meeting once a week (except in late November at the beginning of the SALT negotiations) and got a sixty-seven-page report completed in February 1970. The report was unanimous, and both the practitioners and the researchers felt that they had learned a lot in working on it.

The full report is composed of six sections and two lengthy appendices: 'Introduction', 'The objectives of news activity', 'Informational news criteria', 'News acquisition', 'News broadcasts' and 'Suggestions for practical measures', with a survey of research into program comprehension and an analysis of the traditional news criteria as appendices. In the following only parts of the report will be reproduced. Sections omitted include a survey of the history of news transmission, originally part of the introduction, and the sections on news acquisition and broadcasting (describing the present system and suggesting an application of informational news criteria to the gathering and presenting of news). Also omitted is the section suggesting practical measures for implementation of the new policy into practice. Parts of the appendices have been incorporated in the introduction and in the section on informational news criteria below (in the original report the appendices are elaborated supplements to the introduction).

The report: introduction

The starting point of this report is the recognition of the fact that news diffusion through mass communication is in a worldwide state of crisis. The problems to be faced can be reduced to two main categories: comprehension and news criteria.

Comprehension

It has been shown that news broadcasts are among the most popular programs on the basis of both audience size and appreciation. Over 80 per cent of the Finnish population over fifteen follow at least one news broadcast a day over radio or television. The news is also followed with concentration. Around 90 per cent of listeners and viewers follow the most important news broadcasts with concentration.

Seventy per cent of listeners and viewers rate radio and television news as the most reliable, compared to other news media. About 80 per cent of the adult population is satisfied with the Broadcasting Company's news programs. The figure is about 90 per cent for domestic news and seventy per cent for foreign news.

When we start to measure comprehension of the news, however, the situation is different. Interviews carried out immediately after the news have shown that in general little if anything is remembered of the content of the news. It also appeared that the unsystematic details which are retained are subsequently formed into a whole which may be faulty. Even with some help from the interviewer, 48 per cent of television-news viewers remembered nothing of the content of the news. The questions were easy ones: e.g. 'Who are fighting in the Near East?' (38 per cent knew the answer, most of them probably knew it before). The study, in fact, concluded that 'the main thing retained from the news is that nothing special has happened'.

This telephone interview study is also supported by other interviews carried out by the LRP section. The concluding estimate in these is that news concerning general issues (which forms the basis of news material) offers essential information to only about 10–15 per cent of the audience.

This is in agreement with the observation that for many Finns, following the news is a mere ritual, a way of dividing up the daily rhythm, and a manifestation of alienation. According to a report,

Many people follow the news because in this way they gain a point of contact with the outside world – a fixed point in life – while the content of the news is indifferent to them.

Accordingly, despite widespread interest in the news and close attention to news events among the public, it is frequently questionable whether the content of the news has been understood. This is so especially in the case of the public at large, which usually lacks the informational background necessary to a comprehension of the abstract concepts involved in the news. In such a situation, news programs do not fulfil their function, which is the transmission of information; they begin to serve a completely different purpose, whereby the following of news broadcasts becomes a ritual, a custom serving to maintain a feeling of security.

Large audiences and interest or confidence in the news thus do not necessarily testify to successful news activity. The final criterion must be comprehension, i.e. the question whether news programs enable the audience to form a truthful picture of the events described. It should especially be noted that in the case of radio and television, as mass media with an exceptionally wide distribution, comprehension should be examined in all population groups, rather than, for example, only from the point of view of the elite. Only a stream of information which penetrates the entire society can serve to advance the democratization which has been set as one of the basic goals of the program activity of the Finnish Broadcasting Company.

Four main factors have been identified in research as important for comprehension of the news message: interest (in so far as it affects the decision to follow the news), concreteness, identification and linguistic factors (including the TV picture).

But although taking these factors into consideration is of great help, even their most skillful application will not solve all problems. There will still be important issues, about which news does not reach a majority of the people. Here we come to the effects of alienation. Several Finnish researchers have independently come to the conclusion that alienation is an important obstacle to comprehension of the news message. Tiihonen:

We observe that those who use television as their main news medium are passive individuals with little education, who lack motivational stimulation.

Pietilä:

Not many read the newspaper in order to find out what has really happened and in order to organize and control their view of the world on the basis of this information; more often it is in order to feel that they belong to something, whether this be a restricted environment or the whole world. This need for contact is very close to the concept of alienation. Without doubt those who in one way or another feel themselves to be isolated from their social environment and whose normal contacts are weak or unsatisfactory often seek a substitute for these in the mass media. . . . Alienation also includes the experience that the world cannot be controlled. According to Morris Seeman, the individual's state of alienation is indicated by the fact that he feels unable to control and organize his world – it feels uncertain – a world in which anything can happen for any reason and without any single individual being able to do anything about it. . . . This uncertainty can be resolved by withdrawing from the sphere of information which demonstrates this state of affairs to him, i.e. by avoiding the mass media either completely or at least concerning information which would reinforce this state. But there are also alienated individuals who use the mass media even more than normally; for them the content of the news is indifferent, what matters is a fixed point in life. These alienated and high news-consuming individuals were the most disturbed during TV and newspaper strikes.

Both Pietilä and Tiihonen recommend that in order to improve this situation more background material be included in news broadcasts than at present. Tiihonen:

The expansion of televised news broadcasts so as to include more interpretative commentary material would thus reach primarily passive viewers. Thus it would seem to make sense to program possible new broadcasts in such a way as to arouse even the most passive viewer.

This would probably be a good step, but this alone is not enough. According to Peltola,

Alienation is largely due to a real lack, for many people, of ways of affecting the social reality surrounding them. This is due in turn to lack of education, low economic status, perhaps also distance from centers of population, and the practical inadequacies of democracy. People have learned that voting alone is not enough to provide political influence, and they lack the experience, the daring and the information to try anything else. Furthermore, the channels of influence in remote areas are few and narrow. The causes of alienation will not disappear until our society is considerably more democratic than is at present the case.

The problem of comprehension, in news as in other messages, has often been seen as a purely linguistic one. According to this point of view, comprehension can be ensured by using easily understood and graphic language. This way of thinking, however, oversimplifies and trivializes the comprehension problem, since it pays no attention to the quality and 'degree of difficulty' of the content of the message as an 'idea whole'. It must be remembered that the simplicity of an idea – for instance of a news item – is not the same thing as the simplicity of the language in which it is described. Language usage must of course receive continual attention in news transmission, but this in itself is not enough; other means are also necessary to ensure comprehension of the message and simultaneously fulfillment of the purpose of news transmission.

News criteria

The other problem in news activity, which has been more in the foreground than comprehension, is the actual definition of news value and thus of news activity as a whole – the criteria by which news items are selected for transmission from the material available. News editing is specifically a process of selection, but the factors which determine this selection have not been very thoroughly examined either by news editors or by mass communication scientists. Thus the criteria applied have been based on the 'eye for news', the 'news instinct' or 'rule of thumb'; mainly unwritten rules, shaped by journalistic tradition, which have determined the order of importance and manner of presentation of news items.[4]

Now, however, it is becoming apparent everywhere that the old practice is no longer sufficient to guide present-day news transmission. The improvement of national and international communication and the acceleration of technological, economic and social development have placed the mass media in a new situation, in which their task and working criteria must be re-evaluated. This is so especially in the case of television news transmission, which at its birth stepped into the traditions shaped by the press and the radio, but which has turned out to be in many respects more effective than its predecessors. Newsmen are now asking more and more often what to tell and how to tell it. These problems are especially acute in the sphere of publicly controlled broadcasting companies, where attention must be paid to a balanced information diffusion. An ability to make quick decisions and an instinctive 'news eye' are no longer enough; what is needed is an analytic approach to news activity, based on broad information and on rational decisions, along with increasing technical skill.

Although the traditional news criteria do not exist as written rules, we can discover their character by examining how they work in practice. In order to understand their background, however, it is necessary to recall the conditions under which news diffusion had its origin: the history of news activity.

A survey of the history of news diffusion indicates that the news judgements of traditional journalism are based, on the one hand, on commercial factors – the courting of public favor – and, on the other hand, on deference to the conditions defined by the political decision-makers (a group which in practice includes a considerable proportion of the leaders of private business and public administration). This way of thinking measures success by

4. In the Program Activity Regulations of the Broadcasting Company, the term 'news value' is frequently used, but its content is never defined. The way of thinking described above is also followed in textbooks of journalism; e.g. Charnley (1966): '... the experienced newsman has his rules of thumb ...' and '... a fairly good idea of what makes a news ...' (p. 31). In some textbooks, a news item is actually defined according to what a person with such a 'news eye' considers news.

the yardstick of audience size and of the confidence felt in the news by both the public and by the political elite.

The unwritten 'journalistic ethic' resulting from these two main factors has, at its best, nevertheless produced news reports unpalatable either to commercial or to political leaders. The principles of these ethics include: strict adherence to facts, an attempt to bring out concrete social grievances which concern the reader, and a rapidity which serves to evade the censor. A journalist presenting sensitive facts has been able to act with the support of the audience and to lean on the income and prestige provided by a large public. An editor who applied these 'journalistic ethics' in their pure form, however, soon got into difficulties if his reports dug too deep; public popularity was then no longer able to save him from the pressure exerted by strong interest groups. Similar difficulties resulted if his reports, for one reason or another, were not to the public taste.

Demonstrations are in general a theoretically interesting news subject, in the handling of which the criteria discussed above appear with special emphasis. A demonstration is specifically a phenomenon originating outside the power center and it often particularly reflects the demand of a new influence group to make itself heard and obtain political power.

In general, the interests of the political decision-makers have been taken into consideration in two ways. First of all, they have had the use of 'official' information channels, by means of which they can reach the general public. Secondly, they have been offered news in which they themselves are interested. It is obvious that the news information transmitted by radio and television has specifically favored the uppermost social strata. This has been achieved, on the one hand, by selecting items of news which are significant to the decision-makers, but only rarely to the general public. Such 'official news' is represented, for example, by many of the announcements made by the government. Furthermore, the elite group has been unintentionally favored by presenting even news of general interest in concise and abstract language, so that a broad foundation of general information has been necessary for their comprehension (for instance 'official news' is of this nature). The man in the street has had to content himself with 'human interest' stories, which have not been of much practical use to him. Recent development, however, has been away from this situation toward greater consideration of the needs of the general public. These needs, however, have not been sufficiently taken into account in the manner of presentation; news presentation is 'institution-centered' rather than 'people-centered'. Thus, since the general audience does not comprehend the message, the 'people' are unaware of the details of decision-making. A partial reason for this is that even the news editors themselves, under pressure of routine, are unaware of these details.

The traditional news criteria are unconsciously learned and internalized in the process of practical editing work. This learning occurs on the basis of innumerable hints received from the working environment: the preconceived ideas of colleagues, telephone calls, letters from the public, criticism from influential and prestigious individuals, etc. Open pressure from pressure groups has hardly ever occurred; the criteria have evolved gradually and without remark, and continue to do so as new social forces continue to emerge with new political significance.

Guidelines for change

Underlying the ideas and suggestions contained in this report are two basic principles. The first of these is that news activity should be approached from two different points of view: that of the actual *news events* and the process of selection involved in the reporting of these events; and that of the news broadcast itself, i.e. the *means* which are used in transmitting these events to the audience. The first point of view includes the problem of news criteria, the second that of comprehension. The choice of news is naturally a primary question, linked with the goals of news activity as a whole. The manner of presentation is of secondary importance in so far as it is concerned with the means used in news work. In practice of course these means are often decisive, but we must remember that means always serve some end.

The second basic principle has to do with news criteria and objectives: it says that a distinction should be made between the 'objective' importance or significance of a piece of news, and the subjective interest felt in the news by listeners or viewers. Actual news criteria, by which news is determined, should according to this way of thinking be based primarily on the significance of an event, rather than on a consideration of *the interest aroused in the general public*. In choosing the means of presenting the news, on the other hand, the point of departure should be based on what is close to the audience and interesting to it. Only in this way can we ensure comprehension of the news. Evidently more background commentary and explanation of the current news is necessary, both in news broadcasts and in program output as a whole, than is the practice today. The purpose of such background material is specifically to link the frequently distant and abstract events reported in the news to the everyday reality of the world of the audience. In any case, the fact that news criteria are based on significance rather than on interest prevents news activity from slipping in the direction of triviality-oriented sensational journalism.

No report can give precise and unambiguous directions which would enable the news editor to make the 'absolutely right' decision. In this case the editor would again turn into an automaton, similar to the one shaped by the traditional news criteria. On the contrary, the news editor should be capable of independent thinking and should be aware as far as possible of the problems of news activity. The aim of this report is to indicate directions, rather than to come up with binding rules or instructions; these are best formulated by those responsible for practical news work.

The objectives of news activity

According to the Program Activity Regulations of the Finnish Broadcasting Company, the main general objective of broadcasting activity is

to offer a view of the world which is based on correct information and on facts, which changes as the world changes and as our knowledge of it increases, changes or becomes more perfect. The Broadcasting Company should not aim at implanting some particular world view in its audience, but rather at making available the building blocks necessary in the construction of a personal world view.

These general guidelines naturally concern all fields of program activity, including the news. The Regulations specifically touch upon news activity as follows: 'An important part of the Broadcasting Company's activity is the transmission of news and coverage of both cultural and social events.'

What distinguishes news activity from other programming is the fact that news programs and background commentaries on the news are concerned with events which have recently occurred or which have recently become of interest.

By a news item we mean a piece of information about an event which has recently occurred or has recently been brought up, which is of significance to the audience according to the news criteria. News criteria will be defined below.

A news item may concern an event which has recently occurred, or it may give information about an event of older date which has recently become of current interest.

In the case of raw news, recentness generally refers to the span of one day. Background commentary may treat events over a longer time-span.

News activity can be divided into two parts: raw news and background commentary. Raw news means the news item as such, without explanation or background. The background commentary goes more deeply into the topics brought up in the raw news.

Raw news

The function of the raw news is to supply the audience with informational raw material. This type of news generally contains short pieces of information about events and matters existing in the real world. The raw news functions more or less as an extension of our senses; it allows us to perceive things which would otherwise not be reached by our eyes, ears or other senses. Such information is necessary to the individual in his attempt to orient himself in the environment. Just as the information received by our senses in everyday life is not necessarily in any particular order, so the stream of information provided by the raw news does not necessarily form a meaningful whole.

For practical reasons it is useful to distinguish between concrete and abstract raw news. Concrete raw news does not include any difficult concept of a general nature which would have to be separately explained. Abstract news contains either one or more general concepts (e.g. 'family pension'), which the listeners cannot be assumed to understand without a special background commentary. But both concrete and abstract news items refer to some real event or sequence of events which has occurred uniquely at some point in space and in time. (Such an event or sequence of events is often called a singular phenomenon.) For example, a concrete news item may describe the fact that at a certain shipyard on a certain day a new vessel was launched, with such and such properties, which was given such and such a name. An abstract news item will be concerned, for instance, with the fact that on a particular day the cabinet of state presented a bill in parliament for the revision of the family pension plan.

Background commentary

The purpose of the background commentary is to analyse and organize the raw news material so as to make it readily comprehensible. Thus the commentary will explain the general concepts occurring in the raw news (e.g. family pension), so that their content becomes familiar, and will provide general background information. Commentary does not mean commitment to a particular point of view or side in an issue. Such commitment implies support for particular norms, which is not the function of background news commentary.

Thus the background commentary is based on that point in the program activity regulations, according to which the purpose of broadcasting is to offer a view of the world changes, without trying to implant any particular world view. This can briefly be called *intellectual activation*. Intellectual activation means arousing the individual to thinking about reality, about the world in which he lives. The aim is to mobilize the individual's thinking, so that he is able to construct his world picture on the basis of the factual information supplied to him every day; to prevent him from becoming ossified and rigid while the world around him is changing and our knowledge of it increasing. If we call the raw news material 'an extension of the senses', then background commentary can be compared to a switch which 'turns on' mental activity.

The background commentary must provide information which is important from the point of view of the individual's picture of the world, i.e. such information must be relevant to his overall conception of reality. The starting point is what the individual himself considers important, and the aim is to help him link the content of the raw news to his own view of the world. Information which activates the individual intellectually provides evidence of facts which the individual has ignored in his previous beliefs concerning reality, beliefs which are often called prejudices or stereotypes. If the individual receives information about a fact which does not fit in with his stereotyped, preconceived ideas, intellectual activation is possible and the result will probably be a more realistic stereotype. Thus news activity is intellectually activating with regard to the audience as a whole if it provides as much information as possible about such facts as are known to be unfamiliar or ignored among the public.

Service information

Weather, police and betting announcements, together with other such information of general usefulness, do not belong to news activity except in so far as they are possible sources of news items (according to normal news criteria). However, it is often most practical to broadcast such announcements within the framework of the news program. If the news broadcast has enough space, there is probably no particular reason to change the existing practice. It should be noted, however, that the inclusion of these announcements in news programs does not yet make news out of them, so that news criteria cannot be applied to them. The results of sport competitions and event should also be understood as service information.

Informational news criteria

As we have said, the objective of news activity is the transmission of valid information on a current basis, and the intellectual activation which is related to it. News material must be selected and transmitted to the audience according to criteria which enable us to achieve these objectives. By means of these criteria, the value of a given news item can be determined at least with respect to other news, together with the means which will give the best result within the framework of the news material of a given day.

The criteria applied in news activity aiming at these objectives cannot be limited to the transmission of information which is in harmony with some particular ideology or social theory. This would be a political news criterion. Nor can the news be restricted to what the audience wants to hear; the interest of the audience at a given time is determined by what people are accustomed to (or what has been given them before). This would represent a commercial news criterion. The primary criterion of news selection should be the extent to which the event described presumably affects the life of a large number of people, i.e. the extent of the effect of the event among the audience. In this case, we are applying an informational news criterion.[5]

In his elaborated conceptual analysis, based on the semantic information theory, Ahmavaara gives a logically exact formulation to the general objective of the FBC, as expressed in the Program Activity Regulations, e.g. the construction of a subjective world view and the consequences of an accumulation of new empirical evidence upon it. In this framework information is, by definition, understood as messages which are likely to change the world view of a recipient to one which is more realistic, i.e. more consistent with new evidence about the 'objective true world'. This necessarily leads to an emphasis on facts and opinions 'neglected' in the climate of public opinion, and furthermore to a kind of conflict between the medium and the public – this, after all, is essentially what the idea of opposition to (any kind of) conformism or hegemony implies.

The principle of an informational program policy – or of an informational press theory in general – can also be expressed as in the third part of the Long-Range Planning Report for the FBC:

The deliberate aim of informational broadcasting activity is to avoid the censorship which may follow as a consequence of the inclusion of ideological truths in programs. This does not mean that informational program activity should not include such ideological truths, but only that the *censorship* connected with them should be avoided. This can be achieved by allowing various ideological viewpoints to be brought forth within the framework of program activity as a whole, thus cancelling out the information barriers set by each of them. The principles of informational broadcasting activity are derived from the general concept of information, according to which various world views are seen as alternative hypotheses rather than as ideological truths. Only by

5. The informational news criteria described here are based on Ahmavaara (1969).

following this principle can broadcasting activity offer the public the greatest possible amount of the most accurate possible information, about the world around it. Informational broadcasting activity rests on the assumption of the greatest possible independence of all pressure and interest groups, including the state.

Criteria of news value

1. The external criterion. The importance of a news item is determined in the first place by the extent to which the event described influences the life of the listeners and viewers either directly or indirectly, regardless of whether or not the audience is itself aware of this effect.

Thus, for example, the news of negotiations between the ministers of industry of the four largest copper-producing countries in Peru is of considerable value; these four countries are developing countries, which by means of cooperation may be able to free themselves from the tutelage of the industrial nations and reach a stable economic position. Furthermore, copper is of strategic importance; it is therefore possible that the industrial nations will not willingly give up their advantage, and crises will occur the true nature of which will perhaps not be revealed. For all these reasons, the news of the negotiations is important and concerns indirectly also the Finnish public, which, however, cannot be expected to realize the significance of the meeting.

According to this criterion, statistical information which describes in a significant way an occurring process of development may also have news value.

The external criterion should nevertheless not be applied so rigidly that news items providing a general informational background for the audience are eliminated. Such a background is continually necessary, both for domestic and for international news. In this case such events also have news value which perhaps do not concern a Finnish audience even indirectly, but which are part of a general trend of development which is related to various issues and which it is useful to understand.

2. The criterion of generality. A news item must have general significance. This means that it must concern as large a part as possible of the audience which is following the news broadcast. According to this criterion, news of an event which affects the lives of only a few individuals is not particularly valuable. For example, publicizing the names of the people who died when a private house burnt down is not appropriate, unless they happened to be especially prominent individuals.

This criterion should also not be applied so rigidly that it excludes the possibility of transmitting information to minority groups which are especially dependent on the radio news broadcasts for their information; this is particularly the case with the blind.

Reliability, balance, speed

Raw news should be based on the application of these two criteria. In addition, however, the general requirements, applicable to all news activity, those of reliability, balance (neutrality, impartiality) and speed, should also be applied.

Reliability means that individual items of information should be checked whenever possible. In general this can be done with all domestic news. From abroad, however, information is often obtained which is uncertain, in the sense that only the agency supplying the information is responsible for its content. In making such information public the uncertainty involved should always be made clear, not merely by mentioning the initials of the news agency responsible, which are often meaningless to the audience, but in some more explicit manner.

Reliability is closely related to balance in so far as it is often difficult to achieve a reliable picture of an event unless many different points of view are taken into account. Over a period of time a number of different interpretations of an event or issue should be presented, as far as they are available. This places great demands on the editors' ability and on their desire to be as objective as possible. However, since no one individual can be completely objective, even if he makes a sincere effort to be so, many different ways of thinking should be represented on the editorial board. Only this can guarantee balance in the long run.

The most important thing is not to strive toward objectivity in the short run, toward a state of affairs in which every single news item is the Truth. This is not possible. If the partiality, onesidedness, subjectivity and unreliability of each item of news were to be accepted as the starting point, it would be possible to assure impartiality in the long run.

It is thus not advisable to seek after the most reliable source of news and the most objective editor. There is no such thing. All possible sources of news ought to be used and the editorial offices should be staffed with editors who differ from each other in as many ways as possible in subjectivity, philosophy of life and partiality. In this way something essential can be reached by means of the rules concerning demands for impartiality, listening to the other side, similar treatment of parties, verification of information and so on.

Speed is an essential part of news activity. It is important that news information be transmitted to the audience without delay. This nevertheless does not mean that speed should be used as an excuse for inaccurate reporting, superficial commentary or outright errors. In particular, there is no need for the FBC to compete with itself in speed, even if it does compete with other news media.

Criteria of background commentary

In the case of background commentary, additional criteria must be applied, which we can call internal criteria. Since the point of departure of the commentary is the raw news, the external and general criteria are taken into consideration indirectly.

The internal news criterion means that the news value of an item is determined by the significance attached to it by the receiver himself. The purpose of the background commentary thus is to explain the content of a news item to the listener in such a way that he comes to perceive its relevance to his own life. This is simultaneously intellectual activation, which is the actual function of the background commentary.

Conclusions

On the basis of the criteria defined above, part of present-day news material should be treated differently. Such material concerns, for example, crimes, accidents, beauty contests, royal weddings and sports. This kind of news rarely has any relevance as such to the life of the audience or to intellectual activation, unless they reach significantly high proportions or unless they are treated in such a way as to bring out their general significance or lack of it. These news items are also typical of news selected on the basis of traditional (commercial) news criteria, i.e. giving the public what it wants to hear and what it has been made used to wanting.

The use of this kind of material is usually defended by saying that it also gets people to follow more important news. However, there is equal reason to say that the use of such material attracts the interest of the audience away from more important issues to trivialities. Therefore there is reason to exclude these items from news broadcasts. The possible decrease in audience size caused by the elimination of this kind of 'selling' material can be prevented by increasing the interest of more important issues through background commentary. Furthermore, it has been shown that the following of news broadcasts does not depend exclusively on their contents (see studies on alienation and comprehension already noted).

While the news value of crime and accident news and other such material will decrease considerably compared to present practice if informational criteria are applied, this does not mean that such material cannot be used at all. The news value sufficient for publication varies considerably from day to day. Furthermore, we must remember that the news value of an item can be appreciably affected by the way in which it is treated. Thus, for example, an accident report in which attention is drawn primarily to the general causes of accidents and possibilities of eliminating these may contribute significantly to avoidance of accidents in the future.

References

AHMAVAARA (1969), *Informaaties* (*Information: A Study in the Logic of Communication*), Tapiola (in Finland).

CHARNLEY, M. V. (1966), *Reporting*, 2nd edn, Holt, Rinehart and Winston.

LITTUNEN, A. A., and NORDENSTRENG, K. (1971), 'Informative communication policy: the Finnish experiment', paper presented at the International Symposium on New Frontiers of Television, Bled, Jugoslavia.

NORDENSTRENG, K. (1968), 'Communication, research in the United States: a critical perspective', *Gazette*, vol. 14, no. 3, pp. 207–16.

NORDENSTRENG, K. (1971), *Internat. Stud. Broadcasting*, NHK, Tokyo.

19 Stuart Hood

The Politics of Television

Published for the first time in this volume

Television is an industry. A studio complex is an electronic factory for the manufacture of programmes, which are commonly called the product. It is an industry to which the normal techniques of management are applied. Productivity is important. Cost accounting is applied to programme-making as it is to the making of cars. Management processes are computerized. The programmes themselves are commodities in Marx's sense of the word. Their value to the producing companies can be quantified in various ways. Like any other commodity they have a price and are bought and sold. Their effectiveness can be measured statistically by audience ratings. It is from the ratings that the advertisers calculate the notional figure of the cost of each commercial per thousand viewers. In commercial television the concept of the cost per thousand is crucial; in the BBC the concept of the cost per thousand is not officially used, but the ratio of audience size to the cash and resources required to mount a programme or series of programmes plays a by no means negligible role in the scheduling decisions. What distinguishes the television industry from most other industries is the fact that each piece of product is the result of creative effort of some kind and on some level by a team of programme-makers and technicians; this gives rise to certain tensions between management efficiency and programme standards, between profitability and excellence. It is an industry whose product is used by almost every household in Britain. It provides their main source of news and entertainment. Theories as to its effect on this mass audience vary. There are those who believe that television washes over viewers, doing little more than confirm them in their existing prejudices. Others see in it a source of moral corruption on the one hand or of alienation on the other. Politicians and governments, however, believe it to be an important medium capable of influencing public opinion and swaying voters. Television is an industry that operates under government licence.

The politics of television in one obvious sense deals with the relationship of the television industry and the organizations which control it – the BBC and the ITA – to government. Both organizations are allowed to function as broadcasters by virtue of a licence issued by the Postmaster General (as he was when the last licence was granted) under the terms of the Wireless Telegraphy Act 1949 and the Telegraph Act 1869. By granting these licences the government permits the existence of a television monopoly in the field of public-service broadcasting as it does in that of commercial television. The industry is further controlled in that it is not free to produce only the most popular or the most profitable programmes which, in the case of commercial television, is a tautology. Commercial television in Britain – the fifteen contracting companies which constitute ITV – is controlled in this respect by the Television Act 1964 which, reinforcing the Television Act 1954 whereby commercial television was established, imposes certain conditions as to what may or may not be broadcast. These conditions the Independent Television Authority is charged with enforcing. The most important stipulations are that the Authority, as licensee, must provide 'television broadcasting services as a public service for disseminating information, education and entertainment'; that it must ensure that the programmes 'Maintain a high standard in all respects . . . and a proper balance and wide range in their subject matter'; and that the programmes shall include nothing which 'offends against good taste or decency or is likely to encourage or incite to crime or lead to disorder or be offensive to public feeling'. The latter is a very wide clause which begs a number of important questions as to who determines what is decent and in good taste, what the homogeneous entity called 'public feeling' is, and how it is identified except as a hypothesis in the minds of the officials who apply the terms of the Act to ITV programming. The ITA is further instructed to ensure that 'due impartiality' is observed 'as respects matters of political or industrial controversy or relating to current public policy'. The BBC, for its part, is bound by a phrase in its Charter which defines its aims as a broadcasting organization as being to provide information, education and entertainment, by the terms of its licence and agreement with the Postmaster General, and, in a more gentlemanly way, by various undertakings giving in writing to previous postmasters general that the Corporation will observe impartiality in political matters.

Both the Television Act and the licence and agreement contain two important reserve powers. By the first the broadcasting organizations may at any time be required to broadcast at the request of any Minister of the Crown an announcement which it appears necessary in his judgement to disseminate in this way. The second lays down that the Postmaster General may, at any time, by notice in writing require the broadcasting organizations 'to refrain from broadcasting any matter or classes of matter' defined by the Minister. The first power was frequently used during the war for official announcements on such matters as rationing changes and continued to be exercised in this way after the war so long as rationing continued. It also covers ministerial broadcasts, which the government in power requests, and to which, if it considered them controversial, the BBC used to invite an Opposition spokesman to reply; the Opposition now has a mandatory right of reply. The second of these powers is usually dismissed by the broadcasters as theoretical in the sense that (so it is argued) its exercise would postulate the complete breakdown of communication and understanding between the broadcasting organizations and the government. The fact is that precisely because of this understanding it has never proved necessary to use it. That the government of the day should wish to exercise such controls over the broadcasters is not surprising; what is surprising is that the control is not acknowledged. Thus the system of licensing and control to which both the BBC and ITA are subject is generally rationalized on the grounds that the broadcasters are being given a scarce national resource – part of the spectrum of radio frequencies on which to broadcast signals in sound and vision – and must therefore be subject to constraints. It is looked upon as the price the industry pays for its monopolistic privileges. Looked at from another point of view, this system is the method whereby government keeps a hold over the most persuasive of the mass media.

The concept of television as a controlled industry determines the structure of the commercial network. While the licence to broadcast is granted to the ITA, the Authority in turn grants contracts to make programmes to fifteen individual companies which thereby acquire a franchise to broadcast to a specific area for a period to which the Television Act sets a term of six years. The Authority has vested in it the absolute right, in the event of any breach of contract, to determine or suspend it without compensation. In the seventeen years since commercial television began in Britain the right has never been used. In this respect it might be said to be in the same state of desuetude as the government's right to censor the BBC and ITA by forbidding the broadcasting of certain classes of material. Both sanctions are real; neither has been exercised, the difference being that in the case of commercial television the ITA has never, in spite of what many critics consider to have been ample grounds, even threatened to do so. What did happen was that, when the contracts last came up for revision, one was not renewed for reasons which were not made public; another company was spared the indignity of cancellation and edged into a merger. Even this somewhat shamefaced method of using the ITA's powers was sufficient to confirm the businessmen who run and control ITV in their view that television is a high-risk industry, in which there is no certain prospect of being allowed to derive profits in perpetuity – which is what they would wish to see and believed had tacitly been accepted by an Authority more concerned to defend the contractors from criticism than to act as public watch-dog. It is, also, indisputably a high cost industry. The electronic equipment required for an electronic factory for the manufacture of programmes is expensive; programme costs, often inflated, by show-business values, are – or can be – high. The amortization of the equipment within the duration of a contract which, theoretically, may not be renewed is seen as a financial risk. But these are risks only when considered alongside their ideal for the television industry which has been described as requiring, in its purest form, only a telecine machine for showing films and a cash register to clock up the advertising revenue. In spite of complaints of the businessmen that they are hampered in their operations and unable to run their businesses on *laissez-faire* lines, it is significant that when bids were called for for the contracts in 1968, merchant bankers, newspaper proprietors, cooperative societies and a large variety of other business interests, were eager to be given the opportunity of making what seemed to them a reasonable and predictable profit from television. The fact that it is unlikely that there will now be any large-scale inquiry into the structure of the industry before the contracts, prolonged a couple of years to be co-terminous with the BBC's Charter, come to an end in 1976, and therefore unlikely to be any major changes in its working, has done a good deal to allay their misgivings. What is more significant still is that there is every reason to believe that the Commission set up by the Labour government at a late date to examine the broadcasting organizations was an electoral manoeuvre and that neither party's leadership saw much to criticize in either structure or functioning of the television industry.

Cash is a strong and important nexus between broadcasting organizations and government. The revenue of the BBC derives from the sale to the public of television licences, which are collected by the Post Office and handed over to the Corporation under the terms of the licence and agreement, the costs of collection being first deducted. This has not always been the arrangement. During the war the BBC depended on a government grant-in-aid, the licence fee being restored only after the end of hostilities. When the system of licence revenue was renewed the Treasury made it subject to deductions which between January 1947 and March 1960 amounted to nearly £28 million. The deductions were stopped only in 1961. The fact that the whole of the revenue is handed over to the BBC and that the BBC is empowered to spend its income 'according to its own judgement in forwarding its approved policies' is the basis of the BBC's claim to editorial and institutional independence. It is true that there is no control by Parliament on how the money is spent, which would, in practice – as happens in Canada, for instance – mean direct parliamentary control of programme content; but the money is voted by Parliament in the annual broadcasting vote. It is absurd to suppose, as the BBC officials sometimes suggest, that the money flows directly and, as it were, uncontaminated by government, from the viewer to the BBC. It is, in fact, given by Parliament to the BBC. Moreover the size of the licence fee itself is decided by the government from time to time. It is when the BBC asks for the licence fee to be increased or is in a deficit situation that the Corporation becomes vulnerable financially and politically. A deficit situation is one that the BBC has sometimes been tempted to exploit – as it did when it took on BBC-2 – on the assumption that the government will have to step in and save it; it is a dangerous exercise in blackmail, which, if successful, risks antagonizing the politicians. Their retaliatory weapon is to delay the required increase in licence fee so that its effect is reduced. They judge and judge rightly that such a situation will make the BBC anxious not to offend. Conversely it is no accident that the period when the BBC was most adventurous editorially was when the graph of licences was rising steadily at the rate of a million a year and a parallel graph of increasing revenue could be projected into the future. These graphs have now levelled out. The recent increase in the licence fee – a belated one – and the rise in the number of colour licences have lifted it temporarily; but even if the sales of colour sets reach the projected figure of six million, nearly a third of the total number of sets, by 1975, the increment will not in itself be enough to meet rising costs and inflation. The BBC will continue to be vulnerable. The trend towards conformity in programming and editorial policy is one expression of that vulnerability. So too is the pursuit of ratings, which is justified in the following terms: if the BBC is in financial difficulties and wishes to press the government for an increase in the licence fee, the Corporation must be able to demonstrate that it has a considerable share of the audience. If, it is argued, the ratio of BBC:ITV ratings were consistently 30:70 or lower (which is roughly what it was when the full impact of ITV's competition first made itself felt), then the BBC's enemies in the House of Commons of whom there are a number on both sides – enemies of public corporations, members who feel they have been slighted in some way, members who feel the BBC to be too strong and arrogant – would be able to urge that a broadcasting organization which was unable to attract a larger share of the audience should not be given more funds. It is an argument firmly based on expediency on both sides. What is important is that the pursuit of ratings, first seen as a tactical weapon, becomes an end in itself. Ratings are an example of the way in which quantification allows discussions to be diverted from less easily definable but more important issues such as the social and psychological effect of programmes.

Commercial television is also dependent on the goodwill of the government in financial matters. In 1964 a Conservative government imposed a levy on advertising revenue – a step best construed as some sort of act of conscience to set against the undisguised exploitation of a commercial monopoly which had marked the early days of ITV. In spite of the levy profits before tax were running around the £18 million mark up to 1968. In 1969, however, they fell to just over £9 million and in 1970 were down to £5 million. The decline was due to a drop in the volume of advertising which in 1970 earned £94·6 million – the lowest figure for three years. This was, in part, a reflection of the general economic situation, in part the result of the BBC's pursuit of the ratings. The fall in advertising revenue and the impact of the levy, which reached a peak of over £25 million in 1969, were used by the contractors to justify an economy drive in which programme expenditure was one of the first items to be cut back and from which it will take the industry some time to recover. The Conservative government responded to the outcry of the commercial lobby, which was strongly supported by the ITA and the levy was reduced; ITV's profits will rise in 1971 by £6·5 million. There is, however, no guarantee, for none was exacted by government or ITA, that the extra money will be spent on programmes. The levy may not have been planned as such but it is, in fact, an important regulatory device. When the ITA and the commercial companies are financially dependent on government they are no more anxious than is the BBC in similar circumstances to give political offence.

The facts concerning the controls that may be and are exercised over the broadcasting organizations by government, one way or the other, are not in dispute; they are worth restating chiefly because the official ideologies of both BBC and ITA lay claim to a degree of independence not borne out by the realities of the situation. Of the two, the BBC's ideology – sometimes called the

BBC ethos – is the more coherent; a great many people have been working on it for a very long time and it has itself been subsumed into the national ideology along with the monarchy, the parliamentary system and the Anglican Church. It is also the more important of the two because it is an ideology which has been evolved to support and provide a rationale for the operations of a very large corporate body which combines (as the ITA does not) three diverse functions: control of the means of communication from studios to transmitters, policy-making and the making of programmes. The ideology of the ITA is a curious mixture but it is also an accurate reflection of the nature of the system it operates, being based on the proposition that the pursuit of profit is the best incentive for making good television programmes in the public interest. The concept of public service is written into the Television Act; but it is a concept which plays a subordinate role, whereas it is one of the main components of the BBC ethos. Official BBC statements on the nature of public-service broadcasting merely express the truism that the BBC is not a profit-making organization and that those who run it need not let considerations of profitability influence their technical or editorial decisions. They go on to assert that the programmes provided by the BBC are different in character from those of its competitors, being more consciously designed to be of social, political or cultural benefit to the public. Such statements are true in so far as the concept of the cost per thousand, while not absent from the minds of the men who run BBC television, is not as critical as it is in a commercial company. BBC television can therefore afford – both literally and metaphorically – to transmit minority programmes which a commercial company, for reasons that the ITA understands and approves, could not consider putting in its schedules. But since the bulk of those programmes which the BBC aims at a majority audience are indistinguishable from those put out by ITV, the concept of public service cannot merely mean that the Corporation caters for a slightly wider scatter of minority tastes than its competitor. The question arises what service beyond the provision of these minority programmes the BBC provides for the public and, similarly, what service the ITA causes the programme contractors to provide in that sector of their programmes which may be said to have a public-service element. Central to the concept of public service in both cases is impartiality in the presentation of news and current affairs. Impartiality, as we have seen, is laid upon the ITA by the terms of the Television Act; it is a duty the BBC has accepted. The doctrine of impartiality is one of the fundamentals of the BBC's ideology, which – at its most naive – depicts the BBC as a system of extreme sensitivity, responding to political and commercial pressures (e.g. by the motor industry), but balancing them scrupulously and offering, in the words of the chief assistant to the Director General, whose task it is to deal with these pressures at the highest level, 'a convenient machinery for complaint and representation' and providing redress as required. Internally, he added, there is a system for observing 'any developing imbalance . . . at an early stage' and putting it right 'before representations are made'. The picture is one of a marvellous self-regulating mechanism wound up by Lord Reith, its great first mover, and working smoothly, effortlessly ever since, like the universe of the Deists. 'No system,' he concludes

can ensure good broadcasting. The public service system, however, creates conditions in which there are fewer obstacles to good programmes than any other (Crawley, 1971).

This Panglossian view of the BBC and its workings is not shared by those who work in its political and current affairs programmes where the true mechanisms of political pressure – as for instance over Ulster – can be seen operating openly and effectively.

The concept in its ideal form, as formulated above, is that of the BBC as an organization mediating between the political parties and the public and, in particular, between the government and the public. How this role came to be established can best be understood historically. It was at the time of the general strike of 1926 that the BBC's function as a mediator was first defined. Reith had contrived to avert the commandeering of the BBC under the emergency regulations – a step for which Churchill, then Chancellor of the Exchequer in the Baldwin government and advocate of strong measures to break the strike, had been pressing. As a result of being exempted from direct government control the Corporation was, in Reith's words, able 'to give our listeners impartial news of the situation to the best of our ability'. It was the way in which it functioned during the general strike that established the BBC's importance as a source of news. There were no newspapers except Churchill's government-produced sheet. Loudspeakers were set up in public places and people gathered to hear the news. This was indeed a public service. But why did Reith want to provide it and feel that the BBC had a duty to do so? Some light is thrown on his concept of impartiality by the fact, recorded by Asa Briggs in his history of the BBC, that there was a good deal of talk privately at the time of the BBC as 'an organization within the constitution'. This is not a doctrine that has ever been publicly affirmed but it has had a strong influence on BBC thinking. It does much to explain the terms of an astonishingly honest letter sent to his departmental heads once the strike was over. In it he argues that had the BBC supressed news of

any unfortunate situation arising it might only have led to the panic of ignorance . . . But, on the other hand, since the BBC was a national institution, and since the government in this crisis was acting for the people, apart from any emergency powers or clause in our licence, the BBC was for the government in the crisis too; and that we had to assist in maintaining the essential services of the country, the preservation of law and order, and of life and liberty of the individual and of the community.

The document is of great interest. It is first, but not most importantly, an early instance of that distinction between the trade unions and 'the people' which has become one of the commonplaces of broadcast news and comment and has passed over from radio to television. More significantly it is an example of that double game which Gorz has described as the pretence of keeping a balance between a bourgeoisie which is in power and a working class which is not and, as such, a textbook example of mystification (Gorz, 1967). Reith is exceptional in the honesty and accuracy of his description of impartiality; the dubious nature of which is not usually made so explicit. Once again the facts of the case are not surprising; what is surprising is the degree to which the BBC's ideology, in which impartiality plays so large a part, as it does by extension in that of the ITA and its news service, ITN, has come to be accepted at its face value. An important factor leading to the acceptance of the BBC's view of itself was its role in wartime, when it became the main source of news for the nation and was remarkable for its accuracy. Impartiality in wartime was all the easier to achieve because of the strong pressures towards national unity which Churchill and the government interpreted as meaning that any discussion of – far less controversy about – the conduct of the war, or indeed the nature of the peace that would follow it, should be avoided. The BBC fell in with this restrictive view to the extent best illustrated by its handling of the Beveridge Report (see Briggs, 1970). The terms of the report were given in news bulletins (the compilers were rebuked, however, for making a comparison between the cost of Beveridge's proposals and that of the war) but they were not commented on or discussed on the air except in transmissions to the troops abroad, to Germany and the United States: all for obvious propaganda purposes. The governors of the BBC in an astonishing example of weakness – or perhaps of recognition of their true situation – refused to allow Beveridge to give a talk on his scheme unless the government approved the script in detail. Beveridge refused in these circumstances and no talk was broadcast. In the immediate post-war period which saw television transmissions resumed, the concepts of wartime broadcasting still dominated much of the BBC's thinking on the handling of news and current affairs. This was a time when, in certain BBC departments, impartiality was tacitly defined as the acceptance of a Conservative line in politics. It is rarely defined in such philistine terms today. The definition, in fact, has varied according to the security of the Corporation which depended on its financial situation. In general, impartiality (so far as it affects the political parties) has for long been taken to mean that the party in power, as the natural initiator of policy and fount of news, will be favoured in news coverage; Cabinet Ministers, for example, will naturally enjoy more coverage than members of the Shadow Cabinet. This editorial decision, it is accepted, is bound to cause annoyance and resentment in the Opposition, which can expect, however, to be shown the same impartiality when it comes to power. It is a policy which, in the end, antagonizes both parties; the political intervention which ended the Greene regime and the appointment of an ex-Cabinet Minister as chairman of the BBC can be taken as a sign of the politicians' displeasure. The Corporation – like the ITA – runs least risk of annoying politicians when it interprets impartiality to be the duty to reflect that middle-of-the-road consensus in political matters which is spanned by the two-party system and acceptable to the whips on either side. Greene's mistake was to believe in the ideology of the BBC and to act as if it were a true reflection of the place and power of the BBC in the political and social structure of this country.

Fundamental to the concept of impartiality is the assertion that newscasts are objective and neutral. There are certainly a number of news stories of which it can be said that they are objective in that they report facts or incidents which can be verified. Similarly it can be demonstrated whether the reporting of a speech or a statement is accurate or not. But accuracy is not in itself proof of objectivity or neutrality. A news bulletin is the result of a number of choices by a variety of 'gatekeepers'. They include the editor who decides on the day's coverage, on the organizer who briefs the camera crews and reporters and allocates the assignments, the film editor who selects the film to be included in the bulletin, the copytaster who chooses the stories from the tape to accompany the film, the sub-editor who writes the story and the duty editor who supervises the compilation of the bulletin, fixes the running order of the stories and gives it its final shape. Each of the gatekeepers accepts or rejects material according to criteria which obviously, under no system, can be based on individual whim but are determined by a number of factors which include his class background, his upbringing and education, his attitude towards the political and social structure of the country. More specifically his judgements are determined by what he believes to be possible, tolerated and approved by the organization for which he works. It is noteworthy that the television news organizations do not lay down in writing – or do so only on very rare occasions usually concerning 'taste' – what may or may not be included in a bulletin. It is something that the new sub-editor joining the organization learns empirically by seeing what is permitted and what is not and, more indirectly, by absorbing the traditional wisdom of the organization, which he learns from the conversation, comments, anecdotes and reactions of his fellow-workers. He will find that changes in line can occur from time to time. They originate with the editor who is part of the upper management of the organization and is himself, by the nature of his position, required to receive, understand and apply the collective view of his peers and superiors as to what is permissible and what is not. A good and effective editor will be one who is, by his social and political outlook, in tune with the organization, so that his judgements coincide with the collective judgements of the upper management or, to put it in another way, who is able to persuade that management that any changes he wishes to make are a logical extension of accepted positions. Such changes are more likely to be concerned with the general tone of newscasts than with the details of political content. Thus there have been quite sharp changes in the editorial policy of the BBC, which moved from a posture of extreme conservatism and a period when royal stories automatically led the bulletin to a more popular stance and accent adopted as a result of the more demotic idiom of ITN. Successive editors have nudged television news slightly in one direction or another; for instance, ITN has moved (in terms of taste and manner of presentation) towards the BBC's position, while the BBC has moved from a situation near the opposite pole towards a more central one. But the political line of both organizations has remained the same. In practice it is the expression of a middle-class consensus politics, which continues that tradition of impartiality on the side of the establishment so clearly defined by Reith. Impartiality is impartiality within bounds and is applied to those parties and organizations which occupy the middle ground of politics; where impartiality breaks down is when the news deals with political activities or industrial action which are seen as being a breach of the conventions of the consensus. A demonstration of how this happens was provided by the evidence collected in January 1971 as a result of a monitoring exercise carried out by the ACTT, the film and television union. News bulletins in both radio and television, BBC and ITN, were monitored for the week straddling the TUC's demonstration against the Industrial Relations Bill on 12 January; texts were recorded and analysed in terms of content and language. The decision to do so was prompted by the coverage given by the media to the earlier strike against the Bill on 8 December 1970 and, before that, of the power workers' go-slow. In the latter case, in particular, there was a strong feeling in trade-union circles, that newscasts had been used to produce an emotional bias against the workers by concentrating on interviews with doctors who used dialysis machines, incubators and other electrical equipment. The efforts made by the union to avert such difficulties, and the failure of hospital managements to react effectively to the prior warnings they received, were less prominently featured. The outcome of the monitoring, which has since been published, was to show that there was bias in both the language used and in the handling of particular interviews and news items, stronger in BBC bulletins than in ITN's, but demonstrable and pervasive in both. 'militants' attempt to cripple industry has been something of a flop,' said one BBC news summary. 'Fifteen thousand workers took the day off,' said another story in terms which deny any political motivation to the strikers. But the overwhelmingly middle-class protest demonstration against the proposal to site London's third airport at Cublington was described as 'quite incredible' and 'a vast demonstration'. The analysis of the week's coverage confirmed the feeling of many trade unionists that the reporting of industrial disputes is frequently biased, the issues being misrepresented or simply not understood, and the men's case – particularly in unofficial disputes – allowed to go by default. The result is scepticism about the credibility of what they see on the screen and hostility towards television crews when they attempt to cover certain disputes. The bias which trade unionists detect is not to be explained by some conspiratorial theory nor by the assumption that directives must exist which lay down a particular attitude towards industrial matters. The narrow social range from which the staff of television organizations are drawn and the immense pressures the organizations – among them are job security, team spirit, indoctrination with the ethos of the working group – are sufficient to ensure that the ground rules of consensus politics are not broken.

When the rules are broken, consciously or unconsciously, the self-regulating machinery, of which the chief assistant to the Director General of the BBC writes, takes over. Sometimes, as he rightly says, corrections are made internally before any external pressures are applied, although the latter are real and frequently exercised. However, this varies from case to case, for the machinery is nowhere defined and procedures in general are not highly formalized. Pressures may come from a number of sources frequently mediated by members of the Boards of Governors of the BBC or ITA, who are in general selected from a safe list of distinguished representatives of the political consensus; or they may come from the members of the advisory councils which serve both the BBC and the ITA. They may come in the shape of letters or telephone calls directed to the top executives of the BBC, the ITA or the commercial companies. They may be formulated in articles by the press. (It is worth remarking that because there is no sponsorship in British commercial television and because advertising spots are not linked to specific programmes, pressures from advertisers, which exist, are not directly political but concerned to prevent programmes that might tarnish their brand images.) Government departments, as might be expected, are quick to protest if they believe that their policies have been misrepresented or, in their view, unfairly criticized; so, too, are the organizations of the establishment such as the police, the Confederation of British Industry, professional bodies, the armed forces, the churches – although the last of these enjoys a special position in broadcasting in that defined periods are set aside for religious broadcasting of what is called 'mid-stream Christianity' and, through the Central Religious Advisory Council (the first advisory committee to be set up in 1925), which services both the BBC and the ITA, exerts a continuing supervisory check on programmes. The quickest reflexes, however, are naturally those of the political parties whose complaints are frequently dealt with by the chief whips; it is significant that an ex-chief whip from the Labour Party is the present Chairman of the ITA, the appointment being an example of how the broadcasting organizations can be used as part of the political spoils system. The whips deal directly with the Director General's offices at the BBC or the ITA, the latter then taking the complaint up with the company involved in the programme about which the complaint has been laid. The relationship of the broadcasters to whips is formalized at election times when the broadcasting organizations hand over to them the power to decide how much time shall be allotted on either channel for party political broadcasts. This procedure is generally explained as a demonstration of their complete impartiality; it is, however, a procedure which effectively prevents minority views from appearing on the screen – a result which the BBC can then shrug off as being not of its making. At election times the whips are vigilant to detect any suspected imbalance in the reporting of the election campaign and, by their refusal or consent, to dictate which politicians appear on the screen, in what context and with what opponents; they thus effectively use their pressure to determine what type of programme the BBC and the commercial companies are allowed to mount and the public to see. At other times they keep programmes like *Panorama*, *Twenty-Four Hours* or *This Week* under close scrutiny and have at various times taken exception to the appearance on the air of what they conceive to be extremists or untypical representatives from within their own parties or have prevented public debates on specific subjects by refusing to match their opponent by a politician of, as it were, his own weight. This tactic can have the effect of preventing the item from going on the air. The pressures the broadcasting organizations have to deal with are therefore frequent and effective. What is curious is that the trade-union movement and, in particular the TUC, has not yet learned that the broadcasters can be effectively pressurized; a high official in the trade union movement has been heard to express the view that because the BBC is independent it might not be proper to exert such pressures. What the TUC and the individual unions have yet to learn is how to apply them at both national and local levels.

The occasions when the broadcasting organizations acknowledge pressure from bodies of opinion outside the conventional spectrum are rare. This fact lends a certain significance to the decision of the ITA to deal officially with the pressure group headed by Mrs Mary Whitehouse, which is best described as representing a brand of right-wing populism. It is true that the decision to do so and to listen to her representations was probably a tactical move designed to deflect her by a gesture – one which the BBC has not followed although Lord Hill, who was chairman of the ITA at the time is now in the corresponding position at the BBC – but the occasion is perhaps an indication of the direction in which respectable public opinion may be extended in the future. What the BBC did was to invite Mrs Whitehouse to appear on *Talkback*, a programme conceived and managed, as are most viewer participation programmes, to prevent a true dialogue between the Corporation's officials and members of the public, and a true example of technical and psychological manipulation. Appearance on the programme under conditions which are closely controlled by the BBC through the placing of the microphones, the dominance of the chairman and the intervention of the studio director in switching cameras and sound, does very little to satisfy the complainants but perhaps gives to some of the viewers an illusion of public debate. As for the multitude of other groups, minorities and local interests up and down the country, some of them are represented in theory at least on the advisory bodies, both regional and national, of which both the BBC and the ITA have a large number. These councils are the gesture the organizations make to accountability to the community. Like the board of governors they are chosen from a restricted section of the community in terms of social provenance, interests and age. It is the broadcasting organizations themselves who pick the members to serve on the councils; they have no representative, no constituencies, and no responsibilities; it follows that their influence is minimal.

Pressures must exist in any society, for no society is without an element of pluralism in its constitution; what is wrong with the present situation is that the range of bodies with access to the levers of the machinery is so restricted and that bodies which are located socially, politically or philosophically outside a well-defined range of opinion find it so difficult to make their influence felt. It is not, however, a point over which it is possible or necessary to be sentimental; it is of the nature of most societies, and certainly of any society that we can envisage, short of some utopia, that there are those who have access to and those who are excluded from the means of mass communication. Thus, at one time, the BBC made the editorial decision that British Fascism should not be provided with a platform in the mass media of broadcasting, nor should the proponents of racial discrimination; at the same time it was held that, at the other end of the spectrum, communists were outside the accepted political consensus. The question which has not yet been posed in practical terms is how the BBC or the ITA would behave in two situations which might be distinct from each other or might be connected: one is the case of a swing to the right in domestic politics, the other is that of a swing to the left which threatened to upset the balance of powers implicit in the binary parliamentary system. The Reithian concept of the BBC as 'an organization within the constitution' (a position the ITA would no doubt share) or a more recent formulation (never officially recognized) which defines the BBC as 'the national instrument of broadcasting', must lead to the suspicion that in a major political crisis the broadcasting organizations will be seen to have and to exercise considerably less impartiality than that to which they pretend.

The basis for their claim to independence derives from the concept of journalism – it is as publishers of pictures and spoken material in the realm of journalism that the BBC and the ITA are most often subject to pressure – as a fourth estate expressing that 'middle opinion in the mind of the nation' of which Delane considered himself to be the exponent. 'If there is one lesson more than another which the late administration has bequeathed to its successors,' he wrote in 1846, 'it is that it is not in the power of any one party to dictate the policy of the country. In fact the country will govern itself.' Delane saw his function as that of the spokesman of this *spiritus rector*, this governing opinion of the nation, and as such was prepared to hold the ring for the leaders of the two contending but similarly motivated parties. It is a concept of the role of journalists which Reith, consciously or unconsciously, took over in the founding period of the BBC and which has been handed down from his day. It rests, however, upon a false analogy between circumstances in which a newspaper editor works and those imposed upon the editor-in-chief (as some director generals have called themselves) of the BBC, for the BBC does not enjoy – nor for that matter does the ITA – that real degree of independence which Delane and *The Times* could claim (and contemporary newspapers also do) as organs of opinion not subject to legislation or to self-imposed canons of impartiality.

There are within the BBC and the commercial companies men and women who, from time to time, act as if the claims to independence were true; but in the event of a real clash with the political parties or with any of the pressure groups which the broadcasting organizations think it advisable to appease, they will be faced with the need to compromise, to provide balance or to suppress. It is a situation which they are essentially powerless to influence or to alter. Their impotence derives from the internal structures of the bodies for which they work. These vary greatly as between the individual programme companies and between the programme companies and the BBC but they share one characteristic – they are not democratic. There is one not unimportant difference between the programme companies and the BBC, however, which is that the former are very much smaller; management is therefore more personal and what one might call the ethical pressures – in the sense that one can speak of a BBC ethos – are less effective. This had led to certain pockets of anti-establishmentarianism, which, however, operates within fairly narrow limits. Granada Television is a case in point. But such an exception does not disprove the general rule that the organization of the television industry allows those who work in it little scope to influence policy. The BBC differs from the programme contractors in being a very large, highly complex, strongly centralist organization in which the control of news and current affairs programmes, in particular, is closely coordinated and controlled at a high level with the director general either acting as editor-in-chief or reserving the final right to editorial decisions. The authoritarian nature of the BBC's structure is one of Reith's least desirable legacies to British broadcasting and a memorial to his autocratic temperament. In so far as there have been in the BBC's history periods of liberalism when a degree of free discussion took place on the BBC's doctrine of broadcasting and the policies that should flow from it, these freedoms have been confined to producer level and above. Thus there was a period in the development of BBC Television – it has been considerably idealized in retrospect – when the weekly departmental meetings of producers (as for instance the department dealing with current affairs programmes) were forums where programme policy and programme ideas were discussed freely and those taking part had some feeling that they were shaping the attitudes and actions of the BBC in their own area of specialization. With the great expansion of staff which followed the BBC's decision to run BBC-2 alongside BBC-1, the organizational structures became more complex, the chains of command longer and the managerial processes more industrialized. The result has been to erect between the producers and the top management a large middle management, the growth of which has been described in a 76 Group paper on the subject, as 'the proliferation of small empires disguised as functioning departments but, in fact, very often created arbitrarily like native states as bribes for continued service'. This process has been accompanied by a new interpretation of the phrase 'doctrine of devolution and delegation', which has frequently been claimed by the BBC as one of its greatest strengths and virtues. But delegation has always been an ambiguous term as the then director of administration made clear in 1965. 'Delegation means many things,' he stated. 'It means the most careful recruitment of the right staff . . . above all it means delegation of responsibility, to encourage and liberate the talent and genius that may exist at the working level – in the BBC, particularly the producer level.' These talents were not to function without guidance, however, as he made clear in the same statement.

The BBC has had to create the right sort of climate of opinion and reference in which its producers and programme staff operate. This has been achieved by choosing producers with sensitivity as well as technical proficiency (and) trying to appoint above them heads of output departments who are both accessible guides and experienced in all kinds of policy and taste decisions which their producers have to take.

'Sensitivity' in this context means ability to read the prevailing atmosphere, to anticipate pressures and to obviate the need for them to be expressed. Delegation may mean many things but one thing it does not mean is any real exercise of power and decision by 'junior' staff as the Director General made clear when speaking on the subject of 'money, management and programmes' in 1969, that is to say, after the American business consultancy firm of McKinsey had completed its investigation into the management of the BBC. 'It is perhaps cynical,' he went on record as saying,

that the word devolution used by juniors represents a claim to power which they think they should have and which they think is greedily retained by senior management. In the minds of senior management, however, devolution is the art of being able to pin the responsibility on someone else.

It is one of the clearest attributable statements on the lack of industrial democracy within the BBC. It is also – like the statements by the director of administration – interesting as a demonstration of the BBC's views on the relative importance of certain categories of staff. It is an old tradition in the BBC and one which was perpetuated in the contracting companies that the most important category is that of the programme makers or 'creative element'; it is an assumption that obscures the contribution of technicians to any television programme and their role in the production team. The demarcation line between technicians and creative elements is clearly drawn and institutionalized; thus it is extremely difficult to progress from being a cameraman, film editor or sound technician, to being a director. This situation is justified in terms of the 'primacy of programmes' over all other branches of television; in social terms it is a perpetuation within television of the distinction between white-collar workers and technical workers.

The present situation of television in Britain is due in part to the pressures of industrialization, in part to the role assigned to the broadcasting organizations by the political forces which dominate the life of the country. The politics of television is a term which can be applied to the relationship, formal and informal, of these organizations to government and to the parties, but it applies equally to the relationship of the broadcasting organizations to their employees and to the public. In the case of the employees the most important problem is how to introduce democratic processes into the running of the BBC and the commercial companies. The areas of debate – if these organizations were to concede that the subject is debatable – range from participation in decision-making and management expressed concretely in terms of workers' representation on all the controlling bodies up to the board of management; it is a subject which is beginning to be discussed in the ACTT, the film and television union, and which on the workers' side presents a number of problems of which the principal one is whether any form of participation can be said to be properly democratic, short of workers' control.

Where the public is concerned the problem is one of accountability and therefore of political responsibility in the broadest sense. It is one the broadcasting organizations have contrived to avoid except by the token gesture of setting up advisory councils. How empty that gesture is is demonstrated by the fact that the proceedings of the General Advisory Council of the BBC which in theory represents the viewers and listeners, are held in private and are not made public. In the case of the ITA there is similar secrecy on a matter of great public importance – the proceedings of the meetings whereby the ITA, acting on behalf of the public, grants contracts to commercial interests to set up local broadcasting monopolies, are held in secret; no reasons are given for the granting of a contract or for the withdrawal of one. No serious thought has been given to the setting up of broadcasting councils which would be representative, with members answerable to the bodies and organizations which had appointed them, given them a mandate and a duty to report back. Democracy of this kind runs counter to the Reithian tradition which is by nature elitist and undemocractic. There are obvious problems connected with the extension of democracy in broadcasting – they are illustrated by the stranglehold party caucuses have established over the advisory councils in the West German broadcasting system; but the real difficulties which democracy presents are not a good reason for refusing to consider democratic procedures.

Connected to the question of accountability is the question of access. Debates in Britain on the virtues and defects of the broadcasting systems embodied in the BBC and the ITA do not commonly raise in principle the question of monopoly. It is true that in assuming that monopoly is necessary and desirable British opinion is in line with what one might hear in most West European countries, where after the war monopoly of one sort or another was established, the one exception being Holland, which continued a tradition of pluralistic broadcasting which came into being when radio was first started there in the 1920s. It is natural that the broadcasting organizations and the politicans should be unwilling to initiate a debate which would perhaps lead to the dissolution of the monopoly; what is surprising is that so little attention has been given elsewhere to the discussion of alternative models. One obvious proposal envisages a BBC which no longer combines in one organization such disparate functions as control of the means of communication – the studios and transmitters – and control of both the making of programmes and their content. This concentration of power has in the past been justified (apart from the argument for monopoly which has already been discussed) on the grounds that the production of television programmes is impossible without the concentration of extremely complicated and costly electrical equipment which an organization like the BBC has installed in its studios; but technical advances – in particular the miniaturization of equipment – have led to the production of less bulky equipment and cheaper models. The capital cost of equipment which is perfectly adequate for programmes which do not aim at the scope, technical virtuosity and production values of prestige television is now low enough to bring the making of programmes on tape within the reach of a large number of groups and organizations. If the BBC's functions were split in two, giving an organization which ran the production facilities in the public interest, and another organization responsible, again in the public interest, for drawing up a schedule and for the supervision of balance in the sense of seeing that the 'mix' of programmes was good and varied – in other words with exercising a broad editorial function – then programmes would be available from three main sources: from groups and organizations which used their own equipment; from production companies and organizations making more sophisticated programmes in their own studios or in hired studios; or from production companies and organizations which hired the facilities now used by the BBC. Similarly, and more easily, the studios and facilities of the commercial companies could be made available to production companies which would provide programmes to fill a schedule drawn up by the ITA as editorial body working in the public interest. There is indeed an argument for proposing that the editorial function should be minimal and that, as happens now in the case of party political broadcasts, editorial responsibility should be surrendered so far as programme content is concerned, it being made clear that the views expressed were that of a particular group, production company, documentary film-maker or political party. Such a system would require a broadcasting commission to oversee the operation. Composed, ideally, of members of the public appointed on a representational basis and of representatives of the men and women working in television, this council would act as a court of appeal to which any group or member of the public might turn if it felt it had been unfairly treated in programmes, as might programme-makers who felt that they had unreasonably been refused access to the medium or that their programmes had been kept off the air. It would also have to act as mediator between the broadcasting organizations engaged in operating the technical facilities or drawing up the programme schedules and the government, negotiating on their behalf on matters of finance and control.

What makes the need to discuss alternative models for television broadcasting is that technology is likely to force change upon us which will carry with it the need for new structures. Television as it is at present organized is an example of how a new technological process can be confined within the limits of its predecessor. Television signals are distributed by cable to a transmitter and then by 'wireless' to a receiving antenna on a house-top; this was the method adopted for radio and taken over by television. Technically a much better signal would be obtained if it were conveyed by cable to the viewer – a system which is used for community television in the United States and Canada and one which is being provided in some of the new towns in Britain. The latest type of coaxial cable which is required to distribute television signals can take a very large number of signals – fifty or more at one time – together with telephone, telex and facsimile messages. Cable is likely to be superseded in its turn by waveguides, which are essentially hollow tubes along which signals can be transmitted at various frequencies and which are capable of carrying up to two hundred television channels at one time. Such technical advances present the opportunity of distributing television signals by common carrier. How such a common carrier will be used will depend on the social, political and economic structure of the country that instals it. In the United States wired television is already being discussed in terms of free enterprise and access controlled by the ability to pay for the lease, for a shorter or longer time, of a channel. In Canada it is seen as a method of making possible – to some extent at least – a new kind of community television, drawing communities together by debate of matters of local significance and interest. Such television must almost certainly be less polished, less technically perfect than the highly polished productions of the large organizations which now provide us with the bulk of our viewing and have come to equate technical proficiency with excellence, to value presentation more than content – a judgement which the viewer has come to share. It may be that it requires a crisis of a kind that the television organization faced in Czechoslovakia in 1968 to demonstrate that what is important is precisely the content and not the form.

Any far-reaching change in the nature and structure of television cannot be envisaged without a similar change in the nature and structure of the society that produces it. Unfortunately the experience of the socialist countries of Eastern Europe and elsewhere has demonstrated that it is possible to have social and economic changes of a radical nature which are not accompanied by radical transformations of the media either – as in the Soviet Union – because a strongly centralized, authoritarian regime demands total control of the medium or – as in the case of Cuba – because the reform of television has been given a low priority for reasons which may be partly economic. If there are large stocks of old American films and cartoons, why bother to make new ones for television? There are, it is true, examples from other socialist countries – notably from Poland and Hungary – of television being used as a means of direct communication between representatives of the government and the managers of industry, and the people, as a weapon of social criticism. Thus in Poland ministers have appeared in the studio along with their advisers and there have answered questions phoned in by viewers. In Hungary the managers of factories have been faced in the studio with complaints about the quality of their product and exposed to the criticisms of consumers. It is difficult to envisage either of these programmes in a British context; here criticisms of goods and services stop short of absolute candour for a variety of reasons, some legal, some institutional. It is obvious of course that programmes of the kind which have been mounted in Poland and Hungary are easy to control and censor as are the 'phone-in' programmes in the United States. The fact is that television broadcasts under the technical conditions with which we are familiar and by the type of organization which has almost universally been set up to regulate it must be subject to this kind of restraint, that feedback will be minimal or so controlled as to be merely a method of confirming the views and aims of authority. The question is whether television, which is a linear method of communication from which, so far, the possibilities of feedback have been excluded, can have a positive and useful part to play in any society or whether it is in the nature of the medium that it lulls, hypnotizes and defuses the viewer – whether, as has been suggested, the medium is the message. There are people working in television in both capitalist and socialist countries who would deny the allegation and point to the amount of information conveyed by the medium if only in the fields of news, documentaries, scientific and medical programmes, to the educational role it can play in countries with an illiteracy problem, or to its effect in increasing the viewers' awareness of the world and world politics. Others are more cynical, and, while recognizing its power to convey information, are aware of its sedative qualities. Thus at a recent international conference a high television executive from Yugoslavia remarked that television has an important part to play in damping down radicalism and cited as an example of its beneficial effects a European Cup broadcast which had, in his view, kept young people off the streets and prevented them from taking part in a student demonstration in one of the federal capitals of Yugoslavia. It is a view which has been expressed in the United States and which was implicit in the kind of television which was produced in France under de Gaulle – an escapist avoidance of the realities of the French situation.

The case against television is a formidable one. As we know, it is a reductive medium, bringing down to the same level of unreality political discussion, quiz competitions, World Cup matches and beauty contests, in all of which the competitive element is stressed, all of which are treated with the same degree of seriousness. The presenter at the Miss World contest is no less serious, no less convinced (apparently) with the importance of the occasion than the presenter who presides over an election results programme. If everything is equally important, then nothing is important. It is because they have perceived this that many radicals refuse to appear on television, arguing that what they have to say, the films they make, the plays they perform in the streets and before groups of workers as agitational theatre would be devalued in precisely the same way, assimilated in the viewer's mind to the last instalment of *Peyton Place* or the last edition of *Sportsview*. It is from such perceptions that the critique of television developed by the New Left has sprung. They point to its manipulative power and to its reinforcement of that atomization of society into tiny family groups. These twin qualities are logically connected, for it is precisely in the small family group that citizens of the developed industrial countries absorb those images of life, politics and culture, which are projected into their homes with the approval and consent of the ruling class. Much of the indoctrination achieved by television is explicit in the limitation of the discourse of politics to certain narrowly defined areas, in the constant propaganda of the commercials which suggest that the family unit developed by western civilizations is the ideal social group, that sexual gratification and love can be purchased by drinking the right beverages, wearing the right perfumes, using the right bath salts; but much of it is implicit in the assumptions that underly the telefilms, the teleplays, the comedy shows, which subject the viewer to a view of the world where emotion is supreme and thought (particularly political thought) discounted, where the symbols of success are material and sexual, where certain staid forms of virtue will always triumph over the paper tigers of evil, and fundamentally the individual can best live by accepting the established order. It is in the child viewers that the indoctrination begins; the rejection of television by teenagers is a positive reaction. The tragedy is that, with marriage, so many of them settle down with the television set as their freedoms disappear with marriage, mortgages and children.

The radical critique of television is well grounded and accurately describes how it is used in both capitalist and socialist societies at this time. It is frequently accompanied by the suggestion that the viewers are not themselves capable of understanding the process to which they are being subjected. This is a deeply pessimistic view which is not borne out either by the reactions of children who have grown up with television and appear to be able quickly to distinguish between what is real and what is not, or by the deepseated distrust displayed by workers and trade-unionists of anything on the screen which touches on their interests or experience – a reaction which springs, in part, from their experience of the medium as represented by television reporters and cameramen. The main onus of the traditional attack rests on two closely related theses – those of manipulation and of repressive tolerance as defined by Marcuse. The former has already been discussed; of the latter there are obvious examples in the 'critical' programmes, the inquiries, probes, inquests (they are variously described) which the great broadcasting organizations mount from time to time with a great deal of publicity provided the criticism is kept within limits and confined to certain defined targets. They are, in any case, normally followed by a discussion to provide 'balance' or by a programme placed soon after in the schedules which cancels the points they made or suggests that both points of view are equally valid, counterpoised, equivalent. Balance, in this sense, is the technique of denying the truth of any criticism and suggesting that all views are equally acceptable provided they do not lead to political action. They are, as Gorz has pointed out, an alibi which helps to consolidate the existing system, to arbitrate its conflicts and to absorb the anticapitalist forces. The most interesting counter-argument from within the Left to radical pessimism about the medium of television has been advanced by Hans Magnus Enzensberger, who has suggested that the manipulation thesis may be used as an excuse for inaction and for a refusal to understand and exploit television. 'To cast the enemy in the role of the devil,' he comments, 'is to conceal . . . (one's own) weakness.' So, too, the theory of repressive tolerance can, in his view, become a vehicle for resignation. Certainly there is some evidence on the Left of the desire to keep one's hand clean where television is concerned, leading to a refusal to explore the capabilities of the medium as some underground groups are already doing (outside the confines of the broadcasting organizations) and exploiting the new types of equipment. It also leads to the refusal, which is by no means free of a suggestion of puritanism, to consider the role of entertainment in

Stuart Hood 433

society, including a socialist society, or how television might be used in it to perform the functions of informing, entertaining and educating. Whatever the future shape of society, it is unlikely that television will disappear or be abolished. The need is for a discussion of the medium within the framework of a critical theory based on the supposition, as Horkheimer explained of the theory of the Frankfurt school, that men can alter being and that the conditions for doing so already exist.

References

BRIGGS, A. (1970), *The War of Words*, Oxford University Press.
GORZ, A. (1967), *Strategy for Labour*, Beacon Press.
CRAWLEY, J. (1971) 'Pressures on public service broadcasters', in the *Listener*, vol. 85, 10 June.

20 Paul Hartmann and Charles Husband

The Mass Media and Racial Conflict

Paul Hartmann and Charles Husband, 'The mass media and racial
conflict', *Race*, vol. 12, 1970–1.

Introduction

Discussions about the role of the mass media in society are
inevitably concerned with questions of attitude and public
opinion, for if the media do influence events they seldom do so
directly, but through the way people think. We therefore think
it appropriate to make some remarks about communication,
attitude and culture at the outset of this paper, and then to
mention some research findings about mass media and attitudes,
before going on to our main argument.

Communication between people is possible to the extent that
they share common frameworks of interpretation. They need to
have similar meanings for the same symbols, and a way of thinking
about things in common before they can communicate. Our
perceptions are structured by the mental categories available to
us for making sense of our world.

Research into attitudes commonly concentrates on differences
in attitude between people and groups, and the interpretive
frameworks within which such differences occur are either taken
for granted or ignored. Where racial prejudice is concerned this
emphasis may produce a tendency to seek the origins of prejudice
in the personality of the individual or the immediate social
situation rather than in the cultural framework itself. This approach was evident in the *Colour and Citizenship* survey (Rose,
1969) and made possible the comforting but misleading conclu-
tion that intense prejudice is a phenomenon rooted in the
personality of the individual, an irrational solution to the
inadequacies of an undermined personality (Deakin, 1970). But

This paper is based on an earlier paper presented at the Fifth Annual
Race Relations Conference of the Institute of Race Relations, 1970.

prejudice is not in the first instance the result of immigration, personal pathology or social strain; it is built into the culture. Our whole way of thinking about coloured people, influenced by the colonial past, constitutes a built-in predisposition to accept unfavourable beliefs about them. The very notion of 'tolerance' betrays this cultural bias, for it implies that there is something nasty that requires special virtue to put up with. Even 'authoritarianism', so often cast as the villain of the piece, is not some purely personal aberration; for the beliefs and values that serve to define it are related to our particular social and industrial history and are well embedded in British culture. They have much in common with 'social Darwinism' and the 'Protestant Ethic'. Only after the underlying cultural predisposition to prejudice has been taken into account does it make sense to ask how variations in prejudice relate to other factors.

The attitude scores given in the Appendix show, for instance, that among white working-class secondary schoolchildren, at least, prejudice towards coloured people is more common in areas of high immigration than in areas of low immigration, and in schools with appreciable numbers of immigrant children than in schools with few or none. The data show that immigration into an *area* is more strongly related to prejudice than is personal contact in school.[1] This means that white children with little or no *personal* experience of coloured people who live in areas of high immigration are on the whole more prejudiced than children with considerable personal contact living in areas of low immigration. These results suggest that competition, generated by large-scale immigration into an area, leads to more negative attitudes. It does not show that competition causes prejudice; only that competition (real or imagined) may serve to activate or intensify the existing cultural tendency to view coloured people negatively.

The mass media and attitudes

A considerable amount of research effort has been devoted to assessing the influence of the mass media on attitudes and opinions. Results, on the whole, have shown that social attitudes,

1. For a review of relevant studies and a discussion of the complexity of contact as a variable see Amir (1969).

including prejudice, are relatively resistant to influence through the media. What effects have been demonstrated have typically been of a limited kind. Trenaman and McQuail, for instance, in their study of the effects of the 1959 election campaign on television showed that this produced increases in political knowledge, but were unable to find any effects on attitudes or voting behaviour (1961). Blumler and McQuail's important and complex study of the 1964 election campaign found that various kinds of attitude change did occur as a result of exposure to election television, but the particular kind of attitude change depended on the characteristics of the voter, particularly his motivation, and it was not possible to make across-the-board generalizations that applied to the electorate as a whole (1968). In an early study on prejudice, Cooper and Dinerman found that although many of the *facts* presented in an anti-prejudice film did get through to the audience, this was not associated with change of attitude, and there was even evidence of 'boomerang' effects (1951).

One of the main explanations for findings of this kind is selection. People select what they read and what they view and tend to avoid communications that they find uncongenial. They are also selective in what they perceive and what they remember. Where the 'message' clashes with existing attitudes or beliefs it is typically the existing outlook that remains intact, while the 'message' is rejected, or distorted to fit the outlook. A study of viewers' reactions to a programme in an ITV series, *The Nature of Prejudice*, carried out in 1967 found that prejudiced viewers evaded the intended anti-prejudice message by a variety of means, ranging from becoming hostile towards the interviewer (who was opposed to prejudice) to finding in the programme confirmation of their own views.[2]

In reviewing research on the effects of mass communications Klapper came to the conclusion that they are much more likely to reinforce existing attitudes (whatever the attitude and whatever the 'message') than to change them (1960). Attitudes may be expected to be particularly resistant to change when they are

2. The study was carried out by Dr Roger Brown in connection with a production study conducted by Philip Elliott. [See Reading 11.]

supported by strong group norms or the prevailing cultural climate.

Work of our own confirms that direct effects on attitude following short-term exposure to media material are unlikely. We studied the effects of the six-part television series, *Curry and Chips* which caused some controversy in November and December 1969. We gave questionnaires to about two hundred secondary schoolchildren, both before the beginning of the series and after it had finished. They had no reason to connect us or the questions with television. The questionnaires included attitude measures as well as open-ended questions designed to elicit beliefs and information about Pakistanis. On the second occasion they were also asked how many of the programmes they had seen. Differences between responses on the two occasions were analysed in relation to the number of programmes viewed. We expected that children who had seen all or most of the series would show changes in information and attitude not found in those who had seen none of the programmes. We found no effects that could be attributed to viewing the programmes. Even when analysed in relation to initial attitude, to whether the children had discussed the series with others, to how true-to-life they had thought it, and other variables, the data yielded no positive results.

This is not to say that the series had no important effects, but only that it appears not to have had the type of effect studied. We do not know the extent to which children's initial opinions were strengthened by viewing the programmes, for instance. It may be that the series helped to make it more acceptable for both children and adults to make fun of immigrants. Letters of complaint appearing in the press and anecdotal evidence suggest that for a time at least this was so. And going on press reports and letters, we have the impression that one of the main effects of the series was to affront the Asian communities. A further possibly important effect was that the programmes provided a focus of discussion in which the questions of immigration and race were aired in informal groups up and down the country. Sixty per cent of the children we surveyed claimed to have discussed the series with others. This must at the very least have resulted in greater awareness of race as a controversial topic and greater familiarity with prevailing norms. All that emerges clearly from our study is that to look for effects in terms of simple changes of attitude may be to look in the wrong place.

More generally we should not conclude from the type of research that we have been discussing that the media have no important influence on public opinion or race relations. Part of the reason for the high incidence of null results in attempts to demonstrate the effects of mass communications lies in the nature of the research questions asked and the limitations of the theoretical orientations of the research tradition. Much of this work was influenced by a view of man as an atomized unit of mass society, whom stimulus–response psychology saw as responding in a straightforward way to the stimuli or 'messages' of the media. The tradition is characterized by a search for direct effects, short-term effects, and an over-reliance on attitude as the index of effect.[3] This kind of model of mass media influence is still the basis of much thinking on the subject. It may be that the media have little immediate impact on attitudes as commonly assessed by social scientists, but it seems likely that they have other important effects. In particular they would seem to play a major part in defining for people what the important issues are and the terms in which they should be discussed. Thus the debate surrounding race in Britain has come to be defined as hinging on immigrant numbers and the threat to existing social patterns, rather than on integration, housing, or other issues.

We now present, with some supporting evidence, an outline of one of the main ways in which we believe the mass media influence the race relations situation in Britain at the present time. We are concerned with the news media in particular because these relate directly to the present social situation, have wide circulation and enjoy the high credibility that enhances their capacity to influence how people think (see e.g. Klapper, ch. 5, 1960; Hovland, Janis and Kelley, 1953). They also provide a steady stream of race-related information. Preliminary content analysis shows that the typical popular national daily contains on average

3. A good review of work in this tradition is to be found in Klapper (1960). For general reviews and discussion of mass communications research and theory see McQuail (1969), Defleur (1966), and Halloran (1970).

two items a day in which coloured people in Britain or the USA figure, or that deal with explicitly race-related topics.

The argument

Briefly, our thesis is that the way race-related material is handled by the mass media serves both to perpetuate negative perceptions of blacks and to define the situation as one of intergroup conflict. In communities where there is a realistic basis for conflict (e.g. competition for housing) black-versus-white thinking about the situation will be reinforced by the media and existing social strains amplified. In multi-racial communities where there is no 'objective' basis for conflict, conflict may be created because people come to think in conflict terms. People in all-white communities are particularly liable to accept the interpretation of events offered by the media because they lack any basis of contact with coloured people on which to arrive at an alternative way of looking at things – apart, of course, from the view of blacks provided by traditional culture.

Mass communications regarding race will be interpreted within the framework of meanings that serve to define the situation within any social group. At the same time the way race-related material is handled in the media contributes towards this definition of the situation. Attitudes and interpretations prevailing in a community are therefore seen as the result of the interplay between the on-the-ground social situation and the way race is handled by the media. 'Media influence' is seen as operating on interpretive frameworks – the categories people use when thinking about race-related matters – rather than on attitudes directly. The way the media define the situation is seen as resulting from the definitions prevailing in the general culture and from institutional factors that stem from the media themselves.

The media are social institutions located within the overall socio-economic structure, and they have their own characteristics which influence the form and content of their output. In the first place, the nature of the medium itself, the kind of production ideology this generates, together with simple physical limitations of time and space, and the need to attract readers and viewers, imposes constraints both on what events make the news and on the kind of treatment they receive. The well-known preference for action visuals over 'talking heads' in television production, for instance, means that television coverage of a riot, say, is likely to emphasize the violence to the neglect of the causes and background. This was the major criticism made against the television coverage of the 1967 disturbances in America by the Kerner Commission (National Advisory Commission, 1968). The Commission concluded that the type of coverage given contributed to the definition of the disturbances as simple black–white confrontations. This is still the generally accepted view, even though the Commission found that the situation was in fact far more complex.

In fact almost all the deaths, injuries and property damage occurred in all-negro neighbourhoods, and thus the disorders were not 'race riots' as that term is generally understood (National Advisory Commission, 1968, p. 365).

The cultural legacy

There are two main strands to our argument. They are intertwined but it will make for clarity to illustrate each separately. Briefly, the first is this. The British cultural tradition contains elements derogatory to foreigners, particularly blacks. The media operate within the culture and are obliged to use cultural symbols. Hence it is almost inevitable that they will help to perpetuate this tradition in some measure. The prevalence of images and stereotypes deriving mainly from the colonial experience and at least implicitly derogatory to coloured people may be guaged from the existence of a number of traditions of cartoon jokes. These include the missionary in the pot, the fakir on his bed of nails, the snake charmer, and the polygamous Eastern potentate with his harem. Similar themes and images are to be found in nursery rhyme, idiom and literature.

We do not think that these examples are particularly important in themselves, except as an index of the widespread familiarity with, if not acceptance of, the image of coloured people that they carry. It does, however, become disturbing to find this kind of outmoded image obtruding itself into the media handling of current events concerning real people; so that elements of the cultural legacy that are at best ethnocentric and at worst racist come to influence reactions to and interpretations of race-related events in Britain today. The tendency may most clearly be seen in headlines and in cartoon comment, where the use of a phrase or image that will evoke a similar set of associations and meanings in virtually all members of the society to which it is directed enables a complex point to be crystallized unambiguously and memorably in a few words or a single picture. In its front page report of the discovery of the forty illegal Indian immigrants in a Bradford cellar last July the *Daily Express* of 2 July used the heading 'Police find forty Indians in "black hole"'. This is an instantly recognizable allusion to the 'black hole of Calcutta', which, by evoking colonial associations suggests that the appropriate attitude to adopt towards these Indians is that adopted toward the natives in the days of Empire. We are not suggesting that this is what the *Express* intended, only that this is the sort of reaction that the heading is likely to have achieved. The importance of headlines in influencing the way news items are interpreted has been demonstrated by Tannenbaum (1953), and by Warr and Knapper (1968). Headlines have a particularly strong influence when the item itself is not thoroughly read. In the illegal immigrant story, a similar effect was created by the cartoon in the *Sun* on 3 July in which an illegal immigrant asking the way addresses a white man as 'Sahib', and in the cartoon in the *Mirror* on 6 July which showed two lovers on a beach, one of whom was saying 'I thought you said this was a quiet beach' while the beach was being overrun by illegal immigrants in turbans, including a man riding on an elephant, a snake-charmer complete with snake, and a man carrying a bed of nails. The reiteration of this kind of image, not merely at the level of joke or fantasy, but in relation to actual events involving real people, can only perpetuate an outlook which is not only outmoded but antithetical to good race relations and likely to influence perceptions of current events. These examples illustrate the way in which a cultural tradition may be at least partly self-sustaining. The image is used because it exists and is known to have wide currency and therefore enables easier communication. By virtue of being used it is kept alive and available for further use.

News value

The second strand of our argument concerns the concept of 'news value' which influences the pattern of coverage of race-

'Scuse please, sahib – is this England?'
Reprinted by kind permission of the *Sun*

related topics. We might regard news value as composed of some of the major criteria by which information about events is gathered, selected and published. Galtung's famous analysis of what factors make events newsworthy includes the concepts of unambiguity, meaningfulness, consonance, continuity and negativeness (Galtung and Ruge, 1965). Though we shall not use these terms our approach is essentially the same. A similar approach was used by Lang and Lang, who showed that the television coverage of a parade in Chicago bore a closer resemblance to the newsmen's anticipations of what the event would be like, than to what actually happened (1953). Similarly, Halloran and his colleagues in their recent study of the anti-Vietnam war demonstration in London in October 1968 showed how the event came to be defined by the media in advance as a violent one, and once this news framework was established, how it structured the coverage of the event itself so that violence was emphasized, and the issues involved and the predominantly peaceful nature of the march neglected (1970).

For present purposes we may distinguish two kinds of characteristics which make events newsworthy. Firstly, conflict, threat and deviancy all make news, both because information about these has a real importance to society, and because, for various reasons, people enjoy hearing about them. Conflict is the stuff of news just as it is the stuff of drama and literature. Material that can be couched in terms of conflict or threat therefore makes better 'news' than that which cannot. Hence for the story of the forty illegal Indian immigrants referred to above, the front page of the *Daily Mail* of 2 July 1970, carried the headline '40 Indians "invade"'. The word 'invade' manages to imply that society is somehow threatened by them. This theme was echoed in the *Sun* of 3 July which headed its story 'The Invaders', and in the *Daily Sketch* of the same date which had the headline: '"Invasion of Migrants" Fear in Bid to Beat Ban'. Similarly, the police were said to have 'seized' the Indians in the same way as drugs, firearms and other dangerous commodities are seized (*Sun* and *Express*, 2 July). This story was big 'news', being carried on an outside page of seven of the eight major national dailies. That it could be made to carry the inference of threat and conflict would seem to be at least part of the reason that it was thought so newsworthy.

A second feature that makes events more newsworthy is their ability to be interpreted within a familiar framework or in terms of existing images, stereotypes and expectations. The framework and the expectations may originate in the general culture, or they may originate in the news itself and pass from there into the culture. The situation is one of continuous interplay between events, cultural meanings and news frameworks. The way events are reported helps structure expectations of how coloured people will behave and how race relations situations develop. Subsequent events that conform to the expectation stand a better chance of making the news than those that do not. Thus new events may be interpreted in terms of existing images even if the existing image is not in fact the most appropriate. The use of the image of ethnic conflict derived from the American disorders of the sixties as the framework for reporting the British situation is a case in point.

In January 1970 the Birmingham *Evening Mail* published a series of feature articles on the race relations situation in the Handsworth area, which explained the background to the social problems there. This was a positive attempt to foster better community relations and was rightly commended as such. The first article of the series, which gave an overview of the situation, provides a good example of what we have been discussing. Its first sentence was 'Must Harlem come to Birmingham?' In the subsequent fifty column inches there were four further explicit parallels drawn between Birmingham and the United States. There were also fourteen separate sentences in which explicit reference was made to violence (this excludes generalized references to crime and robbery). Effectively the situation is defined as one of potential riot. Thus the image of black–white confrontation derived from the media coverage of the American disorders becomes the model for thinking about the British situation, both because it is known to be familiar to the audience, and because it fulfills expectations of how race-relations situations develop. The question is, is such an image the most appropriate one for Birmingham today, and does its use not have all the elements of the self-fulfilling prophecy? Might it not be that any benefits resulting from the in-depth explanation and pro-tolerance tone of the *Evening Mail* series were bought at the expense of confirming expectations of civil disorder and amplifying conflict in the area? The author of the article himself seems to be aware of the danger, for he writes:

The trouble about violence in a multi-racial area like those we have in north Birmingham is that it may be dangerous to the community. People start using emotive words like 'race-riot' and take sides according to the colour of their skins. Reports appear in overseas newspapers. Before you know it the community is split into bitter factions. The problems of the Handsworth area are bad enough as it is.

The fact that he is effectively doing with the best of intentions what he fears might be done by others and the overseas press, illustrates the apparently unconscious nature of many of the assumptions that go to structure the news.

The numbers game

Public perceptions of the race-relations situation depend very heavily on the type of material made available through the media, the relative prominence given to different types of material and the way it is handled. All these factors are influenced by considerations of 'news value'. A comparison of the coverage given to two events by the eight major national dailies provides an illustration of this process in a particularly important area.

The events were the publication on 10 March 1970 of the Registrar General's returns which showed that the birth-rate among immigrants was higher than the national average, and the announcement by the Home Secretary on 14 May 1970 of the immigration statistics which showed that the rate of immigration was decreasing and that the number for the previous quarter was the lowest on record. Our comparisons are of the coverage of the events on 10 March and 15 May respectively, the days on which the news was first carried.

Seven of the eight national dailies carried the birth figures, five of them on the front page. Only four carried the news about the reduction in immigration, only one of these on the front page. The average headline for the birth figures occupied four times as much space as the average headline for the low immigration figures. Altogether there was about five times as much news-space given to the birth figures and reactions to them as to the immigration figures (approximately two hundred and fifty column inches as compared to about fifty). Five of the seven papers carried Enoch Powell's reaction to the birth figures, of which only one, *The Times*, went to the trouble of trying to balance the story by eliciting reactions from other sources. This pattern of coverage meant that almost no one who opened a newspaper on 10 March – or even glanced at his neighbour's on the bus – could fail to become aware that the coloured population was increasing and that this was regarded as a matter of great importance; while only the most diligent newspaper reader on 15 May would have discovered that the rate of immigration was low, and reducing.

Even if we accept that the birth figures were of greater social significance than the reduction in immigration and therefore warranted greater coverage, and allow that Enoch Powell did make a statement, a reportable event, it would still seem necessary to invoke other factors to explain this pattern of coverage.

Specifically, events that carry or can be given connotations of conflict or threat are more newsworthy than others. 'More coloureds' is thus better copy than 'fewer coloureds'. That the threat image was important in making the birth figures newsworthy is clear from the opening paragraph in the *Telegraph*'s front-page report where it was stated that 'there was no sign of panic over the fact that nearly 12 per cent of the 405,000 babies . . . were conceived by mothers born outside the United Kingdom'. And the front page of the *Sketch* carried the assertion that 'The report adds fuel to Mr Enoch Powell's previous warnings of the rapid breeding rate among coloured families.' Note the use of the word 'warnings' and the acceptance of the Powell definition of the situation. The idea that coloured people constitute some kind of social threat is simply taken for granted – it has become one of the unspoken assumptions of the news framework. The birth figures made a story that fitted this framework, and so the story got big play. The reduction in immigration didn't fit the framework very well, and so it got little play. But even in the reporting of the immigration figures the framework is evident. All four papers that carried the story also reported the Home Secretary's determination to keep the figures low.

Finally the amount of newspace devoted to Powell's statement must be partly explained by the fact that Powell on race has come to be newsworthy in himself. Once a particular kind of news has hit the headlines there appears to be a lowering of the threshold for subsequent news of a similar kind. With Powell one has the impression that since his first immigration speech his every utterance on the question is now thought worth reporting, even if what he says differs in no important respect from what he said the previous week.

Some results

It is one thing to argue from an examination of the media themselves that their handling of race effectively defines the situation in conflict terms, and another to show that this pattern of coverage does in fact influence people's view of the matter. We now present evidence based on a partial analysis of some of the data from our ongoing research that provide support for our general argument. These results cannot be taken as conclusive because our sample is small and confined to white working-class secondary schoolchildren, and the differences we have found do not always reach a high level of statistical significance. A rigorous evaluation of our argument must await the completion of our data collection and analysis. However, the results we have available show a sufficiently coherent pattern to make them worth presenting now.

Unless otherwise stated, the quantitative evidence that follows is based on a combined group of two hundred and eight eleven to twelve-year-old and fourteen to fifteen-year-old children, both boys and girls. Half of them come from areas of high immigration in the West Midlands and West Yorkshire and half from Teesside and Glasgow where immigration has been very low. Schools were chosen in pairs from each area so that one contained an appreciable number of coloured immigrant children (at least 10 per cent, normally 20–40 per cent) and the other few or none. So we have fifty-two children from 'high-contact' schools in 'high-contact' areas (high-highs), fifty-two low-highs, fifty-two high-lows and fifty-two low-lows. We shall make our comparisons between 'high' and 'low' types of *area*, and our sampling design ensures that the children are roughly equated for amount of personal contact with coloured people, and for social class.

The first thing that has become evident from our interviews is the widespread conviction that the number of coloured people in the country or the rate of immigration is very high and that this poses some kind of threat. This is true even of places where there has been no immigration. In a school in a County Durham village for example (not part of the sample described above) as many as 35 per cent of children expressed something of this kind in response to general open-ended questions. When specifically asked whether they thought anything should be done about coloured immigration to Britain, nearly half (47·4 per cent) advocated restricted entry or more stringent policies. In areas of high immigration the impression of vast numbers is understandably even greater and a clear majority want the numbers limited or reduced. But in an area like our Durham village the only possible major source of this impression is the media. Even apart from that, what is striking is that the idea that 'there are too many here' or 'too many coming in' should be taken as self-evident by such large proportions of children wherever they live. Clearly the message about numbers and their implied threat has got through. It has been equally evident that the message that there is little threat (promoted from time to time, usually in editorials) has not got through. Nor has it got through that whatever threat was posed by unrestricted immigration is now being dealt with. We were confronted with people recommending, as a matter of urgency, the adoption of policies that have been in operation for five years! This is clearly the result of the pattern of reporting about 'numbers' discussed earlier. The inference of threat that any increase in numbers has come to carry is also evident from the fact that when asked how they thought the presence of coloured people in Britain would affect their lives in the future, 23 per cent of all answers referred explicitly to increasing numbers or expressed the fear that the blacks would 'take over'.

Other findings show an interesting pattern. Firstly, children in areas of high immigration are more aware of the major points of 'realistic' competition or conflict between black and white – namely, housing and employment – than are children in 'low' areas. When asked, 'How do you think the presence of coloured

Paul Hartmann and Charles Husband 449

people in Britain might affect your life in the future?', firstly fewer of them foresaw no effect (thirty-eight compared with sixty-one of the 'low' group), and secondly they were more likely to say that their housing or employment opportunities would be threatened (25 per cent of one hundred and thirty-eight answers given compared with 13 per cent of one hundred and seventeen answers – these include 'no effect' answers.[4] When 'no effect' answers are left out, the percentages change to 35 per cent of one hundred in 'high' areas, and 27 per cent of fifty-six answers in 'low' areas.[5] Some children gave more than one answer). This fits the commonsense expectation and is also consistent with the pattern of attitude scores (see Appendix) which shows that there is more hostility in areas with a realistic basis for conflict.

On this basis we might expect that the ideas of white children in areas of high immigration would be relatively more dominated by the notion of conflict than those living elsewhere. To test this we examined the responses to one of our first questions. 'Can you tell me what you know about coloured people living in Britain today?' Ten per cent of each group gave no answer. Of the remainder we counted the responses having a conflict theme. These fell broadly into three groups: 1. references to direct conflict, e.g. 'They cause trouble.' 'They make riots.'; 2. responses implying incompatibility of interests between black and white, e.g. 'They take all the houses.' 'They take white people's jobs.' 'They'll take over the country soon.' and 3. responses that showed awareness of hostility of whites to blacks, e.g. 'People dislike them; are prejudiced against them; discriminate against them.' These were counted whether they were said with approval or disapproval. The essential criterion was whether the response explicitly or implicitly contained a definition of the situation in terms of conflict. This is not the same as attitude. Contrary to the hypothesis we found that conflict themes were more common in areas of *low* immigration (29·6 per cent of one hundred and fifty-nine responses, as compared with 23·0 per cent of one hundred and sixty-one responses in areas of high immigration –

4. For difference between proportions $z = 2·48$, $P = 0·014$, two-tailed.
5. $z = 1·065$, $P = 0·29$, two-tailed.

some gave more than one response).[6]

For each response a child gave we asked him also for the source of his information. Of the one hundred and ninety sources mentioned in 'low' areas 27·4 per cent were media sources, against only 17·5 per cent of one hundred and seventy-seven sources in 'high' areas.[7] Taking both groups together, 54·2 per cent of the eighty-three responses attributed to a media source were 'conflict' responses, as against 45·1 per cent of the sixty-two attributed to other people, and 16·7 per cent of the two hundred and twenty-two claimed as personal experience, 'own idea', or 'don't know'.[8] So of all the information children were able to give us, that obtained from the media was more likely to contain the conflict theme than that obtained elsewhere. Looked at in another way, there were one hundred and ten responses in all that had the conflict theme of which forty-five (41 per cent) were attributed to a media source. There were forty-one answers that mentioned cultural differences (religion, clothing, life-style) of which only five (12 per cent) were attributed to media sources. This suggests that while the media seem to play a major role in establishing in people's minds the association of colour with conflict, their role in providing the kind of background information that would help make the race-relations situation, including its conflict elements, more understandable, is relatively small.

The picture seems clear, and is what might be expected if our analysis of the handling of race-related matters in the mass media is correct. Children who live in areas of low immigration rely perforce more heavily on the media for their information about coloured people than do others. Media-supplied information carried the inference of conflict more often than that from other sources. As a result these children are more prone to think about race relations in terms of conflict than are those in 'high' contact areas, even though they (the 'lows') live in places where the objective conditions for inter-group competition or conflict are absent. It would seem that while *attitudes* are responsive

6. Testing for difference between proportions $z = 1·34$, $P = 0·18$, two-tailed, under the null hypothesis of *no difference*. Our prediction was for a difference in the other direction.

7. For difference between proportions $z = 2·266$, $P = 0·02$, two-tailed.

8. Comparing the proportion of conflict themes derived from the media with those from elsewhere, $z = 5·5$, $P < 0·0001$, two-tailed.

to the characteristics of the local situation – i.e. the extent of immigration – interpretive frameworks, ways of thinking, are heavily structured by the mass media, particularly in areas where there are few immigrants.

Conclusion

The news media have a crucial role to play in maintaining an informed state of public opinion, upon which the effective functioning of democracy depends. They do this by providing information, defining issues and interpreting events. The generally high credibility which they enjoy enables them to perform this function. Their role is particularly important on subjects which are not matters of common experience – such as the consequences of immigration, and the state of race relations.

We have argued that a number of factors pertaining to traditional culture, to the media as institutions, their technologies and their related ideologies, and to the interplay between these factors, operate to structure the news coverage of race-related matters in a way that causes people to see the situation primarily as one of actual or potential conflict. Blacks come to be seen as conflict-generating *per se* and the chances that people will think about the situation in more productive ways – in terms of the issues involved or of social problems generally – are reduced. The result is that real conflict is amplified, and potential for conflict created. For the media not only operate within the culture, they also make culture and they help shape social reality.

Clearly the factors that we have discussed are not the only ones that structure news coverage. There are obviously others, including the nature of events themselves and editorial policy, but the ones we have discussed do influence what is reported and how it is reported. Although there may be political and other motives at work in the media that influence the coverage of race, it is not necessary to invoke these to explain the kind of pattern we have described. A main point of our argument is that this kind of result may be produced in a quite unintended fashion. The media do not need to *try* to define the situation in terms of conflict. They need merely unreflectingly to follow their normal procedures of news-gathering and selection and to apply their normal criteria of news value.

We do not, however, believe that the type of consequence we have outlined need be inevitable. It is something the media themselves can do something about. There is no reason why the (apparently) unconscious assumptions that underlie the sense of 'what is news' need remain unconscious, or the unintended consequences of news reporting should go unrecognized, or that unwitting bias should remain either 'unwitting' or 'bias'. It is also not inevitable that the sort of media ideology that defines the media as passive and impartial mirrors of society, reflecting but not affecting events, should hold indefinite sway.

Advice to the communicators from social scientists is seldom taken kindly, so in conclusion we quote Harold Evans, Editor of *Sunday Times* (1970):

We need a better understanding of their responsibilities from, for want of a better word, I have to call communications people. We need a discretionary code of conduct. This is not because bad race relations are less acceptable than bad housing or bad crime, certainly not because we can hope to gloss over genuine difficulties, but because experience has shown that the way race is reported can uniquely affect the reality of the subject itself . . .

It is not enough to rely on what we call 'news value'. We have to ask why there is news in a racial or religious identification. What assumptions are we making about the readers and about society? It is not enough to rely on the accuracy of the facts assembled. We have to ask whether, as presented, they represent truth. All facts may be true but some combinations of facts are truer than others. And any single collection of facts is itself susceptible to dramatically different treatments. We have had some vivid instances of all these things in the way race and immigration are reported. This has demolished once and for all any idea that matters of race can be left to report themselves.

Appendix

Attitude scores of white secondary school children

Scores are derived from a ten-item Likert scale that we have every reason to believe is a good measure of attitude to coloured people in general. The higher the score the more negative the attitude. The scores were obtained at interview from a combined group of white eleven to twelve and fourteen to fifteen-year-old children (half and half), both boys and girls, randomly selected from fourteen schools – eight from areas of high immigration in the West Midlands and West Yorkshire, and six from areas of low immigration – Glasgow, Teesside and Sheffield. Schools were chosen in pairs from each borough used so that one had a relatively large number of coloured pupils (at least 10 per cent, and in most cases 20–40 per cent) and the other similar school, few or none. The means are given below with standard deviations in brackets.

Table 1 **Type of area**

	High immigration	Low immigration	Total
			High-contact schools
High-contact schools	23·60 (6·06) N = 104	20·23 (5·86) N = 78	22·15 (6·21) N = 182
			Low-contact schools
Low-contact schools	21·83 (6·31) N = 103	19·00 (5·87) N = 78	20·61 (6·28) N = 181
Totals	High immigration areas 22·72 (6·00) N = 207	Low immigration areas 19·62 (5·90) N = 156	Overall mean 21·38 (6·29) N = 363

Significance of differences: High versus low areas, $z = 4.921$, $P < 0.0001$, two-tailed.
High versus low schools, $z = 2.347$, $P = 0.02$, two-tailed.
High area–Low school versus Low area–High school, $z = 1.76$, $P = 0.08$, two-tailed.

References

AMIR, Y. (1969), 'Contact hypothesis in ethnic relations', *Psychol. Bull.*, vol. 71, no. 5.
BLUMLER, J. G., and MCQUAIL, D. (1968), *Television in Politics: Its Uses and Influence*, Faber & Faber.
COOPER, E., and DINERMAN, H. (1951), 'Analysis of the film *Don't be a sucker*: a study in communication', *Pub. Opinion Q.*, vol. 15, no. 2.
DEAKIN, N. (1970), *Colour, Citizenship and British Society*, Panther Books.
DEFLEUR, M. L. (1966), *Theories of Mass Communication*, McKay.

EVANS, H. (1970), *The Listener*, 16 July.

GALTUNG, J., and RUGE, M. H. (1965), 'The structure of foreign news', *J. Peace Res.*, no. 1. –

HALLORAN, J. D. (ed.) (1970), *The Effects of Television*, Panther.

HALLORAN, J. D., ELLIOTT, P., and MURDOCK, G. (1970), *Demonstrations and Communications: A Case Study*, Penguin.

HOVLAND, C. I., JANIS, J., and KELLEY, H. H. (1953), *Communication and Persuasion*, Yale University Press.

KLAPPER, J. T. (1960), *The Effects of Mass Communication*, Free Press.

LANG, K., and LANG, G. E. (1953), 'The unique perspective of television and its effect: a pilot study', *Amer. Sociol. Rev.*, vol. 18, pp. 3–12.

MCQUAIL, D. (1969), *Towards a Sociology of Mass Communications*, Macmillan Co.

NATIONAL ADVISORY COMMISSION ON CIVIL DISORDERS, (1968), *Report*, Bantam Books

ROSE, E. J. B. (1969), *Colour and Citizenship*, Oxford University Press for the Institute of Race Relations.

TANNENBAUM, P. H. (1953), 'The effect of headlines on the interpretation of news stories', *Journalism Q.*, vol. 30, pp. 189–97.

TRENAMAN, J., and MCQUAIL, D. (1961), *Television and the Political Image*, Methuen.

WARR, P. B., and KNAPPER, B. (1968), *The Perception of People and Events*, Wiley.

Further Reading

Part One
General Perspectives

B. Berelson and M. Janowitz (eds.), *Reader in Public Opinion and Communication*, Free Press, second edition, 1966.

L. Bryson (ed.), *The Communication of Ideas*, Harper & Row, 1948.

F. E. X. Dance (ed.), *Human Communication Theory*, Holt Rinehart & Winston, 1967.

M. L. De Fleur, *Theories of Mass Communication*, David McKay, second edition, 1970.

L. A. Dexter and D. M. White (eds.), *People, Society and Mass Communications*, Free Press, 1964.

H. D. Duncan, *Communication and Social Order*, Oxford University Press, 1962.

A. Edelstein, *Perspectives in Mass Communication*, Copenhagen, Einar Harcks Forlag, 1966.

M. Janowitz, 'The study of mass communication', *International Encyclopedia of the Social Sciences*, vol. 3, 1968, pp. 41–53.

D. McQuail, *Towards a Sociology of Mass Communication*, Macmillan, 1969.

J. W. and M. W. Riley, 'Mass communication and the social system', in R. K. Merton (ed.), *Sociology Today*, Basic Books, 1959.

W. Schramm (ed.), *Mass Communications*, University of Illinois Press, 1960.

W. Schramm (ed.), *The Science of Human Communication*, Basic Books, 1963.

J. Tunstall (ed.), *Media Sociology*, Constable, 1970.

B. H. Westley and S. Maclean, 'A conceptual model for communications research', *Journalism Quarterly*, vol. 34, no. 4, 1957, pp. 31–8.

C. R. Wright, *Mass Communications: A Sociological Perspective*, Random House, 1959.

Part Two
Mass Media and Mass Society

F. Alberoni, *L'Elite Senza Potere*, Milano, Vita e Pensiero, 1963.

R. A. Bauer and A. Bauer, 'America, mass society and mass media', *Journal of Social Issues*, vol. 16, no. 3, 1960, pp. 3–66.

L. Bramson, *The Political Context of Sociology*, Princeton University Press, 1960.

G. Friedman, 'Leisure and technological civilization', *International Social Science Journal*, vol. 12, 1960, pp. 509–21.

N. Jacobs (ed.), *Culture for the Millions?*, Van Nostrand, 1961.

M. Janowitz, *The Community Press in an Urban Setting*, University of Chicago Press, 1952.

W. Kornhauser, *The Politics of Mass Society*, Routledge & Kegan Paul, 1959.

D. Lerner, *The Passing of Traditional Society*, Free Press, 1958.

L. Lowenthal, *Literature, Popular Culture and Society*, Prentice Hall, 1961.

H. Marcuse, *One Dimensional Man*, Routledge & Kegan Paul, 1964.

R. Park, *On Social Control and Collective Behaviour*, collected papers edited by R. H. Turner, University of Chicago Press, 1967.

T. Peterson, J. W. Jensen and W. L. Rivers, *The Mass Media and Modern Society*, Holt Rinehart & Winston, 1965.

B. Rosenberg and D. M. White (eds.), *Mass Culture*, Free Press, 1957.

H. L. Wilensky, 'Mass society and mass culture', *American Sociological Review*, vol. 29, no. 2, 1964, pp. 173–97.

R. Williams, *The Long Revolution*, Chatto & Windus, 1961; Penguin, 1965.

Part Three
The Audience of Mass Communications

M. Abrams, *The Newspaper-Reading Public of Tomorrow*, Odhams, 1964.

W. A. Belson, *The Impact of Television*, Crosby Lockwood, 1967.

B. Berelson, 'What missing the newspaper means', in P. F. Lazarsfeld and F. M. Stanton (eds.), *Communications Research 1948–9*, Harper & Row, 1949.

H. Cantril and G. W. Allport, *The Psychology of Radio*, Harper & Row, 1935.

J. Curran, 'The impact of television on the audience for national newspapers, 1945–68', in J. Tunstall (ed.), *Media Sociology*, Constable, 1970, pp. 104–31.

B. P. Emmett, 'A new role for research in broadcasting', *Public Opinion Quarterly*, vol. 32, pp. 654–65.

L. Handel, *Hollywood Looks at its Audience*, University of Illinois Press, 1950.

P. F. Lazarsfeld and F. M. Stanton (eds.), *Radio Research 1942–3*, Duell, Sloan and Pearce, 1944.

P. F. Lazarsfeld and F. M. Stanton (eds.), *Communications Research 1948–9*, Harper & Row, 1949.

D. McQuail, 'The audience for television plays', in J. Tunstall (ed.), *Media Sociology*, Constable, 1970, pp. 335–50.

J. P. Mayer, *British Cinemas and Their Audiences*, Dennis Dobson, 1948.

H. Mendelsohn, 'Listening to radio', in L. A. Dexter and D. M. White, *People, Society and Mass Communications*, Free Press, 1964.

K. Nordenstreng, 'Consumption of mass media in Finland', *Gazette*, vol. 15, no. 4, 1969, pp. 249–59.

V. Pietila, 'Immediate versus delayed reward in newspaper reading', *Acta Sociologica*, vol. 12, 1969, pp. 199–208.

G. Steiner, *The People Look at Television*, Knopf, 1963.

W. L. Warner and W. Henry, 'The radio daytime serial: a symbolic analysis', in B. Berelson and M. Janowitz, (eds.), *Reader in Public Opinion and Communication*, 1953, Free Press, pp. 423–37.

S. D. Wiebe, 'Two psychological factors in media audience behaviour', *Public Opinion Quarterly*, vol. 33, 1969, pp. 523–36.

Part Four
Mass Communication Organizations

W. Breed, 'Social control in the newsroom', *Social Forces*, vol. 33, pp. 326–35. Reprinted in W. Schramm (ed.), *Mass Communications*, University of Illinois Press, 1960.

T. Burns, 'Public service and private world', *Sociological Review Monographs*, ed. P. Halmos, vol. 13, 1969, pp. 53–73.

M. Cantor, *The Hollywood TV Producer*, Basic Books, 1971.

P. Elliot, *The Making of a Televison Series*, Constable, 1972.

J. D. Halloran, P. Elliot and G. Murdock, *Demonstrations and Communications*, Penguin, 1972.

P. Halmos (ed.), *The Sociology of Mass Media Communicators*, Sociological Review Monograph, no. 13, 1969.

L. C. Rosten, *Hollywood: The Movie Colony, the Movie Makers*, Harcourt Brace & World, 1940.

J. Tunstall, *The Westminster Lobby Correspondents*, Routledge & Kegan Paul, 1970.

D. M. White, 'The gatekeeper: a case study in the selection of news', *Journalism Quarterly*, vol. 27, no. 4, 1950. Reprinted in L. A. Dexter and D. M. White, *People, Society and Mass Communications*, Free Press, 1964.

Part Five
Structural Analysis and Mass Communication

Communications, Journal of the Centre d'Études des Communications de Masse, Paris.

G. A. Huaco, *The Sociology of Film Art*, Basic Books, 1965.

J. Mitry, *Esthetique et Psychologie du Cinéma*, Paris, Éditions Universitaires, 1963.

E. Morin, *The Stars*, Grove Press, 1960.

H. Powdermaker, *Hollywood: The Dream Factory*, Little Brown & Co., 1950.

J. Viet, *Les Méthodes Stucturalistes dans les Sciences Sociales*, Mouton, 1965.

Part Six
Issues of Policy or Social Concern

J. G. Blumler and J. Madge, *Citizenship and Television*, Political and Economic Planning, 1967.

P. Clarke and L. Ruggels, 'Preferences amongst news media for coverage of public affairs', *Journalism Quarterly*, vol. 47, no. 3, 1970, pp. 464–71.

J. Dumazadier, *Towards a Sociology of Leisure*, translated from French by S. McClure, Free Press, 1967.

R. Fagen, *Politics and Communication*, Little Brown & Co., 1966.

J. Galtung and M. H. Ruge, 'The structure of foreign news', in J. Tunstall (ed.), *Media Sociology*, Constable, 1970, pp. 259–98.

B. S. Greenberg and B. Devlin, *Use of the Mass Media by the Urban Poor*, Praeger, 1970.

K. and G. Lang, *Politics and Television*, Quadrangle Books, 1968.

J. Macleod, S. Ward and K. Tancill, 'Alienation and uses of the mass media', *Public Opinion Quarterly*, vol. 29, 1966, pp. 583–94.

R. MacNeil, *The People Machine*, Macmillan, 1970.

E. Ostgaard, 'Factors influencing the flow of news', *Journal of Peace Research*, vol. 4, no. 1, 1965, pp. 39–65.

R. Sainseaulieu, 'Les classes sociales défavorisées en face de la télévision', *Revue Française de Sociologie*, vol. 7, no. 2, 1965, pp. 201–14.

W. Schramm (ed.), *Mass Media and National Development*, Stanford University Press and UNESCO, 1964.

C. Seymour-Ure, *The Press, Politics and the Public*, Methuen, 1968.

E. G. Wedell, *Broadcasting and Public Policy*, Joseph, 1968.

R. Williams, *Britain in the Sixties: Communications*, Penguin, 1962.

Acknowledgements

Permission to reproduce the following Readings in this volume
is acknowledged to the following sources:

1 Association for Educational Communications and Technology
2 Holt Rinehart & Winston Inc.
3 Polish Scientific Publishers
4 Instituto Agostino Gemelli
5 Suhrkamp Verlag
6 American Academy of Political & Social Science
11 Constable Publishers
13 British Broadcasting Corporation
14 NHK Theoretical Research Centre, Tokyo
16 *Journalism Quarterly*
17 *Communications* and Professor H. J. Gans
18 *Educational Broadcasting Review*
20 Institute of Race Relations

Author Index

Subject Index

Penguin Modern Sociology Readings

Industrial Man
Edited by Tom Burns

Kinship
Edited by Jack Goody

Language and Social Context
Edited by Pier Paolo Giglioli

Mythology
Edited by Pierre Maranda

Peasants and Peasant Societies
Edited by Teodor Shanin

Political Sociology
Edited by Alessandro Pizzorno

Poverty
Edited by Jack L. Roach and Janet K. Roach

Social Inequality
Edited by André Béteille

Sociology of Law
Edited by Vilhelm Aubert

Sociology of Religion
Edited by Roland Robertson

Sociology of Science
Edited by Barry Barnes

Sociology of the Family
Edited by Michael Anderson

Television and the People
Brian Groombridge

Television is a mass medium. Is it possible, after many disappointments, that it can do some real mass communication?

Brian Groombridge argues persuasively that it can, and that, given the precarious state of our participatory democracy, it is high time it did. But first, television must escape from the superficial and the newsworthy, from confusing timidity with 'balance'. At the same time, viewers must become actors rather than onlookers.

In a series of case studies of what he calls 'participatory programming', drawn from broadcasting and educational experiments in America and Europe, Brian Groombridge shows how, by involving the community in the *production* of programmes, genuine participation in public affairs can be encouraged, and television itself reinvigorated.

This is a remarkable and richly argued book. It comes at a time of mounting concern over the future of our broadcasting services and the state of our democracy. At root it is a book about people. If the full potential of television was made use of, it could be an instrument through which we learn to talk to each other as well as to our leaders.